Sanderson Miller
and his Landscapes

Sanderson Miller
1716-1780

Sanderson Miller
and his Landscapes

Jennifer Meir

Phillimore

2006

Published by
PHILLIMORE & CO. LTD
Shopwyke Manor Barn, Chichester, West Sussex, England
www.phillimore.co.uk

ISBN 1-86077-387-7
ISBN 13 978-1-86077-387-7

Printed and bound in Great Britain by
CAMBRIDGE PRINTING

Contents

❧·❧

For
Aylwin

List of Illustrations

❧ · ❧

Colour Illustrations

Acknowledgements

❧·❧

I would like to thank The King Henry VIII Endowed Trust, Warwick, for a generous grant towards the cost of publishing this book.

Many people have helped me in the production of this book and I am most grateful to them all. My initial thanks must go to Paul Edwards, whose lectures on garden history first introduced me to Sanderson Miller and the gap in our knowledge concerning Miller's landscape designs. William Hawkes has encouraged me in my aim to uncover the story of Miller's landscaping as a complementary study to his own on Miller's architecture. I am grateful to Mavis Batey for her initial encouragement on my work on Miller at the University of York, and Peter Goodchild was very helpful with my early studies at York, from where I obtained my PhD on Miller's landscape work. I owe particular thanks to Tim Mowl, of the University of Bristol, both for his encouragement for the whole project, his invaluable criticism of the text for this book, and his Foreword.

Many other people in the world of garden history have helped me in my quest for the evidence which remains of Miller's work. Sandy Haynes has provided detailed information on Enville, and allowed me to use her own hand-drawn maps of Enville and Hagley. Among those who have helped me in various ways are Dianne Barre, Nick Bennett, Michael Cousins, Fiona Cowell, Kate Felús, Keith Goodway, the late Linden Huddlestone, David Jacques, David Lambert, Jonathan Lovie, Shirley Stirling, Michael Symes, Sophie Piebenga, John Phibbs, Philip White and Harriet Wyatt.

Owners of the houses and estates where Miller worked have been most generous with their hospitality, allowing me access to the grounds and to private papers which have provided fresh insights into the mid-18th-century landscaping of their estates. In this respect I would like to thank Mrs Camilla West of Alscot Park, Viscount Daventry of Arbury Hall, Mrs Dominic Collins of Adlestrop Park, Lord Bathurst of Cirencester Park, Mr and Mrs Peter Williams of Enville, Lord Cobham of Hagley Hall, Mr Benjamin Wiggins of Honington Hall, The Earl of Aylesford of Packington Hall, Mr David Richards of Radway Grange, Mr R. Waley-Cohen of Upton Viva, Lady Elizabeth Hamilton of Walton Hall, the late Mrs Brunner of Wotton Underwood, the staff at the Bishop's Palace, Hartlebury and the staff of Fairleigh Dickinson University at Wroxton Abbey. I would also like to mention Mr A.L. Lain, of Gopsall Hall Farm, and Mr R.F. Bayley, of Castle Farm, who gave me assistance in interpreting what is left of the landscaped grounds at Gopsall Park, Leicestershire.

The National Trust kindly allowed me to photograph Miller's portrait at Lacock Abbey, and to see the archives at Wimpole, where David Adshead discussed Miller's work with me. I have also been fortunate enough to have access to unpublished reports commissioned by the Trust on Farnborough Hall and Lacock Abbey.

I owe special thanks to the Warwickshire County Record Office for their unfailing assistance with the large Miller archive and other papers, and to Miss Caroline Sampson, Head of Archive Service, for her generous help with the publication of archival images. The Shakespeare Birthplace Trust Records Office, the library at the King's Manor, York, and other record offices and libraries have also been very helpful.

I would like to thank Noel Osborne, Managing Director of Phillimore and Co. Ltd, for his support and also for initially having faith in the publication of a book on Miller, and also Daniel Finch for the design, and for his tolerance over delays concerning the illustrations.

Finally I owe a great debt to my family, various members of whom have provided ideas, editorial assistance, proof reading and instruction with computer problems, and without whose help and support this book would never have seen the light of day.

My grateful thanks are due to the following for the use of their illustrations, in particular the Warwickshire County Record Office (WCRO): WCRO, 2 (CR1382/1: Diary of Sanderson Miller, 1749-50), 7 (CR1382/2: Memoir to James Stuart Menteath by Sanderson Miller, c.1770), 9 (CR 125B/826: Letter from Miller, 1779), 43 (CR1596/197: A General Map of Radway Field, 1756, G.Salmon), 48 (Z939/2 (L): Map of Radway Inclosure Award, 1997, S.G. Wallsgrove), 53 (Z403(U): Volume of maps entitled A Survey of the Estate of William Holbech Esq, Situate at Farnborough in the County of Warwick by Edward Linnell 1772), 67 (CR351/11BR: Honington, plan by Buck and Buck, 1731), 71 (HON HAL 1: Print of Honington Hall and grounds by Neal, c.1829), 99 (PV.WAR.Shi.1: Plan and Elevation of the Shire Hall, Warwick engraved by Edward Rooker after drawings by Francis Hiorn), 108 (CR125B/149: Letter from Lord Deerhurst to Miller, 1740s), 118 (CR 351/633A: Warwick Castle from Lodge Hill, 1776, aquatint, Paul Sandby), 119 (C820 JAG: taken from Richard Jago, Edgehill, the Landscape Delineated and Moralised, 1767); Lord Cobham: 5, 31; National Portrait Gallery: 6, 10, 11, 24, 63; The British Library, 25,66; Mrs C. Cottrell-Dormer, 34; London Borough of Lambeth, 35; The Provost and Fellows of Worcester College, Oxford, 38; Shakespeare Birthplace Trust Records Office, 39; Oxford University Department of Continuing Education and James Bond, 40; Oxfordshire County Council, 41; Buckinghamshire County Museum Collections, 42; English Heritage, National Monuments Collection, 46, 90; The President and Fellows of Magdalen College, Oxford, 59; The Bodleian Library, University of Oxford, 62 (Gough Maps 26, fol.69r); National Gallery of Ireland, 64, 65, 117; Hestercombe Gardens Trust, 75; The British Library of Political and Economic Science, 76, 77; Sandy Haynes, 78, 89; Royal Institute of British Architects, 81, 82, 83; The National Trust, 87, 88; Mr and Mrs P.B. Williams, Enville, 91; Oxfordshire Record Office and Mr J.H. Norman, 97; The Ashmolean Museum of Art and Archaeology, 101; Trustees of the Croome Estate, 109, 110; The Duke of Beaufort, 116. I would like to thank John Harris for kindly lending me his slides for the colour pictures of Honington, nos XII and XIII.

All other line drawings, colour, and black and white photographs not acknowledged above are by the author.

Foreword

࿐ · ࿐

Sanderson Miller, like William Kent and Batty Langley before him, has suffered from the 'Strawberry Hill Gothick' syndrome. Most 20th-century commentators have equated all experiments in that theatrical, curvaceous revived Gothick of the mid-18th century with Horace Walpole's Thameside villa at Twickenham. Because of Walpole's shameless self-publicity, early pioneers in the style have only recently been given their due. Even now, at the beginning of the 21st century, with the serious study of architectural history over 50 years old, Kent's Esher Place has only just been given its due as the first major domestic work of the style, while the influence of Batty Langley is still largely underplayed.

And then there is Miller, called in his time the 'Great Master of Gothick', the gentleman amateur ready to throw off sketches for his friends and acquaintances, which his trusty mason Hitchcox would then realise in stone. His rehabilitation began with *Country Life* articles on his estate at Radway and his work at Adlestrop, and then William Hawkes, a Stratford architect and Georgian enthusiast, began to research Miller's life and wrote a thesis on his architectural influence in the Midlands. Hawkes has followed up this groundwork with a carefully edited volume of his diaries published by the Dugdale Society in 2005, and now we have Jennifer Meir's rounded study, which takes in Miller's architectural work, but also his landscape designs. These last have, apart from Meir's own seminal articles, received little attention, and they present a significant advance in our knowledge of mid-century landscape aesthetics. At long last we are now able to see how Miller contrived the landscape settings for his buildings and can judge his early appreciation of the value of the wider prospect. In this, of course, he was following Kent's lead at Esher and at Rousham, but here he is accorded a pivotal role in that 1740-60 cusp period in landscape design as a precursor of Capability Brown – Miller is seen as the link between the 'Rococo' layouts, so beautifully illustrated by Thomas Robins, and the ideal parkscapes of the Brownian revolution.

Walpole was right when, in a rare moment of generosity for a fellow Gothic enthusiast, he remarked that Miller's Sham Castle at Hagley had the 'true rust of the Barons' wars'. But Miller's attention to the real medieval Gothic was never slavish – his quotation of Guy's Tower at Warwick Castle for his own Radway Tower on Edgehill is for its silhouette rather than for its scholarly detail. Safe in the amateur airs of the Midlands, his best work retains that theatrical elegance of the Rococo-Gothick, which prized associations of the past above an antiquarian desire to copy. Walpole, influenced by his informed 'Committee of Taste', was to make his Gothick too archaeological, and in its later phases Strawberry was compromised by the dead hand of scholarship. Miller was a true pioneer of the Gothick, Walpole merely a follower. This important book will finally set the record straight and Sanderson Miller will take his place in the development of revived Gothic, where he belongs, as the 'Great Master'.

Dr Timothy Mowl

1

Introduction

❧ ⋅ ❧

This book is about the landscape work of Sanderson Miller (1716–80), gentleman architect and designer, and his contribution to the development of a natural style in the design of gardens and estate grounds. Most of Miller's work was carried out in the English Midlands, where many men who were leaders in politics and the army had their estates. Miller's approach to landscaping was considerably in advance of current trends, and the Midlands were to become increasingly important as a focus for the new ideas in estate improvements.[1]

Miller's home was a small estate at Radway, in south Warwickshire, bought by his father at about the time of Miller's birth. Radway, although comparatively isolated in the 18th century, was nevertheless fairly centrally situated in that area of the Midlands where some of the most influential estates associated with the beginnings of the new natural landscape style are situated. During the 18th century, the style developed, with many variations, as a strong movement away from the formal designs previously introduced into England from continental Europe. It may be defined as the laying out of grounds in an informal manner so that the appearance of the landscape is greatly enhanced, and the design in maturity would seem as if created by natural means.

Some Midlands estates where landscapes were being newly laid out in this informal style include Hagley, Enville and the Leasowes to the north west of the region, Croome, in Worcestershire, to the west, Warwick Castle in the centre of the region, and to the south the great gardens at Stowe, in Buckinghamshire, and large estates such as Blenheim, Ditchley, and Heythrop in Oxfordshire. Other estates of particular interest in this context, and which were considered to be more important in the 18th century than they are today, include Wroxton Abbey, near Banbury, Wotton Underwood, near Stowe, Shotover, east of Oxford, and Hartwell, near Aylesbury.[2]

Although Miller's interest in landscaping had developed through his visits to Stowe when an Oxford undergraduate, Miller has long been known as the architect who designed mock ruined castles for the nobility and gentry. In the late 1730s Miller began to landscape his own park at Radway, which ran up to the northern scarp of the Cotswold outcrop known as Edgehill. Here Miller built a mock medieval Tower and its associated ruinous buildings, on the site where tradition says that Charles I raised his standard before the battle of Edgehill in 1642. The Tower overlooked Miller's estate, the site of the battle (the first battle of the Civil War), and the south Warwickshire plain beyond. Following the success of his Tower and its ruins on Edgehill, and his landscaping of his estate, Miller began to gain a reputation not only for designing mock ruins, but also for his ability in the laying out of land. The idea of a mock ruin to embellish an estate became increasingly popular, and many of Miller's friends and acquaintances asked him to design mock castle ruins for their own estates, setting a precedent for a trend which still continues today. Miller's mock medieval castles and eyecatchers, although not the first to be built, were among the very earliest of such buildings.[3] Miller also designed other landscape buildings in a variety of styles, varying from the classical to the Chinese, sometimes as part of a landscape scheme, but also as a single building requested by a client for a particular site.

Miller's architectural abilities are central to his landscaping, for the two went hand in hand. At his more important sites, in terms of what can still be seen today, his landscape buildings have an intrinsic merit, both in their design and their situation within the general plan, which adds greatly to the effect of the whole designed landscape. Purely as an architect Miller's output was not great. Apart from buildings in the landscape, he only designed two complete buildings, the Palladian mansion Hagley Hall, near Stourbridge, Worcestershire for George, later Sir George Lyttelton, and the Shire Hall, for his native county of Warwick. Miller also carried out various improvements to existing houses, mainly in the Gothic style, including his own Radway Grange, and he designed some additions to churches, including part of the interior of Kilkenny Cathedral. Miller's architecture, as distinct from his landscaping, has been discussed in some detail by modern authors, in particular by William Hawkes, the architect responsible for the restoration of two of Miller's buildings: the Museum at Enville, Staffordshire, and the Bath House at Walton, in Warwickshire.[4]

Miller's complete landscaping output has not hitherto been examined in detail. This neglect is partly due to the fact that, as a gentleman, Miller declined to ask for fees; consequently, no bills were sent out for his work. He did record in his diaries the fact that he was drawing plans for friends and acquaintances, but it appears likely that detailed architectural drawings were left to the master masons and craftsmen who worked for him, as was normal for men of his social status. Only a very few of his architectural sketches still exist,[5] and no drawings of landscape designs have been found to date.

1 *Miller's Tower and gatehouse, with Egge Cottage just visible beyond. A view copied from an old postcard, c.1910.*

It would not have been possible to write this book without the availability of the archival material held by the Warwickshire County Record Office (WCRO), and the work and publications carried out by William Hawkes and Anthony Wood in the 1960s. The WCRO holds upwards of one thousand letters written mainly to Miller from his many friends and acquaintances, dating from the early 1740s to 1779, the year before his death. Hawkes wrote his undergraduate thesis on Miller's architecture in 1964, and Wood subsequently discovered the existence of two of Miller's diaries. The diaries are for part of the years 1749-50, and part of the years 1756-7 respectively, and are held in the WCRO. Their WCRO access references are given in the chapter notes, and the published transcripts of the diaries are given in the bibliography. To avoid repetition, since constant reference is made to the diaries throughout this book, no reference details will be given in later chapters. The WCRO also holds a Memoir written by Miller to his old university friend, James Stuart Menteath.[6]

Miller's letters provide a valuable source of information, but they are virtually all personal letters. As such they rarely touch on matters of business. The number of letters from each of Miller's correspondents varies a great deal. The majority contain personal news, details concerning travel arrangements for forthcoming visits, and sometimes references to the politics of the day. Only occasionally do they refer to Miller's landscaping. These stray references, often difficult to locate among much which is irrelevant, can provide vital clues to his work. In some cases the reference is the only one tying Miller's name to a site, as in the letter from Lord Guernsey, of Packington Hall, in Warwickshire, in October 1748, discussing Miller's forthcoming visit to Charles Jennens at Gopsall, in Leicestershire.[7] The date of this letter also accords well with the known dates for several of the verified drawings for Gopsall which are held in the Royal Institute of British Architects (RIBA) Drawings collections,[8] underlining the likelihood of Miller's involvement, for several of these drawings were carried out by the Hiorns, master masons from Warwick whom Miller is known to have employed at other sites. It is this type of connection which has proved so important in narrowing down the attribution of work at a particular site to Miller himself.

Collections of a large number of letters from a single correspondent include those from Sir George Lyttelton, Lord Coventry of Croome, and Lord North of Wroxton Abbey. These letters contain some useful references to the landscaping and the landscape buildings at these particular sites. In addition, some letters also refer to requests for designs from other men which the writer duly passed on to Miller. These include the initial request from Lord Chancellor Hardwicke for a castle ruin at Wimpole, his Cambridgeshire estate, and that from Lord Chetwynd for a Gothic design at Ingestre, in Staffordshire, both made to Miller through George Lyttelton. Several letters from Lord Hardwicke give interesting details concerning the castle ruin at Wimpole, and Miller's annual visits to stay with him there. Miller also received a request from William Pitt (the elder) for an eyecatcher on the hills outside Bath for Ralph Allen, who had made his fortune excavating Bath stone for building.[9]

A few letters are particularly revealing concerning Miller's landscaping. Among these are several letters from William Pitt. A quote from one of these, written in 1755 when Miller was planning to bring in his Enclosure Act for the parish of Radway, is given below:

> … I particularly rejoice … that you are descended from the cloud capt Tower to the
> fertile plains beneath, that is, in plain English, that you are up to your knees in the

2 *A double-page spread from Miller's diary for 1749-50.*

improveable dirt of Radway-Field, tracing ditches and mounds, and planting Gate Posts instead of all the vegetable Tribes of America ... [10]

A single letter from two of Miller's Oxford friends, Oswald and Vansittart,[11] together with brief diary entries, provides most of the information concerning Miller's involvement at Honington, in south Warwickshire, one of the few sites where most of Miller's work can still be made out, although largely in a decayed state. Details in two or three letters from George Grenville, Lord Cobham's nephew and later Prime Minister, show the importance of Miller's contribution to the landscaping of Grenville's estate at Wotton Underwood, about which we should know nothing were it not for this correspondence. The landscape at Wotton has undergone an extensive restoration in recent years.[12]

The two diaries, the first of which covers part of 1749 and most of 1750, and the second a large part of 1756, shed a great deal of light not only on Miller's way of life and his daily activities, but also on what was important to him. They list all the people with whom he came in contact, showing the value of these connections to him, and providing an insight into his social life, his visits to other estates, and also to London, where he went at least annually. The diaries complement the correspondence because they reveal for these particular years not only the pattern of Miller's life, but also the exact dates of his various visits and tours. The correspondence often indicates his landscaping activities during his visits, when the diaries are silent on this subject. A typical diary entry recorded how long Miller spent riding round an estate in terms of hours, for example with Lord Hardwicke at Wimpole, but not the all important details of exactly what he was discussing. Miller recorded that such estate rides often took three to four hours, much longer than would be expected if the men were simply out for exercise within the park. It is more than likely that Miller and Hardwicke were discussing the improvements, if only because of Hardwicke's great interest in landscaping the park at the time.

Judging from similar brief diary entries, which refer more often to the time taken when walking or riding around the estates of his friends than to any other details, it seems probable that Miller usually gave his advice verbally on his visits. It was only very occasionally that he recorded actually planning some planting, or marking out the site for a building, and often when referring to a design he was drawing out he described it simply as a plan. We are left guessing as to whether the plan was for a building or a landscape. The diaries also show how much time Miller spent on his own estate, either overseeing the work of others or doing some of the work himself, for example planting trees, weeding newly set quicks (hawthorn), or checking to see if his new trees were all growing satisfactorily. A typical entry is that for the morning of Saturday, 10 March 1749: 'plantg. [planting] the Firs at the Long Walk at the Mt.[Mount]'.[13] The Mount was a raised area below the Tower. Although the diaries give a breakdown of Miller's daily activities, including his social life, his building work on his Tower at Edgehill on his Radway estate, and such matters as attending church, and his daily reading material, the entries are very brief and give little indication of his thoughts or of the ideas behind his work.

The Memoir to Menteath was written in 1774, when Miller was confined due to suffering recurrent fits of 'madness'. Although a little rambling, there seems no reason to doubt the veracity of the text. It is not as revealing as the diaries, but provides an insight into Miller's activities during his student days at Oxford University, and in particular his frequent visits to Stowe during this formative period in his life. There is also some account of later visits to Menteath at Barrowby, near Grantham, in Lincolnshire, where Menteath was the incumbent for many years.

In 1910, Lilian Dickins and Mary Stanton wrote the only book which has been published solely about Miller: *An Eighteenth Century Correspondence.*[14] Using quotes from the collection of Miller's letters, the authors build up a chronological picture of Miller, his correspondents, and the historical, social and political background of his period. This picture, particularly the thumbnail sketches of Miller's friends, has provided interesting background material to my work.

While various authors have written on Miller's architectural output, published work on Miller's landscapes is scanty. In 1969 two articles were published on Miller: a biography, by Anthony Wood, and an account of Miller's work at one of his major sites, Wroxton Abbey, near Banbury, by William Hawkes. In 1986 Paul Edwards wrote on Miller's work at Wroxton, when Edwards himself was responsible for extensive restoration work carried out at the cascade to the Great Pond and in the upper valley gardens. Edwards did not discuss the work attributed to Miller in the lower valley, which was an important

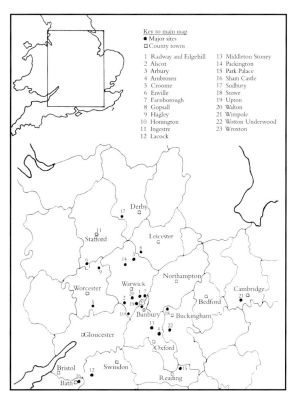

Key to main map
● Major sites
□ County towns

1 Radway and Edgehill	13 Middleton Stoney
2 Alscot	14 Packington
3 Arbury	15 Park Palace
4 Ambrosen	16 Sham Castle
5 Croome	17 Sudbury
6 Enville	18 Stowe
7 Farnborough	19 Upton
8 Gopsall	20 Walton
9 Hagley	21 Wimpole
10 Honington	22 Wotton Underwood
11 Ingestre	23 Wroxton
12 Lacock	

3 *A map showing the distribution of the major sites at which Miller worked between 1736 and 1760.*

part of the landscape scheme but now lies neglected and unrecognised. It is now held in different ownership from that of the upper gardens. In 1987, Wood and Hawkes together published a comprehensive account of Miller's landscaping of his own estate at Radway prior to 1757, the date of the Radway Enclosure Act.[15]

Other modern garden historians have not paid Miller's landscape work much attention, with the exception of a few perceptive comments by Batey (1989), Batey and Lambert (1990) and Symes (1991),[16] who says that Miller's work 'typifies much of the Rococo spirit'. Mavis Batey sees Miller as 'essentially a romantic antiquarian', who saw 'turrets, buttresses and battlements with poetic feeling'. She notes the influences of Oxford in the buildings that Miller designed for his friends, and sums up Miller's work by saying that 'Sanderson Miller had anticipated picturesque vision by seeing buildings in relation to landscape ...', a succinct conclusion that emphasises the importance of landscape in his estate designs. Other writers who have discussed Miller's work include Cousins, who has written several articles on sites where Miller worked, but who comments more on aspects of the design and siting of Miller's buildings, rather than the planning of the landscape as a whole. Neither Williamson nor Mowl in their recent books on landscape and garden design mentions Miller's landscape work at all.[17]

What is known of Miller's work is tantalisingly incomplete. Little research of a practical nature has previously been carried out on Miller's landscapes, which have either been ignored or relegated to a very minor place in the literature concerning the development of 18th-century landscape design. However, there is a surprising body of work with which Miller is associated. His name is connected with at least 35 estates, where his work varied from designs for the whole estate to a plan for a single building, although today there are only a few of these sites where his work still exists in anything like its original conception.

Field research on Miller's sites has been based initially on Hawkes' original list, for often the buildings Hawkes discusses in his thesis were part of a landscape scheme. Additional properties were added to the list as more references to Miller's landscaping were found either in the diaries, the Memoir to Menteath or in Miller's correspondence. Using the characteristics of a 'Miller' landscape, an assessment has been made as to whether the landscaping with which Miller's name is associated is actually likely to be by him or not, and therefore how important his work is in the overall development of what may be called the 'natural landscape style'.

The widespread development of this style in garden design, which was just becoming fashionable in the 1740s when Miller started his work, is traditionally associated with the work of Lancelot 'Capability' Brown in the second half of the 18th century. It was in the Midlands that Brown first came to prominence, while working as head gardener for Lord Cobham at Stowe.

Although Brown did not start up in business on his own until 1751, he and Miller were exact contemporaries. Brown also made at least one visit to Miller at his home at Radway, in 1750. After 1760, when Miller had his first attack of temporary insanity, his work was seriously curtailed. In the previous decade, Brown had been laying down the foundations of his own spectacularly successful career. The documented association between the two men, together with circumstantial evidence, suggests an appreciable influence by Miller on both Brown's work and his business connections between 1750 and 1760.[18]

2

A Biographical Account

☙ ' ❧

Sanderson Miller was born in 1716 at Radway, a small village in south Warwickshire. His father, also called Sanderson, was a mercer selling cloth, buckram, gloves, buttons etc. who had moved from Banbury a year or so previously. Miller senior was the youngest son of John Miller, who owned land at Boycott in Buckinghamshire, adjacent to Stowe. The navigation of the Thames to Oxford had been greatly improved, and Miller senior brought his goods to Oxford by water, and thence to Banbury in flat bottomed boats designed by himself. Both Miller senior and his father-in-law, a solicitor, became mayors of Banbury. Miller senior's wife was Mary Welchman. Her grandfather, a master baker, had created the famous Banbury cakes in the early 1600s.[1]

By 1715 Miller senior had made enough money to buy the estate of Radway Grange for £3,671 from the Goodwins, who owned the adjacent estate of Arlescote.[2] The Grange had in the early 17th century belonged to the Washingtons of Sulgrave, in Oxfordshire, ancestors of George Washington, of American fame. At the time of Miller senior's purchase, the Radway estate consisted of 240 acres held in the common unenclosed fields, and 70 acres of enclosed land, which included a small park to the south of the house running up towards the scarp of Edgehill, on the parish boundary.[3] Miller senior gradually enlarged the estate with purchases of extra land, and by 1728 he had obviously obtained some standing in his adopted county, for in this year he became High Sheriff of Warwickshire.[4]

Sanderson Miller junior and his sister Anne were the only ones to survive to maturity of a family of at least six children, of whom Miller was the youngest. Nothing is known of his early life and schooling, but in 1734 his father sent Miller to Oxford to finish his education. At the age of 18 Miller entered the college of St Mary Hall (now a part of Oriel College) as a Gentleman Commoner,[5] and matriculated on 6 April 1734.[6]

He was a good student, for in 1737 Walter Harte, presumably Miller's tutor, wrote to his father suggesting an advantageous purchase of books for him, adding:

> …. your son, of all the young Gentlemen I ever was concerned with, bids the fairest
> to make a Learned, and an honest valuable man.[7]

Miller's love of learning was to remain with him all his life, and his two existing diaries reveal a regular pattern of daily study. In an age when the university had a bad name for excesses of all descriptions, Harte's comment is particularly illustrative of Miller's character. He was fortunate in both his tutor and in the Principal of St Mary Hall, William King.[8] The latter encouraged Miller in his enthusiasm for classical studies and, although a Jacobite while the majority of Miller's friends were Whigs, he and Miller remained friends for many years.

Previous to his arrival at Oxford Miller would probably have been familiar only with the small provincial towns of Warwick, where he would have seen the castle, and Banbury. Oxford, with its wealth of fine buildings, its academic interests and challenges, and the fellowship of other bright minds obviously made a great impression on him. Impressed by the sheer number of beautiful and historic buildings in Oxford, Miller began to study architecture on his own account. His own college of St Mary Hall, adjacent to Oriel College, dated back to 1325, when Edward II gave the Hall to Oriel College. In 1333 St Mary Hall became a separate college, which it remained until the early 19th century, when it was again incorporated with Oriel College.

During Miller's time at Oxford there must have been an air of excitement concerning the magnificent new buildings which were being constructed. Sir Christopher Wren had built the Sheldonian Theatre in 1664-7, the first building in the city to be modelled on a building from classical antiquity, and in 1681 had designed Tom Tower over the entrance to Christ Church, founded by Cardinal Wolsey. The first part of the 18th century saw the construction of the Clarendon Building (1711-13), and the Great Quad and the Hall at All Souls College (1716-30s), all by Nicholas Hawksmoor, who had been introduced to Oxford in about 1708 by George Clarke. In the early years of the 18th century, architecture in Oxford was greatly influenced by Clarke, the knowledgeable amateur architect and Fellow of All Souls, and much of the new building work was carried out by the master mason William Townesend. Between 1716 and 1760 the Codrington Library, also designed by Hawksmoor, was built, and in 1739, just before Miller left Oxford, the Radcliffe Camera was begun by James Gibbs.[9] It is not surprising that Miller was inspired to study architecture to the point where he felt that he could have taken it up professionally had he so desired.

Miller was following well known precedents in determining to educate himself in the principles and practice of architecture: both Sir Christopher Wren and George Clarke were self-educated architects. Miller wrote that he had applied himself so closely to 'his

4 *St Mary Hall, Miller's old college in Oxford, now part of Oriel College.*

5 *Sir George Lyttelton, 1709-1773, by Benjamin West.*

business of building' that he could always 'make publick profession of it for money', although he had in fact never accepted money for his plans or journeys, nor been at the call of any gentleman who would employ him.[10] Miller's own buildings, with their use of architectural details from the Oxford colleges, illustrate his eye for detail and the application of his observations.

At Oxford Miller made many friends among the sons of the landed gentry and nobility. Men such as Sir Edward Turner of Ambrosden, near Oxford, Sir Roger Newdigate, of Arbury, in north Warwickshire, George Coventry, of Croome, and James Leigh, of Adlestrop, in Gloucestershire, whose branch of the family was to inherit Stoneleigh Abbey in Warwickshire in the early 19th century, were all well known to Miller and to each other. These men, together with many others such as Henry, later Colonel Conway, cousin to Horace Walpole, George Lyttelton of Hagley and the Grenvilles of Wotton Underwood, whom Miller met through his Oxford and Stowe connections,[11] were all to profit in future years from Miller's talents in the embellishment of their houses and estates. The Lytteltons and the Grenvilles were relations of Lord Cobham, Richard Grenville inheriting his uncle's estate at Stowe on Cobham's death in 1749.

Miller was a regular visitor to the Temples at Stowe, where the important developments in the gardens had a great influence on Miller's own future work. Not only was his family neighbours of Richard Temple, Lord Cobham, but the Temples also owned land at Burton Dassett,[12] near Miller's own property at Radway and adjoining the estate of Farnborough, where Miller carried out one of his most important landscape designs.

Miller was a most hospitable man. Many people visited him at Radway, and guests often walked up the hill to see the Tower and its ruins. In the evenings, when he had company, Miller liked to have music and dancing. Miller was a competent musician, playing the spinet, harpsichord and flute, and was in demand as a guest for these skills. On 8 October 1749, Lord North asked him if he would bring his flute when he came to Wroxton. On 28 January and 4 February 1750, Miller recorded in his diary that he was tuning the harpsichord at home, and on Wednesday, 6 May he was 'tuning spinet and sent it to the Castle'. On Thursday, 31 May he 'went to the Wkm[n] [workmen] at the Ruin[d] Tower. practising spin: [spinet] in Castle …'. When Colonel Henry Conway visited Radway, he and Miller used to play duets together, Corelli's music being a favourite. Later that summer, Miller's diary entry for Monday, 13 August, when Conway was staying with him at Radway, reads, in Miller's typical shorthand: 'Corelli's Son [sonata] with C.Con …'. On the following Tuesday, both men went to Hagley for a week's visit, walking round the Park, visiting Shenstone's adjacent estate at The Leasowes – 'a charming place of natural beauties' – with their host George

Lyttelton, and enjoying musical evenings. A typical diary entry during this visit was that for the evening of 15 August: 'After dinner … playing duets with Col.Conway …'.[13] In that same year Miller recorded travelling to Oxford to hear an oratorio composed by Mr Handel. Handel's patron was Charles Jennens, of Gopsall, in Leicestershire, whom Miller knew and whose property he visited in 1748 to advise on the landscaping surrounding Jennens' new mansion.

During the year, other than in the wintertime when the condition of the roads made travelling very difficult, Miller would make several visits to friends who lived within a day or two's ride of home. On Miller's visits to Hagley there were always house parties, and it is likely that it was at Hagley, where the new landscaping of the park was influenced by advice and designs from several of George Lyttelton's friends, that Miller first became acquainted with William Pitt

6 *William Pitt the elder, 1708-1778, by William Hoare.*

and the poet Alexander Pope. Both men were particularly interested in the laying out of grounds, and Pope's writings and also the design of his own garden at Twickenham had a profound effect on men's thoughts concerning this new style. Pope was a regular visitor to Hagley and was commemorated in a portrait, with his dog Bounce, which still hangs in the library, and also by a seat in the park. The latter no longer exists. Miller's personal friendship with William Pitt is shown both in the few letters from Pitt to Miller which have survived, and also by his gift of laurels for the Radway estate, and the fact that in 1754 Pitt visited Radway and planted three trees in the park there.[14]

From Hagley Miller visited Lord Stamford at Enville, west of Stourbridge. Miller designed several landscape buildings for Lord Stamford, who was carrying forward extensive improvements to his park. At Hartlebury Castle, just north of Worcester and the seat of the Bishops of Worcester, Miller visited Bishop Maddox, who was building a new chapel and also redesigning the parkland in the 1750s. From Worcester it was a short ride south to Croome to see his old friend George Coventry, who inherited Croome in 1751, but had begun to improve the grounds in the late 1740s. Several of Lord Coventry's letters to Miller mention both his alterations and plans for the estate, and also their personal friendship.[15]

Miller used to make at least one annual trip to London, often combining this with a visit to properties near London or in the east of the country, such as William Pitt's estate at Enfield Chase, Lord Hardwicke's estate at Wimpole, and Lord Dacre's at Gosfield in Essex. On 2 May 1750, when he was staying in London, he recorded in his diary a visit to Mr Pitt: 'at Enfield Ch: dined there with L^d .Cobham J Granville Mr Legge Nugent, Elliot. Walked there. c h [came home] at 10.' Robert Nugent, MP, lived at Gosfield Hall, in Essex. Miller visited Gosfield several times, and designed both Gothic alterations to the Hall, and improvements to the park. In London Miller was part of the social scene, visiting many people and going by river to the fashionable pleasure gardens at Ranelagh and Vauxhall. In his diary entry for 3 May, he 'went with S[r] Ed. by Water to Ranelagh', and the following day he was 'abt. alterations to VauxH.' though he gives no further details as to what this enigmatic remark might mean. 'S[r] Ed'. was Sir Edward Turner, a friend from Miller's undergraduate days.[16] Miller designed his new house and laid out his landscaped park at Ambrosden, in Oxfordshire. Miller's diaries are full of lists of those people he met, always referred to by their titles where this was appropriate. These contacts were the source of many of his invitations to visit and give advice. On such occasions Miller was always entertained as a friend of the family, whether it was to one of his friends from Oxford days, or to a more recent acquaintance such as Chancellor Lord Hardwicke at Wimpole. Despite his status as a country gentleman with only a small estate, Miller was treated as an equal by members of the nobility and prominent politicians, and formed friendships with some of the most able minds of his generation.

Two contemporary quotes will serve to illustrate the high regard in which Miller was held by his friends. As a preface to the Memoir to James Menteath, Menteath himself wrote, after Miller's death:

> This gentleman was eminent in all branches of Literature, & particularly by his Skill and Taste in Architecture, of which the Town County Hall in Warwick and Lord Littletons House at Hagley Worcestershire are lasting proofs. He was at one time the intimate Friend of Lord Chatham, Hardwick, Littleton, Gilford [Guilford] and Temple, as likewise the acquaintance of almost every Man of Taste or Literature, in the Kingdom, beloved by all who had Happiness to know him, & who were sure to find him a most useful friend. He was learned, religious, benevolent, just & good.[17]

7   *Pages from Miller's Memoir to James Menteath, his Scottish friend from his undergraduate days at Oxford.*

On 25 April 1744, Thomas Leonard Barrett, of Belhus in Essex, one of Miller's friends of longstanding, perhaps best summed up the attitudes of those who knew him when he wrote:

> You ask me how upon such little acquaintance I repose such trust in you; my answer to this shall be, the character Lords Deerhurst and Coventry gave of you which I experienced viz. that there is a certain simplicity and ingenuity in your cariage and discourse which in a week discovers you worth and goodness as much as if one had known you a year; and without compliment from the first time I saw you I became so prejudiced (if I may call it prejudice) in your favour that I from thence forward desired nothing more than the happiness of your friendship.[18]

Miller was also concerned about those beneath him in social status. He gave to the poor, and looked after his own tenants well. In a memorandum to his executrix, he advised:

> Let my old Tenants have such good bargains as may be a sufficient Encouragement to manage the Land in a husbandlike manner, being well convinced that the racking of Land Tenants too hard is as great a prejudice to the Landlord as it is to the Tenant, and that an industrious Tenant has as good a right to a reasonable Profit in his Farm as the Landlord has to the Farm itself.[19]

In an age of excesses and liberality, Miller lived in a regular and reasonably abstemious way. His main occupations were the running of his estate, and his landscaping and architectural plans for his friends and acquaintances, both of which he took very seriously. He read widely, recording his daily reading material in his diaries. His reading material varied from books on local history, such as Dugdale's *History of Warwickshire*, 1659, and Butler and Keyworth's description of 'Edgehill Fight', to works on heraldry, law and religious subjects. His taste in literature varied from classical authors such as Pliny and Horace to Milton's Paradise Regained, and contemporary literature such as novels by Henry Fielding, and Thomson's popular poem The Seasons. Miller was religious, attended church regularly, even when away from home, and often commented on the sermons in his diary.

In 1737 Miller's father died and Miller inherited the estate.[20] Reluctant to leave the academic life, Miller stayed on at Oxford intermittently until after 1740, although in common with many others at this period he did not take a degree.

In 1739, his friend Deane Swift, from undergraduate days in Oxford, a cousin of Jonathan Swift, wrote:

> From your last letters I endeavoured to form a judgement of your present self, Quantum mutatus ab Antiquario, Metaphysico Academico

Miller had already started to landscape his estate by this date, for Swift goes on to say:

> Methinks I see my old friend laughing with Epicurus under the shadow of Edgehill with all his fountains roaring and cascading before him[21]

Evidence of a man of many interests, Miller's library at Radway was extensive, and he himself wrote that it contained 3,000 volumes. His books, in several languages, ranged over subjects as diverse as agriculture, history, Greek and Roman classics, religious writings, poetry, Shakespeare and modern drama. He owned three of Henry Fielding's novels, and the author is traditionally supposed to have read aloud the text of *Tom Jones* to Miller

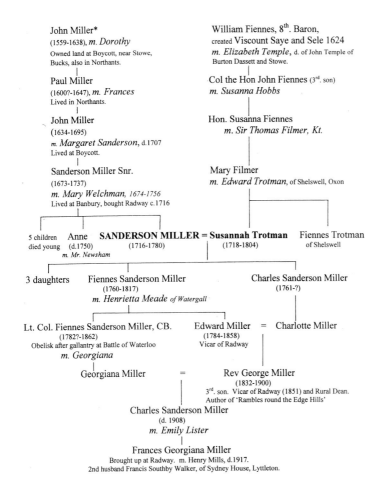

John Miller*
(1559-1638), *m. Dorothy*
Owned land at Boycott, near Stowe,
Bucks, also in Northants.

Paul Miller
(1600?-1647), *m. Frances*
Lived in Northants.

John Miller
(1634-1695)
m. Margaret Sanderson, d.1707
Lived at Boycott.

Sanderson Miller Snr.
(1673-1737)
m. Mary Welchman, 1674-1756
Lived at Banbury, bought Radway c.1716

William Fiennes, 8th. Baron,
created Viscount Saye and Sele 1624
m. Elizabeth Temple, d. of John Temple of
Burton Dassett and Stowe.

Col the Hon John Fiennes (3rd. son)
m. Susanna Hobbs

Hon. Susanna Fiennes
m. Sir Thomas Filmer, Kt.

Mary Filmer
m. Edward Trotman, of Shelswell, Oxon

5 children | Anne | **SANDERSON MILLER** = **Susannah Trotman** | Fiennes Trotman
died young | (d.1750) | (1716-1780) | (1718-1804) | of Shelswell
| *m. Mr. Newsham*

3 daughters | Fiennes Sanderson Miller | Charles Sanderson Miller
| (1760-1817) | (1761-?)
| *m. Henrietta Meade of Watergall*

Lt. Col. Fiennes Sanderson Miller, CB. | Edward Miller | = | Charlotte Miller
(1782?-1862) | (1784-1858)
Obelisk after gallantry at Battle of Waterloo | Vicar of Radway
m. Georgiana

Georgiana Miller = Rev George Miller
(1832-1900)
3rd. son. Vicar of Radway (1851) and Rural Dean.
Author of 'Rambles round the Edge Hills'

Charles Sanderson Miller
(d. 1908)
m. Emily Lister

Frances Georgiana Miller
Brought up at Radway. m. Henry Mills, d.1917.
2nd husband Francis Southby Walker, of Sydney House, Lyttleton.

and his friends at Radway before its publication in 1749, possibly basing the character of Squire Allworthy on that of his host.[22] Miller also collected Civil War pamphlets, for he was enthusiastic about the history of the war and in particular that of the first battle, at Edgehill, which had taken place over his own land in 1642.[23] Miller's books on architecture included *Vitruvius Britannicus*, written by Colen Campbell in 1715, and the translation by Giacomo Leoni of Palladio's *Quattro Libri dell'architettura*, originally published in 1570. Campbell's book and Leoni's translation of the *Quattro Libri …* were published in consecutive years, and both were greeted with acclaim and widely consulted by all who were interested in the newly popular Palladian style. Miller also owned a copy of Serlio's writings on architecture, first published in 1537.[24] Miller thought highly of Inigo Jones, the first English architect to introduce Palladian design to England with the design for the Queen's House at Greenwich, in 1638. In 1736, when Miller was still up at Oxford, a large collection of Jones' drawings, including the annotated copy of the *Quattro Libri …*, were bequeathed to Worcester College. On 6 January 1750, when visiting Oxford, Miller mentioned in his diary that he was: 'at Worcester to see Jones' designs'.

In 1746 Miller married Susannah Trotman, whose family owned land at Bucknell and Shelswell in Oxfordshire, and Siston in Gloucestershire. She brought with her a marriage settlement of £5,000.[25] Her mother was Mary Fiennes, of the family of Lord Saye and

Sele of Broughton Castle, near Banbury, and her grandmother was Elizabeth Temple, of Stowe. Miller had known her since his undergraduate days when visiting Stowe. Miller himself was related to the Fiennes through a marriage dating from the reign of Edward II, and could thence trace his ancestry back to William I. Connections such as these were very important to Miller, for they established his position in a hierarchical society, enabling him to mix easily with the aristocracy in a way which would have been impossible had he been only a tradesman's son made good. Susannah was an asset in more ways than one, for she was a good manager, and played a charming hostess to Miller's many friends, besides having a lively mind herself. She was often specifically included in invitations to Miller from his friends, and Sir Edward Turner wrote a delightful poem in praise of her, the first couplet of which runs: 'Assemblage soft of every grace, Angelic Miniature of Face …'. The children of the marriage surviving to maturity included four daughters and two sons, the eldest called Fiennes Sanderson. Fiennes' son, Miller's grandson, was also given the name Fiennes.

At Radway Miller began to translate some of his ideas into reality. The actual management of land, a necessary prerequisite to any successful landscape design, had formed a part of Miller's upbringing from his earliest years. In adult life Miller had a reputation not only with his own friends but throughout the Midlands and beyond for his ability in the management of land and his expertise in land drainage. He was involved with legal aspects of estate management for Lord Saye and Sele at Broughton Castle, near Banbury, and for Henry Grenville he managed both the legal side and the practicalities of the Enclosure Act for land at Moreton Morrell, a few miles north of Radway, which Grenville had purchased from him.[26]

Miller's expertise in land drainage had particular importance for the farming of the period.[27] Heavy clay was the predominant soil type both in Radway and in much of south Warwickshire. Although clay soils are fertile, drainage is poor, and cultivations were restricted to reasonably dry periods due to the inherent physiological properties of these soils. Even in favourable conditions, heavy clay could require as many as four strong farm horses to pull the plough. According to his diaries Miller took an active interest in his estate, going to the field to see how his men were progressing with haymaking or other farm work, even on occasion doing practical work himself, such as hoeing his newly planted quicks (hawthorn plants). On 26 February 1750, Miller recorded 'sowed Beech Mast [seed] at Oxhouse'. In the summer he often got up early – on 14 July he was 'up at 4. water^d Trees at the Castle at 6'. On 25 October 1756, Miller 'w^d [walked] to ye Bank on ye Hill. Wale and Ned W. at w^k there weed^s… direct^s Smith to Cut Trees on ye Sand Walk'.

Fired with enthusiasm for both Gothic architecture and the laying out of grounds, Miller added Gothic windows and detailing to the old Grange, then gradually transformed his land from the Grange in the valley up to the top of the scarp at Edgehill, before starting to build Egge Cottage (1743-4) on the hill above. He built his Tower with its associated ruins from 1745-7. Following the success of Edgehill Tower, George Lyttelton requested Miller to design a mock ruin for him, and it was the fame of the castle 'ruin' at Hagley, where the park was already a popular venue on the gentry tourist trail for visiting newly improved estates, which led to Miller being commissioned to design the mock ruins for Lord Chancellor Hardwicke at Wimpole.

Two of the first properties which Miller was asked to landscape were Wroxton Abbey and Farnborough Hall, both situated near Radway. At Farnborough Miller altered and improved both the hall and the estate for William Holbech, creating new lakes and two hillside terraces. At Wroxton, Miller assisted in the redesign of the gardens from 1744, the year in which he first met Lord North. Miller was involved in landscaping at Farnborough for at least ten years and at Wroxton until 1760.

From 1745 onwards Miller was assisting Sir Edward Turner, whom he had known from their undergraduate days, with the building of his new house and his landscape improvements at Ambrosden. Among other buildings he designed a sham ruin, probably the first he designed other than his own Edgehill Tower. In 1745/6 Miller was advising Lord Coventry at Croome, Lord Guernsey on his improvements to his park at Packington, north of Coventry, and was also planning alterations for Lord Dacre's house at Belhus, in Essex. The year 1748 saw the construction of the ruined castle on the high ground in the park at Hagley. In 1748-50 Miller visited Gopsall, in Leicestershire, where he probably designed both landscape details and buildings for Charles Jennens.

Between 1748 and 1750 Miller was involved with Sir Roger Newdigate's improvements to his house and estate at Arbury, in north-east Warwickshire. In 1749 the Gothic Lodge at Middleton Stoney, in Oxfordshire, was designed for Lord Jersey, and also in this year Miller designed the Bath House in the woods at Walton, not far from Radway, for his friend Sir Charles Mordaunt. Work traditionally attributed to Miller at Honington Hall, in progress by 1749, included a complete redesign of the formal gardens which ran down to the river.

By 1750, Miller was busy fulfilling requests from many quarters. In this year came the commission to design the castle 'ruin' at Wimpole, although the building was not actually put up until 1772. At Wroxton, Miller and Lord North were involved with the construction of the Temple on the Mount, one of Miller's most important garden buildings. At Alscot Park, near Stratford-upon-Avon, Miller stayed overnight when drawing a plan for James West, who was extending his house and improving the grounds. Miller designed a 'Gothic Greenhouse' in this same year for Lord Stamford at Enville, near Stourbridge, and his name is connected with two or three other buildings in the park there. Hagley and Enville, together with Shenstone's estate The Leasowes, were the most popular places to visit for tourists who wished to see the new improvements in this part of the country.

Another design carried out in 1750 was for the Vernons at Sudbury Hall, in Derbyshire. While not identified beyond doubt, this probably refers to the Deercote in the park, which was radically altered at this time. Between 1755 and 1758 Miller was asked to provide designs for a sham castle at Bath for Ralph Allen, a design for a Gothic Greenhouse and arch for Henry Talbot at Chart Park, Dorking, and a design for a Gothic 'eyetrap' at Portsmouth for a family friend, about which little is known. He was also involved with several designs for buildings in the parkland at Wotton Underwood, Buckinghamshire, for George Grenville.

In 1756, Miller's diary entries were already recording the onset of unusually severe headaches, for which he was seeking medical help, and in 1760 he had his first seizure, which, followed by further ill health, severely limited his future capacity for work.

Miller's three largest architectural designs were for Hagley Hall, West Midlands, which replaced the Lyttelton family's old Elizabethan house, for the new Shire Hall in Warwick, and for a new Gothic Hall and entrance at Lacock Abbey, Wiltshire. The Palladian design of Hagley Hall, 1756-60, is similar to that of Croome Court, Worcestershire, built from 1751 onwards.[28] In c.1753 Miller designed the Shire Hall, built between 1754 and c.1770. In 1755 Miller designed a new Gothic entrance front and Gothic Hall for John Ivory Talbot at the old monastic Lacock Abbey, in Wiltshire.

Architectural additions or alterations to houses include the Gothic work mentioned above for Sir Roger Newdigate, and Gothic bay windows for the Leighs at Adlestrop, near Stow-on-the-Wold. Similar windows and a Gothic porch, which have been ascribed to Miller, were built for Ambrose Isted, at Ecton Hall, near Northampton. At Rockingham Hall, adjacent to Hagley, Miller carried out alterations to the façade for Admiral Smith, Lyttelton's half-brother, at All Souls College, Oxford, he provided Gothic alterations to the library for Robert Vansittart, and at Teston House, in Kent, he gave advice on alterations for Sir Philip Boteler. Miller also assisted with Gothic alterations to the mansion and with 'improvements' to the grounds at Gosfield for Lord Nugent, and at Belhus for Lord Dacre, both in Essex. At Barrowby in Lincolnshire, he designed Gothic windows for the rectory, the home of his friend Menteath, and also new stables. Miller designed the classical stables and some alterations to the house at Beckett, in Berkshire, for Viscount Barrington, and his name is associated with the design of the stables at Packington, for Lord Guernsey. The

9 *A letter written by Miller to his wife when staying at Beckett, in Berkshire, with William, Lord Barrington. Between 1763 and 1770 Miller had designed both alterations to the house, and new stables.*

latter still appear today much as they must have looked when first built by the Hiorns. Miller carried out alterations and designed additions for several churches, including those at Wroxton, for Lord North, at Kineton, near Radway, at Hagley, for George Lyttelton, and at Kilkenny Cathedral in Ireland.[29] Much of his church work has been destroyed by Victorian improvers, including that at Kineton Church, near Radway, where his own great-great-grandson, Francis Miller, vicar of Kineton, was responsible.

Although Miller had a reasonable income from his estate, his expenses with the new building, planting and landscaping at Radway were sufficient to cause him concern, particularly since he was also buying more land, adding to the estate left him by his father. In 1756, Miller decided to increase his income by applying for an enclosure award, which necessitated an Act of Parliament. He wished to consolidate his holdings so that his tenanted land was all together instead of held in separate strips in the open field. Although the enclosure procedure was in itself expensive, Miller stood to gain from the increased income he could expect from renting out the newly enclosed land, and he also wanted to exchange some of his land in the valley for that adjacent to his park on the hill, so that he could enlarge his landscaped area. After enclosure, Miller's estate comprised about 865 acres from the Radway common field out of the total enclosure for Radway of 1,335 acres.[30]

Despite the fact that many of his friends held high political or public offices, politics do not seem to have been particularly important to Miller. He supported his Whig friend, Sir Edward Turner, in the Oxford Election of 1754, but probably more from friendship than from active political leanings. In 1761 he was on the Warwickshire Commission of the Peace, but his main contribution to public life was his design for the new Shire Hall in Warwick, a fine classical building which still stands today. He was also in charge of both the building and obtaining the necessary finance for its construction. In 1770 Miller took the post of Deputy Commissary of Musters, at ten shillings a day and a travelling allowance of £50 a year, procured for him by his friend Lord Barrington.[31] This is thought to be the only salaried post Miller ever held.

By 1756 Miller was already recording in his diary increasing bouts of debilitating headaches, although he continued to work as if nothing was wrong. When he went to London that year he consulted a doctor about headaches. In the following years these attacks began to affect his mind, however, and were giving his friends cause for grave concern. In early December 1759, he had an attack in Warwick when he appeared to be 'raving mad'. Charles Talbot, writing to Miller's nephew Clement Newsham, Miller's sister Anne's son, reports 'with infinite concern' of the 'melancholy and deplorable situation' of his uncle San. Talbot goes on to say:

> The Disorder he has been struggling with at particular periods for sevl. years past has at last got the better of him & made him raving Mad and He is now under Confinement at Hogsden about a Mile out of London. It is impossible to Form any Judgement at present whether he is curable or not. He was seized with the Frenzy but about a fortnight ago in Warwick Town where he gave such publick proofs of his being disordered in his Senses that it was impossible to conceal his Misfortune from the world.[32]

Following this attack, Charles Talbot's brother, the Rev. William Talbot, rector of Kineton, brought Miller up to London to the doctor he had previously been consulting for 'melancholy' – what would today be called depression. However, Miller 'grew so outrageous' that he alarmed the neighbourhood and it was found necessary to put him in a private madhouse. In spite of the severity of this attack, Miller was back at Radway six months later, perfectly himself again and refusing to believe that he had ever been affected. Both Miller's wife Susannah and his friend Menteath, concerned about his health, entreated him to do less. Miller felt he had pressing amounts of work to do; Hagley Hall was not complete, nor the County Hall, and his estate required his attention.

In the Memoir to Menteath, Miller writes:

> It was suggested that I should be stop'd in my Carreer and prevented from Wearing myself, as she [his wife Susannah] thought I certainly must if I went on at that Rate, and therefore it was thought proper that I should be stopped before I wore myself out.[33]

Menteath records that Miller was subject to fits of insanity 'of the most particular kind' from about the year 1760, and on that account had been confined four or five times by his friends and family. In 1774 Miller was confined on account of insanity at the house of Dr Willis at Dunston near Lincoln. Perhaps he had had another attack when staying with Menteath, whose living at Barrowby was not far from Lincoln. It has been suggested that Miller's repetitive illness may have been the result of a condition known today as congenital cerebral arterio-venous malformation. This condition leads eventually to severe migraine attacks, which are sometimes followed by seizures or epileptic fits. These symptoms seem to fit the descriptions of Miller's complaint, about which, of course, nothing would have been known in the 18th century.

Few details are known concerning the last twenty years of Miller's life. The last letters from both Lord Dacre and Henry Grenville were written in 1761. Sir Edward Turner died in 1766, and Lord Lyttelton in 1773. Miller made fewer visits which required extensive travelling, spending more time at home with his family, which by 1761 included the two sons who grew to maturity. He visited Beckett, where he carried out plans for Viscount Barrington,[34] and he continued to visit Stowe. He obviously felt fit enough at the age of 53 to take on the post of Deputy Commissary of Musters, which involved a certain amount of travelling.

Miller died at Doctor Duffield's at Chelsea on 23 April 1780, at the age of 64. He was buried at his home at Radway. His obituary notice in *The Gentleman's Magazine* stated:

> At Mr Duffield's in Chelsea, Saunderson Miller, esq; of Radway, near Edge-Hill in Warwickshire. He was possessed of an estate of 2000L. per Ann. And was very intimate with the lords Temple, Lyttelton, and Mr Shenstone, for whom he planned several buildings, which they erected, having had an exquisite taste in architecture.[35]

The wording of the obituary is probably not quite accurate, for there is no record of Miller having designed any buildings for William Shenstone. Miller's memorial in Radway church, removed to the present church when it was built in 1865, states that he 'acquired the sincerest regard of great and good men' and that it was his constant wish to employ his talents in the service of his friends. It continues: 'Although chiefly devoted to polite Literature yet so great was his Thirst after Knowledge that no Road which led to Truth through the Sciences was left unexplored by him.' The testament further mentions Miller's skilful application of mathematics to architecture, his sincere study of theological pursuits, and 'the tenor of a Life carefully adapted to the Rule of Sacred Writ'. Miller's wife outlived him by many years, dying in 1807 aged 86, and his estate remained in the family until 1916, when the male line died out and the estate was sold. It is now in divided ownership.

3

The Historical Background

A New Society, a New Approach to Science and a Reborn Architecture

❧ · ❧

Miller's ideas and designs in architecture and the laying out of grounds became very popular among the aristocracy and the important politicians of his time, yet he was only a country squire, the son of a draper who had entered the ranks of the landed gentry through the acquisition of a small rural estate. How was Miller able to rise to such a position of influence? How did he come to be in a position where both his friendship and his advice on architectural projects and the laying out of grounds were sought by those in high places? How did it come about that his mock ruined castle at Edgehill, in the depths of the south Warwickshire countryside, generated so much interest that even the Lord Chancellor asked him for a plan for a similar mock ruin on his great estate at Wimpole, in Cambridgeshire?

The major alterations in government during the second half of the 17th century, together with the great advances made in the sciences, meant that by Miller's time a society had emerged which was based on a new philosophy and the importance of the ruling classes. This approach meant that men of Miller's status and intellectual ability found themselves for the first time with a freedom which enabled them to enter society as gentlemen and rise to a position of influence. The last decades of the 17th century heralded great changes both in the government of the country, and also in intellectual attitudes towards science, philosophy and the arts. These changes were to play an important part in framing the society in which Miller found himself towards the end of the 1730s.

Prior to the Civil War, the royal court was the centre of national power, with the monarch at its head. The monarch had a monopoly of power, underlined by the belief in the divine right of kings, to which even his courtiers were subservient. Nobles spent a large part of the year in London, and the court was not only the centre of government, it was also the centre of all that was artistic. The king possessed a fine and extensive art collection, and his elaborate court masques praised the powerful royal image and the mysteries of kingship.[1] After the Civil War, the restored Stuart monarchs endeavoured unsuccessfully to recreate a new monarchy along lines similar to those of Charles I. On his accession in 1685, James II's efforts to re-establish an autocratic monarchy, his conversion to Catholicism, and his pro-Catholic policies finally led to such concern in Parliament that in 1688 a coalition of Whigs and Tories invited the protestant William of Orange to take the throne. James fled ignominiously to France. After 1688 the country estate became increasingly important for the aristocracy and members of Parliament, both as a setting in its own right and also as a venue for the reception of guests.

This revolution spelled the end of absolutist monarchical power and the transference of the power of government from the monarch to Parliament.[2] Liberty had been safeguarded and the supremacy of the Anglican faith maintained, but such was the concern that the Catholic Stuarts might mount an effort to regain the throne – as indeed they did in both 1715 and 1745 – that Roman Catholics were henceforward excluded from politics and from university appointments. Although William and Mary, and also Queen Anne, were still able to wield a certain amount of power against the decrees of Parliament, the political dominance of Parliament became assured on the advent of George I in 1714. The new king neither spoke English nor had as much interest in his English domains as he had in those of Hanover. This historical shift in the centre of power in the country from monarch to Parliament had an effect upon the position and importance of the country estate.

Between 1690 and 1714, the Whigs and Tories alternated in holding power, but after the accession of George I the Whigs held political power until 1762. Many of the Whig politicians had commercial interests both at home and abroad, commercial supremacy and the dominance of the Whig aristocrats being two of the important characteristics of this period. Concurrently with these changes, the intellectual approach to philosophy and religion in the wake of new scientific discoveries was beginning to challenge the whole concept of man's place in the universe.[3]

Following the upheaval of the Civil War, great strides were made in the advancement of science. In 1666, working in Cambridge, Isaac Newton established the law of gravity, and worked on the laws of motion and the movement of the planets. In Oxford there was a group of outstanding scientists with wide-ranging interests. Robert Boyle, working at his laboratory in the High Street, discovered the law relating the pressure and volume of gases, among many other scientific achievements. Robert Hooke, his assistant, used a microscope to make the first identification of the biological cell. William Harvey, who came to Oxford as physician to Charles I after the battle of Edgehill in 1642, discovered the circulation of the blood. He and George Bathurst carried out experiments on the embryology of chickens at Trinity College. Boyle and John Evelyn, who had been a student at Oxford, both had interests in the planting of fruit trees and of forest trees. Evelyn's *Sylva, or a Discourse on Forest Trees* (1664), on the planting and care of trees, was influential in encouraging landowners to plant to provide replacement timbers for the Navy, and this and Evelyn's other publications on many different aspects of gardening and husbandry were widely read. Evelyn and Boyle regularly visited the Oxford Botanic or Physic Garden, which had

10   *John Evelyn, 1620-1706, by T. Bragg.*

been started for the study of plants as early as 1621.[4] Oxford was the first English city to have a physic garden where plants were grown specifically for study.

In 1649, Christopher Wren came to Oxford University as an undergraduate when he was 17, and devoted himself entirely to mathematics, astronomy and natural philosophy. After taking a post as astronomer at Gresham College in London, he returned to Oxford four years later, in 1661, to take up the post of Savilian Professor of Astronomy, before being asked by Archbishop Sheldon to design the building now known as the Sheldonian Theatre for the presentation of degrees. Wren planned this building in the classical style, his ingenious design illustrating his ability to find practical solutions to architectural problems. In order to span 70x80 feet without visible supports the ceiling was suspended from a series of concealed triangular trusses. In 1660, the Royal Society was founded in London

11 *John Locke, 1632-1704, by Michael Dahl.*

'for the promotion of Physico–Mathematicall Experimental learning'. Charles II granted it a royal charter, John Evelyn gave the fledgling society its name, and Christopher Wren was asked to draw up the wording for the charter.[5] The new spirit of enquiry, experiment and deduction led to the development of an empiricist approach both to practical science and to philosophy. Boyle wrote in praise of separating scientific truth from alchemy, and others began to search for liberty and truth, and the existence of order and rationality in the natural world, as opposed to the mysticism of previous ages, and a belief that a Divine Providence governed all things.

There developed a profound sense of the conception of man's place in the universe. Hitherto the earth had been thought of as the centre of the heavens, and the ancient world had been obsessed with a sense of original sin, and the need to be humble before Almighty God. But it became less easy to remain humble before an all powerful God when men were achieving such great scientific triumphs, and advances in worldwide trade were bringing increasing prosperity.[6] To the west, the Americas were being opened up and settled, and in the east trade prospects were also improving. The East India Company, originally founded in 1599 to compete with the Dutch for the profitable trade with the Spice Islands, had expanded through trade with China and had established a firm trading base on the Indian subcontinent. Throughout the 18th century the East India Company was becoming more and more powerful through trade and local political alliances backed up by a military presence.[7]

John Locke (1632-1704) was a leading light in the promulgation of the new philosophical ideas. An Oxford scholar, Locke became a physician, and was able to save the life of his patron, the Earl of Shaftesbury. In 1683 Shaftesbury was forced to take political asylum

12   *Heythrop House, the main entrance. This Baroque house, situated near Enstone, Oxfordshire, was designed by Thomas Archer (1668-1743) in the early years of the 18th century for Charles Talbot, 1st Duke of Shrewsbury.*

13   *Blenheim, the approach to the palace from the north.*

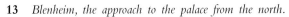

in Holland for his views on limiting royal power, and Locke accompanied him, spending these years in exile writing treatises, including his *Essay Concerning Human Understanding*. In the *Essay ...* he argued that human knowledge was limited to the world as revealed by the senses, showing that innate ideas on their own were inadequate as a means of understanding. Locke's philosophical liberalism and religious toleration, his thoughts on the possibility of moral improvement in society, his ideas concerning the potential equality of men to one another, and his empiricist approach to the theory of knowledge became the accepted views of philosophers and politicians for many years to come. His ideas heralded a revolutionary approach to the understanding of the sources and boundaries of knowledge, and ushered in the beginnings of the so-called 'Enlightenment'. Shaftesbury himself, whose main work *Characteristics of Men, Manners, Opinions, Times* was published in 1711, believed in the English spirit of Liberty, and praised the high spirit of a people who were in the habit of judging for themselves both spiritual matters and the works of man in both arts and science.

These ideas illustrate the beginning of a concept which allows men of intelligence and education, no matter what their background, to become part of intellectual and polite society. If not quite the acceptance of the 'noble savage' into society, then this new approach at least allowed men from lower stations in life but with particular abilities to become accepted by their social superiors in a way which had been impossible in previous centuries.[8] If all men were equal apart from having been born into either riches or poverty, Miller was as good as the next man. The appreciation of his exceptional abilities

14 *Ditchley, the house across the park from the lake.*

15   *Chiswick, Lord Burlington's villa.*

by aristocrats and important politicians, and their ready acceptance, on equal terms, of the friendship for which he seemed to have been renowned, underlines this concept.

The conviction became widespread that a beneficent Providence regulated both the course of Nature and the fortunes of men, and that there was in all men a benevolent spirit. Great value was placed on reasonableness and polite conversation, combined with intellectual speculation. Both English intellectuals, and the French *philosophes*, placed their faith in the hope that the slow progress of education would gradually lift the more intelligent members of the common people to become part of polite society, the stability of which, in the first half of the 18th century and before the whisperings of revolution, was taken for granted.[9]

Even with the existence of financial resources, it requires both the availability of capital and the existence of a comparatively stable and peaceful society for men to consider expending much money on building and estate improvements. By 1714 the War of the Spanish Succession had been brought to a triumphant conclusion and the Duke of Marlborough had been granted the estate and promise of the new mansion at Blenheim in reward for his military successes. The Treaty of Utrecht had forced Louis XIV to recognise the Protestant succession in England, and England had secured access to her trade centres in Europe, the Mediterranean and in the New World, setting the scene for her imperial expansion.[10] Sir Robert Walpole, the first minister, made certain that England enjoyed a long period of peace in which to allow her commercial interests to flourish. New money was coming into land, often at the expense of old Tory families with royalist sympathies who had been impoverished by the Civil War and then later by the Land Tax which had been imposed to raise money for the War of the Spanish Succession. A pertinent example of this provided Miller with one of his first commissions: the improvement of Farnborough. In 1684 William Holbech's grandfather, a lawyer, had bought the estate of Farnborough from the Raleghs, an impoverished royalist family who had been forced to mortgage their estate to him. Farnborough lay across the valley from Miller's own estate at Radway.

Between the first years of the 18th century and the early 1740s there was a boom in country house building, resulting in the building of around one hundred and fifty new houses.[11] Important mansions dating from the early years of the century, all with notable gardens, include, among many others, Castle Howard (designed by John Vanbrugh and actually begun in 1699), Blenheim (designed by Vanbrugh and begun in 1705), Heythrop, north Oxfordshire (designed by Thomas Archer for the Duke of Shrewsbury and started about the same date), and Ditchley, also in north Oxfordshire (designed by James Gibbs and finished in 1722). Miller visited Ditchley, and almost certainly would have seen both Blenheim and Heythrop, the latter being of particular interest as a probable source of inspiration for Miller's own landscaping. Many owners of new houses were members of Parliament, the importance of a new house being directly connected to political success and the enhancement of the owner's prestige in the country district from which he would seek re-election.

The English Baroque style in which these great houses were built was soon to be superseded

by a revival of classicism marked by the introduction of the Palladian style, harking back not only to Vitruvius, who wrote his treatise on architecture c.27 BC, but also to the work of Inigo Jones in the 17th century. Jones was the first English classical architect, although initially a painter and decorative artist responsible for the production of masques at the court of King James I. His second visit to Italy, 1613-14, confirmed his interest in the study of architecture, and in 1615 he became Surveyor of the King's Works. One of his first commissions was the classical Queen's House at Greenwich, finally completed for Henrietta Maria, Charles I's Queen, in 1635. The Queen's House, together with the Banqueting House, in Whitehall, and the much altered St Paul's church in Covent Garden are among his very few surviving works. Jones had been particularly interested in the Roman 'antique', as described by Vitruvius. His own architectural drawings, together with his annotated copy of Palladio's *Quattro libri del'achitettura*, were deposited at Worcester College, Oxford, in 1736, during

16 *Chiswick, statue of Inigo Jones (1573-1652) outside the villa. Jones was the father of English classical architecture.*

17 *Chiswick, statue of Andrea Palladio (1508-80) outside the villa. Lord Burlington based his neo-Palladian revival on Palladio's famous Italian renaissance architecture.*

18 *Hagley Hall, a view from Milton's Seat, part way up the hill towards the castle ruin.*

the time that Miller was an undergraduate at Oxford. Later, when visiting Oxford on 6 January 1750, Miller mentioned in his diary that he was 'at Worcester to see Jones' designs'.

The amateur architect Lord Burlington, who had purchased most of Inigo Jones' architectural designs as well as the majority of Palladio's drawings, was the leader in the development of the Palladian revival in England. Two publications mark the emergence of the Palladian revival, published in 1715 and 1716 respectively: the first volume of Colen Campbell's *Vitruvius Britannicus*, the first book on purely British architecture, and the first part of Giacomo Leoni's edition of Palladio's *Quattro libri del'architettura …*, which had been translated into English by Nicholas Dubois. *Vitruvius Britannicus* was subscribed to, among others, by 22 dukes, and the illustrations showed many classical and Palladian plans and elevations of great houses. Miller's own library included both books, and in one entry in his diary for 17 September 1750, he recorded reading *Vitruvius Britannicus*. Following his tours abroad, particularly in Italy, Burlington drew upon Roman antiquity for the design of his new villa at Chiswick, which at the time of its inception was unique in Europe.[12] This building had a great influence on the subsequent popularity of the Palladian style, often chosen to replace an earlier house. A new mansion with a classical exterior would be complemented by a symmetrical interior layout of reception rooms, replacing the old medieval asymmetrical style of hall and cross passages.

Miller's biggest architectural achievement, Hagley Hall, was built between 1756 and 1760 for Sir George Lyttelton, who wished to replace his old Tudor half-timbered house. It was modelled on similar lines to those of Wilton House, rebuilt in 1636 by Isaac de Caux with advice from Inigo Jones,[13] and also of Houghton, built almost a hundred years later for Sir Robert Walpole. Hagley Hall had a simple Palladian exterior, a tower at each of the four corners, and an interior of interconnecting rooms with fine decorative plasterwork.

Part of a contemporary description of Hagley Hall by Philip Yorke, who succeeded his father at Wimpole as the second Earl of Hardwicke, reads:

> … a most excellent house for which Mr Miller of Warwickshire was architect. The hall, salon, eating-room, gallery and drawing room on the first floor are remarkably well proportioned and pleasant rooms. There are two complete apartments for strangers besides; the attic floor is the best I ever saw; and the rooms in the four towers very good. Lord Lyttelton told me he could make twelve or fourteen *lits de maitres*.[14]

The bearing which the architecture of Oxford had on the development of Miller's architectural abilities and style cannot be underestimated. The architecture of Oxford's buildings was often both of the highest quality, and innovative for its period, since the city was so important to church, crown and academia. Miller's interest in architecture appears to have stemmed directly from his time as an undergraduate at Oxford, for he started to alter his own house, Radway Grange, very shortly after inheriting his property and while he was still studying at Oxford. Among the oldest buildings in Oxford were the castle, dating from 1071, and parts of the 13th-century city walls. Several medieval buildings, for example Mob Quad, Merton College, date back to this period, and the Gothic style, which had originated in France *c.*1140,[15] continued to be the dominant architectural style for the Oxford colleges well into the 17th century. Oriel College, adjacent to Miller's own

19   *Oxford Botanic Gardens, the main entrance arch seen from the gardens, built 1632-3 by Nicholas Stone, master mason to Inigo Jones.*

college of St Mary Hall, was rebuilt at this period (1620-42) in the Gothic style.[16] The entrance to St Mary Hall, and also a bay window at Oriel, were probably the inspiration behind Miller's own Gothic bay windows built as extensions to Radway Grange, and his work in a similar vein at Arbury in Warwickshire, Adlestrop in Gloucestershire, and Ecton Hall in Northamptonshire. The Gothic style had reigned supreme until in the 17th century Inigo Jones introduced the classical Italianate style, and Gothic continued to be the traditional style in cities such as Oxford.

The first buildings constructed in Oxford in the classical style were the gateways to the new Botanic Gardens, 1632-3. Based on the Roman triumphal arch, these were designed by Nicholas Stone, Inigo Jones' master mason for the Banqueting House, in London. In 1664-7 Wren's classically inspired Sheldonian Theatre was built, followed in subsequent years by a new library for Queen's College in the classical style, and Tom Tower, the entrance gate to Christ Church, designed in Gothic to complement the existing college architecture. Wren was also responsible for the new Gothic entrance to the Divinity School, opposite the Sheldonian Theatre, where he repeated the ogee-shaped arch used in his design for

Tom Tower. Miller may have been inspired by Wren's ogee arches, for he used ogee arches successfully in the entrance to the Hall at Lacock Abbey, Wiltshire, in 1753, and also in the design for the Museum, a garden building at Enville, built in 1750.

During Miller's time at Oxford, impressive new buildings, built between 1700 and 1737 in both classical and Gothic styles, came to dominate the academic centre of the city. The earliest neo-Palladian building was the Peckwater quadrangle at Christ Church (1707-14), designed by the Dean of the College, Henry Aldrich, who had travelled in Europe, and whose designs imitated to some extent those of Italian Renaissance palaces. In the following three decades, major innovative architectural designs were carried out by Nicholas Hawksmoor (1661-1736), George Clarke (1661-1736) who with the master mason William Townesend was responsible for major new work at Queen's College, c.1713-20, and James Gibbs (1682-1754), who designed the Radcliffe Camera, begun in 1737. Hawksmoor's Clarendon Building, 1712-13, with its large Doric portico, stood as the entrance to the heart of the University. It was followed by other monumental classical buildings after the Roman manner, including a new college, Worcester College, founded in 1714, and a new library at Christ Church, 1717. Hawksmoor frequently adopted a variety of styles for buildings

20 *Oriel College, main quadrangle. The buildings of St Mary Hall adjoin one of the inner quadrangles.*

coinciding in date, sometimes using forms directly based on antiquity while at other times using inventive adaptations. Besides his work with Vanbrugh at Castle Howard, dating from 1699, Hawksmoor had had a long connection with Oxford, commencing in 1709 when he advised on the rebuilding of the front quadrangle at Queen's College. In 1714 Hawksmoor was asked to design the extensions to All Souls College. The design which was finally accepted for the new quadrangle and the Codrington Library was in Gothic, but was a stylistic compromise, for the exterior is Gothic, but the interiors are classical in inspiration.[17] Hawksmoor used lanterns on top of towers in a dramatic composition at All Souls, perhaps inspiring Miller to add the lanterns to Gibbs' towers on the Gothic Temple at Stowe.

Hart has an interesting comment on Hawksmoor's consistent use of the octagon as a model for his lanterns: 'Given Wren's link between form and symbolic meaning, this relevance may well have rested with its octagonal shape … The octagon had long

21   *The Divinity School entrance, Oxford. The building is 15th-century; the entrance was designed by Sir Christopher Wren.*

been associated in the Christian tradition with the *octava dies* or eighth day.'[18] This referred to the time of the risen Christ from the tomb, beyond the earthly cycle of seven days, as given in the Authorised Version of the Bible, St John 20:26. Christian associations between resurrection and the octagon were, at the very least, perfectly compatible with the use of an octagonal model for open church lanterns, especially one connected with wind, or *spiritus*. Hawksmoor had used the octagonal tower of Andromachus at Athens, known as the Tower of the Winds, as the model for his proposed bell tower for the chapel at Worcester College in Oxford. Miller used the octagon form repeatedly in his designs; the Shire Hall at Warwick, his own Tower at Radway, and the upper room of the Bath House at Walton all furnishing examples. Miller's library reveals his interest in religious writings, and he not only attended church every Sunday, but also commented on sermons in his diary entries. Although his use of the octagon is not reserved specifically for religious buildings, his obvious liking for the form may well have been associated with this background. The Shire Hall, for example, which was to be used for the judiciary, could be said to have had a spiritual background in the sense of the triumph of good over evil.

Miller himself designed buildings in both the classical and the Gothic style, his greatest number of works being carried out between the years 1740-60. His output ranged from the classical Hagley Hall and the new Shire Hall for Warwick, which has an interior design based on the octagon, to his idiosyncratic mock castle ruins. His many small landscape buildings varied from classical to Gothic, and were designed in a mixture of styles, occasionally even venturing into the Chinese.

22   *All Souls College, Oxford, the towers with lanterns in the north quadrangle. The quadrangle was designed in the Gothic style but with classical symmetry by Nicholas Hawksmoor in 1715.*

During Miller's lifetime, Gothic as a style took on a new popularity, which became known as the Gothic Revival. The Gothic Revival, which had its origins in a literary movement interested in fantastic and romantic history, manifested itself in a renewed interest in the architecture of castle and monastic ruins,[19] and became associated with the rights and freedoms of our ancient forbears. In the 17th century, the Parliamentarians had revived the idea of what they took to have been ancient prerogatives of government by tribal assembly, thought originally to have been introduced into England by the Germanic invaders. Jonathan Swift, writing in 1719, stated that Parliaments were a peculiarly Gothic institution, implanted in England by the Saxon Princes.[20] The Saxons, together with the Jutes and the Angles, were a Gothic people who had brought with them the principles which had become enshrined in the traditional idea of freedom and embodied in English law. King Alfred, the greatest Saxon monarch, was identified with the best traditions of the English constitution, and to study Saxon history thus became not only the preserve of antiquaries but also the duty of patriots.[21]

Although the Saxons had submitted to the Romans, they never gave up the freedom of their Gothic institutions of government, and it is this contrast between Gothic freedom, associated with the Saxons, and Roman tyranny that gave to the 18th century the idea of 'Gothic' to denote liberal, or 'enlightened', thought. Interestingly, the two terms 'Saxon' and 'Gothic' appeared to have been more or less interchangeable in the 18th-century mind. Batty Langley, writing in his 'Gothic Architecture Improved' suggested that it was 'reasonable to believe … that … there was no distinction of Goths from Saxons, but in general all were called Saxons'.[22] The Gothic style of architecture was seen as a historical link back to the ancient British freedoms so important to the Whigs of Lord Cobham's persuasion. A preference for the Gothic style of architecture might be therefore be characterised as a 'Whiggish' taste.[23]

By the 18th century, a knowledge of local antiquities and of heraldry had become a subject in which most educated country gentlemen were expected to take an interest, and with Miller this was certainly so. Antiquarians had long had an interest in Gothic, as is shown in the depiction of the monuments of medieval architecture in *Monasticon Anglicanum*, 1655, by Sir William Dugdale and Roger Dodsworth, and Dugdale's own work, the *History of Warwickshire*, published in 1656.[24] Miller himself had a copy of Dugdale's *History of Warwickshire*. Miller corresponded regularly with Charles Lyttelton, who had studied the antiquities of Worcestershire, the county of his family's seat at Hagley. Younger brother to Sir George Lyttelton, Charles was later to become both the Bishop of Carlisle, and in 1765 the president of the Society of Antiquaries.

At Stowe, Lord Cobham commissioned James Gibbs to design him a Gothic building, named the Gothic Temple or Temple of Liberty. In striking contrast to Stowe's great classical garden buildings both in style and colour, it was built in a deep reddish brown ironstone to a three-cornered plan, with Gothic windows and battlemented corner turrets, and a tower. Gibbs (1682-1754), although a Tory and a Catholic with Jacobite sympathies, was a versatile and outstanding architect, and was employed by Lord Cobham after Vanbrugh's death to design various other buildings in the classical style at Stowe. Gibbs was also responsible for some London churches, including the church of St Martin-in-the-Fields in London, basically classical with a steeple reminiscent of the Gothic. Oxford's Radcliffe Camera, built between 1737 and 1748, based on an original design by Hawksmoor, was one of Gibbs' finest works. Miller would have been conversant with the construction of the Radcliffe Camera, started as he was finishing his studies at Oxford, and also, of course, with the Temple of Liberty at Stowe. Between 1748 and 1756, the Temple of Liberty was altered and embellished with architectural and heraldic additions which are attributed to Miller himself. Miller's friendship with George Ballard, the Saxon specialist from Oxford University, underlines Miller's interest in history and the Saxon past.

Beyond the cities, the Gothic traditions of local builders were a firm link in the chain of the survival of the style. At a distance from London were men who had established reputations and were craftsmen in their own right, and the Gothic had often survived continuously as a style used in country districts where there was a local supply of good building stone and a strong tradition of building.[25] In the Midlands such men were represented by the Woodwards of Chipping Campden and the Hiorns of Warwick. The Hiorns carried out some of Miller's own designs, and the Woodwards built James West's Gothic additions to the house at Alscot Park in the 1750s, work which may well have been designed by Miller. Edward Woodward was also responsible for the Gothic remodelling of the local church for West at Preston-on-Stour.

Why build a *ruin*? The answer to this question is partly answered by the perceived value of Gothic history to the new democratic power of government. William Stukeley, first president of the Society of Antiquaries, fostered a general interest in ruins in the first half of the 18th century through his interests in ancient stone circles and their religious significance. Michel Baridon[26] shows that the creative imagination of the 18th century appears to have attributed a great power of stimulation to ruins, who were 'sung by Gray, described by Gibbon, painted by Wilson, Lambert, Turner, Girtin … they adorned the sweeps and the concave slopes of gardens designed by Kent and Brown, … and graced the pages of hundreds of sketchbooks …'. Ruins were an essential element of the landscape of sensibility, giving it an element of nostalgia which was part of its essence, for ruins in themselves create a romantic aura. The vogue of this taste was inseparably linked with the English garden, and its influence was felt in most countries of Europe and in America. Ruins of both English castles or monasteries, and also the classical ruins of antiquity in Italy, which were depicted in the paintings of Claude Lorraine and Gaspard Dughet, had ideological connections with the political myths of the time. Baridon mentions the connection between Gothic pointed architecture, the gloom of forest groves, and the traditional freedom associated with woods by the northern peoples, the Saxons and the Goths. Horace Walpole referred to the 'gloomth' of his Gothic chapel at Strawberry Hill, set in a small grove of yews. Literary developments, such as Horace Walpole's Gothic horror novel *The Castle of Otranto* (published in 1764), also lent the Gothic style a certain association with romantic melancholy.[27]

The importance of including genuine ruins in the creation of a landscaped estate had been noted by others before Miller, men such as John Aislabie and Thomas Duncombe. Aislabie, who turned to landscape gardening in 1720, after his resignation, when Chancellor of the Exchequer, over the disastrous affair of the South Sea Bubble, utilised views of the impressive ruins of Fountains Abbey in his gardens at Studley Royal, in Yorkshire. Thomas Duncombe was prompted by the presence of the ruins of Rievaulx Abbey in the Rye valley, also in Yorkshire, to incorporate views of them into his own landscaped terrace grounds at Duncombe in the 1750s.

John Vanbrugh praised both the historical interest and the romantic appeal of ruins when he made his unsuccessful appeal to the Duchess of Marlborough for the preservation of the ruins of Woodstock Manor, in the grounds of Blenheim Palace. Alfred's Hall at Cirencester, built by Lord Bathurst in memory of the model patriot king who served the free Saxons, was the first mock ruined castle to be built, in 1721-34. As political power became centred more and more in the hands of the landed aristocracy and gentry, and the landscaping of grounds became increasingly important to those in power, so a romantic interest in mock ruins became more popular. Following Miller's lead, others took up the design of mock ruins, men such as Robert Adam, William Chambers and John Soane.

The social scene, and indeed the whole approach to life, had changed markedly since the 17th century. A spirit of scientific enquiry and a search for truth had led to a philosophy of liberalism towards all men. Men of Miller's status in life, with education and ability, were able to mix easily with the nobility. The first quarter of the 18th century had seen a period of initial military success, followed by peace at home. As the century progressed, the arts and architecture flourished, and financial expansion and success abroad encouraged an optimistic approach to the future which men such as Miller were able to grasp.

4

Developments in Garden Design
between 1700 and 1740
and their Influence on Miller's Work

❧·❧

The background to Miller's interest in a natural style in the laying out of grounds must be sought in the history of garden and estate design immediately prior to the 1730s, a period when attitudes towards the design of ornamental grounds were undergoing rapid change and the informal approach was gathering momentum.

At the start of the 18th century gardens were completely formal in design. Subsequent decades witnessed a transition away from this formality, and during the early years of Miller's active working life, in the 1730s and 1740s, experiments were being made with many different styles of 'natural' or informal gardening. No single definite style predominated. By the time that Miller's ill health had forced him into early retirement, Lancelot Brown's large-scale landscape plans, the first of which was produced in 1751, were fast becoming the norm to which every fashionable man of taste with landed property aspired.[1]

The development of this new informality can be traced through the intellectual ideas of the 17th-century scientists and philosophers. After the restoration of the monarchy in 1660, garden design in England was influenced by French ideals, exemplified by the work of Andre Le Notre, designer to the French King Louis XIV. Le Notre's grandiose plans featured parterres laid out in complicated geometric designs, with long avenues of trees radiating out from the main house. Garden design underlined the centrality of power, whether at the Royal Court or the great house. Between 1689 and 1702, during the reign of William and Mary, the royal garden at Hampton Court was developed after the Dutch style, the popularity of which was to be seen in the increased use of clipped evergreens, ornamental canals and formal pools.[2]

After her accession Queen Anne altered the gardens at Hampton Court, greatly simplifying the intricate designs and removing the ubiquitous box edging, which she disliked. She also instructed her gardener, Henry Wise, to enlarge the informal wilderness to the north of the Palace.[3] The word 'wilderness' in the 18th century was used to denote an area of trees, or trees and bushes, often enclosed by a clipped hedge, with paths within the planting. It was usually on the outskirts of the ornamental grounds, and the trees within the wilderness were allowed to grow to their full height, though the lowest branches were often pruned away.

Royal gardens had always exerted an influence on general gardening trends, but during Queen Anne's reign (1702-14), the writings of Joseph Addison and Alexander Pope also exerted a strong influence on gardening fashions. Addison, writing in *The Spectator* in 1712, criticised topiary, and described his own garden as 'a Confusion of Kitchin and Parterre, Orchard and Flower Garden, which lie … mixt and interwoven with one another …'.[4] He believed that simple pleasures, among which he numbered architecture, art, statuary, natural scenery and gardening, stimulated the imagination. In 1713, Pope, commenting on how the ancient Romans such as Virgil, Horace and Pliny preferred the simplicity of unadorned Nature, wrote: 'how contrary to this Simplicity is the modern Practice of Gardening; we seem to make it our Study to recede from Nature … And are better pleas'd to have our Trees in the most awkward Figures of Men and Animals, than in the most regular of their own.'[5] Pope came to be seen as the epitome of Britain's own Augustan age of stability and literary eminence, and his publications, in which he referred to gardening with Nature, affected current attitudes to both the natural world and to garden design.

Pope utilised some of the ideas of the Ancients in his own five-acre garden, which led down to the river Thames in fashionable Twickenham, where he lived from 1719 onwards. He referred to his house and garden as 'my Tusculum' after Cicero's villa outside Rome. Pope directed that the 'genius of the place' should be consulted in the design for any garden or estate, and that the designer should work with Nature, who:

> Calls in the country, catches opening glades
> Joins willing woods, and varies shades from shades;
> Now breaks, or now directs, the intending lines;
> Paints as you plant, and as you work, designs.[6]

23   *Het Loo, Holland, the palace of William of Orange and Mary, a restored parterre. This parterre illustrates the Dutch style introduced at Hampton Court when William and Mary took the English throne in 1688.*

Pope introduced informality and perspective into his own garden, and also created his famous grotto, using many different and unusual rocks and shells. The grotto, which still exists, although unfortunately vandalised of many of its treasures, joined the two parts of the garden in a tunnel under his house and the road. 'By linking scientific, classical and romantic nature,' Mavis Batey wrote, 'Pope's grotto was important in the 18th-century search to establish man's relationship with nature.'[7] Pope's ideal estate is described in the following extract of his poem based loosely on the first few lines of Jonathan Swift's 'Imitations of Horace':

> I've often wished that I had clear
> For life, six hundred pounds a year,
> A Handsome House to lodge a Friend,
> A River at my garden's end,
> A Terras-walk, and half a Rood
> Of land set out to plant a Wood.[8]

24 *Joseph Addison, 1672-1719, by Michael Dahl.*

Pope's poetry and philosophy would have been known to Miller, who was himself interested in poetry and philosophy. Both were friends of George Lyttelton, and both assisted Lyttelton in his improvments for Hagley. Pope died in 1744. Miller's first recorded visit to Hagley is noted in his diary as 21 October 1749, but Dickens and Stanton refer to Miller having visited Hagley before the death of Lyttelton's first wife Lucy in 1747,[9] and probably he had visited Hagley earlier than this.

Stephen Switzer, designer and author, advocated extending the ornamental design nearer the house by the use of long avenues, often associated with adjacent strips of woodland. He suggested the planting of such rides or avenues, interspersed with small woodland, across working farmland in a manner which he referred to as 'extensive gardening' in his *Ichnographia Rustica*, first published in 1718. Switzer's plans for this ideal 'extensive gardening' included complicated winding paths joining his extended avenues – 'a little Regularitie' near the main house, and then many 'Twinings and Windings' in the outer grounds.[10] In a design of his for Caversham, in Berkshire, however, published in Colen Campbell's *Vitruvius Britannicus, III*, in 1725, the long radiating avenues stand alone. The upkeep involved with many intersecting paths and hedges and the difficulty of working in small agricultural fields formed in awkward shapes meant that this type of extensive design never became popular.

During the early years of the new century, Lord Carlisle began to create his grand heroic landscape at Castle Howard, in Yorkshire, to the designs of John Vanbrugh, with Nicholas Hawksmoor as his architectural draughtsman. This new landscape contained many innovative informal features. Carlisle eschewed George London's formal plan for the new gardens, and rather than levelling the site in the traditional manner, he and Vanbrugh took the natural topography as their guide in their informal design for the grounds. In the plan for Ray Wood, an ornamental wood close to the house, Carlisle broke new ground, again deciding against the initial plan, that of a regular star-shaped system of paths within the wood, in favour of groves threaded with winding paths.[11] A traditional network of avenues was, however, established in the parkland to the west and south of the house, outside the ornamental landscape. These long avenues added to the stately impression given by the approach drive, with its castellated gateways.

At Castle Howard, the statues set along the terrace created from the old main street of the village of Henderskelfe, together with the Temple of the Four Winds at the end of the terrace, give an air of importance to the countryside. Worsley comments that the individual landscape buildings, such as the Temple of the Four Winds, the Mausoleum, and the Pyramid and Pyramid Gate, are imbued specifically with Roman overtones, and of course the area had once been part of a Roman province.[12] The mock fortified walls and tower, built 1719-25, appear medieval, however, not Roman. It seems much more likely that these were intended to give the appearance of having been part of the walls of a medieval castle whose grounds were on the site of the grand new estate, rather than harking back to the walls of old Rome, as has been suggested elsewhere. They look similar to many an old English castle ruin, and help to confirm the new estate in the noble traditions of English history.[13] It is particularly in Miller's creation of similar mock castle-like buildings that his work can best be compared with that of Vanbrugh at Castle Howard.

Designed grounds in the early part of the 18th century often incorporated features such as terraces with bastions, or strong stone walls and towers which, despite their ornamental

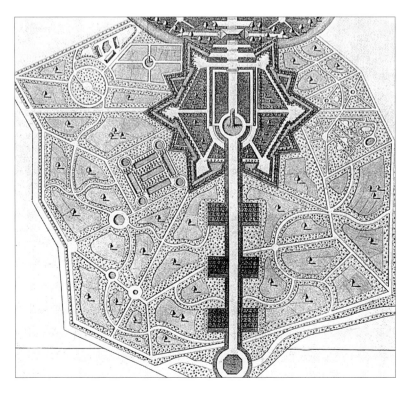

25 *The Manor of Paston divided and planted into Rural Gardens', an engraving by Stephen Switzer in* Ichnographia Rustica, *1718. This imagined plan encapsulated Switzer's ideas for the perfect design for a gentleman's seat.*

26 *Castle Howard, the viewing terrace, which was formed along the line of the old main street of the village of Henderskelfe.*

context, had obvious military origins. The War of the Spanish Succession, 1702–13, had been conducted with many sieges which required fortified earthworks and bastions from which the besieging army could open fire on the city or fortress it hoped to overcome. Some of these military style devices were copied in garden design by Vanbrugh, such as the mock fortifications with bastions around Ray Wood at Castle Howard, and a diamond shaped bastion at Claremont, in Surrey. At Seaton Delaval, in Northumberland, a ditch with a platform above it was constructed. This was interrupted by four circular bastions, which may even have been intended for actual defence, since the Jacobite rising of 1715 was a very recent event, and the Scottish border was only a few miles away. Vanbrugh's designs may even have been based on the Elizabethan walls with star-pointed bastions around the border town of Berwick. Vanbrugh's great kitchen garden at Blenheim, with its solid walls and bastions, was partly military in inspiration, as befitted the estate of a great general. In 1711, Stephen Switzer designed earth ramparts with viewing bastions in the Dutch style around the ornamental grounds at Grimsthorpe, illustrated by William Stukeley in 1736.[14] These are similar to those shown in his plan of the manor of Paston. Miller recorded having visited Grimsthorpe when staying with his friend Menteath some time after 1759, though he does not comment on the landscaping.[15]

27   *Castle Howard, the Temple of the Four Winds (Vanbrugh, 1728). From this point, at the far end of the terrace, there were spreading views over the estate and its landscape buildings.*

In Yorkshire, terrace walks were used to great effect at Studley Royal, where John Aislabie created walks on the wooded hillsides which overlooked his valley water garden. In the same county, Thomas Duncombe also created a remarkable terrace three decades later, at Duncombe, overlooking the Rye valley. Other estates with terraces included the grounds at Oatlands, in Surrey. Here a fine terrace, dating from before 1730, of about half a mile in length, overlooked a 'canal' and the prospect beyond. From about 1740, the Earl of Lincoln began to landscape the gardens, retaining the terrace, enlarging the 'canal' to give the appearance of a natural lake called the Broad Water, and creating an intricate grotto. A much smaller garden which Miller would probably have seen when visiting relatives at Siston, near Bristol, was that at Clifton. In 1705 Thomas Goldney, son of a Quaker merchant of the same name, bought the property at Clifton and began to create the garden, which was enlarged and developed by his son, Thomas Goldney the third. Although small, it was popular with 18th-century visitors for its intricate and impressive shell grotto and waterworks. Mrs Delany visited the garden in 1756, and a description by the Duchess of Northumberland after her visit in the early 1760s included a list of the 'Shells Fossils Oars Sparrs Petrifactions &c' decorating the grotto, many of them collected from the sides of the Bristol Gorge. She also referred to 'a Lyon carv'd in stone as large as the Life' within the grotto. It is still there, a rather incongruous inmate. The Goldney garden had a small elevated terrace with a watch tower from which Goldney could view his shipping in the Bristol Channel.[16]

Miller's use of terraces and bastions in his designs can therefore be seen to follow an existing tradition in the ornamental use of these essentially military structures. The views

28 *Goldney, the bastion wall at the end of Thomas Goldney's viewing terrace, c.1740s.*

which could be enjoyed from an estate were particularly important to Miller. Viewing terraces, and also the use of raised mounds to elevate an individual building to improve the view, are found throughout his work. Examples of terraces can be found at Radway, at Farnborough, where the great terrace had repeated bastions along its whole length, and at Alscot Park, where there is a fine view from the terrace across the river towards the house and the countryside beyond. The application of military terms to contemporary landscaping is illustrated in Henry Grenville's letter to Miller concerning his landscaping at Radway following the Enclosure Act of 1757. Grenville mentions 'the inclosure of the Greenfields and the lines of circumvallation which you have been drawing about your banks …'.[17] Circumvallation, or the surrounding of a city or fortress with ditches and earth mounds, was a military term which was obviously generally understood in ordinary correspondence. With the Civil War in mind, Miller's bastions along the terrace at Farnborough were appropriate as mock lookouts, though in Miller's time one would have been looking out to admire the view, rather than to keep watch for the enemy, as it might have been (in the mind's eye) a hundred years previously. Such a repeated row of bastions would have been considered striking, but would not have appeared as unusual in the mid-18th century as they appear to the modern eye.

In 1726 Charles Bridgeman, the most prolific designer in the second and third decades of the century, became Wise's partner in charge of the royal gardens, and subsequently became Royal Gardener on Wise's retirement. Following the accession of George II to the throne in 1727, Queen Caroline employed Charles Bridgeman to create the Serpentine from Queen Anne's ten formal ponds in Hyde Park. At Richmond, Bridgeman's extensive garden design for the Queen was: 'revolutionary in introducing cultivated fields, and even tiny pockets of seeming forest, within the garden vista. Old-fashioned straight lines were still included, but symmetry had virtually gone'.[18] Horace Walpole, that indefatigable commentator on the period, wrote in his *History of the Modern Taste in Gardening* that Bridgeman 'banished verdant sculpture, and did not even revert to the square precision of the foregoing age. He enlarged his plans, disdained to make every division tally to its opposite, and though he still adhered much to strait walks with high clipped hedges, they were only his great lines; the rest he diversified by wilderness, and with loose groves of oak, though still within surrounding hedges.'[19] Bridgeman designed numerous estate layouts, often on a very large scale, but he always imposed his plans on the landscape, as had traditionally been done by designers before him, rather than utilising the diversity of the topography as a base for the creation of his design. Among the best known of his designs, beside his work for Royalty, were those at Blenheim and Rousham, in Oxfordshire; Eastbury, in Dorset; Boughton, in Northamptonshire; Claremont, in Surrey; and his extensive work at Stowe, in Buckingham.

With Bridgeman, garden and estate design began to move away from the Baroque, and the formal approach with impressively large garden buildings. The use of impressive garden buildings had characterised most of Vanbrugh's work, not only at Castle Howard, but also, for example, in the imposing design for the Belvedere at Claremont, in Surrey. Bridgeman used brilliant adaptations of the formal style, creating solutions to problems such as the design for Stowe, where he worked from 1714 onwards for upwards of twenty years, and where Vanbrugh designed some of the garden buildings prior to his death in 1726. At Stowe, Bridgeman simplified the formal layout and combined the awkward outlines of Lord Cobham's grounds into a comprehensive design. The novel use of ha-has along the boundaries opened the gardens out to extensive views of the rural Buckinghamshire countryside which could be enjoyed from the raised terrace walks. Bridgeman's work

29   *Goldney, the tower at the end of the terrace, from which Goldney could see his shipping coming up the river.*

30 *The Goldney Grotto, begun 1737. Shells were obtained from captains returning from overseas, and Goldney used 'Bristol stones', diamond-like quartz crystal clusters, collected from the nearby Avon river gorge. There was also the lion's cave. There were two lifesize plaster lions in the grotto.*

was much admired. A typical response was that by John, Viscount Perceval, who wrote to Daniel Dering on 14 August 1724 explaining that:

> ... The Cross walks end in vistos, arches and statues, and the private ones cut thro' groves are delightfull. You think twenty times you have no more to see, and of a sudden find yourself in some new garden or walk as finish'd and adorn'd as that you left. Nothing is more irregular in the whole, nothing more regular in the parts, which totally differ one from the other ... What adds to the bewty of this garden is, that it is not bounded by Walls, but by a Ha-Hah, which leaves you the sight of a bewtifull woody Country, and makes you ignorant how far the high planted walks extend.[20]

Bridgeman died in 1738, the year after Miller inherited Radway and started his own landscaping career. From the beginning of his work at Radway, Miller's designs differed from Bridgeman's concept of introducing informal areas within a basically formal design. Miller's plantings are not imposed upon the landscape in a geometric outline, but his designs utilise the existing landforms, his paths are laid out to follow the banks of a stream and his plantings the contours of the hill.

Lord Burlington's gardens, developed concurrently with his new villa at Chiswick which was built during the 1720s, were also influential in the development of new ideas. Like those of Pope, his gardens looked back to the antique Roman ideal. Burlington commissioned Robert Castell to translate the letters of the younger Pliny, in *The Villas of the Ancients*, published in 1728. Judging from his writings, Pliny's gardens appeared to be formal, with exedras and a hippodrome, but further from the villa was an area designated as 'Imitatio Ruris', which was supposed to represent natural surroundings. Burlington tried to reproduce these ideas at Chiswick. The Chiswick gardens in their early form were still predominantly formal, with a central avenue which led away from the house, dividing into a patte d'oie or goose-foot of three smaller avenues each terminated by a different classically inspired building. In 1733 Burlington, assisted by Kent, who trained initially as a painter and whose career as an architect and garden designer began with his employment by Lord Burlington, gradually began to alter the gardens to a more naturalistic design, perhaps with Pliny's 'Imitatio Ruris' in mind. Extra land was taken in, the Bollo Brook was widened and 'serpentined', the cascade created, and a raised boundary terrace made on which flowering shrubs were grown.

Concurrent with these moves towards the introduction of informality into garden design, there arose a new interest in Gothic buildings. The Gothic style was associated with the idea of a liberal approach to government supposedly inherited from our Saxon forbears, as has already been discussed. Where better to reintroduce the style than in a distinctive garden building on the estate of a prominent politician or military man? The style became associated with the

31   *Alexander Pope, 1688-1744, by Jonathan Richardson. This portrait hangs in Hagley Hall, where Pope was a regular visitor. The dog Bounce was his constant companion.*

movement away from the corrupt government of Sir Robert Walpole, and though it was a predominantly Whig idea it was very much a part of those Whigs who clustered round Lord Cobham in his move against Walpole.

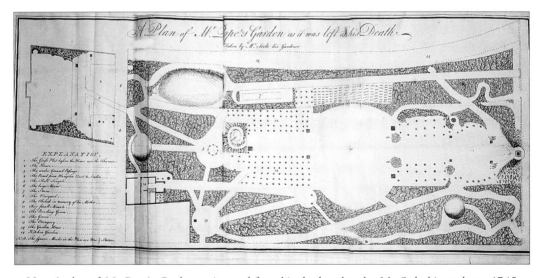

32   *A plan of Mr Pope's Garden as it was left at his death, taken by Mr Serle his gardener, 1745, London.*

33   *Alfred's Hall, Cirencester. The first mock ruin, completed by 1721, it was built by Lord Bathurst as a romantic site for entertaining. It is now undergoing restoration.*

The first Gothic Revival garden building in Britain was the Gothic Temple, built *c.*1720 at Shotover. This building initiated an 18th-century fashion for erecting Gothic buildings in the grounds of country houses. Gothic buildings in the garden engaged issues of great social, political and cultural moment, and were crucially distinct from 17th-century Gothic architecture in that they had no medieval tradition to evoke, but were capable of assuming a new range of identities for the present. The estate at Shotover, just east of Oxford, belonged to Lt. General James Tyrrell. His father had been friendly with Boyle and a member of the academic and scientific group in Oxford of which Boyle was also a member. The Temple, probably designed by the Oxford mason Townesend, celebrated the political triumph of the Whigs over arbitrary government. Behind the house, the garden had wilderness areas intersected by informal paths in the manner of Bridgeman and Stephen Switzer, and within these Kent designed an obelisk and an Octagon Temple. The gardens at Shotover retain some formality, yet also illustrate the beginnings of the move towards informality. They are a rare survival of the period, due to little interest being taken in the estate after 1742, when Tyrrell died childless and the property was left to Augustus Schutz, whose father had been Hanoverian ambassador to the English court.

The Gothic Temple at Shotover was the forerunner of those buildings with a similar message later constructed by Lord Cobham at Stowe. Townesend was also responsible for the garden buildings at Rousham, north of Oxford, where William Kent made extensive alterations to the gardens for General Dormer in 1738. Miller, with his Oxford connections, would have been familiar with both Shotover and Rousham.

Bathurst's extensive planting schemes at Cirencester, covering more than 2,000 acres, were carried out on the old sheep pastures of the upland estate. The long intersecting grass rides created a similar effect to that of the great avenues of the previous century, such as those at Badminton House, depicted by Knyff and Kip in *Britannia Illustrata*, 1707. Lord Bathurst was greatly influenced in his improvements by Alexander Pope, who first visited Cirencester in 1718, by which date Bathurst had already begun his improvements. The buildings, situated among the great woodland rides, were a mix of the classical and the Gothic. The best known of these was Alfred's Hall, the first purpose-built castle ruin, completed by 1721.[21] King Alfred, whose system of civic liberty was lost following the Norman invasion in 1066, was a suitable hero after whom to name the 'castle', as he was associated with the idea of historic British freedom, although the site has no particular associations with King Alfred. The castle, deep in woodland and not in any elevated position, probably owes its situation to the fact that Bathurst liked to entertain his friends there, and so it was built near the only natural source of spring water on the whole estate.[22] As well as its castellated exterior, the Hall had stained glass windows, and fine panelling inside. Around it some small mock ruins were also erected to add to the medieval effect. Other Gothic creations at Cirencester included Ivy Lodge, an old Elizabethan barn converted into a romantic Gothic castle with one wing built as a castellated façade, and the castellated Square House and the Round Tower, both of which hid farm cottages behind a castle-like exterior. Pope's Seat, where he used to write his poetry on his frequent visits was, however, built in the classical style.

It is not known if Miller ever visited Cirencester, but it is quite possible, since he had relatives living locally. Bathurst's extensive plantings on such an open site would perhaps have encouraged Miller, who although working on a much smaller scale, also clothed his own previously open hillside at Radway with woodland composed of a variety of native trees. Miller's mock castle ruins at Edgehill and Hagley had similarities with Alfred's Hall, for all three were designed for entertaining, had strong historical allusions and were built in a medieval style with stained glass windows. In 1736 Bathurst constructed a lake of an informal outline, one of the very first.[23] Miller designed informal lakes at Farnborough in the early 1740s, only a few years later, as a pivotal point of his new landscape there. Mrs Delany (1700-88), the niece of Lord Landsdowne, often visited the Millers at Radway when staying with her sister and brother-in-law at nearby Wellesbourne Manor. She had visited Cirencester Park in 1733 and had written to Jonathan Swift about it,[24] so it is likely that she discussed the improvements with Miller. Gardener, botanical artist and collage maker, Mrs Delany was an indefatigable letter writer and observer of her times.[25] She was involved with the interior of the Bath House at Walton, near Wellesbourne, designed by Miller in 1749 for Sir Charles Mordaunt.

In the 1730s, William Kent designed new garden buildings with views across the Serpentine which were carefully framed with planting, and at Richmond he also designed several buildings, including Merlin's Cave, designed in 1735, another early Gothic garden building. The use of Gothic in garden buildings, with its historical symbolism, was becoming increasingly popular, and it was a form which Miller used not only in his mock castle ruins but also in other more purely decorative landscape buildings, such as the Gothic Greenhouse (known as the Museum today) and the Boathouse at Enville. Capability Brown later used the form in several buildings, some examples being the new stable block and the greenhouse at Burghley, in the late 1750s, and at Blenheim, the Gothicised High Lodge *c*.1764, and the castellated design for the granary at Park Farm in 1765.

In 1732 Frederick, Prince of Wales commissioned Kent to design his new garden at Carlton House, in London. The existing formal plan was replaced by a long central lawn with arbours, flower beds, and informal groves of trees and shrubs, terminated by a classical temple. This novel design created a sensation among the Prince's friends and acquaintances.

In 1734, Sir Thomas Robinson wrote in a letter to his father-in-law, the Earl of Carlisle:

> There is a new taste in gardening just arisen, which has been practised with so great success at the Prince's garden in Town that a general alteration of some of the most considerable gardens in the kingdom is begun, after Mr Kent's notion of gardening, viz., to lay them out, and work without either level or line … The celebrated gardens of Claremont, Chiswick and Stowe are now full of labourers, to modernize the expensive works finished in them … [26]

This five-acre garden at Carlton House, 'an apparently simple *Rus* in the *Urbe* of the capital, confirmed Kent's reputation, and … gave instant fashionable authority to the new taste in gardening'.[27]

Kent worked on several estates outside the capital, including Holkham, the seat of Sir Robert Walpole, the classically inspired and politically motivated landscape at Stowe, and Rousham, the garden which Kent adapted for General Dormer from Bridgeman's earlier and more formal layout. His work was generally carried out on estates where Bridgeman had worked before him. Kent's approach was to produce an overlay on Bridgeman's designs. He introduced a more informal series of sylvan scenes, often with classical buildings harking back to those which he had admired in Italy, with a background of evergreen planting. Kent's designs were predominantly small-scale, and were created as a series of composed views, each as in an individual painting. At Rousham, the garden was redesigned following Bridgeman's initial plan. The outlines were softened with new planting, and flowering shrubs, statues and temples were introduced. Two Gothic 'eyecatchers' drew attention to the countryside beyond the garden: an old mill beyond the river boundary had castellated extensions added to it, and a Gothic arch was set up on the distant skyline.[28] In his own designs Miller could be said to build on this idea, designing his own landscapes to include even the distant horizon. Such ideas echoed the move from an autocratic society to a situation where 'polite society' had taken control, even of the view.

Kent's use of flowering plants and shrubs deserves comment, since it has previously been supposed that 18th-century landscapists did not use flowering shrubs to any extent. Recently, evidence has come to light revealing that many designers, including Charles Hamilton, Henry Hoare, Capability Brown, Richard Woods, William Emes and others all used ornamental shrubs in their landscape designs.[29] These plantings could be in association with tree planting in the wider landscape, or planned in more detail within a garden area, as in Charles Hamilton's exotic shrub beds for specific areas at Painshill, in Surrey, or Brown's specialised flower garden, designed in 1772 for Brocklesby, in Lincolnshire.[30] In 1738, Hamilton, who over a period of time held several posts under the Prince of Wales, purchased an area of poor heathland at Painshill. He first improved the quality of the ground by planting turnips and feeding sheep on the crop, then began to landscape the grounds, which extended to about 170 acres (80 hectares). He planted trees in great variety, introducing both native species and also exotics from North America, many of which were imported for the first time during this period. A tour of the estate involved a succession of distinct scenes, characterised by buildings such as the Gothic Temple, the Turkish Tent, the Hermitage, the Gothic Tower and the ruined Abbey. Hamilton successfully carried out the artificial raising of the river Mole to provide a lake of a natural appearance, within which was an island reached by a Chinese bridge. The island contained a large grotto overlooking the lake which was created by Joseph and Josiah Lane of Tisbury, in Wiltshire. It was made of artificial stalactites and stalagmites, with tufa, spar and fossils. It has recently been restored to its full splendour, but when originally illuminated by candlelight it must have been a glittering and fantastic sight. Painshill was much visited and admired by Hamilton's contemporaries, and there is a record of Miller having planned a visit there with George Lyttelton.[31] Hamilton's estate was probably the nearest contemporary design, at least in spirit, to Miller's own work. It was laid out to appear as natural as possible, apart from two areas which had borders of exotic flowering shrubs, and a vineyard, respectively. The planting and the buildings were used to frame and emphasise the views. The expense of Hamilton's building projects must have been a major cause of the financial difficulties which forced him to sell his estate in 1773.

The design of the landscape garden at Stourhead, created by the banker Henry Hoare, is thought to have been inspired by the landscape paintings by Claude Lorraine and Gaspard Dughet. Hoare inherited the estate at Stourhead, with its Palladian villa, on his father's death in 1724. The creation of the present large lake and the circuit path around it, with its classical buildings, was carried out over a period which is contemporary with Miller's own work, starting in the early 1740s. The valley with the main lake (formed by a dam in 1754) is naturally picturesque, with steep hillsides rising from the water's edge, and small streams feeding down into the lake. The garden is built around a theme, based on scenes from the Aeneid. Hoare's classical buildings around the lake include the Temple of Flora, the Grotto of the Nymph, the River God and his cave, the Pantheon, and, in the 1760s, a Temple of Apollo and the five-arched bridge. Hoare also erected the 14th-century Bristol High Cross in his landscape, discarded by the people of Bristol as having associations with popery. On the slopes above the lake were sited various other buildings in different styles reminiscent of the Rococo: Chinese, Venetian, Turkish. By the 1780s these had become unfashionable, and Hoare's grandson had them removed from the gardens. Over the hills above the lake there was also an outer circuit ride of seven miles, taking in King Alfred's Tower – King Alfred making an appearance here as well as in Cirencester Park. Around the lakeside walk the views are magnificent, backed by the hills crowned with hanging woods. They are indeed reminiscent of the paintings by Claude Lorraine, Poussin and Gaspard Dughet which Hoare had in his collections. In describing the improvements in the gardens to his daughter Susanna in 1762, Hoare thought the view from the Pantheon towards the bridge over the river, with the village and church, would make a charming 'Gaspard' picture.[32] Rousham, Stourhead and Painshill can be thought of as Arcadian picturesque creations. They are basically enclosed landscapes with an air of fantasy about them, with individual scenes created to represent either antiquity, at Rousham and Stourhead, or different periods of history and settings from foreign lands, as at Painshill. To this trio might be added the earlier garden of Studley Royal, begun in about 1722, for that also was an enclosed landscape, with its formal lakes in the valley and its temples set on the steep valley sides. The addition of the magnificent ruins of Fountains Abbey, seen from the hillsides but only actually incorporated into the gardens when bought by Aislabie's son William in 1768, completed the romantic scene.

The most influential garden in the Midlands in the 1730s was undoubtedly that of Lord Cobham at Stowe. From about 1714 onwards, Cobham had employed both Vanbrugh and Bridgeman to redesign the existing formal gardens at Stowe. In his journal of 1725, Sir John Evelyn, grandson of the great diarist, described the gardens at Stowe as 'very noble, and adorn'd with Temples ... Statues, Obelisks, Pillars and Porticos, and consisting of 30 acres ... There being no walls to be seen, the prospect of the Country is very extensive – from the garden, as well as from the House ...'.[33] Horace Walpole cited his father Sir Robert Walpole's newly designed estate at Houghton, in Norfolk, where the plan is attributed to Bridgeman, as one of the first where the ha-ha had been introduced. He commented that the sunk fence, or ha-ha, was 'the leading step' in designing 'the contiguous ground of the park ... to be harmonised with the lawn within'.[34]

After 1733, Cobham began to create the politically inspired and informally designed Elysian Fields, with William Kent as his architect. The design included the Temple of Ancient Virtue, and a ruin entitled the Temple of Modern Virtue, symbolising the corrupt modern state, with a headless statue supposed to represent Sir Robert Walpole. The Temple of British Worthies had busts of Whig heroes from the past. Two with particular importance in the present context were King Alfred and Inigo Jones, the father of English Palladianism and revered by the Whigs. There were also busts of two living 'heroes': Alexander Pope and Sir John Barnard – the latter had voted with Cobham over the Excise Bill.[35] The development

34   *Rousham, William Kent's Gothicised old farmhouse and distant Gothic arch, drawing the eye from the gardens out towards the countryside beyond.*

35 *Drawing by William Kent thought to be The Temple or Bagnio in the garden at Carlton House, part of the new informal design carried out for Frederick, Prince of Wales c.1734.*

of Hawkwell Field, the area adjacent to the Elysian Fields, took place largely during the 1740s. The great temples built on this area included the Temple of Friendship, the Ladies' Temple, the Palladian bridge, and, most importantly, the climax to Lord Cobham's political scene, the Gothic Temple (1741-4). The Gothic Temple was triangular, with towers, turrets, and pointed arches, the style representing the ancient 'Gothic' liberties of England, emphasised by the placing of Rysbrack's statues of the seven Saxon gods in front of the building. It had a sharply contemporary Gothic meaning in its political focus, constituting a Whig claim on national history, and a political ideology borrowed from the medieval past.[36]

During the last years of his life, Cobham began to create the Grecian Valley, an informal landscape created by earth moving and tree planting. His intention was to create a Grecian Vale of Tempe. The 1746-7 accounts show that huge quantities of earth were excavated to shape the valley, and trees were brought to it from elsewhere in the gardens.[37] The completed scene was also reminiscent of the landscape paintings of Claude Lorraine (although it lacked a water feature). These paintings had become popular with 18th-century collectors, many of whom had purchased them when in Italy on the Grand Tour. Capability Brown, who was Lord Cobham's head gardener from 1741-9, was responsible for the practical work of creating the Grecian Valley. It was Brown's last major undertaking for Lord Cobham before setting up in private practice on his own account following Cobham's death in 1749.

By the time that Miller began his landscaping career in the late 1730s, experimental trends in informality had resulted in what Mowl has described as 'an eclectic free-for-all where classical garden buildings are joined by Chinese, Gothic and Mohammedan structures, all set in an asymmetrical fantasy against backgrounds of artfully placed trees and natural seeming lakes'.[38] Garden historians have given this period of creativity the name Rococo, though this term was not used in the 18th century to describe gardens. The word 'Rococo' comes from the French words 'rocaille', rockwork, and coquille, a shell, and grottoes using both were often found in Rococo gardens. The Rococo style was informal; serpentine or

'S' shapes were used – Hogarth's 'line of beauty' – in an effort to simulate those found in Nature, and a playfulness, an enjoyment of experiment and the use of an element of surprise were all seen in the mix of designs. The majority were smaller gardens rather than designed estates or parks, and elements of the style can be found in many designs of the period, including Miller's own work.

Although few of these gardens survive today, we have some knowledge of them due to the romantic mid-century paintings created by Thomas Robins (1716-70), known as the 'limner of Bath'. Robins painted in a fashion entirely different from the detailed and precise views of illustrators such as Kip and Knyff, or Samuel and Nathaniel Buck, working in the earlier decades of the century. Miller's own design at Honington Hall was illustrated by Robins in two paintings.

Among the gardens painted by Robins were those for Benjamin Hyatt of Marybone House in Gloucester and of Painswick House in Painswick, Gloucestershire, dating from the late 1730s and 1740s. These two paintings give an idea of the scenes which were included in Rococo gardens; geometric areas, paths which were serpentined to an extreme, canals, and buildings in a variety of different styles. At Painswick, the Red House, built in a whimsical Gothic style, was so asymmetric that even the front façade was divided and sloped two different ways. The garden is not large, but contains several different areas, more or less secluded, which provide variety and interest, surprise and also an element of privacy for the visitor. They have recently been recreated and the buildings restored using Robins' painting as a guide. Other owners, anxious to keep up with the fashion, built in such a variety of styles that the result was an odd collection of buildings dotted about a park rather than of any preconceived design. An example can be found at Shugborough, in Staffordshire, where the gardens and park boasted, among others, a Chinese temple, a copy of the Greek Tower of the Winds, a Shepherd's monument, a Lysicratic monument, a small mock ruin and a Doric Temple, scattered about the grounds with little attempt at a coherent design.

As the 1730s progressed, Chinese influences began to appear in garden design. During this period there was a craze for Chinese imported pottery and porcelain, and Chinese designs were popular in fabrics, furniture – 'Chinese Chippendale' – and even clothing, so it was not surprising that this influence began to be felt in gardens. The popularity of Chinese inspired design was also due to some extent to recent publications of reports from travellers to China. The Jesuit Father Matteo Ripa, who returned to London from China in 1724, had published 36 prints of the Imperial Chinese Palace Gardens at Jehol.[39] In 1735, Father Gerbillon's recollections from his time in China were published in French, referring to Chinese beauty as consisting of 'a great Propriety and Imitation of Nature as Grotto's, Shellwork and craggy Fragments of Rocks …', while in 1743 a description of Yuan Ming Yuan by Father Jean-Denis Attiret, translated by Joseph Spence, described the gardens as having irregularities in the design and bridges which generally wind about and 'serpentise'. This description caused Horace Walpole to remark, after having studied Spence's translation, that Chinese gardens had a determined irregularity, but that there was nothing in them that gave any idea of attention being paid to Nature. He continued: 'methinks a straight canal is as rational at least as a meandering bridge'.[40]

Chinese buildings appear to have been more popular than actual Chinese gardens. One of the first Chinese garden buildings to be constructed was that at Stowe, erected on stilts

36 *The Beech Water, one of the pools on the circuit around William Shenstone's* ferme ornée *at The Leasowes.*

in the Alder river in 1738. Several buildings in the Chinese style were constructed at a similar date for Richard Bateman at Grove House, Old Windsor, in Berkshire.[41] Duke John, the 2nd Duke of Montagu, purchased a Chinese summerhouse on 29 November 1745. Made in London for the garden of his London house it has, remarkably, survived and can be seen at Boughton House in Northamptonshire. In 1746-8 Thomas Anson built his Chinese House at Shugborough, following the return of his brother Admiral George Anson with treasure from his circumnavigation of the globe. The admiral was able to describe the design of Chinese houses and temples with authority, following his stay in Canton. Lord North, at Wroxton Abbey, where Miller worked, also had Chinese garden buildings at an early date.

The first English *ferme ornée*, or ornamental farm, a term used to indicate an area where crops were grown or animals tended as on a normal farm, but where in addition certain areas of the farm were devoted to purely ornamental cultivations, is thought to have been that of Philip Southcote, at Woburn Farm, in Surrey, begun after 1733. The farm had some ornamental buildings within the central farmland, but was chiefly known for its ornamental belts of trees and sand walks surrounding the farm. Alongside the walks were flowers, flowering shrubs and small trees, planted in bands depending on their height and protected by a thorn hedge at the back.

In Scotland the *ferme ornée* began with the developments at North Merchiston, a small enclosed park outside Edinburgh, bought by William Adam in 1730. The agricultural fields were surrounded with ornamental shrubbery and walks, with 'tasteful and well contrived intricacies'.[42] Adam had visited William Shenstone at the Leasowes, in what is now the West Midlands, some years before the latter had begun work on the Leasowes in around

1743. The *ferme ornée* at the Leasowes came into existence several years after Miller had first begun his landscaping, but is mentioned here because Shenstone is contemporary with Miller and because his *ferme ornée* has become well known through his own writings and through the descriptive guide books of the time. Shenstone's farm was not large, but it had mature woods on the highest land, from where small streams ran down small attractive narrow valleys. The topography was ideal for Shenstone's ideas, which were to embellish this landscape with small features and designed areas such as Venus' Vale, interpreting each scene with a literary or personal allusion. The imagination was the single most important idea behind Shenstone's landscaping, and, as with William Kent, the picture before him was likened in his mind's eye to a painting. The practical considerations with which Shenstone achieved his aim are subservient to this central thought, and his created landscape lived through the experiences of his visitors. They were invited to enter into Shenstone's flights of imagination which had led him to create the scenes in front of them through the various inscriptions placed at each viewpoint.[43]

Shenstone never had enough money to build as he would have liked to have done, and was critical of both Hagley and of Miller's work at Radway. At the Leasowes, the designed routes with their views and their specific messages were all important, and without a constant supply of appreciative visitors – so important to Shenstone – the whole creation had significantly less meaning.

The upkeep on a *ferme ornée* must have been considerable, and farming and poetic inscriptions attached to urns do not really go together. Although Shenstone assisted Lord Stamford in the layout of his cascades at Enville, not far from Hagley, and Lord Plymouth with his estate at Hewel Grange in Worcestershire, the general concept of an ornamented farm was short-lived, and even the Leasowes itself was considerably altered after it was sold on Shenstone's death in 1763.

Having seen the ways in which the approach to garden design and the laying out of estate grounds altered over the first decades of the century, Miller's own work can now be assessed against this background. How and why did his designed landscapes differ from those of previous designers? Naturally his work had similarities with the work of others who were more or less contemporary with him, for no man lives in a vacuum, yet he also introduced novel ideas which broke away from what had gone before. Miller had grown up in the unenclosed agricultural landscape of south Warwickshire. Judging by his landscape plans, which clothe the countryside with extensive planting and new water features, he was very much aware of the bare appearance of the open field system in the Midlands countryside with which he was so familiar. This perception had a major impact on his approach to landscape improvement.

Prior to the beginning of the 18th century, only a comparatively small percentage of the south Midlands had been enclosed.[44] Between 1700 and 1757, the latter being the date of Miller's Enclosure Act for Radway, there had been only 11 Enclosure Acts passed for the whole of south Warwickshire, Oxfordshire and Buckinghamshire, the area where Miller carried out most of his work.[45] The countryside of enclosure, which is essentially the modern agricultural landscape of the Midlands, is very different from that of the spreading and featureless appearance of the old open field system. The working countryside where the large open field system predominated had few hedges and trees.[46] There were three or four large fields for each parish, with trees restricted to commons, or field boundaries, and lopped for fodder and other agricultural uses – which did nothing to improve their beauty. Remnants of such old hedge pollards can still be seen at Honington, where Miller was involved in a new design for the estate in 1749.

In the Cotswolds, the original tree cover had largely been cleared from the upland wolds by 1200, and by the 14th and 15th centuries the prosperous Cotswold wool merchants were keeping their great herds of sheep on large pastures enclosed by stone walls. Apart from the actual topography, the appearance of the land in the early 18th century, whether under unenclosed arable or extensive sheep farming, was open and comparatively featureless.

Although there were a few areas of woodland, woods were a vital primary resource, rather than an ornamental feature in the landscape. To exist at all they had to be enclosed from the depredations of animals grazed on the communal fields. Apart from ancient hunting forests, woods were managed to produce timber for the building of houses and ships, and the basic needs of agriculture and domestic life. Ornamental groups of mature trees were only seen in the enclosed parks and gardens of larger estates. Large bodies of water, apart from estate fishponds, such as those near Radway at Compton Verney and Compton Wyniates, were almost non-existent, particularly in the Cotswolds.

Contemporary sources confirm the fact that the landscape outside the parks of the great estates was often bare of trees, uninteresting, or even bleak, whether open field agriculture or uncultivated common land or heath. Between Hagley and Enville the countryside was open heathland, with only sparse settlement. An anonymous writer discussing the journey from Hagley to Enville, Staffordshire, in 1789 wrote:

> Our approach towards Enville is over wild heath, nearly barren. As we get sufficiently near to discover his Lordship's grounds, the contrast is extremely fine: opposed to the bleak desert, the verdant sloping lawns of Enville appear with ten-fold lustre, edged and interspersed with luxuriant woods, from whence peep forth, with singular beauty, various grotesque Alcoves.[47]

Lady Newdigate, the wife of Miller's friend and fellow undergraduate Sir Roger Newdigate of Arbury, near Nuneaton, discussing their approach to Stowe in 1748, wrote:

> The countryside hereabouts is very unpleasant, but began to improve within two miles of Buckingham. Very near the town lies Finmore, the seat of Mr Poulett. The house is situated in the middle of a small park very full of Timber which comes up close to the Great Road. From hence we had a fine view of Stowe …[48]

Lady Newdigate does not define 'very unpleasant', but it was certainly a countryside which contrasted badly with the beauties of Stowe.

In Miller's time it is recorded that between Radway, with its bare hillsides and open field system, and the village of Kineton, about three miles distant, there was only one hedge.[49] The nearby estate of Farnborough, which Miller laid out for William Holbech c.1742, had a similar view to that from the hills above Radway, since a map of the Farnborough estate, dated 1772, shows that the lands of Avon Dassett, the parish forming the western boundary to the estate, were also unenclosed at this date.[50] Miller's new landscapes, with earth moulding and terracing, lakes and belts of trees, must have appeared in dramatic contrast to adjacent unenclosed agricultural land.

5

Miller's Approach to Landscaping
and his work at Radway

❧·❧

In 1737, when Miller left Oxford, there were few men who could be called upon both to design buildings and lay out grounds. Vanbrugh and Bridgeman were dead, and William Kent's plan for the grounds at Rousham, in 1738, was his last major landscape design. New or enlarged designs for the grounds of country houses were becoming more important, as it became necessary to provide entertainment and outdoor activities for increasing numbers of summer visitors. Travelling had become much easier, with improvements in the design of carriages and the introduction of better roads due to turnpiking.[1] Despite Radway's comparatively isolated situation, Miller's wide circle of friends could visit him frequently, at least in the summer months, and so were able to see for themselves both his new landscaping and his Tower at Radway.

Miller became known firstly as an inventive architect. He had made Gothic additions to the exterior of his own house at Radway, and was designing new houses or new architectural features for the old houses of his friends in both classical and Gothic styles.[2] His reputation spread as his ability in the laying out of grounds, together with his practical skills in land management and drainage, became known through his work at Radway, Farnborough and Wroxton, and also at Belhus, near Brentwood, in Essex. Miller's architectural flair was most apparent in the design of garden buildings, which were still considered an essential feature in ornamental grounds. During the 1740s and early 1750s, the Gothic style was becoming more popular, particularly for buildings in the landscape, where the style evoked a feel both of fantasy and historic allusion very much in tune with the period. Even before Kent's death in 1748, Miller's reputation had spread far beyond his native Warwickshire. In March 1746 his friend T. Lennard Barrett, later Lord Dacre, of Belhus, wrote to Miller saying: 'Your fame in Architecture grows greater and greater every day and I hear of nothing else; if you have a mind to set up you'l soon eclipse Mr Kent, especially in the Gothick way in which to my mind he succeeds very ill ….'[3]

Since there are no existing plans of the landscaping at Radway – or indeed of anywhere else – drawn by Miller himself, it is perhaps pertinent to look at what evidence there is for attributing the landscaping at Radway to Miller. Much of the evidence stems from his entries in his two diaries, which note briefly his daily activities. They give details about his practical work on the estate, his supervision of his men, and in particular the building of the Tower at Edgehill.

A few short examples are given below:

23 Nov 1749: 'Walked to the Castle and to the Clumps at Knowl end yᵉ trees all alive.'

3 July 1750: 'Set out the Work for Bridge with Hitchcox.'

4 July 1750: 'Drawing up … a Design for my Castle Draw-[bridge].'

9 July 1750: 'Up at 4. Waterᵈ Trees at the Castle at 6.'

25 October 1756: 'W. ye Sawyers and Carpenters Hewᵍ posts &c. … wᵈ to yᵉ Bank on yᵉ Hill. Wale and Ned w at wk there weedᵍ yᵉ Qᵏˢ [quicks, or Hawthorns]- directᵍ Smith to Cut Trees on yᵉ Sand Walk … cutting wood in yᵉ Mount.'

Although there are only remnants left of Miller's landscaping, his work can be made out with the help of the O.S. maps for 1886 and 1900, and also a detailed map commissioned by Miller himself in 1756,[4] prior to his Enclosure Act for the parish. This map confirms much of what is mentioned in the diaries, and also illustrates the scattered Miller landholdings within the parish prior to enclosure. The landscape work at Radway is also mentioned in letters, such as those from his university friend Deane Swift in December 1739, referring to Miller's new cascades, Henry Grenville, Lord Cobham's nephew, referring to Miller's work at Radway following the Enclosure Act, and William Pitt. A typical quote from Pitt's letter written on 30 October 1755 referring to Miller's work on his land prior to the coming Enclosure Act, reveals that he is pleased that Miller is:

> … up to your knees in the improveable dirt of Radway-Field, tracing ditches and mounds, and planting Gate Posts instead of all the vegetable Tribes of America …[5]

Miller, although he used predominantly native trees and shrubs, had by that date a growing reputation for the number and variety of his trees, which included some of the imports newly arrived from North America.

Wood and Hawkes, when discussing the landscaping of Radway, attribute the design to Miller himself. Hawkes also describes Egge cottage, the Tower and the mock ruins at Edgehill as Miller's own work in his discussion on Miller's Gothic designs.[6]

The style of the landscaping at Radway was quite informal. A path led from the Grange up through old parkland to the summit of Edgehill. From here, the site of the Battle of Edgehill could be seen and also the spreading view of the valley beyond. The Tower and its mock ruins, commanding the view from the top of the hill, was the dominant factor in the design. There was no attempt at symmetry or pattern; features of interest, such as the cascade, and a levelled viewing area being placed where the topography dictated a suitable site. Planting was extensive, and included a wide belt of mixed indigenous trees clothing the hilltop.

A similar approach was followed in all Miller's designs: the interesting views which could be obtained within the site or across the adjacent countryside were of prime importance in the consideration of the design, and the topography was taken as the basis from which to create the new landscape. Today, this informal approach appears quite natural and unsurprising, but when Miller started to landscape Radway there were only a few large estates, such as Cirencester, or Rousham, where any type of informal approach had been used before.

Traditionally, ground had always been levelled or terraced to take a formal patterned layout which had been designed with complete disregard for topography. An illustration of this approach is seen in the formal design by Isaac de Caux in the late 1630s for the

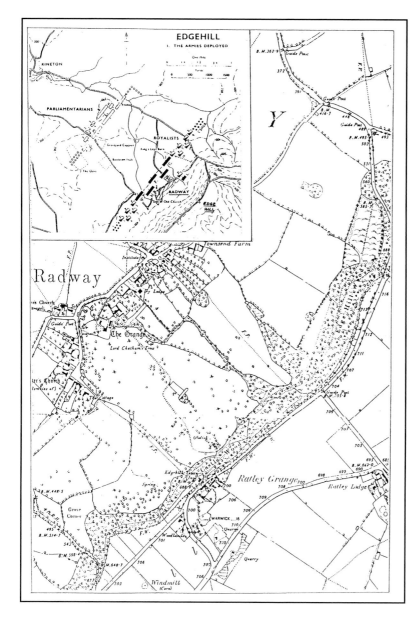

37 *Part of the six-inch O.S. map for 1886, showing Radway and, inset, the plan of the Battle of Edgehill, 1642.*

garden at Wilton House, Wiltshire, where the river was treated more as an inconvenience than a feature, simply flowing through a geometric design which ignored the river itself.[7] This formal style had been fashionable for over a century, and was to continue in use, both for newly laid out grounds and also on those estates where owners did not wish to introduce change, well into the later years of the 18th century. It has been said that 'at all social levels the dominance of a formal style remained unchallenged for the first three decades of the century'.[8] The serpentine irregularity thought of as 'natural' took time to develop as a conscious style in garden design. Ornamental grounds were often altered by the simple expedient of adding a 'wilderness' area in which there were complicated

38   *Wilton House, the gardens drawn by Isaac de Caux, late 1630s. The river Nadder flows across the middle of the gardens, but the formal pattern has been superimposed, completely ignoring the course of the river.*

networks of paths, and there were many country gentlemen as late as the 1770s who still maintained completely formal gardens.

Miller worked mainly in the English Midlands. Several men who were influential in politics and the army owned land in the Midlands, for example: Lord Cobham of Stowe, in Buckinghamshire; Lord Brooke, later Earl of Warwick, and Sir Roger Newdigate of Arbury, in Warwickshire; George Lyttelton of Hagley and Lord Coventry of Croome in Worcestershire, and Lord Chetwynd, of Ingestre, in Staffordshire. The English Midlands were set to became an important focus for the new ideas in estate 'improvements'; and it was here, in the 1750s, that the abilities of Lancelot, or 'Capability', Brown first came to prominence. To set Miller's work in context it is instructive to look at the existing state of design in ornamental grounds in this general area at the time when Miller first began to take up landscaping.

In the late 1730s the grounds of most Midlands estates were formal, although some, such as the Warwickshire estates of Honington and Packington, had deer parks. Although attractive features in themselves, deer parks, often medieval in origin, were essentially functional, and had never been thought of as an attempt to mould the landscape for aesthetic reasons.[9] By the 1730s and 1740s the significance of the park as an essentially attractive area had overtaken its importance as a place where deer were kept, and in these 'transitional parks' new ornamental features began to appear as old deer parks were altered into new landscaped parks laid out for pleasure. It was not easy to introduce informal new features which blended satisfactorily into the old parkland. Landscaped grounds of this period had often more of an artificial than a natural appearance. Some examples include those at Holkham, in Norfolk, where Kent had designed clumps of trees for the grounds in a pattern compared rather mockingly by Horace Walpole with the ten of spades, at Painshill, where Charles Hamilton had formal terraces for growing vines and shrub borders with a great variety of foreign plants,[10] and even Lord Cobham's extensive gardens at Stowe.

The style in which ornamental grounds were laid out at several large properties in Warwickshire and the adjacent counties is known through early 18th-century illustrations and maps. These include: the formal grounds of Arbury Hall, Castle Bromwich, Charlecote Park, Compton Verney, Edgbaston Hall, Honington Hall, and Newnham Paddox in Warwickshire; Croome Court in Worcestershire; and Wroxton Abbey in north Oxfordshire.[11] At all these estates the formal gardens were later swept away in favour of the new natural landscaping, with the exception of the gardens at Castle Bromwich, which were left unaltered when the Bridgeman family moved to Weston Park as their principal seat. Miller himself provided new designs for Honington Hall and Wroxton Abbey, and was involved in the landscaping of the grounds at Arbury Hall and Croome Court.

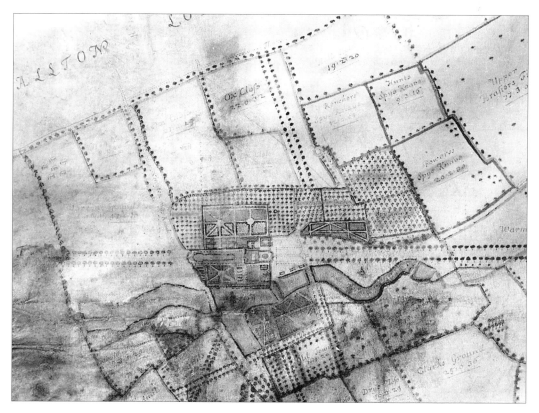

39   *Compton Verney, detail from the estate map by James Fish, 1736. Compton Verney is about five miles from Radway, so Miller would have been familiar with these formal gardens, laid out in the 1720s. Capability Brown later landscaped the grounds, working here from 1768.*

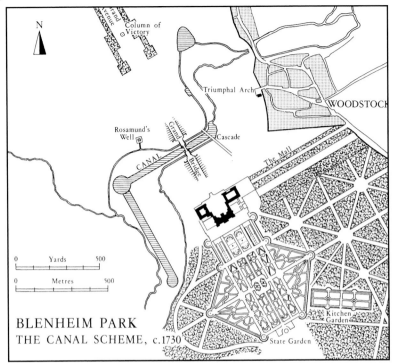

40 *Blenheim Park, a plan showing the canal scheme for the grounds, designed by Colonel Armstrong, the Duke of Marlborough's chief engineer, for the Duchess in the 1720s. The formal gardens and wilderness are to the south.*

41 *A vertical aerial photo of Blenheim Park, taken in 1961. The outline of the earlier formal canal can be seen through the waters of Capability Brown's lake, designed in 1765.*

At Stowe, where Lord Cobham was considered to be in the vanguard of the new ideas in the laying-out of grounds, Jacques Rigaud's views of the gardens, commissioned in 1733 by Bridgeman and published by his wife Sarah in 1739, show long avenues, clipped hedges, and ornamental pools in geometric shapes within a layout which was still largely formal. At Hartwell House, not far from Stowe, formal walks and pools were surrounded by high hedges clipped into repeated classical arches. At Blenheim Palace, where John Vanbrugh, Henry Wise, and Bridgeman had all worked, the formal gardens of the early years of the century were unaltered. To the north west of the palace, both Colonel Armstrong's right-angled canal, and the grand north avenue towards the Ditchley Gate were determinedly formal. Other estates where Bridgeman had produced formal plans with long avenues included Boughton, in Northamptonshire, and Wimpole, in Cambridgeshire. As late as 1729-31, Bridgeman's plan for Lodge Park, Sherborne, in Gloucestershire, imposed geometric blocks of woodland on this isolated and undulating Cotswold landscape, and the lake, although serpentine, had parallel sides. At Cirencester, the great new woodlands were bisected by straight avenues, although Lord Bathurst's park buildings, constructed in both classical and Gothic styles, were disposed without recourse to symmetry.[12]

These examples suggest that in the 1730s and early 1740s, as a general rule, ideas concerning informality in the laying out of grounds had barely begun to reach the rural shires, underlining the innovative nature of the ideas behind Miller's new landscapes.

Miller's approach to the landscaping of Radway, although undoubtedly influenced by Lord Cobham and by Kent, was more radical in its move away from formality. Miller's first work on the estate was in 1736 when he planted a group of trees known as The King's Ley Copse beyond the village of Radway to the north west to mark the spot where King Charles passed the night after the Battle of Edgehill in 1642. The copse was cut down in 1863.[13] A further copse was planted on Knowle End, beyond the Kineton to Banbury road, to mark the spot from where King Charles surveyed the enemy positions before the battle. Miller made an informal path leading up his hillside to the summit of Edgehill, with its panoramic view. Beside the path was a small stream. As the path left the Grange, it ran between hedges on both sides for some way up the hill. William Shenstone, from the Leasowes near Hagley, visited Radway in 1750. He wrote to Lady Luxborough, of Barrells, near Ullenhall, describing the scene as the party left the Grange on the way up the hill:

> His Farm lies betwixt his House & yᵉ Hill. He has therefore, rightly enough, taken yᵉ advantage of some *double* Hedges which surround his Farm to make a shady Path betwixt yᵗ conveys you to his Hill. This path very *fortunately* begins as soon as you come out of his Library or Parlour an advantage (I mean this of getting immediately into Shade.) which *I* can never obtain not *much;* Before I go further, let me mention that his trees are detestable, viz: old *Ashes* stunted & crop'd & newly sprouting out again: such as ought by all means be destroyed for ye sake of Trees of a more agreeable *Form*; more early *vegetation*, & more lasting *verdure.*[14]

The old ashes which Shenstone so disliked may have been in the boundary hedge between Miller's land and that of his neighbour, John Sargent, whose close is shown on the 1756 map and who probably had the right to lop the ashes for his own use. On the map there are also double hedges shown on either side of part of a second footpath up

42   *Hartwell House, Buckinghamshire, the great exhedra, by Balthazar Nebot, 1738. One of eight paintings commissioned by the Whig landowner Sir Thomas Lee, illustrating the amazing forms achieved by the use of formal topiary.*

the hillside to the south. In the existing Radway estate accounts there are lists of many of the shrubs and trees which Miller was using on the estate. On 1 May 1743, there is an entry of £3 for ten loads of thorn, which may well have been used in the planting of these hedges.[15] They would have had time to grow well between 1743 and Shenstone's visit in 1750. Double hedges are nowhere apparent on the 1756 map except on Miller's land. As a decorative feature the hedges had several uses: they channelled the view up towards the summit of the hill to the Tower, they provided shade and an attractive border to the paths, and they kept animals out.

Just below the top of Edgehill, Miller created a mount with a small pool, below which was a cascade and fountain. This semi-formal layout, a design which Miller did not repeat, belongs to an earlier period, stylistically, than the rest of his work, and had similarities with the water features in Venus' Vale at Rousham, near Oxford, designed by William Kent in 1738. Miller's diary entry for 26 June 1750, reads: 'w. with Nanny [his niece] to yᵉ Mᵗ [mount] to get the roses', which suggests that there was ornamental planting associated with the design. Around the top pool trees were planted. There still exist five old limes to the south and three to the north of the pool, but the pool has now only a little spring water in the bottom of it. Below the cascade, the water was led into a small pool further down the hill, known as the Long Pool, which had originally been a fishpond for the monks who had, in the middle ages, maintained a small convalescent cell for brethren on this site. At the time of the dissolution of the monasteries, both Edge Grange (or 'Egge', an older name of the same meaning) on Edgehill, and Radway Grange were part of land owned by the abbey at Stoneleigh, which included small granges within Radway and the adjoining parish of Ratley.[16] Today the stream leaving the pool no longer runs the length of the hillside, and is actually dry for most of the year. Water off the hill is led under the Grange into an ornamental pond (once the old farm horsepond) in the Grange garden. It appears to have been culverted underground well before it reached the Grange through a large stoned culvert, thought to be 18th-century in origin, which was seen during excavations on a recent visit to the site. The culvert may well have been put in by Miller. An old resident of Radway can remember much more water coming off the

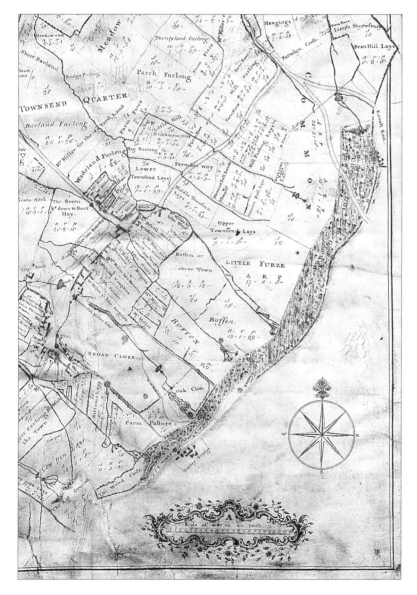

43 *Radway, part of the pre-Enclosure map surveyed and drawn by George Salmon, 1756.*

hill from several springs than there is today. The whole village used this water before the arrival of mains water, and the supply never ran dry. However, in times of heavy rainfall the houses stood in some danger of flooding. Today all the water approaching the village in small streams is culverted or piped under or around the houses.

The cascades and the water garden were installed by 1739, for on 27 December of that year Miller's old university friend Deane Swift, nephew of Jonathan Swift, wrote to Miller from Ireland: 'Methinks I see my old friend laughing with Epicurus under the shadow of Edgehill, with all his fountains roaring and cascading before him …'[17]

There are only a few humps and bumps left in the field below the Mount today, and we need Swift's enthusiastic description, balanced by Shenstone's rather critical appraisal, to provide us with a picture of the scene. Shenstone mentioned Miller's 'artificial Piece of ground & waterwork, ' then continued:

> … Tis a detach'd thing; utterly unlike, & I think inconsistent with ye genius of his Land in general. At ye Top of this is a Reservoir (which … may spurt forth a little frothy water on some gawdy Day & be dry ye rest of ye year.) It falls over 3 rustick arches, runs down, thro broken stone-work, to a Bason in ye midst of wch is a Jetteau; and on each side tumuli or little mounds of Earth artificially cast up. But this is a juvenile Performance, & only retained because it *is* there & has cost him money.[18]

This early feature emphasises how radically Miller's plans changed from his first attempts, as he began to find his own style in his interpretation of how the art of design could be used to transform a landscape.

The terrace, shown clearly on the 1756 map, is above the cascade on the north side. On the O.S. map for 1886 the terrace can also be made out, but it is within the fenceline. It is probable that lack of maintenance over the years had led to trees encroaching here,

44 *View from Edgehill Tower to the west. The old park trees are in the foreground, with Radway Grange and the village and valley beyond.*

and so the modern fence keeping cattle out of the hillside woodland has been moved down the slope. It was quite a feat for Miller to create such a terrace on this steep slope, stabilising the downhill edge so well that 250 years later the terrace is still there. Miller's choice of site for the terrace depended on the lie of the land, for above this level the slope of the hill becomes markedly steeper. The outlines are quite clear on the ground, with three large horse chestnuts spaced along the outer built-up edge, and the bastion curving out into the grassland. The middle part of the terrace is some yards wider than the rest, with a very gentle slope upwards.

The summerhouse and the stable were both situated just within the woodland edge, on the hill below the castle complex. The summerhouse is described in George Miller's book *Rambles round the Edge hills* as: 'below the tower, where in the summer months a resort was often made for tea and the flow of conversation that accompanies the cup that cheers but does not inebriate. On such occasions the host and his clever, charming consort showed off to great advantage.'[19] The 1756 map shows a round building below the Tower, surrounded by trees. Although the summerhouse has gone, there remains a partly circular bastion on the site, about five yards in diameter, projecting out from the pathway. It is still surrounded by five ancient limes. The ornamental plaster finish applied to the stable was described by Shenstone in glowing terms:

> … you pass by a winding ascent until you have a view of a hanging Lawn enclosed on all sides with Wood-Work. It has a wild & *Forest-like* appearance, and is terminated at yᵉ End by a kind of *Eye-trap*, namely yᵉ End of a stable finish'd in yᵉ way of a Door & Pediment, but slightly & in Plaister-work. I lik'd this Scene yᵉ best of any, & I had yᵉ comfort to hear yᵗ Mr Lyttelton had done so before me[20] …

The classical disguise of the stable suggested an importance it obviously did not possess. It was probably built simply for a pony bringing the tea things to the summerhouse. This make-believe or pretence in the exterior appearance of a landscape building was deemed quite acceptable; indeed, it was a ruse which had been practised by Kent at Rousham, with his ordinary farmhouse masquerading as an important Gothic building beyond the gardens,[21] by Lord Bathurst, who had several castellated farm buildings at Cirencester and also by Lord Cobham at Stowe, who hid workers' cottages behind the simple castellated façade known as Stowe Castle, a mock castle wall built *c.*1738 and intended to be seen only in the distance from the gardens themselves. Miller's own mock castle ruin, his Tower at Edgehill, was to be built in this same vein, with more than a hint of make-believe and the enjoyment of a historical frisson about its conception.

Other than his cottage and Castle on Edgehill, Miller had few buildings in his landscape, underlining the importance of this new style of design where the natural features combining to form the landscape itself became the most important element, rather than simply a backdrop of scenery for an iconographic interpretation of an artistic or political idea. Shenstone commented unfavourably on the lack of urns, remarking: 'There is in his Churchyard [the churchyard at Radway] ye remains of a Monument to Captain Kingsmill [killed in the Battle of Edgehill] … Is it not astonishing yᵗ. Mr Miller does not remove this … to some solemn Area in his wood…?'[22] Miller would never, surely, with his respect for his local parish church and the tenets of the Church of England, have considered transferring Kingsmill's remains from the hallowed ground of the churchyard to adorn his own landscape.

A wide grass track leads from the top of the hill down past the Long Pool to Radway Grange. Too steep for carriages at the top, it was probably originally created by the monks. The sunken appearance of this track today gives credence to its having been in existence for a long time, though Miller may have improved the surface, for it is stoned beneath the grass. The track would have been used regularly by horses and carts, if only to collect furze from the hillside for fuel. One of the upper enclosures on the hill is shown on the 1756 map as 'little Furze', and the top of the hill was marked as 'the Lot Ground'; villagers would have cast lots each year for the right to gather furze from this area. Furze, or gorse, was a cheap and valuable fuel when wood was in short supply, for the top of Edgehill was bare of trees before Miller's planting plans,[23] and there was little spare fuel to be had among the open fields.

Evidence of Miller's extensive planting plans for the estate are shown by the entries in the accounts. Purchases of trees and shrubs appear in Miller's accounts from 1743 onwards. In that year he bought ten loads of thorn (hawthorn, or quicks), and in June he acquired firs and spruce, and also paid Wells of Faringdon six shillings for flowering shrubs. Miller's use of flowering shrubs is interesting, since it demonstrates that Miller, also, was using decorative shrubs well before the middle of the century, as well as designers such as Hamilton and Hoare mentioned previously. Other shrubs which Miller acquired between 1743 and 1756 include laurels and laurestinus, mezereum, and yews bought with some financial aid from William Pitt, and laurel seedlings and 'gelder roses' from Lord Guernsey, of Packington. Spanish broom was also grown from seed.[24] Miller's landscapes were essentially a part of the countryside, and as such his use

45 *Egge Cottage, from the south west, taken from an old photograph c.1910. The two rounded towers were intended to give the cottage the appearance of having been constructed from ruins. To increase the 'authenticity', pieces of masonry were left against the walls beside the front door.*

of flowering shrubs was sparing, similar in feel to the flora of a rural hedgerow.

In January 1744 Miller paid Lord North's gardener five shillings in connection with a purchase of hornbeam and horse chestnut which Lord North had sent over. In later years Strong, Lord North's gardener, came over to Radway from Wroxton several times to help with Miller's plantings. In May 1744 Miller was planting willows – rather late in the year, but on the Radway land where springs proliferated no doubt willows would grow when planted at most times in the year.

In about 1743, Miller built Egge Cottage on the top of Edgehill with mock rounded tower bases at the corners, and a thatched roof.[25] The cottage was intended to look as if it had been made out of existing old ruins, and from inside, framed by the Gothic windows, there is a magnificent view of Radway, the battlefield and the spreading south Warwickshire plain beyond. Egge Cottage, or the Thatched House, as Miller often referred to it, was both Miller's first Gothic building and also one of the very

46   *Edgehill, the old archway. Miller adapted these genuine ruins of Ratley Grange to provide stabling for his guests arriving at the Tower opposite.*

first *cottages ornés*. This descriptive term, since Miller's time, has been applied to estate cottages or small buildings with a stylised ornamental exterior, which became a popular genre as the century progressed. Egge Cottage itself, completed in or before 1744, was designed as a quiet retreat for study. Miller continued his regular reading and studying habits all his life, encouraging his sons and nephews to do the same. Besides offering the use of his Thatched House to friends, Miller also entertained his friends there. On 7 October 1749 he recorded holding a concert at the cottage. The Oxford poet James Merrick wrote a poem on the cottage entitled: 'Upon the thatched cottage in the wood of Sanderson Miller Esq., at Radway in Warwickshire'.

The last verse of the poem reads as follows:

> Within this solitary cell
> Calm thought and sweet contentment dwell,
> Parents of bliss sincere;
> Peace spreads around her balmy wings,
> And banish'd from the courts of kings,
> Has fixed her mansion here [26]

Lord North, who lived at nearby Wroxton Abbey, was obviously impressed by the building, since he often used to ask Miller if a servant would bring the key up the hill so that he could show the cottage to his guests.[27] The cottage is still lived in, but its romantic outlines have largely been lost by changes made in the late 20th century, when the roof was raised and tiled, leaving the towers looking oddly truncated.

In 1743 Miller was able to purchase 'Edge or Ratley Grange' as it is described in the conveyance; a group of buildings comprising the remains of the monastic grange situated across the road from Egge Cottage, adjacent to Miller's own land but just in the adjoining parish of Ratley. Miller also obtained a cottage and a close (or small piece of land) with his purchase.[28] Miller had now sufficient level ground on Edgehill to build both his mock tower, and provide the stabling for horses and carriages within the genuine old ruins of Edge Grange. Old photographs show a large Gothic arch forming an entrance to the stables, above which was an oriole window, and beside the arch were the tumbledown remains of the old Grange, which Miller left to give verisimilitude to the supposed antiquity of the whole site.

Between 1745 and 1750 Miller built the Tower, with its mock ruins and historical associations, to crown the summit. The Tower was also a prominent eyecatcher on the hilltop ridge as seen from Radway Grange and the approach from the north. The Tower was built on the site where tradition states that King Charles had raised his standard on 23 October 1642.[29] The foundations were started in October 1745. The tower was built in an octagonal shape, although the design is thought to be based on that of the 14th-century Guy's Tower at Warwick Castle, which has 12 sides. Miller's tower, like Guy's, had crenellations at the top, underpinned by machicolations, but the windows had Gothic arches, not medieval arrow slits as in Guy's Tower. Beside the main Tower a smaller square tower was built as a gatehouse. The upper room of the main tower, which was the main reception room for visitors and which overlooked the view, was reached from the gatehouse via a drawbridge over the drive beneath. On 8 May 1747 Miller wrote to his friend George Ballard, the antiquary and expert on the Saxon period, offering him hospitality and the use of the Thatched House and the Gothic Room in the Tower.[30]

On 5 December 1749 Miller was reading about the Saxon Heptarchy. George Miller, in *Rambles Round the Edge hills*, states that the centre of the ceiling in the Gothic room held the royal arms, and in the divisions around the centre the arms of the kingdom of the Saxon Heptarchy were displayed.[31] Old painted glass was used, and the arms of eight local families of ancient lineage were emblazoned around on shields, their arms facing the direction in which each family lived. The names represented[32] were: Francis, Lord North, 1st Earl of Guilford, of Wroxton and Shotteswell; Sir Charles Mordaunt, 6th Bart., of Walton; Heneage Finch, 3rd Earl of Aylesford, of Packington; Thomas Lennard-Barret, later 17th Lord Dacre, of Belhus in Essex; William Leigh of Adlestrop; Ivory Talbot of Lacock Abbey in Wiltshire; Matthew Wise of Warwick Priory; and Richard Wykeham, of Swalcliffe, a local village.

To add authenticity to the idea of the battle a century before, Miller ordered cannon balls to be sent from Birmingham. Lord North commissioned a carving of Caractacus, the last British leader to hold out against the Romans, for one of the niches in the Tower. When delivered, however, the statue was found to be too big, so it has spent the rest of its days in the garden at Radway Grange, where it still stands, now rather weathered. On 3 September 1750, the anniversary of Cromwell's death and also of two of his victories, Miller celebrated the building of the Tower with a ball. The date was chosen carefully, Miller hoping to please those of both Royalist and Parliamentarian sympathies. His diary

I   *Studley Royal, with the ruins of Fountains Abbey closing the vista.*

II   *Chiswick, the main garden path leading from the villa.*

III   above: *Shotover, the Gothic Temple, built for James Tyrell c.1720. This was the first garden building designed in the Gothic style, and is attributed to the Oxford master mason William Townesend.*

IV   left: *Rousham, the ornamental fountain at the head of Venus' Vale. The gardens were re-designed by William Kent c.1738.*

V   below: *Cirencester, a castellated façade built to look like an ancient castle, but hiding workers' cottages on Lord Bathurst's estate.*

VI *Shugborough, the Chinese House, 1747, built by his elder brother Thomas to commemorate Admiral Anson's visit to Canton on his circumnavigation of the world (1740-44).*

VII left: *Painswick, the Red House in the Rococo Garden. This asymmetric little Gothic garden-building draws the eye along the main path towards the far end of the garden.*

VIII below: *Painshill, a view in the grounds with the Gothic Temple in the distance.*

IX   *Edgehill Tower, built in the local ironstone. The wooden staircase and bridge are modern. The 'ruins' were to the right of the road. Egge Cottage is just beyond the red pub sign.*

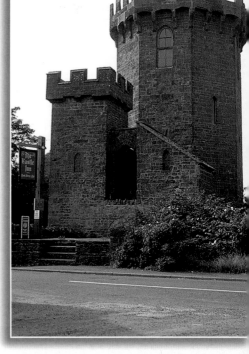

X   *Stowe Castle, probably built by Lord Cobham, c. 1738. This façade can be seen in the distance from the gardens. Estate cottages, built as part of the structure, are hidden behind the façade.*

XI   *Edgehill Tower is similar to Guy's Tower, Warwick Castle. Miller's Tower has Gothic windows and smaller crenellations than Guy's Tower, and is smaller overall. This photograph was taken before the insertion of modern bedrooms in the gatehouse.*

XII *Honington Hall, the pleasure grounds, by Thomas Robins, c.1750s. The painter is painting the scene from beyond the Grotto, looking back at the Hall across the river. His companion may be the owner Joseph Townsend's wife. There is a pleasure boat on the river, and the Hall and the parish church can be seen beyond. The church spire to the left is that of Tredington church. It would not be visible in this view, but has been added to the painting for effect.*

These two informal paintings, with their naturalistic borders of flowers, birds and butterflies, represent a complete change in artistic style from that of the 1731 drawing by Buck and Buck of the formal gardens, comparable with the dramatic change from formality to informality in the laying out of the grounds.

XIII *Honington Hall, the pleasure grounds, by Thomas Robins, c.1750s. A picnic is taking place in front of the Chinese Seat, beyond which is the river and the cascade, with the two river gods reclining on plinths on either side of the latter. On the far side of the river can be seen (r to l) the Chinese bridge, the Grotto, and the Temple.*

XIV *Farnborough Hall, west front and south front (to the right). The house was altered and the estate was landscaped by Sanderson Miller from c.1738.*

XV *Farnborough Hall, view from the Game Larder over Island Pond towards Farnborough church*

XVI *Farnborough, a view from the terrace showing the long avenue (replanted) leading away from the canal. Beyond the valley the ridge of the Edge Hills can be seen.*

XVII *Farnborough, one of the old stone sluices on the 'serpentine river' shown on the map of 1771. This widened stream flowed west from the 'River', now known as Rookery Pool, taking the overflow water to join the other stream on the estate boundary.*

XVIII *Wroxton, the small Gothic bridge at the site of the Chinese seat on the double 'river'. The mound on which the Chinese seat was built is still there, just to the left of the bridge, but it is not visible in this picture.*

XIX   *Wroxton, the Drayton Arch on the hilltop beside the old Banbury to Wroxton road.*

XX   *Wroxton, the Dovecote, which has recently been restored. From this point can be seen the Abbey, the Prince's Obelisk to the south, and on high ground to the south west one of Miller's typical hilltop clumps of oaks and Scots pines.*

entry for the date reads: 'Ball at Castle 48 People – went to bed ½ after 5'.

Miller used a camera obscura to draw a pictorial record of the landscape he had created. He recorded in his diary on 26 May 1750 that he was: 'drawing Lands. with Cam. Obsc.' The drawing was of his landscape as seen from his Tower. Miller took both the camera obscura and his drawing to Hagley, finally recording on 14 June 1750: 'Finished my Landskip'. No record of this drawing survives.

When he visited Radway in 1750, Shenstone was quite critical of Miller's Tower. He described the upper room as 'highly finish'd in ye Gothick Taste'. He then complained that:

> yᵉ Height is so excessive yᵗ I cou'd not endure to look out of yᵉ windows; next, yᵉ arch of yᵉ Ceiling does not please me; & lastly yᵉ wretched Laboriousness & inconvenience of yᵉ Ascent makes it not desireable to compleat a Room so expensively at that *Height* ...'[33]

47   *The statue of Caractacus, the last British leader to stand against the Romans, by James Lovell.*

Paintings of Shenstone reveal him as somewhat corpulent. No doubt the 'wretched laboriousness' of the ascent had left him so hot and out of breath that he was in no mood to admire what he saw. Others thought differently. On 29 September 1756, Bishop Pococke[34] visited Miller and reported on the Radway scene:

> I went ... through the field of battle of Edghill, which was in the grounds under the hill, where they find many bullets, and came to Mr Miller's house at Radway. This gentleman, who lives on his estate, has a great genius for architecture, especially the Gothic, and I waited on him to consult about the adorning the Cathedral of Kilkenny, the design of which he had been so kind as to undertake. He has embellish'd his own house with Gothic architecture, and has made a fine lawn up the hill, with shady walks round it, up to the ruined castle on Edgehill, which he has built adjoyning to the houses of some tenants. But he has erected a very noble round tower, which is entire, with a drawbridge, to which there is an assent as by a ruine, and there is a very fine octagon Gothic room in it, with four windows and 4 niches, and some old painted glass in the windows. In one of these windows is to be placed Caractacus in chains, modeled, under Mr Miller's direction, by a countryman of great genius, now settled in London; it is executed in the yellow free stone.[35]

The Tower is still in a good state of preservation, but is now a pub, and planning permission was unfortunately granted recently to convert the gatehouse tower into modern bedroom accommodation, in spite of objections from the Garden History Society and others. The stabling and the ruins across the road have all now been demolished, cleared away to make room for car parking and modern housing, with complete disregard for the historical importance of the site.

Miller's Tower soon became well known, both through the admiration of his many visitors and also through George Lyttelton's request for Miller to design a mock ruin to be built on the highest point of his park at Hagley, in Worcestershire. The success of the latter led to

Miller being asked to design other similar structures, the best known of which is the mock ruined castle for Lord Chancellor Hardwicke's park at Wimpole in Cambridgeshire.

Why did Miller choose to build a mock ruined castle tower, and why did he choose this particular time? After the Civil War, several local castles in the Midlands had been 'slighted', or destroyed to the point of becoming uninhabitable, including Kenilworth, Oxford and Wallingford. Locally, there were also the ancient ruins of the castle at Kineton, so the mock ruins at Edgehill fitted well into the local scene. Both Lord Bathurst at Cirencester, and Lord Cobham at Stowe had introduced sham castles into their landscapes, Lord Bathurst's Alfred's Hall, 1721, being the first purpose-built mock ruin. These, however, did not generate the same popularity. Interest in the Gothic past had been growing, especially since 1733, when Lord Cobham had fallen out with the Government over the Excise Bill and had begun to develop his gardens as an iconographic tribute to the presumed high ideals of the ancient Gothic past, as against the corrupt government of Sir Robert Walpole. Miller had conceived his Gothic Tower and its ruins at the right time to appeal to these ideals as seen by his friends and acquaintances among the landed gentry, most of whom were Whigs who sided with Lord Cobham. Although ruins have always had a romantic and historical appeal, a further reason for the popularity of Miller's Tower was its appeal to the imagination of those looking to improve their estates at this period. A mock ruin, if an owner had not the genuine article, could suggest a long and noble family line, well established on the estate. If one did not possess this ancient lineage, this suggestion was by no means unwelcome to a man whose rise to power had perhaps been comparatively recent.

Miller continued to plant trees and to work on his landscape after the completion of his Tower. The Laurel Walk is mentioned several times in Miller's accounts. William Pitt is recorded as providing money for laurels to line a walk which Mrs Miller enjoyed, and also strawberries for a 'Strawberry Bank'. He also helped Miller with his landscaping, by lending him his man to help with some of the estate work. On 19 May Miller's accounts show that he paid 'Mr Pit's Richard Palmer for work at the Sand Walk and levelling the ditches, 2.13.03.' Perhaps the ditches were part of the ridge and furrow out in the field below the terrace. On 14 January 1753 Pitt expressed pleasure in a letter to Miller that 'Mrs Miller already enjoys the laurels'. He went on to say: 'I make no doubt the myrtle still blooms at Radway and that all the laurels there are not sufficient to bind your victorious brow'[36] referring to Miller's increasing fame for his buildings and mock ruins. The Laurel Walk may be the path from the terrace to the Summerhouse, for there are a number of very old laurels growing alongside it.

In January 1756 Miller noted in his accounts that he had received 103 beeches[37] to set on the top of the hill from his great friend Sir Edward Turner, whose improvements to his estate in Oxfordshire had been one of Miller's first projects. Miller planted these trees along the top of the scarp as far as the road up Knowle Hill. Above his house, within the old park, Miller planted several groups of trees. Mature specimens of limes, sweet chestnuts and horse chestnuts still growing today probably mark some of these plantings. A group of trees, known as Lord Chatham's Trees, was planted in the park near the Grange. Although marked on successive Ordnance Survey maps into the 20th century, they have now all disappeared. The trees were planted in 1754 by William Pitt, later Lord Chatham, on the occasion of Henry Fielding's reading of the manuscript of his novel *Tom Jones* at

Radway to Pitt, Miller and George Lyttelton. Some years after the planting, an urn was sent to Warwickshire by Pitt's nephew, Thomas Pitt of Boconnoc, to commemorate this ceremony, and set up by Miller in 1779, the year before Miller's death. In 1908 a note was discovered in the urn which read:

> In the year 1754 the Right Honourable William Pitt Esq. planted three trees, two Scotch Firrs and one Mountain Ash, being then on a visit to Radway with Sanderson Miller Esqre. In the month of July 1778 Thomas Pitt Esq. of Boconnok in Cornwall being at Radway thought it would be proper to place this urn under these trees and sent it from Bath and it was set up April 21, 1779 by Sanderson Miller Esq.[38]

Miller's wife and family witnessed this event, together with Edward Trotman, George Ransford and also 'Master Hiorns', the mason Miller used for several of his projects. The urn is now in the garden at Radway Grange, and the letters CHATHAM can still be made out on it. Tradition has it that the Radway landscape was used by Fielding in his novel as the model for the landscape around Mr Allworthy's house. Prior Park, on the outskirts of Bath, has also been accorded this honour. The description of the house and its surrounds are as follows:

> It [Mr Allworthy's house, described as being in 'the Gothick stile of building'] stood … nearer the bottom [of the hill] than the top of it, so as to be sheltered from the northeast by a grove of old oaks, which rose above it in a gradual ascent … in the midst of the grove was a fine lawn, sloping down towards the house, near the summit of which rose a plentiful spring, gushing out of a rock covered with firs, and forming a constant cascade of about thirty foot … tumbling in a natural fall over the broken and mossy stones …'. [a view] 'terminated by one of the towers of an old ruined abbey, grown over with ivy, and part of the front, which still remained entire … 'the left hand scene presented the view of a very fine park, composed of very unequal ground, and agreeably varied with all the diversity that hills, lawns, wood, and water, laid out with admiral taste, but owing less to art than to nature, could give.[39]

During the early 1750s Miller planted a mix of conifers and deciduous trees, including cypress, larches (from seed), New England firs, Scotch firs (pines?), pinasters (grown from seed), Weymouth pines, pines, spruce and yews, alders, ashes, beeches (some from seed), birches, sweet chestnuts, horse chestnuts, mountain ashes, elms and oaks (some from sets). Quantities of 100 alders, 400 elms and several hundred oaks were used. In 1758 Miller wrote to Lord North describing the planting he had been carrying out at Radway of laurels, firs, Weymouth pines, cedars and beeches.[40]

Miller mentions his garden several times in both the accounts and in his diary for 1750. Growing fruit oneself was the only practical way of obtaining it in a small rural community, and it was important to the Miller household. Miller purchased several mulberry trees in 1746 and 1748, and in 1748 and 1749 orange trees came over from Wroxton. In 1754 'pineapple trees' were also sent from Wroxton – Miller must have had a frost free glasshouse for the oranges and heated frames, probably using manure as a source of heat, for the pineapples. In February 1750 Miller was planting both gooseberries and grapes, and on 2 August he 'Gathered 66 abricots', probably a bumper crop.

Despite the success of his Tower, Miller was constrained in his designed landscape, since his land was held predominantly in strips in the common field. To develop the design further he needed to own the hillside in one piece from his own parkland to the north as far as the Kineton to Banbury road, which marked the end of the parish boundary as it ascended the hill. At this date the hillside beyond his park was bare of trees, and comparatively difficult to cultivate because of the steep slope. However, for Miller's purposes it was excellent, for there were further streams coming from springs on the hill, and a belt of trees could be planted along the scarp as far as Knowle End.

Miller's financial situation had been at times sufficiently difficult for him to have considered selling his estate. In 1748 a letter from Deane Swift had suggested that Miller was having financial troubles, and in 1750, just before the opening Ball at the Tower, Miller's great friend Sir Edward Turner wrote: '… But could you find no other person as a purchaser of Radway than Mr Bumshead? I little thought his prophecy wou'd so soon have been completed.'[41] Bumpsted owned the estate at Upton, a mile or so distant from Edgehill. Miller managed to avoid this calamity, but he felt that the only way to increase his income from his land, both tenanted and in hand, was to consolidate his holdings into large blocks. If tenants were able to farm a fenced holding, without having to agree with others the management of communal grazing rights and cropping, they were then masters of their own farming. Furthermore they would not have to graze their animals with those of others, with all the problems of disease and poor inter-breeding which the old communal field system entailed. In his diary for 1756, Miller mentioned that he had been discussing the fiscal benefits of enclosure in other areas, including Norton and Bicester. On 3 September he was at Adlestrop, talking to Mr Thornton about the latter's enclosure at Norton, where: 'His estate improved from £50 to £150 per an. at 500d. expense.' If Miller could obtain anything approaching that percentage increase it is obvious why he was anxious to have the Radway land enclosed. In 1756 Miller applied for an Act of Enclosure for Radway, asking William Pitt's help with bringing the Act before Parliament, and then commissioned a parish survey which was carried out by the surveyor George Salmon, from Long Itchington, a village 11 miles north of Radway.[42]

Throughout Miller's second diary, which runs from April 1756 to the first few days in January 1757, there are constant references to the coming enclosure. Miller, together with his surveyor, had to assess the quality of the land and decide with other owners how it was to be allotted. Miller, of course, wanted all the hill. He also needed to consolidate his arable valley land. With the help of the 1756 map, and a modern map prepared in 1997 which shows the final allotments,[43] it is possible to follow many of Miller's deliberations with his neighbours and to see how the land was finally parcelled out. The new hedging and fencing had also to be considered, for it would all have to be put in place around the new holdings following the award. In March Miller purchased several thousand quicks, or hawthorns, and 6,000 more in the following November. Throughout May and June Miller recorded his men cleaving posts and rails, and he himself was weeding quicks on 19 May. George Salmon may have owned a part of the large wood at Itchington, known as Itchington Holt, as Miller bought 50 young oaks from him for £8 12s. 0d. on 31 May – presumably to move and plant in the coming winter – and on 29 June five loads of wood arrived from Itchington. On 5 August: 'Smith counted ye rails – 6021/2 p^r. Of Mr Bumpsted's Wood 600 p^r of my own 34^p more at J. Hunts. 146 posts at Hunts.' Miller was weeding quicks again himself at the end of the month. On 7 November Miller visited Mr Clark's nurseries at Thame on his way home from

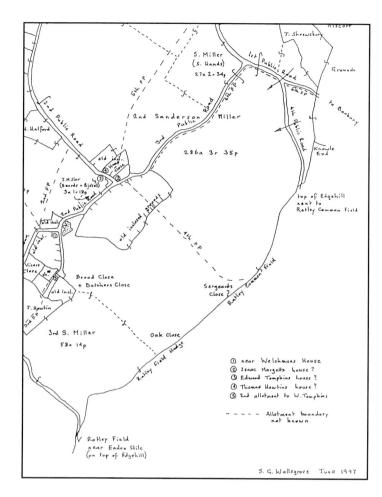

48 *A map of the parish of Radway, by S.G. Wallsgrove, 1997, showing the distribution of the Enclosure awards, and also the parish footpaths.*

a visit to Stowe and Wotton Underwood. He lists the prices: 'Quicks 3s.6d – Small Firs 5ˢ a Thᵈ. [thousand] Laurus Tin: [laurustinus or Viburnum tinus] & Laurˡ. 20 a hundᵈ – bargnd [bargained] for 60,000Q. [quicks] to be sent by Eagles.' Hawthorn (quicks) were the species of choice for hedges, for hawthorn grows quickly, is completely hardy, forms a good and prickly hedge against animals, and is ideal for 'cutting and laying'. This system, used predominantly in the Midlands, involved cutting the hedge plants of about 15 years' growth part way through near the ground, then bending or laying the plants diagonally along the length of the hedge, weaving them in and out of upright stakes thrust in to the ground, then trimming and finishing the tops to make a stock proof barrier. Every man allotted land under the Act had to fence and hedge his new property. For Miller this was a large and expensive undertaking.

On 13 July Miller recorded that he was 'walking in Boveton', or 'Buffon' as it is named on the 1756 map. The name was a shortened form of 'above town', i.e. above Radway. Prior to the Enclosure Act, Miller did not own this field, which was adjacent to and immediately to the north of his parkland. It is the first mention of this field in Miller's diaries. Miller must have been assessing its potential if it were added to his park, for it was to be an important part of his enlarged landscaping scheme after the Enclosure award.

On 1 November the Commissioners convened in the Tower at Edgehill, and again on 16 November. On 1 November Miller spent his day going up and down the hill, attending the Commissioners, directing his men cutting trees on the hill, and entertaining both the Commissioners and Sir Edward Turner and his family, who were staying at Radway, to breakfast, then a much more sociable meal than nowadays. The deliberations of the Commissioners were not without problems, for there was some argument involving Mr Welchman about the division of land, but the diary entry for 2 November finally stated: 'atten^g ye Com^rs who made their Allotments much to my Satisfaction …'. On 16 November: 'all our Allotments concluded'. Miller had been awarded 344 acres on the hill besides nearly 400 acres of the arable land in the valley. He now owned all the hillside in the parish, running right up to the Kineton road.

In the next few days Miller was preoccupied with seeing prospective tenants and discussing the land to be let, breakfasting 'on Milk Por^ge [porridge] w. neigh^r Ennock' and seeing to everything which had to be arranged. There was much to do concerning the changing ownership of land within the parish. The Act laid down the allotments, but individual settlements obviously required some negotiation. Miller's diary entries reveal that on 22 November the trees in Tomkin's close (a name for a small piece of land, sometimes adjacent to a cottage) were being counted, and on the evening of 26 November: 'Mr Tomkins c. in ye Ev^g.[evening] w.[with] Salmon [the surveyor] Con^n.[conversation] Ab^t.[about] value of his Timber and exchanging his Closes…'. However, Miller even found time during this period to read Jethro Tull's book on husbandry, and his headaches, which had been persistent earlier in the year, seem to have been relegated to the background.

In December 1756 Miller wrote the following poem[44] based loosely, as was Pope's earlier poem, on the first few lines of Jonathan Swift's 'Imitations of Horace', written in 1714 as a translation from Horace's *Satires*, Book 2, no.6.

Obviously not intended as serious poetry, it does encapsulate Miller's achievements and aspirations concerning his estate and its landscaping in a way that none of his other writings – his diaries and his few existing letters – manage to convey:

> Epistle to --------, London, December 13th, 1756.
> At last I find that I have clear
> In Land six hundred pounds a year
> Besides a Piece for Wife and Daughters
> And something more for Woods and Waters.
> My House! 'tis true, a small and old one
> Yet now 'tis warm, 'tho once a cold one.
> My Study holds three thousand Volumes,
> And yet I sigh for Gothick Columns,
> Such as Sir Roger, learned Knight of Taste,
> At Arbury so well has placed,
> Or such as Dacre, Gothic Master,
> Has introduced instead of Plaister.
> With here a large Settee for sleep'
> A window there to take a peep
> Of Lawns and Woods and Cows and Sheep.
> And Laurel Walk and Strawberry Bank

For which the Paymaster I thank.
The Paymaster well skilled in planting
Pleas'd to assist when cash was wanting.
He bid my Laurels grow, they grew
Fast as his Laurels always do.
The Squire still said, 'get Ground in Front.'
By dint of Parliament I've don't –
But still they say, 'No piece of Water,
No Duckery for wife and daughter!'
Should that be done, they'd still cry out
And hourly put me in a pout,
The Place is still not worth a farden,
No Mortal has a Kitchen Garden
So full of weeds, so void of Cabbage Plants,
You can't supply your scullions' wants.
No Turnips freshen salted Beef …[45]

The Radway Enclosure Act was passed and the Award signed on 17 May 1757. Miller's bill, as the largest landowner, came to £330, which included the expenses of obtaining the Act, surveying the new enclosures and preparing and enrolling the Award. Sir Edward Turner was surprised that he was not charged more. However, Miller told Sir Edward that this bill was only about a third of the total expense he had incurred in bringing the Act before Parliament. Miller's old friend George, Lord Lyttelton sent him some money to help with the expenses, and hoped he was enjoying his enclosures. Miller must have been considerably worried about meeting his expenses, for the very day after the Act became law he took out two separate mortgages of £850 each on a total of 670 acres and four messuages in Radway to Henry Grenville. Later in the year, in August, he mortgaged 130 acres and one messuage, also in Radway, to his cousin John Welchman of Brackley.[46]

The Millers also owned land in Moreton Morrell, a village not far away from Radway. This land had been owned by the Lords Saye and Sele, and it appears to have come to the Trotman family through marriage, and been given to Miller's wife Susannah as part of her marriage portion in 1747. Henry Grenville came to Miller's assistance again over this property. In 1757 Miller obtained an Enclosure Act for Moreton Morrell and in April 1758 Henry Grenville bought the property from him. Letters from Grenville indicate that Miller continued to manage the land for him, including dealing with tenants and the hedging and fencing required for the enclosures. On 22 August 1759, Miller wrote to his nephew Clement Newsham that the sale of the land at Moreton Morrell had eased him of much financial burden and that it would pay for the costs of the enclosure at Radway. Miller was able to raise the rental of his estate from eight shillings an acre to 30 shillings an acre (there were 20 shillings to the pound) following enclosure.[47]

Miller's grounds were always short of water features of any size. The steepness of the hillside, and the impossibility of making pools on the lower land of the parish, which was occupied by the village houses and by land belonging to others, precluded any extensive lakes. Even if he had had the resources, Miller's philanthropic and kindly nature would not have allowed him to remove the village wholesale to another site for his own ends, as did some contemporary landowners.

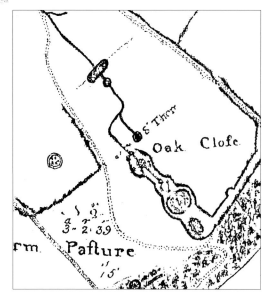

49   *The Long Pool, with the cascades, enlarged from the Radway pre-Inclosure map of 1756*

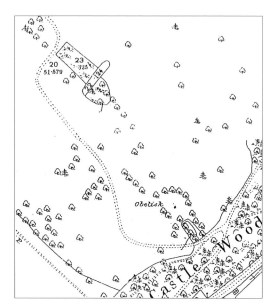

50   *The Long pool with the new pools above and below, taken from the 25-inch O.S. map, c.1900. This map is at the same scale as the 1756 map above, and shows the outline of new pools (by this date no longer holding water) and the trees around the remains of Miller's cascade area.*

It has been suggested that farming and financial problems might have been the reason why there are no large pools at Radway.[48] However, since so much of the water coming off the hill was culverted under or away from the Grange it is unlikely that Miller would have considered creating any large piece of water in the park immediately above his house for fear of flooding.

In 27 December 1756, Miller's diary entry reads: 'Woodw^d. c.[came] d.[down] w.[with] me to talk ab^t.[about] Pond making &c. H spd [supped] w us.' This discussion may well have been about the monks' old pool on the hill, for, after this date, major alterations were made to this pool. These are clearly shown by comparing the outlines of the pool area as shown on the 1756 pre-Enclosure map with those on the 1900 25-inch O.S. map. The pool on the old map is smaller, and is shown higher up the hillside. Measurements between fixed points have shown that the old map, drawn at half the scale of the O.S. map, is remarkably accurate in all other respects. On site, boggy areas, now filled with trees, correspond exactly in shape to those new larger outlines on the O.S. map. It seems certain that these areas had been excavated to form new pools, the top one the original Long Pool, altered in shape, and separated from the lower, larger pool by a dam with a gap in the middle, probably once crossed by a bridge. Water still trickles through this gap into the lower pool area, though beyond this the old watercourse is now dry. Trees were planted along the dam, and a shady walk with water on either side was thus created, a feature which was to become one of Miller's hallmarks. The whole pool system had been altered, explaining the difference in the positions of the long pool on the two maps. Miller – for it was surely he – had succeeded in creating his 'piece of Water', his 'Duckery for Wife and Daughter'.

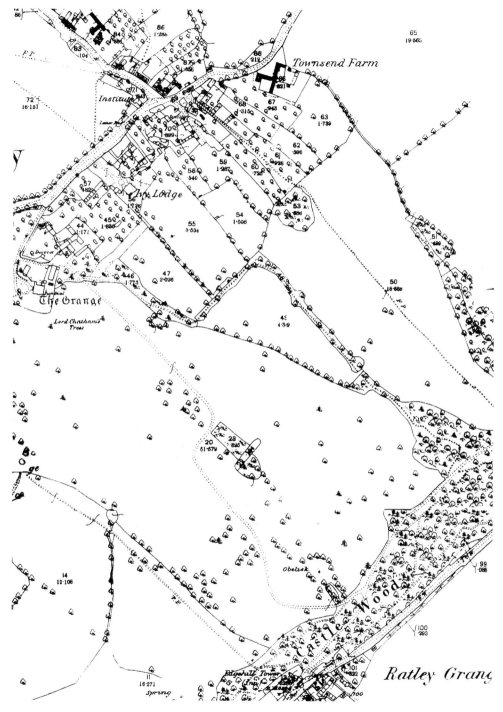

51   *Radway, taken from the six-inch O.S. map for 1900. Miller's new landscaped path can be seen beside the stream running from high on the hillside, along one side of the triangular field in the middle of the map, and down to Radway Grange. This path was made following the extra land exchanged into his ownership following the Enclosure Act. Extensive planting has also been carried out on the upper slopes within Castle Wood.*

Having created a larger pool system, Miller then needed to divert the track down the hill. The new section had to be constructed to run right in front of his new lower pool. Comparing the line of the track on the 1756 map and the O.S. map for 1900, it can clearly be seen that on the latter the track at this point has been altered significantly, describing a more angled bend halfway down the hill to pass around the new pools. This new section can be seen today as a raised bank but, above this, the track is sunk.

Miller had been planning to turn some of his arable land over to improved pasture for sheep or cattle, at least on the hill, to bring in a better return. On the 1906 25-inch O.S. map there are two areas where sheep pens are marked, one at the top of Sargents' old close and one near the springs in the field marked 'Buffon'. (See the 1756 map.) There is also a new pool by the pens nearer the Grange, which would have been useful for washing the sheep. Dickens and Stanton quote a verse written to Mrs Miller, probably by Sir Edward Turner *c.*1756, addressing her as 'Sweet Consort', then describing the changes on Edgehill:

> At first, indeed, the varied Scene
> May please of Fallow chang'd to Green;
> And Herbs improving since the Act,
> May make him feel himself compact.
> But are you sure Content will last
> When you reflect on all that's past?[49]

Today the fallow (land which is left bare of a crop for a period of time to allow weeds to be killed by cultivations) is still 'changed to green' on a large part of the hill, but the ridge and furrow remains, giving testimony to its former arable status. The old parkland has no ridge and furrow, and the line of Miller's footpath which ran up the hill from the Grange can still be made out on the ground, for it ran along the last of the ridges adjoining the old parkland to the north.

Miller was carrying out a great deal of work on trees both before and after the Commissioner's allotment days. Wood was being cut on the Mount, trees were being marked and cut down in the 'Sand Walk', trees were being felled 'under the wood', and on 10 November Miller himself was: 'cutting the Horse Chesnuts at ye Long Walk w. Pole Ax'. On 12 November he was with the men cutting ashes at the end of 'the green terras'. On 26 November he had 30 men working on the ornamental grounds. Perhaps he was cutting down the old trees misshapen by many years of lopping, which Shenstone had complained about. This work, of course, does not include the essential ditching, fencing and hedging which had to be carried out around Miller's newly enclosed agricultural fields in the lower valley land.

On 25 November 1756, Henry Grenville wrote mentioning the 'operations under Edgehill, the inclosure of the Greenfields and the lines of Circumvallation which you have been drawing about your banks …'.[50] This seems to refer to the new hillside land to the north which Miller had acquired through the Enclosure Act. A new path was created which followed along the backs of the town 'closes' and then wound up the hill along a stream which issued from springs shown clearly on the old 1756 map between two areas marked 'buffon' – or 'above town'. Any group of houses forming a small settlement was often referred to as the 'town', a term frequently found on old maps. Looking at the 1886 map, this area can clearly be seen, the narrow band of woodland marking the course of the stream. Just short of the steepest area the woodland was expanded and the path meandered through it to join the walk along the woodland clothing the steepest part of the ridge.

Most of this new 'pathscape' is still quite clear on the ground today, and many of the trees are still standing. Where it begins to ascend the hillside the path has obviously been deliberately raised and levelled above the stream, which is now only a trickle even in winter. It looks as if the stream had been deepened and widened to provide more interest, with the spoil thrown up on the bank to make the new path, as is suggested by Grenville's use of the military term 'circumvallation'. There is an interesting variety of trees on either side: horse chestnuts, beeches, oaks, crabapple, and towards the higher end there are many old laurels in thick undergrowth. There are a few signs of ancient cut and laid hedges alongside the path. From the top of this path one could, and still can walk back to the terrace, the cascades, the Tower and the other buildings, or down to Radway along one of the other paths. One could also walk the whole length of the hill within the woodland as far as Knowle End, and there are several points at which it is possible to scramble up a steep path to the summit, where some of Sir Edward Turner's beeches still adorn the ridge.

Since Miller's last diary ends so soon after the Radway Enclosure Act had been settled, there is little to indicate the extent of his new planting in his extended landscape. Some few details in his accounts for 1756, 1757 and 1758 show that he was thinking of planting on a large scale, quite apart from all his hedging. In early January 1757 crab kernels arrived ready to be sown, and 100 Weymouth pines came from Lord Barrington. In the spring of 1758 Lord Barrington sent some pines which were six feet in height, and also some firs, and Lord Guilford provided oak sets from his nursery at Chipping Warden. Four years later more than a thousand seven to eight feet high young oaks arrived from Chipping Warden. The results of Miller's extensive work can be seen today not only along the landscaped paths and within his park, but also on the whole hillside and particularly along the length of the ridge itself.

The Radway landscape illustrates the development of Miller's ideas, and all the main characteristics of his later work can be seen here. The complete informality of the design is the most important aspect, showing an advance in the development of a 'natural' landscape style over anything which had gone before, and which would lead eventually to the designs of Capability Brown. The landscape was formed around the idea of the dominant buildings on the top of the hill, and the views to be obtained both from here and lower down the hillside. The style of the buildings was carefully chosen to make a statement, and to underline the historic and also the romantic aspect of the situation. The buildings served the additional purpose of providing both shelter and a place where refreshments could be served. Both the Tower and Egge Cottage were designed with the purpose of providing hospitality for Miller's many friends and visitors, an important part of their raison d'être. The creation of new water features made the best use of the topography the site offered, although at Radway Miller's options in this direction were limited. Shady paths were made alongside streams to make pleasurable summer walks. No 18th-century gentleman or lady would have considered taking a walk among labourers working in the open fields, and before enclosure only a small part of the Radway hillside had been available to Miller to create his walks, so his post-enclosure work along the hillside greatly extended the walks which he could now offer his guests. Miller's landscapes were intended to be enjoyed particularly by walking within them, a favoured pastime of his contemporaries and one which is underlined by the entries in Miller's own diaries. In these he often refers not only to walking at Radway or with his friends on their estates, but also notes the time taken, which was sometimes two or three hours.

In 1767 Richard Jago published his poem Edge-hill, eulogising Warwickshire's finest estates of the period. Edgehill itself takes pride of place:

> Like a tall Rampart! Here the Mountain rears
> Its verdant Edge; and, if thy tuneful Maids
> Their Presence deign, shall with Parnassus vie,
> Level and smooth the Track that leads to thee!
> Its adverse Side a Precipice presents
> Abrupt, and steep! Thanks, MILLER! To thy Paths,
> That ease our winding Steps! Thanks to the Rill,
> The Banks, the Trees, the Shrubs, th'enraptur'd Sense
> Regaling, or with Fragrance, Shape or Sound,
> And stilling ev'ry Tumult in the Breast!
> And oft the stately Tow'rs, that overtop
> The rising Wood, and oft the broken Arch,
> Or mould'ring Wall, well taught to counterfeit
> The Waste of Time, to solemn Thought excite,
> And crown with graceful Pomp the shaggy Hill …
> The Summit's gain'd! and, from its airy Height,
> The late-trod Plain looks like an inland Sea,
> View'd from some Promontory's hoary Head,
> With distant Shores environ'd; …
> Such is the Scene! that, from the terrac'd Hill,
> Whose Sides the Dryads, and the Wood Nymphs dress
> With rich Embroidery, salutes the Eye …[51]

At many of the properties Jago described, including Honington, Alscot, Packington, Wroxton and Arbury, Miller himself had been influential in sweeping away their previous formal grounds and planning the introduction of naturalistic and informal designs. By 1767, the date of Jago's poem, an informal approach to landscaping was becoming accepted everywhere, fuelled by the success of Capability Brown, who with his naturalistic designs had followed where Miller had led the way.

6

Farnborough, Wroxton and Honington

❧ · ☙

Miller is associated with the landscaping of more than 35 estates.[1] At some estates he designed a landscape complete with buildings, at some he designed buildings and gave advice in collaboration with several other men, as at George Lyttelton's estate at Hagley; and at others he was asked to design just one building for an important situation, such as the Ruined Castle at Wimpole. Three estates where Miller's landscaping

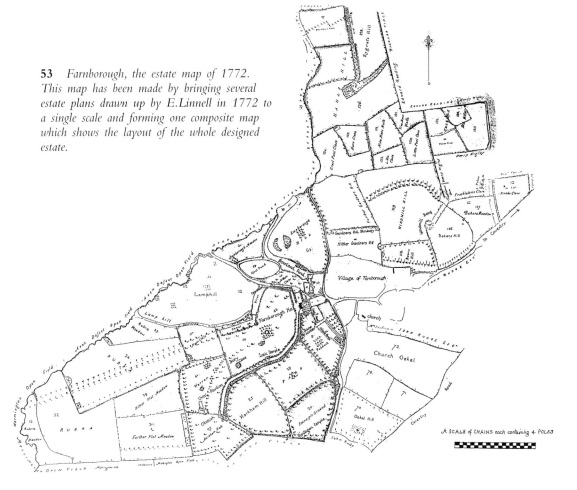

53 *Farnborough, the estate map of 1772. This map has been made by bringing several estate plans drawn up by E.Linnell in 1772 to a single scale and forming one composite map which shows the layout of the whole designed estate.*

has survived the passage of time and can best be seen today are at Farnborough and Honington, in south Warwickshire, and Wroxton, in north Oxfordshire, all newly laid out between the late 1730s and the early 1740s.

Miller possessed a great ability to visualise the possibilities inherent in a site, and to design a plan which would make the most of both the potential of the site and his client's aspirations. He was also capable of complex engineering feats to achieve the realisation of his plans. The management of water and the erection of stable dams to form lakes are matters which still cause problems today, yet Miller was able to construct solid and enduring dams at a time when there was no power or machinery to assist him other than manpower and draft animals. His scheme at Farnborough provides an excellent illustration of these abilities.

Farnborough

Farnborough Hall, built of dark honey-coloured marlstone, is situated six miles from Banbury and four from Radway, on the edge of the Burton Dassett Hills, a northern spur of the Cotswolds. The estate varies in height from about 400 feet to over 600 feet (183m). Both the Hall and its landscaped setting remain largely unaltered from the mid-18th century. In 1684 Ambrose Holbech, a successful lawyer who lived in the adjacent parish of Mollington, bought the estate from the Raleghs (related to Sir Walter Raleigh), who had become impoverished due to their Royalist sympathies. William Holbech, Ambrose's grandson, succeeded to the estate on the death of his father in 1717. On his return from the Grand Tour in the late 1730s William decided to enlarge the old Hall as a setting for his Italian collections, and to landscape the estate in the latest fashion. He appears to have had no particular political or social aspirations and was content to spend his money on his estate after his extensive travels.

Archival records during the earlier part of the 18th century are fragmentary.

The attribution of the alterations to the Hall and the layout of the new landscape to Sanderson Miller relies largely on family tradition – the Holbech family still lives at Farnborough – and on the word of Miller's great-grandson, the Reverend George Miller, who wrote in *Rambles Round the Edge Hills*:

> William Holbech was one who was good and wise in his generation. He had ample means and used them wisely. The old house of the Raleghs he altered, enlarged and improved, giving it its present shape and internal arrangements. He decorated the principal rooms with works of arts, some of Canaletti's paintings being brought from Italy for that purpose. The grounds were freshly laid out; the old formal style, with its belts of trees to shelter the house and gardens, when all the country round was open field, gave place to the expanse of lawn, and the opening out of beautiful vistas and extensive views, a characteristic feature of the place.
>
> One of the chief beauties of Farnborough, and the greatest work of William Holbech, is the terrace, at the end of which stands the handsome, well-proportioned obelisk. The views from the terrace are fine and extensive. The shrubberies by its side are interspersed with alcoves and summer-houses, after the custom of the period, the whole forming an ornament to the place hardly equalled in England. In these works Mr Holbech was assisted by the advice and taste of his friend and neighbour Sanderson Miller, of Radway.[2]

The Hall itself was enlarged and partly rebuilt on classical lines, and the interior was also remodelled. A new north front, and a new and enlarged south front were constructed. The central doorway in the latter has an elegant skirted architrave, the stonework being allowed to curve out at the base of the doorway, a feature Miller was to repeat for the windows of the piano nobile at Hagley Hall. The timing of the landscape improvements at Farnborough, which were begun in about 1740[3] when Miller had completed his first landscaping works on the Radway hillside, and the proximity of the Farnborough estate to Radway, add further support to the attribution of the designed landscape to Miller. Miller was only in his early 20s, but Holbech obviously had faith in the young man's abilities.

An unpublished modern report on the history of that part of the site now administered by the National Trust, which includes the hall, the pools, and the main terrace to the south west of the Hall, also designates Miller as the author of the work at Farnborough. The date 1738 is suggested for the start of the improvements following Holbech's return from his Grand Tour, and the report notes similarities between the work at Farnborough and Miller's own work at Radway; also the fact that craftsmen working on the Hall had worked at other sites for Miller.[4] There is nothing in either of Miller's two surviving diaries which refers back to the actual landscape work, although there are references to visits to Farnborough, for example on 21 July 1750,[5] when Miller brought Lord Cobham over to see the estate. Miller and Holbech visited each other quite frequently, but Miller's earlier diary only begins in the autumn of 1749, by which date it is likely that the work at Farnborough was complete, and Miller's diary entries are brief, usually referring only to whom he had met and to what happened on the day in question.

The earliest plans of the estate known to exist were commissioned by William Holbech's nephew, also William, who succeeded his uncle in 1771. These plans were made in 1772 by Edward Linnell.[6] There is no reason to suppose that any significant changes had been made to the layout of the landscape. The plans were of the land in hand, adjacent to the land let to tenants, and were made to several different scales. These have been brought to a common scale and put together to make one map. It is from this map, and the O.S. map for 1886, together with evidence on the ground, that the interpretation of the landscaping of the estate has been made.

Miller faced several problems at Farnborough. The hillside rising behind the house was windy and exposed, and the foreground, meadow land leading down to the strip farming of the unenclosed Dassett Fields, was lacking in interest. There were, however, spreading views from the higher land across the valley to Edgehill in the distance. The only pools were probably the two large fishponds, adjacent to the walled garden and situated out of sight behind the house. The approach roads were rather uninspiring, and one led through the village – which with its unkempt and perhaps squalid appearance would not have provided the picturesque scene to the 18th-century traveller that it does today.

The scheme at Farnborough was built around the concept of making the most of the spreading views, particularly from the higher land. All over the estate, the eye was drawn to the high points, which were emphasised by the planting of clumps of woodland. Two long terraces were created along the hillsides. The main viewing terrace runs south-west from the Hall, and the second terrace approaches the Hall over the hill from the north. In the valley, which has a heavy and intractable clay soil, three new lakes with cascades were

54 *Farnborough,
the old clump of
Scots pines and oaks
on Oakal Hill. These
groups of hilltop trees
are typical of Miller's
schemes. Similar
groups can also be
seen at Wroxton and
Upton.*

constructed, two of them requiring the formation of large dams. When viewed from the terraced hillsides above, these lakes make a prominent feature in the middle distance.

The earliest mention of the main terrace in contemporary literature is on 24 July 1742, when John Loveday, the writer and antiquary, was invited by William Holbech to bring his family from nearby Arlescote to drink tea and inspect the terrace. The men were asked to ride along it three days later.[7] The creation of the terrace must have taken a protracted period of time, and required an able eye to oversee its construction. It was laid out south-westwards from the Hall along the edge of the scarp for about three quarters of a mile, and was constructed in three separate levels. The upper terrace, some 15 yards wide, starts above the present fenceline at the back of the trees. It begins part way up the hill and continues round to the site of the Pentagon Temple. Below the upper terrace there is a ditch and bank. Continuing downhill, through mixed plantings of mature trees and shrubs, there are two more terraces of the same width as the top terrace, about 15 yards, joined by slopes. A winding path runs the length of the second terrace, under the trees. The lowest, or main viewing terrace, is contained by repeated bastions all along its outer edge, which give a sense of security to the viewer. Such a number of bastions is unusual, but the idea of bastions all along the terrace may have been inspired in part by the current military use of bastions, and in part with the Civil War connections at Edgehill across the valley. Today their value as viewing platforms is greatly diminished by modern plantings of laurels which have been allowed to grow up and obscure the view.[8] A watercolour of the terrace and the obelisk painted by Mary Holbech, *c.*1860, shows bushes clothing the terrace bank, but, significantly, they are not growing above the level of the terrace itself. Each bastion was originally planted with a central tree, and there were also eight specimen trees adorning eight larger bastions in the middle length of the terrace. Behind the obelisk at the end of the main viewing terrace there is a small gate which opens onto the top terrace in the field. The top terrace may have been for carriages to bring less able visitors up from the Hall to the obelisk to admire the view. Carriages, if allowed onto the main terrace, would have cut up the fine turf badly in wet conditions.

55 *Farnborough, the Oval Pavilion, and Ecton, the Pavilion. The Oval Pavilion appears to have been inspired by the similar pavilion (now roofless) thought to be by Inigo Jones on the Ecton estate, Northamptonshire. Miller was probably responsible for the Gothic alterations to Ecton Hall in the mid-1750s.*

Walking the length of the terrace from the Hall, which most visitors would have done, several small buildings are revealed, each built in stone and of a different design. William Holbech, with his love of all things Italian and classical, was obviously not interested in the new vogue for Gothic. His buildings were to be predominantly classical. While it cannot be said for certain that the terrace buildings were designed by Miller, the likelihood of his being the architect has been confirmed by several authors.[9] Each building is sited to make the most of the views, the view from each being different. Coming along the terrace from the Hall, the Ionic Temple is the first building to be seen. This has a pediment supported by four Ionic columns shading a loggia. It is built of limestone ashlar, with imitation ashlar render. There are similarities in the design with that of Hawksmoor's monumental Clarendon Building in Oxford, built in 1712-13 opposite the Bodleian Old Library. From the Ionic Temple there is a view down to the lakes, across part of the valley to the Dassett Hills, and also back to the Hall.

From the temple, the line of the terrace then turns towards the south west and the whole of the valley spreads before the

56   *Farnborough, rococo plasterwork of beautiful quality in the upper room of the Oval Pavilion. The ceiling is similarly decorated. The work is comparable with that in the dining room of the Hall, much of which was carried out by William Perritt.*

onlooker. A Prospect Room was required! Accordingly the Oval Pavilion was constructed; an unusual building with an open loggia framed by four Tuscan pillars, set back from the terrace to gain extra height. The building is of ironstone ashlar with limestone ashlar dressings, and has a lead domed roof. To the rear a stone stairway winds up invitingly to the enchanting small 'prospect room' above, where the rococo plasterwork, picked out in white against a blue background, is a riot of baskets of flowers and asymmetric festoons with cornucopias and shells. The plasterwork may be by the Yorkshire stuccadore William Perritt who worked at the Hall,[10] or even by the Italian Vassali, who worked later at Hagley Hall. The Oval Pavilion is similar to the oval pavilion at Ecton, near Northampton, variously attributed to Inigo Jones in the 1630s, and to Sanderson Miller himself, the latter being acquainted with Ambrose Isted, who owned Ecton. It is more likely that Miller knew about the attribution of the Ecton pavilion to Jones, whose architecture he admired, and he therefore used it as his model for the Oval Pavilion at Farnborough. To mark the end of the main terrace, the Obelisk was erected, noted first by an unknown observer in 1746.[11] From here there is a view across the valley to the south, towards the Warmington scarp. In the immediate foreground one looks across a narrow deep valley, the hillside beyond being in the adjacent parish of Mollington. Holbech's brother lived at Mollington, and tradition says that Holbech used to come to the Obelisk each morning to call 'good morning' across to his brother on the opposite bank.

At the highest point of the hill, behind the Obelisk, the Pentagon Temple, or summerhouse, was built. It was described with detailed measurements by Lady Newdigate in her journal, when she and Sir Roger Newdigate were on a tour of country estates in 1747:

> We had no intention of stopping before we got to Banbury, but were tempted to do so by ye sight of a temple wch. made a pretty appearance and wch. on our enquirey we found belonged to Mr Holbech, it lies a mile from his house whc. is a very indifferent one the Temple is lately built and not yet completed it is in ye form of a Pentagon without and a Rotunda within the diamr. 16 foot and ½ the height about ye same, a little narrow winding staircase brings you into this

57 *Farnborough, the Game Larder. This hexagonal building has an alcove containing a seat overlooking the newly landscaped old fishponds, and the hillside with the village church beyond. The louvred top allowed for aeration of the game.*

room which is four windows and a chimney, over this is a pentagon room 12 foot from ye side to ye angle 10 foot high with a ballustrade round wch. commands a pretty good prospect, the building stands upon five arches in a little Garden of flow'ring shrubs on an emminence at ye foot of wch. quite in a hole stands ye house.[12]

Sir Roger Newdigate was friendly with Miller; they had both been up at Oxford together and had similar interests in both architecture and landscaping. The anonymous visitor who commented on the obelisk in 1746 described the Pentagon temple as 'an elegant and costly building, the ornaments within being of carved wood, but the edifice of stone'. The site is now no more than a bump located in a small area of trees. The Temple is shown on Yates' map of Warwickshire (1793) as a building with a roof in the Chinese style, curved concavely and coming to a point at the top. The Pentagon Temple was the only terrace building big enough to entertain guests. The pentagon room at the top, with its 'ballustrade' would indeed have commanded a 'pretty good prospect', with panoramic views across the Warmington valley and the Vale of the Red Horse and back over the estate both to the north and the east. The Temple, with its intriguing design, was surely the centre of the whole estate plan. Miller's visit on 29 January 1750 suggests that it was used all round the year, so adequate means of heating must have been provided. Miller's diary entry for 29 January 1750 reads: 'Went with W.B[r]. [brother] & Sister Trotman to dine with M[r] Holbeach at Farmb: M[r] Bolton there. drank tea at ye Sum[r]. House. came h. by moonlight.'

Returning to the Hall along the main terrace, and opening a door in the wall at the back of the terrace near the Hall, the visitor would find another little building. This is the Game Larder. It is a small hexagonal brick building which has an open viewing loggia on three sides giving on to the fishponds. The roof is supported by Tuscan columns and the louvered sides of the roof turret provided aeration for the game when hung inside. The Tuscan order was thought by Palladio to be suitable for rural buildings, so this was a suitable choice for such a building.[13] The building faced north, ideal for both the game and for the visitor taking a shady seat to admire the view north across the ponds to the church, rising amongst the trees.

On 30 September 1756 Bishop Pococke went on to Farnborough following a visit to see Miller at Radway. In his journal he records:

> … on the 30th I went to see Farnborough, Mr Holbeche's, a good house in a narrow valley; there is in it several ancient busts and very beautiful fineer'd ancient marble tables; he has made a very grand grass terrace, winding round the hill for half a mile; there is an obelisk at the end which may be 80 feet high, and in another part an oval open summer house, with a room over the colonade. This terrace commands a fine view of the rich country, which is called the Vale of Red Horse, from a red horse, near Tysoe, cut in the hill.[14]

Apart from the Pentagon Temple, which is no longer in existence, the other buildings are still in a good state of preservation, though the Obelisk, which collapsed in 1823, has been rebuilt.

The south-west approach to the Hall was already attractive, but the northern approach led through the village. When the different plans from the 1772 survey were brought to a common scale and fitted together, the presence of an unsuspected second carriageway was suggested by the double row of trees curving round Windmill Hill. A visit to the site confirmed that there was indeed a wide level terrace, still quite marked, which followed the contour line around the hill. None of the trees remained, but there were several great stumps in the correct positions as shown on the old map, and the levelled track was quite wide enough to have taken a carriage with ease. Approaching from the north, the terrace leaves the road before the first village houses were reached, enjoying views as spectacular as those from the main terrace. The views are revealed gradually as the track rounds the hill before descending alongside 'Gardners Shrubbery' towards the Burton Dassett road and the Hall, which itself would not have been seen until the carriage rounded the last bend before the entrance gate. The summit of Windmill Hill was planted, and there may even have been a windmill still remaining here at this date. There are no remains of the windmill today. From the hilltop there is a magnificent all round view of 360 degrees. This second terrace may have been made as a level track following the contour line, from which to enjoy further panoramic views over the estate, the eye attracted to an old farmhouse to the south west, to more distant points by specific planting on the high land towards the Burton Hills, or back towards the Pentagon Temple. The terrace may also have been constructed to provide a new approach drive to the Hall from the north, avoiding the workaday sight of the village and making the most of the views from the hilltop. Either way, the presence of the terrace would explain why 'Gardners Shrubbery' was planted here, apparently in the middle of a field. On the ground, it looks as if the

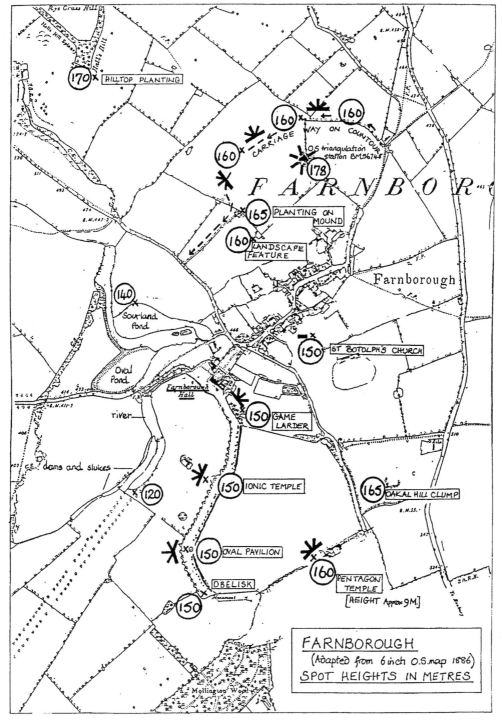

58 *Farnborough, a map adapted from the six-inch O.S. map for 1886. The marked spot heights identify the views to be obtained from each vantage point across the estate.*

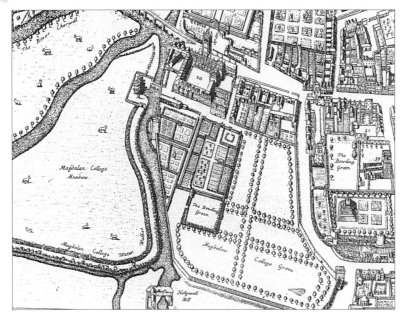

59 *The Magdalen Walks, Magdalen College, Oxford, taken from Loggan's* Oxonia Illustrata, *1675. The ornamental pattern of planting trees within and parallel to the field boundaries was a pattern with which Miller would have been familiar. On the Farnborough estate map of 1772 it can be seen that several fields have been treated in a similar way.*

old drive has been levelled and the earth thrown up to make a bank – still there – on which shrubs were planted to make a feature. There is nothing left today of the planting except for one or two old windswept yews marking the northern end of the bank. Miller used yews frequently in association with other planting, for example at the Bath House at Walton and at Honington. The bank may have been formed to cut off the sight of the village, previously hidden by the hill but just coming into view at this point, but it may also have been made to provide height for a layered shrubbery, with tiers of shrubs of differing heights. Both Batty Langley in the *New Principles of Gardening* (1728) and Philip Miller in *The Gardeners Dictionary* (1731) had described the use of layered planting of flowering and evergreen shrubs in gardens.[15] Earlier formal gardens had used tiers of flowering plants, and this type of planting, using shrubs and trees as well as herbaceous plants, had been used by Philip Southcote at Woburn, in Surrey, to line the paths around his *ferme ornée* in the late 1730s. Flowering shrubs had been used by Kent at both Carlton House, for the Prince of Wales, 1734-5, and at Rousham, in 1738, but the early 1740s was still a surprisingly early date for the creation of such a shrubbery at Farnborough.

The other approaches to the Hall, from the village of Burton Dassett and from Banbury, were made more attractive by the planting of trees along their margins from the points at which the roads entered the estate. Other ornamental plantings which stand out on the 1772 map are the lines of well spaced trees round the edges of some of the fields near the Hall. When the trees mature this type of planting produces an elegant parklike appearance. The planting is similar to the pattern of trees planted along the boundaries of the meadows comprising the Magdalen Walks in Oxford, shown on Loggan's *Oxonia Illustrata* map of 1675. Both Joseph Addison and Philander had enjoyed daily walks around the Magdalen meadows, Philander delighting in a 'prospect which is well laid out and diversified with Fields and Meadows, Woods and Rivers', where he could enjoy the 'rough careless Strokes of Nature'.[16] Miller would naturally have been familiar with the Walks from his time at Oxford.

The harnessing of the water resources at Farnborough provided the Hall with a girdle of lakes on three sides. The fishponds were redesigned, forming part of the view from the road approaching the Hall from the east, and also from the Game Larder on the hillside above. Two streams ran through the estate, one running south-west along the western boundary and the other flowing north-west from the fishponds. The water from these two streams was utilised to form two large pools below the Hall to the north west, Sourland pond and the Oval Pond. The stream leaving the fishponds leads underneath the Hall gardens, into Sourlands Pond where it emerges through two separate inlets under small stone arches. This use of two inlets is also found at Wroxton Abbey, and there are the remains of two similar constructions for water above Miller's own pool at Radway. The culvert under the Hall gardens is not known to have been repaired or investigated in living memory, so the work must have been done well.

Sourland Pond and the Oval Pond were created by damming both streams mentioned above. Sourland Pond is the largest pool on the estate, and was presumably formed from land that was 'sour', i.e. boggy and unsuitable for cultivation. Its construction, together with that of the adjacent Oval Pond into which the water was fed by a sluice and waterfall, required building up the lower banks to a height of 18-20 feet for a considerable distance. Instead of forming lakes along the course of the existing valley streams, which would seem the obvious way to create lakes, Miller excavated his three lakes part way up the slope so that the water was visible from the Hall. The Oval Pond itself is now dry, the water running through it as a stream. The earth dams of the ponds slope outwards and have wide bases. Miller made a virtue of the retaining banks, which were levelled to a width of at least six feet wide along their tops to take a path. Trees were planted closely along the sides of the dams, both to stabilise them and to provide an attractive shady cover. There is a large bastion at the western end of the Oval Pond. From here there is an excellent view over the lower part of the property, and across the 'river', now Rookery Pool, to the terrace and the obelisk, picked out against the skyline.

In the valley, there are still traces of a path which winds alongside the brook which leaves Sourland Pond by a small waterfall at the western end. Beside the path are Scots pines and other trees, shrubs and also ferns. The name Farnborough is supposed to have come from the abundance of ferns locally. Although modern farming has removed much of the evidence, this path probably continued along the western estate boundary. The stream is now no longer composed of little pools, as shown here on the 1771 map, but there are damp low-lying areas adjacent to the stream, and here and there are small raised mounds on which old Scots pines are growing. The Scots pine is not a common tree to find along watercourses, but it was a tree which Miller used repeatedly where he wanted to emphasise a feature in his plans.

From the Oval Pond water passes under the road and into the 'River', known today as Rookery Pool. Originally there used to be a mill on this site. Water also entered the 'River' via an iron pipe over a stepped cascade in an adjacent artificial rock cliff, the terminal point of the ancient yew walk from the Hall gardens. Although no records remain, the gardens themselves were probably greatly simplified at this time, leaving only the old Bowling Green, which is marked as such on the 1772 map and forms what is today the south lawn, separated from the park by a ha-ha. Beyond the lawn to the west there is also an ice-house dating from this period.

60 *Farnborough,*
the stepped cascade,
leading to the 'river'.

The artificial rock cliff is almost hidden in the landscape, for it is not visible either from the Hall or the Yew Walk, and it is not visible even coming from the Oval Pond, for the water flowed under the road into the River and beside the artificial cliff, which was planted with trees and shrubs. The cascade is only a few feet across at the top, and gradually widens in steep unevenly spaced steps of stone towards the base. There may have been a gazebo on the flat stones which still remain here on the level top of the 'cliff'. Approaching it the visitor hears the sound of falling water, and only sees the cascade itself, with shrubs and ferns surrounding it, on approaching the rocky bank at the edge of the 'River'. The waterfall used to be gravity fed by water brought via a lead pipe underground from the Oval Pond, but since the recent restoration of the cascade, water is pumped to it by a modern pump. It is possible that it may have been inspired by the famous cascades at Tivoli, well known to English travellers who had been on the Grand Tour. The design and the siting of the cascade perfectly illustrate one aspect of the Rococo garden style, in which emphasis was laid on the creation of pleasurable surprise in the discovery of the unexpected.

From the River water flows into a formal rectangular 'Canal' aligned on the south front of the Hall. Beyond the Canal is a ha-ha, then a formal avenue (replanted last century) leads the eye away into the distance, the whole seen from the Hall as a long vista, giving the impression of the estate lands stretching into the distance.

The overflow from the 'River' cascades over a waterfall just west of the wooded isthmus which borders the 'Canal' to the west. The water then flows westwards towards the Avon Dassett open fields. Along this lower stretch the stream was widened to form a serpentine 'river', marked as such on the 1772 map, the water levels being controlled by a series of dams and sluices. Substantial remains of most of these are still there, although they are no longer functional. The wooded isthmus between the serpentine 'river' and the Canal was a pleasant place in which to saunter, with water on either side. Miller also designed a shady walk with water on both sides at Radway and at Wroxton. On the map of 1772, the River is joined to the Canal by a narrowing of the water, at which point a bridge is thrown over onto the isthmus. The bridge was removed when the narrow part of the River was widened and both River and Canal were altered to make one informal sheet of water in the early years of the 19th century.

The creation of both terrace and pools was described by Richard Jago, in his poem 'Edge-hill …'

> Where, at yon' smooth-brow'd Hill's remotest Point,
> A tap'ring Column lifts its lofty Head,
> Her spacious Terrace, and surrounding Lawns,
> Deck'd with no sparing Cost of planted Clump,
> Or ornamental Building, FARNBOROUGH boasts.
> Hear they her Master's Call? in sturdy Troops,
> The Jocund Labourers hie, and, at his Nod,
> A thousand Hands or smooth the slanting Hill,
> Or scoop new Channels for the gath'ring Flood,
> And, in his Pleasures, find a solid Joy.[17]

No doubt there must have been 'troops' of men at work to create such a picture from bare hills and wet meadows, but the amount of hard work required makes one question how 'jocund' the labourers themselves would have been about the project. It has been suggested that actual troops may have been used, since Lord Cobham is known to have used soldiers from his regiment at Stowe for work in the gardens there.[18]

The designed landscape at Farnborough is one of the most interesting of its period, the most important of Miller's landscapes, and also the only one of Miller's designs which still remains more or less as it must have been in the mid-18th century. The contrast between the newly laid out landscape and the dullness of the open fields beyond is difficult for us to imagine today. The plan shows an imaginative approach in the making of a new landscape capitalising on the hillsides by creating the terraces, and improving the existing views by the addition of several large lakes. The views over the whole estate, and especially from the terraces and their buildings, are particularly important. Water was introduced in many different forms. Inventiveness is shown in both the designs of the buildings and in the layouts of the walks and the plantings, together with the delights and surprises typical of the Rococo style. The plan of the whole estate represents an important stage in the development of landscape design. Although the plan includes areas which are smaller in scale and Rococo in style, the overall feel is away from formality, ideological design or Greek myth and towards a heightened appreciation of beauty in landscape for its own sake.

Wroxton

The manor house of Wroxton Abbey, near Banbury, dates from the 17th century. It was built on the remains of a 13th-century Augustinian priory and is situated in a sheltered

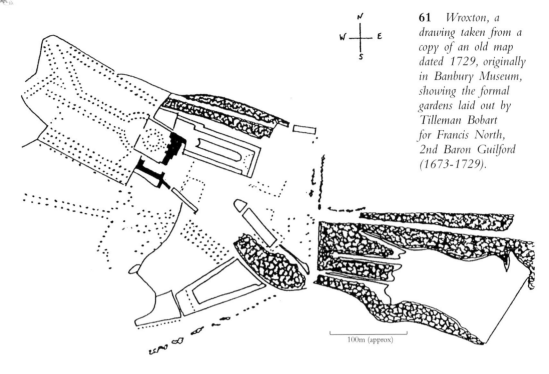

61 *Wroxton, a drawing taken from a copy of an old map dated 1729, originally in Banbury Museum, showing the formal gardens laid out by Tilleman Bobart for Francis North, 2nd Baron Guilford (1673-1729).*

100m (approx)

and well watered valley with deep fertile soil. Sir Thomas Pope, who had acquired the priory in 1537 following the dissolution of the monasteries, gave the property to his new foundation, Trinity College, Oxford while retaining the right of life tenancy for his heirs. In 1671 the leasehold passed through marriage to the North family. In the 1680s Sir Francis North, 1st Baron Guilford, began alterations to the gardens. Celia Fiennes approved of the new gardens on her visit to Wroxton in the late 1680s. In 1729 Francis, Lord Guilford inherited the property, becoming Lord North in 1734 on the extinction of the senior branch of the family.[19]

In 1729, following consultations with Henry Wise, Tilleman Bobart was employed to create large formal terraces and a long canal to the east of the mansion. In 1730 he made a walled garden on high ground to the north east of the main gardens, and he is also thought to have constructed the stone ice-house above the garden terraces. Bobart's father superintended the Physic Garden at Oxford, and Bobart had worked under Wise at Blenheim.[20] A plan dated 1729 held in the museum at Banbury shows the formal layout of the gardens at this time. In 1730 Lord Guilford became Lord of the Bedchamber to Frederick, Prince of Wales, a post which he held until the Prince's death in 1751. The Prince of Wales was in the vanguard of gardening fashion when in 1732 he bought Carlton House, employing William Kent to landscape the 12-acre estate. Lord North decided to follow the example of his employer, and in the late 1730s he filled in the canal, took away the formal gardens and started to replace them with an informal landscape. He had already begun to develop the lower gardens when in 1744 he was introduced to Miller, who lived only a few miles away.

There is good documentation for much of Miller's work at Wroxton. In June 1744, Miller's friend T. Lennard Barrett, whom Miller was already advising on the Gothic alterations at his house at Belhus, in Essex wrote to him saying that he and Lord North were likely to become acquainted that summer.[21] It is from this year that Miller's work at Wroxton went forward. Initial landscaping began with alterations to the cascade below the Great Pond, and Miller was responsible for the Temple on the Mount, below the cascade, and probably three of the other new buildings in the grounds, as well as further landscaping in the lower part of the gardens. In the general improvements Miller was aided by John Strong, Lord North's gardener. Miller also carried out architectural works for Lord North. These included the rebuilding of Wroxton church tower, finished in 1748 with similar Gothic detailing to that which he had used in the extensions to his own house at Radway, alterations to the interior of the Abbey chapel and a design for the new chapel window, finished in 1747, and also a new decorative ceiling in the Hall of the Abbey itself.[22] The chapel window was designed to take Lord North's collection of Van Linge painted glass of 1623. Both North and Miller himself were interested in painted glass. Two pieces from Miller's own collection still decorate the east window in the south aisle of Radway church.

Extensive correspondence exists in the WCRO between Lord North and Miller. The correspondence dates from the mid–1740s and covers both Miller's work for Lord North and their social engagements, documenting a friendship which lasted until Miller's death in 1780. Beside the landscaping, the two families often exchanged social visits, and Lord North assisted Miller in his own work at Radway with gifts of trees from the Wroxton nurseries. One of the last letters Miller kept was dated 1779, when Lord North wrote congratulating Miller on the marriage of his daughter.[23] During 1749 and 1750 there were a number of letters written to Miller, mainly from London where Lord North's parliamentary work detained him, discussing details of the design and construction of the Temple on the Mount.[24] A letter written to Miller from Lord North on 22 February 1749, concerning the Temple on the Mount, illustrates North's appreciation of Miller's abilities:

> The Model is arrived, & I am entirely of your opinion that the Dome appears too heavy, and too big, and must be lessen'd, & that the point at the top had better be left out. … A little open border where I have made a B in the draught, would make the Dome not look so deep: but I don't know whether it would look so well in other respects. Upon the whole I am well satisfied; & persuaded, with the alterations you will direct, the building will have a very good effect. I think to return the Model by Barrat this day sen=night, & order Bannister to bring it to Radway to take your directions … Our best compliments wait on Mrs Miller & my Girls are much yours …

Many other letters testify to their friendship and social gatherings, either at Wroxton or at Radway.[25] Markham describes John Loveday's visit to Wroxton in 1747, when he 'rode to Wroxton Abbey where Sanderson Miller had begun to make extensive alterations for the Earl of Guilford [Lord North]. The architect [Miller] was there to explain to John exactly what was being done and on this occasion he gave him another book – Fletcher's *Purple Island, or the Isle of Man* … published in 1633'.[26] Further testimony to Miller's work at Wroxton is provided by Bishop Pococke on his visit to the gardens in 1756, who wrote enthusiastically about the Gothic Open Rotundo or The Temple on the Mount, 'of Mr Miller's design …'[27]

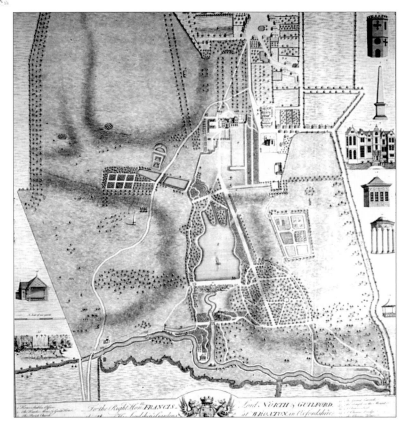

62 *Wroxton, an engraving by Francis Booth, c.1750, showing the newly landscaped grounds, the lower valley with the second waterway on which can be seen a small boat, and small drawings of the landscape buildings in the margins. (NB the map is presented with north to the right-hand side, rather than to the top of the page).*

A site visit revealed that the double waterway shown at the bottom, which had lain neglected and forgotten, was still quite traceable.

The gardens at Wroxton were already well wooded, and had old fishponds and also streams running through the property, but the valley was closed in by the adjacent small hills and had none of the views considered so desirable by the garden cognoscenti. Mrs Delany visited the gardens in 1746, and drew a picture of the dam holding the water in the Great Pond, with a cascade issuing from an arch in the dam, then flowing into a serpentine 'river' which takes the water past a mount covered with flowering shrubs. On the top of the mount is a small construction with trellised sides, probably made of wood, within which may have been a seat. In 1750 Miller's Temple on the Mount replaced this building.

After 1744, further 'improvements' were implemented over the whole estate. In the gardens, spring water was collected from the hillside to the left or south west of the house, and fed into two existing small rectangular fishponds, which were altered in shape. On the 1729 plan there are two other small formal pools leading down from the house. These were filled in. A new curving streambed was dug in the woodland to take the water from the upper pools into the Great Pond. The water levels were retained in the upper pools and the stream by a small bridge which has such a low arch that it is very nearly a dam. This bridge carried the old garden crosswalk, still there today, on which was aligned the Prince's Obelisk on the hillside beyond, donated by the Prince of Wales after his visit to the Banbury Races in 1739. This was rebuilt and engraved in 1769.[28] From the bridge, water fed into the great pond, already surrounded by mature woods.

The great pond was altered in shape, and a boathouse was made on the middle arm of the western bank. These naturalistic alterations in the upper garden were most probably made by Miller, particularly the control of the water levels feeding into the great pond, though Mrs Delaney's drawing suggests that the dam and the 'serpentine river' flowing past the Mount were already there before Miller was introduced to the Wroxton estate. Approaching the dam along the wide path beside the great pond, one can hear the waterfall but cannot actually see it until one has walked past the dam itself. The dam was rebuilt and the cascade was reconstructed, with advice from Miller, c.1744.[29] In the drawing by S.H. Grimm, dated 1781, the formal arch seems to have disappeared, unless it is hidden by the fall of the water. At some stage rocks were placed interrupting the flow of the fall along the top of the waterfall, which would have both increased the sound and improved the spectacle. The fall itself appeared to emerge quite naturally between the bushes and flanking trees covering the dam on either side. At the base of the fall, the water reached a much lower and wider cascade, also with rocks projecting out through the water. The line of the 'serpentine river' appears rather artificial to modern eyes. One can walk along the grassy top of the dam on either side of the cascade, which was restored in the late 1970s by Paul Edwards in a style similar to that in Mrs Delaney's early drawing, but the water is now led over shallow wide steps before falling clear to the base.

The 'serpentine river' stream flows east, past the Mount, under the Chinese bridge and on to the Chinese House, where it is joined by the Sor brook flowing south under the main road from Wroxton to Drayton and Banbury. The Chinese House was built in 1739-40, and sketched by Mrs Delany in 1754. North of the modern bridge over the main road, the ornamental planting associated with the valley design persists for some distance. Starting immediately below the bridge to the south, an ingenious double waterway was constructed, the original stream running parallel to and east of a widened channel. At the beginning of the channel, adjacent to the road and just below it, there is a mound with old yews and a single pine behind. It is typical of Miller's planting, the trees providing shelter and an evergreen backdrop to what must be the site of the Chinese seat. A small pool has been hollowed out below the mound. This marks the beginning of the wider 'canal' or 'river', and is fed from the Sor brook by a small fall of water flowing under a pretty arched Gothic stone bridge built in the local ironstone. The bridge, still extant, is only about a yard in width and has three ornamental stone pieces pointing down from the underside of the curve towards the water beneath. From here the eastern part of the 'canal' or 'river' was made wide enough to take a small boat. Today the water only persists for a few yards, but the wide, dry shallow bed can still be made out as far as the Chinese House, where it is joined by the 'river' flowing west from the cascade below the Great Pond.

On the Sor brook itself, which meanders parallel to the new 'canal', there is one sluice remaining out of several which were originally constructed to control the water levels and feed the new waterway. The central piece of land between was planted with woodland, and an attractive winding shady path can still be followed.

Below the Chinese House, the 'serpentine river' joins the new wide 'canal'. Further south, the ground widens out into a water meadow, the artificial new watercourse joining the Sor brook again, after flowing over small cascades, near the Chinese Lodge, or Keeper's Lodge. Both the Booth map of c.1750 and the O.S. 25-inch map of 1887 show the detail

63   *Mrs Mary Delany, 1700-88,*
by John Opie.

64   *Three Drawings by Mrs Delany:*

Below: *'A view of the great Cascade at*
Wroxton.' The Seat of Lord North of Guilford
in Oxfordshire. M. Delany, Sep 1746'.

Above right: *'The Indian Seat at Wroxton.*
M. Delany, 7 Oct 1754'(?) Usually referred
to as the Chinese Seat; the terms were
interchangeable in the eighteenth century.

Below right: *'A view of the Indian House*
at Wroxton. M. Delany, 7 Oct 1754'. Lord
North always referred to this building as his
'Chinese House'.

described above. The Sor brook was much too narrow to take boats, but by digging out this wider channel and making sure there was enough water to take a boat by feeding the channel from the sluices on the brook, this difficulty was overcome – and a small boat is actually illustrated on the waterway on the Booth map. This feature may not have held sufficient water to guarantee a long life. Bertie Greatheed, who lived at Guy's Cliffe at Warwick, visited Wroxton with the Holbechs in 1822, when he described the gardens as terminating at a 'Chinese Retreat' below the 'little temple, in the taste of a century back'.[30] There is no mention of the double waterway.

The Chinese buildings have all gone, although their sites can be made out on the ground. They were asserted by Walpole in 1753 to 'have the merit or demerit of being the progenitors of a very numerous race all over the kingdom; at least they were of the very first'.[31] Although Walpole was not in favour of such 'paltry' Chinese eccentricities, Lord North was obviously proud of his Chinese house. Inviting Miller over to Wroxton in July 1749 – when it seemed the weather was as variable as it is today – he wrote:

> If you think we shall escape a wet day to-morrow, I hope we shall have the pleasure
> of your company to cold meat and Iced cream at the Chinese House. I am so engaged
> & my time so mortgaged, that I am unwilling to defer so pleasant a party any longer.

65 *'A view of ye winding river & Gothick Temple at Wroxton. M.Delany Sept 1746.' The mound with its flowering shrubs has a small Gothic temple on top, which was replaced by Miller's larger and more substantial Temple on the Mount in 1750. The 'cascade' is shown in this drawing without water flowing down it. The supply of water was limited: Philip Yorke commented in 1748 that it only played occasionally.*

Our compliments wait on the good woman &c, &c. My Chinese House is so warm she will not get cold.[32]

During a site visit, blue and white pottery shards were found in the ploughing on the site of the Chinese Lodge. The first known Chinese garden building in Europe, the Trianon de Porcelaine, built in 1670 by Louis XIV for his favourite mistress, was decorated in blue and white faience in imitation of the supposed finish of the Nanking Pagoda,[33] and the pottery shards may have been part of a ceramic finish used to give a similar 'genuine Chinese' exterior decoration to the Lodge. These three Chinese buildings beg the question, why Chinese? Translations of the writings of Confucius had appeared in England at the turn of the century, and the ideas of the later Taoist philosophers were in tune with the need for a spiritual ideal and a return to Arcadian Nature which was behind much of the search for informality in English garden design. Other contemporary gardens which contained the new Chinese buildings included Stowe, where a small Chinese House had been erected on stilts in the river Alder in 1738, and Richard Bateman's villa garden at Old Windsor which had a variety of Chinese buildings which probably date from the 1730s.[34]

South of the Chinese Lodge and the designed area of the gardens, the old carriageway from Drayton and Banbury crosses the stream where there is a ford and a narrow bridge. From here the land rises on both sides; to the east, near where the line of the old Banbury carriageway enters the estate, the Drayton Arch sits on the hilltop. It is somewhat reminiscent of Kent's Gothic Arch, the eyecatcher visible in farmland from the garden at Rousham, but as a mock Gothic ruin it is much more convincing than Kent's design. Made of ironstone, the arch is flanked by two small towers. The date of construction is not known, but it is probably later than 1750, for it is not shown on the Booth map. Entries in the Wroxton accounts suggest that it may have been built by the Hiorns, in 1770-1.[35] The arch has been ascribed to Miller, who was still carrying out some architectural work as late as 1774, and the Hiorns had often worked for him. However, Miller never made an exact copy of a building, as far as is known, and the side of the Drayton Arch facing west over the park is so very similar to The Spectacle at Boughton Park, in Northamptonshire, c.1770, that it is unlikely that as it stands it was Miller's design alone. Since the Drayton Arch was built, the castellations over the arch have lost their vertical projections, which still existed in 1910, as is shown in an old photograph.[36] To the west, the track of the old carriageway leads up past the Prince's obelisk on the skyline and on towards the Abbey, the Dovecote also coming into view as the abbey is approached. The Dovecote, built in 1746, was one of the earlier landscape buildings, and was sited on the high ground to the south west of the drive approaching the abbey from the village, where it balanced the church tower on the opposite bank. Constructed in the local ironstone, it is an octagonal tower, complete with battlements and slit windows, and its design is typical of Miller's Gothic work. The design was based on that of an old monastic tower in the garden of Idlicote House, near Honington, which stands on the site of a grange of Kenilworth Priory.

Several visitors came to Wroxton and recorded their impressions before Miller and Lord North had started to build the Temple on the Mount. After his visit in 1747, John Loveday wrote in his journal that 'the Gardens have the approbation of all judges, consisting of a piece of water admirably shaded by trees, of a Cascade, of a serpentine River &c.

much of it made out of a bog'.[37] Thomas Salmon, visiting Wroxton in 1748, commented that the abbey was 'a good old House, built after the taste of our Forefathers, secured on every Side by Hills or Groves from tempests, and consequently wants the Prospects that modern seats enjoy; however this is not without its Beauties; for here are most extensive Walks cut through the Groves, fine Slopes, and noble Pieces of Water, which render it a charming retirement'.[38] When the monks originally settled this valley, its protected situation had been a point in its favour, for the monks had been more interested in seclusion and in soils suitable for agriculture than in views. The Yorkes of Wrest Park also came to Wroxton in 1748. Philip Yorke wrote at length in his journal about the grounds:

> The garden is 70 acres and finely diversified with wood and water, and has from the irregularity of the ground many natural beauties which are well improved. There is an irregular piece of water or lake of 7 acres, surrounded with high trees, which ends in a cascade (it only plays occasionally) and falls 20ft. perpendicular; and there is to be a small temple built on the mount against it. A grove of fine old oaks of 12 acres upon the side of the hill is kept rough with paths cut through it that carry you both to the lake and down the hill, at the bottom of which a serpentine river runs through the meadows. It seems to issue (we were told) – [obviously the Yorkes did not walk too far] – from a rustic arch higher up in the garden and a little below this grove it parts into two small streams and upon the banks between them stands a very pretty Chinese summerhouse. At the end of this river is another Chinese lodge which is lived in, and a court with an old wall before it, behind it an open seat which fronts a little natural cascade. The green fields which surround these and the fine trees among them are one great beauty of the place, and in them is a pigeon-house like a Gothic tower, which has a very pretty effect. The parterre before the house rises in several slopes, is bordered with wood on each side, and open to a large meadow at the end.[39]

His report sets the date of the completion of the lower valley design and the two later Chinese buildings as before 1748. Some of the work mentioned in the accounts on the serpentine river and its associated cascades predate Miller's work. However, although the author of the lower valley is unknown, it is reasonable to suggest that the double waterway in the lower valley was by Miller, who started work at Wroxton in 1744. The Chinese Seat, on its small mound and with its typical planting, is another possibility, while the small rustic bridge is very much in Miller's style. The Chinese Seat is similar to that designed for the new grounds at Honington, although the design of the balustrade is different. Miller's advice was first sought at Honington in 1749. In January 1748/9, Thomas Lennard Barrett, later Lord Dacre, wrote to Miller comparing the width of his River with that of Lord North's, but he does not give enough detail to confirm which stream he was referring to, nor the extent of Miller's involvement.[40] Miller had advised Dacre on his estate improvements at Belhus, or Belhouse, in Essex.

Miller designed the new Temple for the Mount in 1750. Both Miller and Lord North went to considerable trouble over the design, Lord North having a wooden model constructed so that Miller could check the proportions. A scheme to decorate the top of the Temple was eventually decided against, and Miller set up poles on the mount itself so that the correct height for the new building could be ascertained:

> I have returned the Model to Banister by Banbury Carrier this day, & order'd him
> to wait on you with it at Radway … I think shortening and thickening the Pillars

66   *The Temple on the Mount, with the Chinese bridge in the distance. A drawing made by S.H. Grimm in 1781.*

a little, making the Pedestals and Capitals neater, not allowing the Roof to rise so high & bulge so much, & putting (if you approve it) a little open border above the Cornice, the building will look very well. If you concur in my opinion, and will take yᵉ trouble to agree with Banister, I shall be infinitely obliged to you … If you chuse it, before you absolutely fix upon the height of the Pillars; you might have some poles the size of the Building set upon the Mount. Our best wishes and compliments wait on you & yours …[41]

The mount was circular, with steep sides. It was about seven metres high and the top was reached by an earth ramp from the path. Now only the foundations for the pillars remain, hidden by grass.

The Temple, an octagon in shape, was constructed of timber with open Gothic arches and a domed roof. Letters from Lord North show that battlements were decided against, and that the roof was made of 'cloath and tarpaulin' dispatched from London in the summer of 1750. The following April Banister was concerned about the roof leaking. A stone dust finish was applied to improve both the appearance and the weatherproofing, and by 30 May Lord North wrote to say that Banister had reported that the building was ready for painting and that he had ordered the painter, and was requesting Miller to 'look in on him'.[42] On 8 June Lord North was writing from London to Miller concerning sanding the building, which was obviously nearly finished. On the back of this letter Miller has drawn some ornamental candlesticks with a stand, together with the price: £6 2s. 0¾d.[43] Were they intended for the interior of the Temple? If so, no expense was spared for the interior decorations, for £6 was quite a sum for candlesticks. The Temple on the Mount, with its classical pillars and Gothic arches, was a mix of the two styles. The building called The Gothic Gateway, or Museum, at Enville, attributed to Miller, was also a mix of Gothic and classic styles. This unusual design approach may have been inspired by the ideas of Hawksmoor for All Souls College in Oxford, where the architect had used Gothic forms in a classical design for the Codrington library designed for the College in 1715.

From the dam the Temple made an attractive picture, and from the Temple itself there were views back across the cascade and the great pond, below the mount to the serpentine river, the Chinese bridge and the Chinese House, along the 'double river' to the Chinese seat by the Wroxton/Banbury road, and south to the Chinese Lodge near the bridge taking the approach road into the park. The views to be seen from the Temple went some way to making up for the enclosed nature of the gardens and therefore the lack of views mentioned by Salmon.

Bishop Pococke, visiting in 1756, was enthusiastic about what he saw:

> But this place is more to be admired without doors … [we] descended to a serpentine river, which is supplied from the large pieces of water and going up by it we came to the Gothic open rotondo of Mr Miller's design, in which he has practis'd curtains, that by turning screws let down so as to afford shelter which ever way you please. This commands a most delightful view of the head that supports the great body of water I have mentioned covered with shrubs, and a cascade falls down 20 ft. from it and forms a serpentine river which runs by the Chinese summer house; and there is another stream and small cascade to the left, which leads to a Chinese seat at a gate of this fine place that leads to Banbury.[44]

At the Temple Lord North's guests could admire the views on all sides, the ladies protecting themselves from the sun or the wind by Miller's ingenious curtains or screens which provided shelter from the elements. After taking their ease everyone could repair to the Chinese House, by way of the Chinese bridge – its Chinese rail has long since gone – for refreshment.

The general planting in the valley was altered to give a more informal feel. The formal avenue leading to the Abbey was removed, and the triple avenue on the bank to the south of the drive was drastically thinned, leaving only two main groups of four trees. This allowed a fine view of the new Dovecote on the bank to the south of the drive. Other formal plantings were left untouched, including that lining the old approach road from the west. Some of these old trees still remain today. From the Dovecote can be seen a clump of trees marking high ground in the park, the trees being a mix of oaks and Scots pines, typical of Miller's work at Farnborough.

It is not possible to ascertain exactly what the planting was like around the great pond in 1729, but by 1750 the plan shows clearly that it was divided into two types. There was woodland to the north of the great pond, and in the area between the Temple on the Mount and the Chinese House. Everywhere else there were groves or open woodland with no under-storey. Walks were cut through the stands of trees. This accords with Philip Yorke's description: 'A grove of fine old oaks of 12 acres upon the side of the hill is kept rough with paths cut through it …'.[45] In the outer parkland there are scattered groups of trees, with belts along the boundaries.

The whole plan, both the ornamental grounds in the upper and lower valleys, and the outer parkscape, represents a creative transformation of a previous formal garden and woodland area into an extended informal designed landscape, with the emphasis on water as a central and unifying theme. The kitchen garden and Lord North's new tree nursery to the south, by the top fishpond, are the only formal enclosed plantings on the whole estate.

The design within the gardens provides a good example of the Rococo style. Miller's buildings, as at Farnborough, are ingenious and well constructed. The layout of the gardens is planned to give both delight and surprise to visitors as they come across unexpected views. The close planting in the woodland area to the north of the Great Pond, where an avenue of yews suggests Miller's hand, imparts an air of mystery.

Mrs Delany visited Wroxton later, in 1753, when she was invited together with 'the good company from Radway'. In 1772 she had no doubt as to her preference for Wroxton as compared with Blenheim, writing: 'I don't find [Blenheim] with all its surprises, improvements and Grandeur stands in any manner of competition with Wroxton'.[46] Perhaps the final accolade should be that from William Pitt, whose poetic tribute to the delights of Wroxton was written to Miller in September 1754:

> I am much honoured by the obliging remembrance of the agreable company at Radway. It is no small mortification to me to think that they will pass tomorrow morning at Wroxton, and that I shall be confin'd to my Dungeon at Kingsutton, by a little medecine that I am obliged to take. As you say you believe in spirits, it will be the least justice you can do me to imagine mine will be on the delightful Banks of Wroxton Lake. May the grand Landskip Painter, the Sun, spread his highest colouring o'er the sweet scene, and the fairest Naiad of the Lake frisk all her frolic Fancy at the Cascade, and be, what you must ever think a pretty Girl, most charming in her Fall.[47]

Honington

The manor of Honington is situated on the river Stour, about two miles (three km) from Shipston-on-Stour in south Warwickshire. The present estate, of about 200 acres (80 ha), rises gradually eastwards away from the river valley to a ridge of higher land. The manor was originally one of the 24 'vills' comprising Earl Leofric's endowment for the Benedictine Priory of Coventry, founded in 1043. The mills on the Stour were locally important; as early as 1086 there were four corn mills, and by the beginning of the 19th century there were eight mills of which four were fulling mills. Weaving was then a locally important industry.

In 1540, after the Dissolution, the manor was bought by Robert Gybbes, in whose family it remained until it was purchased by Henry Parker in 1670. Parker, a successful London lawyer, rebuilt the existing house c.1682, leaving the Elizabethan stables and dovecote intact, and also built a new parish church in the classical style. He constructed stone entrance piers topped with pineapples to mark the entrance to the estate from the highway, and built the stone bridge with decorative stone balls which crosses the Stour. The estate, then comprising about 1,500 acres, was sold in 1737 to Joseph Townsend, the son of a London brewer.[48] In 1744, after his marriage to the heiress Judith Gore, Townsend altered both the exterior and the interior of the house, and also made radical changes to the pleasure grounds, where old formal gardens leading down to the river Stour had included a water garden fed by the river. These are shown in an engraving of 1731 by Samuel and Nathaniel Buck.[49] The gardens were open to the high road along the western boundary of the estate, which meant that the Hall lacked privacy.

The evidence for attributing the greater part of the new landscape design to Miller depends on correspondence between Miller and his Oxford friends John Oswald and Robert Vansittart in 1749, and subsequent diary entries made by Miller in 1750. There is also a tradition at Honington that the landscape design was carried out with Miller's advice. Townsend was 'new money'; he had become an MP, and wished to have his grounds landscaped in the new fashionable informal manner. A romantic landscape was created, with lawns running down to the river. On the far bank a new water garden was made with a large grotto, and a belt of ornamental woodland was planted along the boundary beyond. There are only remains of this landscape to be seen today.

Townsend's improvement schemes were well in hand before the following letter, written from Bath in February 1749, was sent to Miller by John Oswald and Robert Vansittart whom Miller had known at Oxford:

> I reckon myself greatly obliged to you for the trouble you took in going to Honington, and Mr Townsend desires me to give you assurances upon his part, he is pleased with your approbation of his schemes, and no less so with your hints of throwing the Eye over the Kitchen garden wall by evergreen shrubs upon the bank of the fence … he disapproved of the way the water falls at present and intended to have it altered, but did not think of filling up the back water in the manner you propose. My idea for the rock was somewhat different from yours. Yours perhaps is better if it can be done with as natural an appearance, mine is not that of the water coming from a cavern … but as I have not seen Ookey hole … that perhaps may make the other seem more natural to me … I fancy [Mr Townsend] will steal a day to see you at Radway … I should be glad Dear San to hear from you …[50]

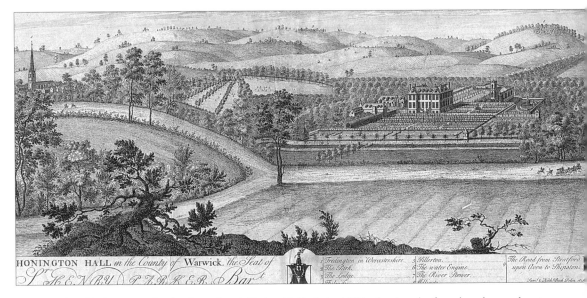

67 *Honington, a plan by Samuel and Nathaniel Buck in 1731, showing the formal gardens and water gardens before the transformation of the grounds c.1750.*

68   *View of Honington Hall across the river Stour from the derelict grotto. The bushes in the foreground have almost obscured what was originally a fine view.*

At Ookey, or Wookey Hole, in the Mendips, a series of caves have been hollowed out of the limestone by the River Axe, which finally gushes out of the rock face. It appears from this letter that Miller had visited the area, but it is not referred to anywhere in his diaries or correspondence. Alexander Pope, in 1739, had used 'a fine and very uncommon petrifaction from Okey Hole' in his famous grotto at Twickenham.[51] The use of the word 'natural' in this letter is important as it is the only reference in Miller's correspondence or his diaries, as far as I am aware, to the *raison d'etre* behind his landscape schemes. That Miller's schemes are natural in appearance is obvious, but here is an actual discussion between Miller and his friends on how best to achieve natural effects.

Miller had already been advising on the 'improvements' and giving detailed suggestions on how to handle the river and 'the back water'. Miller was still working on the plans in 1750. On Wednesday, 17 January 1750 he recorded in his diary that Oswald stayed overnight at Radway, and that evening Miller was looking over Buck's Views, which would have included the estate drawing of Honington and its formal gardens made in 1731. On 7 February, Miller went over to Honington, then in the evening he wrote to Oswald, but his diary entry gives no details of either his visit or the contents of his letter.

69   *Pitted limestone pieces tumbled among weeds at the site of the derelict grotto. These stones would have been specially chosen because of their likeness to tufa, the volcanic material found in many of the old Italian grottos.*

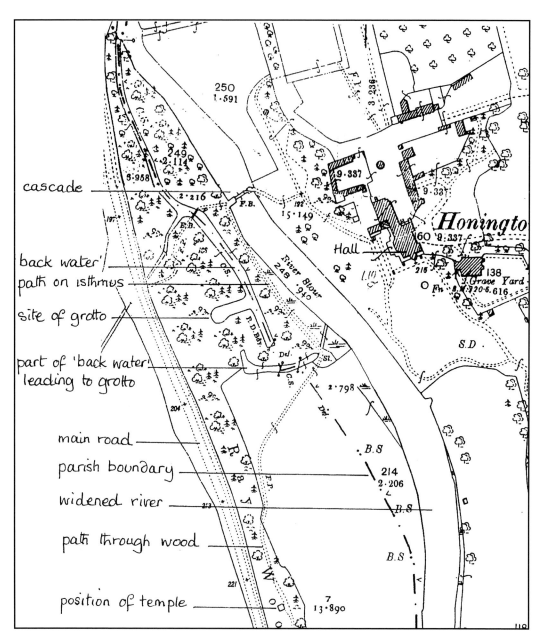

70   *Honington, a map adapted from the 25-inch O.S. map for 1900. The remains of the 'back water' leading to the Grotto area and back to the river is clearly visible. The parish boundary (dashed and dotted line to the west of the river) probably indicates the old course of the river before the mid-18th-century alterations to the course of the river, and the raising of the water levels with the new cascade. A small square to the south of Ray Wood marks the position of the Temple.*

Looking at the 1886 six-inch Ordnance Survey map, the widened and changed course of the river and the 'back water' can be seen. The area is now silted up and overgrown, but it is possible to make out how the whole scheme must have worked. Judging from the evidence of the Bucks' engraving and the 1900 25-inch O.S. map, it looks as if the old river bed had once followed the line of the 'back water', which appears on the 1900 map as a few disconnected long pools. This idea seems to be confirmed by the fact that the dotted and dashed line indicating the parish boundary follows these long pools, and does not go along the present river channel, which would be the obvious line for a parish boundary. From the stone bridge the riverbed was widened along the whole length of the water meadow, and an extra wide area opposite the Hall gave the appearance from the gardens of a small lake. A 19th-century print by J.P. Neal illustrates this feature.[52] The area the 'lake' must once have occupied can be made out in the water meadow, where an abrupt man-made bank is visible in the grass. The main channel was then diverted, leaving the old bed of the river as the 'back water' for Miller's decorative grotto scheme. A new stepped cascade, which still exists, was built further downstream below the Hall gardens to raise the water level for these new features. The maintenance of the levels had also to be considered in relation to the efficient working of the mills along the river.

The 'back water' was altered, and water was fed in from behind the new grotto, pouring into a pool in front through a hole in the grotto face. The grotto itself was made from pitted stone, pieces of which are visible at the site, which can still be made out although now overgrown with weeds and nettles. The stone possibly came from a quarry near Bath which was used to provide similar stone for other contemporary grottoes. This pitted stone resembles the volcanic stone tufa, found in Italy and widely used there in the garden grottoes of the Renaissance popes and princes of the 15th and 16th centuries. These in turn looked back to the grottoes described by Alberti (1404-72) who refers to the designing of grottoes recounted by Pliny and Ovid. In Ovid's *Metamorphoses* (3, 157-62) there is a description of a natural grotto, where 'Nature, by her own cunning had imitated art; for she had shaped a native arch of the living rock and soft tufa'.[53] Although the 18th-century landscapists wanted their inventions to appear 'natural', they also continued to look back to the inspirations of antiquity, and the ideas of the ancients. It is not too far fetched to attribute to Miller the idea of incorporating an arch in his grotto which, although based on the natural rock formation in the Mendips, yet also fitted this description of Ovid's, for he thought highly of studying the Roman texts of antiquity, and encouraged his sons to do the same. In a letter written to his wife in 1779, when his son Fiennes was 19, Miller still thought it important for him to devote some time to studying:

> … I am glad Fiennes looks after the men, they have had such good weather that the work ought to go on well and fast, I hope he does not neglect his Pliny, etc[54]

Statues were placed near the grotto, two of which, supposedly of Joseph and Mary, were moved nearer the house in more recent years and are still to be found in the bushes. The water was fed back to the river Stour further downstream, below the cascade, and a small Chinese bridge allowed access to the central planted area thus formed – a pleasant place to walk, with water on either side, a feature that Miller used both at Farnborough and Wroxton.

71 *Honington Hall, by J.P. Neal. A 19th-century print showing the river forming a 'lake', filling what appears to be the distance between the old course of the river bed, along the parish boundary, and the newly created course. Although today the river flows entirely in the new course as shown on the O.S. map for 1900 (illustration 70) the old course of the river can still be seen as a raised bank in the water meadow.*

Two reclining statues, probably of river gods, originally resided on plinths on either side of the cascade. River gods had decorated Renaissance grottoes, and were also mentioned by Ovid. The effect of the cascade with its river gods is reminiscent of the design of the cascade at West Wycombe, in Buckinghamshire, the seat of Sir Francis Dashwood, though the statues are different. Miller had surely visited West Wycombe, for he was friendly with Sir Francis' brother, Sir James Dashwood, whom he advised on the landscaping of his estate at Kirtlington Park, a few miles north of Oxford, and they had mutual friends in Sir Roger Newdigate of Arbury and Sir Edward Turner of Ambrosden. The statues of the river gods are still in the grounds, but the threat of vandalism has meant that they have had to be moved away from the cascade and nearer the house for security.

Behind the grotto, Ray Wood (was this named after that at Castle Howard?) was planted as a woodland belt screening the property from the road. Within the wood an urn and a small temple were placed, each having a group of yews planted behind, and each with a view across the river. The sites of these, and the foundations of the temple, with the views across the water, as well as a small winding path running through the wood, are still in evidence today, though the urn and temple have gone. Evergreens were used repeatedly by Miller in his schemes, and yews in particular were often chosen to form an evergreen and sheltered background to landscape buildings.

In 1759 Townsend commissioned two gouache paintings from Thomas Robins the elder to record the new riverside scene. Robins was known as 'the limner of Bath', and he recorded several other contemporary scenes, including those at Painswick where the

Rococo Garden has recently been restored. His informal style of portraying the grounds marks a radical change from the precise formality of the Buck engravings, or those of Kip and Knyff made in the early decades of the century. The first painting of Honington shows the view across the river, taken from the lawn below the Hall. In the foreground there is a Chinese Seat, with a party of people on the lawn nearby, and in the distance is shown the river, the cascade, the Chinese Bridge, the grotto and Ray Wood. The appearance of the grotto, with its statues, is hardly 'natural' in modern terms, and certainly would never have formed a part of the natural geology of the Honington valley, but a certain amount of artistic licence was evidently not considered out of place in its design. The Chinese Seat is very like the Chinese Seat at Wroxton, but with differences in the form of the balustrading. The dates of neither are known for certain, but they were built within a few years of each other, and one, or both, may have been designed by Miller. The second painting shows the Hall seen from the far side of the river. On the grass in the foreground is seated the painter himself, pointing out to his fair companion (Townsend's wife Judith?) the arrival of others in a boat crossing the river from the Hall. A single terrace retained from the old formal garden can be seen; also the sundial at the far end. Planting hides an old ha-ha. These three features still exist. This picture shows Tredington church spire, not actually visible from where Robins did his painting. It is, however, important in the design of the whole landscape, as it would have been visible from the Chinese Seat, and was the focal point northwards for a riverside path towards Tredington. Robins encircled his paintings with butterflies, tendrils and stems, and the flowers which he probably saw in the gardens: sweet pea, honeysuckle, nasturtium, ipomea, cyclamen, iris, jasmine, tuberose, polyanthus, and roses. Although there is little left of the landscape on the far side of the river, and there is no sign of the Chinese Seat, nor of the Chinese bridge, these two paintings allow us to visualise in detail the attractive informality of the new landscape.[55]

Looking from the Hall across the river, which had no bridge in the 18th century, although one is shown in the O.S. map for 1900, the question arises: how did people go round to see the grotto on the other side if the boat was not in use? The answer is to be found in a path, now long disused, going along the riverbank north towards the mill at Tredington. Behind the Hall a grand avenue leads past the disused kitchen garden to the old fishponds, now silted up and full of trees. Lower areas among the undergrowth between the fishponds and the river suggest that possibly there were other pools. Fishponds would surely have been adapted as ornamental pools here, for they ran alongside the old entrance to the Hall, now only used as a farm track.

Between the Hall and the village of Tredington to the north, the river bank was originally raised and widened to take a path among mature trees, a path which must have run from the Chinese Seat right up to the weir below the mill. At the weir there are steps constructed either side of a level top making a narrow 'bridge' leading to a small raised tongue of land. The construction work is modern, but the stone base is obviously much older. The tongue of land leads to a meadow, in which, adjacent to the highway, is a raised bank making a useful path above the wet ground, or above the flood water when the river was out. To the south the path enters the woodland and eventually reaches the grotto. The grounds can now be seen to have been laid out with an attractive riverside path nearly to Tredington, where the river could be crossed and the return journey made passing the grotto and the temple in the woods, and returning to the Hall by the stone bridge and the park, where the raised and levelled ground taking the track from the bridge can still be made out. The path continued through a spinney and the old rectory garden back to the Hall.

To the east of the Hall the formal gardens were altered to lawns, to the north the approach driveway was improved with planting. It seems probable that the deerpark was also extended at this period. The line of the driveway can be made out on the 1880s O.S. map by an avenue, which continues, less well marked, with consecutive groups of trees, across the old deer park and the present park, joining the modern drive on the edge of the gardens. It would have made a grander entrance to the Hall than the present driveway which approaches the Hall from the village. Although on the map the avenue appears to be going north to nowhere, east of Tredington the ground rises to the north, then slopes down to a stream. The avenue actually stops beyond the sight line. It would have appeared as if it led on over the immediate horizon, suggesting that the estate stretched away into the distance. There is nothing left today of this avenue east of Tredington.

Other planting on the estate included a belt of trees, known as Hill Clumps, on the skyline to the east beyond the Idlicote road. The Hill Clumps still contain Scots pines and some fine horse chestnuts among other mature trees. Hilltop planting to draw attention to the extent of the estate was typical of Miller's work at Farnborough and in the outer park at Wroxton. The Clumps formed part of a circular route which led from the Hall, across the park and within a double line of hawthorns up to the hillside. This track was in use well within living memory, when the lady of the Hall regularly used to take her pony and trap along it.

Although the grounds nearer the Hall received the greatest attention, the whole estate was included in a general scheme of tree planting and the creation of mixed belts along the hill crest, making the landscape both more attractive and more productive. Close to the Hall the design was typically Rococo, with meandering paths along the river which were full of interest and unexpected views, the whole laid out to provide delight in the pleasures of the waterside grounds, the scenery, the Grotto, and boating.

The river Stour had provided Miller with a good flow of water for his projects, but an imaginative leap was required to make the transformation as recorded in the Robins paintings from those old formal gardens illustrated in the Buck engraving of 28 years earlier. Robins' paintings show how the whole approach to garden and estate design had changed radically. The borders of these paintings, where the scenes are glimpsed through a garland of wild flowers and butterflies, characterise the lightness and gaiety of this Rococo period of landscape design, so different in style from the formality and precision of the earlier gardens. Miller was in the vanguard of this new fashion in the Midlands, the whole plan showing a loosening of form and a much more natural approach to the use of water and landscaping than is to be seen, for instance, at Rousham, where William Kent's design had been carried out only ten years previously.

7

Landscapes and Architecture

⤙·⤚

The years between 1749 and 1756 were Miller's most productive years.[1] During 1749 and 1750 Miller was involved in designs for at least 16 estates, with a dozen or more in the following five years. By the time that the Honington estate was under consideration in 1749, Miller was receiving more and more requests for designs. He had already been working for some years at Ambrosden, north of Oxford, for his friend Sir Edward Turner, at Hagley, in Worcestershire, in assisting George Lyttelton in laying out his park, and at Belhus, near Aveley in Essex, for his long standing friend Thomas Lennard Barrett. All three men were 'improving' their estates and either altering their mansions to the Gothic style or planning to replace their old houses completely. Between 1748 and 1763 Miller's purely architectural work included the Gothic alterations and additions to

72 *The Villa at Chiswick, the Inigo Jones Gateway. Designed by Jones c.1621 for Lionel Cranfield at the Great House, Chiswick, the Gateway was moved by Lord Burlington to his Villa garden in 1738.*

Arbury Hall (1748-55) and Adlestrop House, Gloucestershire (1750-4), and the classical designs for the Shire Hall at Warwick (1752-8) and the new Hagley Hall (1754-63). Other work included alterations to several local churches and, most probably, the large new stable block for Lord Guernsey at Packington House, north of Coventry, built 1753-8 by the Warwick master masons, and brothers, William and David Hiorns.

The most important of Miller's earlier landscape projects during this period were his designs for Hagley, including the famous Castle Ruin; the Ruined Castle and the new landscaping at Wimpole; designs for Lord Stamford at Enville, and for Lord Chetwynd at Ingestre in south Staffordshire, and the Bath House at Walton, in Warwickshire. His clients at this time are nearly all landed nobility. They were important men, and most were also influential politicians. Following the early successes of Edgehill Tower and George Lyttelton's Castle Ruin, Miller's work had become known, and many of the upper members of society began to call on Miller's expertise. It is interesting to comment on this aspect of his 'clientele', for Miller himself, though educated at Oxford, had neither blue blood nor great wealth to recommend him, and his father had made his money through trade. Nevertheless, this background appeared to be no bar to Miller's friendships. Despite the fact that he was carrying out architectural and landscaping designs at a time when these abilities were largely the province of skilled men who were nevertheless definitely below the social status of their clients, Miller was accepted as an equal, and a valued friend by those for whom he worked.

Ambrosden

The estate at Ambrosden is situated about ten miles north of Oxford, on low-lying and poorly drained land. In 1729 Sir Edward Turner, whose family fortune had been made by judicious selling of South Sea stock, bought the estate and replaced the large medieval manor house with a new mansion reputed to have cost £4,000. He also created a park of about five miles in circumference surrounding the mansion. Sir Edward was Miller's closest friend until his death in 1766, and Miller and his family not only used to spend part of each Christmas at Ambrosden, but Miller also assisted Sir Edward in his nomination in the Great Oxfordshire Election of 1752.[2] Neither the site nor Miller's contribution to it is easy to visualise, since the mansion and virtually all of the designed landscape features have gone.

The evidence for Miller's work at Ambrosden rests with the correspondence between the two men between 1743 and 1758, and numerous entries in Miller's diaries. Miller had first made Sir Edward's acquaintance when they were both undergraduates at Oxford. Miller advised Sir Edward about the design and also the interior furnishing of his new mansion, and was responsible for several landscape buildings, including a Gothic Barn, a mock ruin, and a gateway and entrance lodge. In 1747, Miller sent Sir Edward two sketches for the Barn, which had a Gothic front with pediment and pinnacles. The next year Sir Edward was requesting Miller's help with the design of his lodge and entrance gate.[3] Six months later, in April 1749, Sir Edward was complaining about Hitchcock's 'rusticking', requesting Miller to have a model made in wood or stone so that Hitchcock could copy it. The pillars of the Gateway were to be copies of the rusticated pillars of the Oxford Physic Garden, but Sir Edward wanted the rusticating to be either like that at the Duke of Queensberry's or at Lord Burlington's.[4] Lord Burlington had had a gateway, designed by Inigo Jones, moved to his gardens at Chiswick. Perhaps the gateway at Chiswick was what Sir Edward had in mind, for on 6 January 1750 Miller recorded in his diary that he was in Oxford 'at Worcester [College] to see Jones' designs'.

In March 1750 Sir Edward was lamenting the fall of the Gothic ruin: 'Down is fallen, fallen, fallen the Gothick! … Come and deplore the ruin of my Ruins!' and asking whether he should rebuild or substitute something else.[5] In Miller's diary entry for 10 November, written at Ambrosden, Miller commented that 'the Window of the Gothic C. isn't up'. Could this be the rebuilding of the Gothic castle ruin? On the O.S. map for 1885, on the small road leading from Ambrosden to join the modern A41 just short of Wretchwick Farm, 'The Gothic' is marked adjacent to the road on the north side. There are still a few small trees and shrubby undergrowth here, in very wet ground, making a small indentation into an ordinary agricultural field, but there are no signs of any stone construction. Miller was again at Ambrosden on Boxing Day of that year. He stayed for two weeks, and recorded in his diary that he was drawing a plan for a farmhouse and offices during that time. He also walked to the wood, or round the wood numerous times during his stay. There is a pool and a marshy area shown near the Ambrosden to Merton road on the O.S. map for 1885. The marshy area looks as if it was also originally a pool, and the two were crossed by a bridge at a narrow point. Was Miller advising Sir Edward on planting and the creation of his pools? It is almost certain that he was, but there is no actual mention of it either in the correspondence between the two men or in Miller's diaries. Since the work at Ambrosden was one of Miller's major commissions, it is unfortunate that there is so little detail known about the actual design of the landscape and its buildings.

After Sir Edward's death his son pulled down part of the mansion to reduce the running expenses, for he was heavily in debt, and the remainder was pulled down in 1779. There is nothing left of the park except for a few areas of bushes which may mark the sites of previous landscaping or buildings. A housing estate now covers the ornamental horseshoe-shaped planting to the north east of the village visible on the 1885 map, the lakes appear to have been filled in completely, apart from one small area of rushy ground, and modern agriculture has replaced the designed landscape of which Sir Edward had been so proud.

Hagley

The estate at Hagley had been purchased in 1564 by Sir John Lyttelton. In the early years of the 18th century, George Lyttelton's father, Sir Thomas, a direct descendant, had married Christian Temple of Stowe, sister to Richard Temple, 1st Viscount Cobham, and lady-in-waiting to Queen Anne.[6] With such a family connection it would have been surprising if improvements to the park had not been planned. The estate of Hagley is some ten miles south-west of Birmingham, the park itself being about 218 acres in extent. The land rose behind the old Elizabethan house to the Clent Hills (*c.*900 feet), the park being drained by streams in narrow valleys. There may have been some woodland present prior to the 'improvements', but Lyttelton was responsible for a great deal of the planting both within the park and also on the hills beyond the Birmingham road. The combination of small valleys with their streams, the undulating landscape with hills generously covered with woodland, and the wide 'lawns' of grass giving open spaces between, made a secluded landscape of infinite variety. The enjoyment of walking in the park was greatly enhanced by the spreading views towards the Malverns and Wales which became increasingly visible as the visitor climbed higher, leaving the Hall itself nestling in a hollow.

George Lyttelton was one of the first to introduce the new informality into his park. He and Miller were close friends, a friendship likely to have begun through their meeting at Stowe. Subsequently, Miller became a frequent visitor at Hagley. The Hagley landscape is very much a composite design, in which Miller's advice played a major part. Other men who contributed included Alexander Pope, William Pitt the elder, his cousin John Pitt of Encombe, and Thomas Pitt, Lord Camelford, William's nephew, who designed the small Palladian Bridge below the cascades in 1762. On Wychbury Hill, to the north of the main park, James 'Athenian' Stuart designed the Temple of Theseus, one of the very first Greek Doric Revival buildings, between 1758 and 1759.[7] Lyttelton's landscape had poetic associations; he was himself a minor poet, and within his park over the years 'seats' or urns appeared to Milton, to Pope and to James Thomson, author of The Seasons. Pope and Thomson were frequent visitors to Hagley, and the Hall contains the painting of Pope with his dog 'Bounce'.

There were originally 19 buildings and structures in the park. Although today the designed elements of the landscape itself have largely disappeared, the five main buildings, the Castle Ruin (now renovated and used as a private dwelling), the Temple of Theseus and the Obelisk (both outside the main park), the Rotunda and Prince Frederick's column still survive. Paintings, letters, and descriptions made by visitors allow a picture to be built up of what must have been an enchanting, if not enchanted, landscape.

The valley to the south of the park was the first area to be developed, with a small series of lakes and dams, a Hermitage c.1739, a Seat of Contemplation c.1743, and a Pebble Alcove. It is not known who designed the landscaping, but it was possibly done by Lyttelton himself, with the advice of Pope. Pope is known to have made three sketches for garden buildings in 1739, which may well have been for the three buildings mentioned above.[8] These were intended to inspire a sense of retirement and a contemplative mood among verdant scenery. They were of a fairly simple construction, and were decorated with snail shells, sheep bones or pebbles.

Lyttelton had plans to demolish his old house and build a new mansion, and Miller had already designed some of the offices for the latter when Lyttelton decided that he would like a mock ruined castle for his own park similar to Miller's own Tower at Edgehill. Lyttelton may also have been influenced in his desire to have a castle 'ruin' by the fact that there was a castle eyecatcher (not a ruin) on the hill behind the mansion at Castle Hill in Devon, built by Hugh Fortescue. A photograph of the painting by J. Lange, 1741, taken for Country Life, shows what appears to be the castle on the hill behind the house, dating the castle to pre-1741. The actual painting was destroyed by fire in 1934.[9] Hugh was half-brother to Lyttelton's beloved first wife Lucy who died in 1747.

In 1748, Miller designed the Castle Ruin for Lyttelton, Hagley's most important landscape building. The site is the climax of a walk up to the top of the park from the Hall, but the building is carefully positioned so that it can be glimpsed from below from certain points, but is not completely visible until Castle Lawn, the grassy slope actually leading up to the Castle itself, is reached. From the high point chosen for the Castle there were far-reaching views to both south and west. The Castle has two complete round castellated towers, the higher one being narrower and adjacent to the main tower. From the main tower part of a curtain wall joins up with three other low 'ruined' part towers enclosing a courtyard. The whole forms a square with sides of about 25 yards length, the main towers themselves being five yards across. The construction has a genuine appearance, even to the detail of the curtain wall, in which in one section shows a partly exposed rubble filling, a common method of medieval castle wall construction. The attractive reddish sandstone used for the building is said to have been taken from the ruins of nearby Halesowen Abbey, as were also the large windows in part of the curtain wall. At the top of the larger complete tower there was a 'prospect' room. There are small Gothic windows in the prospect room for which Miller supplied painted glass, and it is easy to imagine Lyttelton taking his visitors up the narrow stair to the top room and opening the windows to show his visitors the fine views from this elevated position. Henry Keene, an architect whom Miller had encouraged and given work to when a young man, was asked to make up special Gothic chairs to Miller's design – in June 1749 Lyttelton had emphasised that 'they are not to be common chairs but in a Gothic Form.' In an inventory of the goods and chattels of George Lyttelton's father Sir Thomas, who died in 1751, eight chairs were listed for 'the best room', together with oil cloth for the floor. The lower room served as a bedchamber and below this was probably a dining room, for more chairs were listed, together with two 'elbow' chairs, a table and a fire grate.[10] The building was also used as a lodge for the keeper. The listing of two tables in the adjacent 'Slaughterhouse' suggests that the keeper slaughtered and dressed deer here. The design of the Castle Ruin appears

73 *Hagley Hall, view from Milton's seat of the Hall and the church. The Hall was designed by Miller and built 1756-60.*

74 *Castle Hill,*
Devon, the mock
castle behind the
house, c.1730s, built
by Hugh,. 1st Lord
Fortescue, Earl of
Clinton. His half-
sister, Lucy, was the
much loved first wife
of George Lyttelton of
Hagley.

just as authentic, but is quite different from Miller's own Tower with its ruins. The towers
are round, while Miller's own is octagonal, and a different stone has been used. The design
of one large tower built together with a smaller and higher tower beside it suggests that
Miller may have been thinking of several similar medieval tower constructions in Oxford,
for example St Martin's church tower at Carfax. Although the latter is not round, Miller
always liked to take a building as a model, but alter it somewhat in his own design.

When the Castle was nearing completion, in the summer of 1748, Shenstone, of the
Leasowes, which was adjacent to the Hagley Estate, visited the site, and reported to his
friend Lady Luxborough on 16 June: 'it consists of one entire Tow'r & three Stumps of
Tow'rs with a ruin'd Wall betwixt them. There is no great Art or Variety in yᵉ Ruin, but
the Situation gives it a charming Effect; The chief Tow'r is allowedly about 10 Feet too
low.'[11] Shenstone, critical as ever, was no doubt envious of Lyttelton's Castle, which was
well beyond anything which he could afford. However, a little later, in a letter to his
friend Richard Graves, the criticism is left out – for Shenstone had realised that the Castle
'is *just* seen from my wood; but by the removal of a tree or two … I believe it may be
rendered a considerable object here.[12]

Joseph Heely, writing a description of a walk through the grounds in 1777, described
the picture:

> This gothic ruin is very judiciously situated on the boldest eminence in the whole
> domain; and commands a most unbounded prospect … to wipe away any suspicion
> of it being otherwise than a real ruin, the large and massy stones, which seemingly
> tumbles from the tottering and ruinous walls, are suffered to lie about … in the utmost
> confusion … The ground about this eligible ruin, without exception, surpasses any
> other in the park; to its loftiness is added, the most agreeable variety … the amazing
> profusion of prospect over an unlimited and beautiful country.'[13]

Horace Walpole, able as ever to conjure up a picture in a few words, gave Miller's Castle
Ruin high praise when he wrote after his visit to Hagley:

There is a ruined Castle built by Miller that would get him his freedom even of Strawberry [Walpole's Gothic mansion at Strawberry Hill]: it has the true rust of the barons' wars ... I wore out my eyes with gazing, my feet with climbing and my tongue and vocabulary with commending ...[14]

Below the Castle Ruin, a second valley was laid out. Springs on the hill below the Castle feed into a holding pool held in place by a dam, below which was a Grotto and a series of cascades falling down to a pool crossed by a small Palladian bridge, one of the last structures to be built in the park, near the lower end of the valley. Above the Grotto and the cascades, on a small hill, was situated the Rotunda. Designed by John Pitt of Encombe, it was built in 1749 by Miller's personal mason William Hitchcox, who had also built the Castle Ruin. The Rotunda is built of stone and has eight Ionic columns supporting a domed roof. Miller supervised the construction, and advised Lyttelton on the exterior finishing of the stonework and the associated landscaping. Miller favoured evergreens as a background to the light stone building. Looking back up from the Palladian bridge at the bottom of the valley, the Rotunda would have been visible beyond the cascades, but cannot be seen from here today due to the growth of trees. It is in a poor state of repair, and has lost its domed top.

In 1754 Miller provided materials for a Grotto, for which Sir George Lyttelton wrote to thank him from Hill Street, his London address, in August of that year, writing: 'I thank you for your care to furnish my Grotto; all these materials will make it very fine ...'.[15]

75   *'Ruins in Hagley Park', by C. Warre Bampfylde of Hestercombe, 1784.*

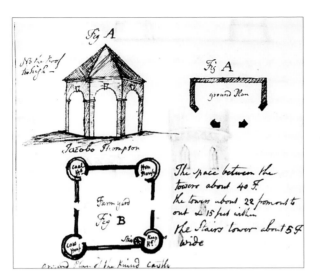

76 *Drawings from John Parnell's 'Journal of a Tour thro' England and Wales, Anno 1769', showing Thomson's Seat and groundplan at Hagley. James Thomson (1700-48) visited Hagley and wrote about the landscaped park in his poem 'The Seasons'.*

77 *Drawings from John Parnell's 'Journal of a Tour thro' England and Wales, Anno 1769', showing Miller's Castle Ruin, 1747-8, at Hagley.*

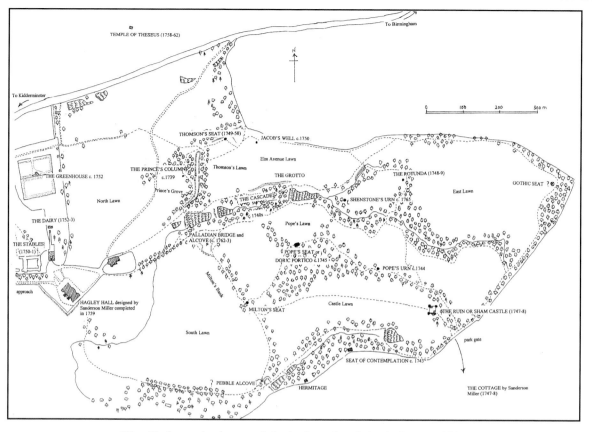

78 *Hagley, a sketch map of the landscaped park by S. Haynes, 2005.*

These materials may have been for the Grotto in the park, but it is possible that they may alternatively have been for a second grotto, which was being constructed under the piano nobile of the new Hall, begun in this year. How much Miller was involved in the actual design of the Grotto in the park, and the cascades, is not known. Pococke, in 1751, described the use of materials from glass works and quarries where the water emerging from the rocks fell about 15 feet, then through a Grotto containing a statue of Venus.[16] A few remnants of these materials can still be found at the site, but all semblance of the Grotto itself has disappeared in small land slippages and recent tree growth. Miller was also involved with Thomson's Seat (1749), built in memory of the poet who died in 1748. A letter from Lyttelton to Miller in 1750 refers to a delay by Hitchcox in sending a man over to stucco the stone built 'octagon'.[17] Having worked out where the position of Thomson's Seat must be from an old 19th-century map, the site was actually discovered by scratching away the grass and uncovering the stone foundations of the pillars – the building itself had long since gone – on a visit to the park in 1994. The ground plan is half a hexagon to the front and half a rectangle behind, and in appearance from the front the building had three open round arched entrances and a pointed roof. From front to back it measured nine feet, across the back wall it measured 18 feet, and the front pillars were six feet apart. The back wall was a double brick construction with a rubble infill,

79   *The south door at Farnborough, and one of the main windows at Hagley showing skirted architraves. A distinctive feature in Miller's work, these architraves, with their bases curving outwards, were derived initially from designs by Inigo Jones. Skirted architraves also occur on the house Miller designed for Sir Edward Turner at Ambrosden, Oxfordshire.*

and the floor was a brick dust and mortar mix, the latter a type of finish which had been used by the Romans. It is possible that Lyttelton and Miller may have been consciously copying this precedent. There is a fine view from the Seat across the valley of the Grotto and the cascades towards Pope's lawn and Seat, and the rising ground behind, with the Castle Ruin peeping out of the trees on the far hillside.

On the flyleaf of a large volume of timber accounts at Hagley was found the following, probably written by Lyttelton's father, Sir Thomas:

> In the year of 1747 I built the Castle and also the Cottage. [This was designed by Miller, and was just outside the park near to the castle Ruin.] The same year part of the plantations upon the Hill were made, the rest in the following year … In 1748 I built the Rotundo and in 1749 the half octagon seat and made the Haha over against it. Mr Miller, architect of the Castle. Mr John Pitt of the Rotundo and the Octagon.

Hitchcox was paid £151 for building the Rotunda.

Miller's work at Hagley continued well into the 1750s. During the second week of June 1756 Miller stayed at Hagley for five days. There are references in his diary to walking in the park, and also 'the shrubbery'. On 13 August 1756, Miller recorded in his diary that he was drawing a 'Gothic Seat'. The following day he fixed up poles for the seat in 'Rushy Lawn' with Sir George Lyttelton. The site of 'Rushy Lawn' has not been identified, but it may have been on the hillside beyond the Rotunda. On 16 August he was drawing another seat. Miller stayed at Hagley for 10 days, from 10-20 August, and referred several times to walking round

80 *Packington, the stables, built by David Hiorn of Warwick, 1756-8. Ascribed to Miller, the design is typically neo-Palladian, with a Tuscan portico. Simple but imposing, the building adds dignity to the setting of Packington Hall, built 1693 but enlarged in the Palladian style in 1763.*

the park, and once to going to see the cascades. It seems likely that he would have been discussing the general landscaping and the planting during these walks, but, as in similar entries made when he was visiting other estates, Miller gives no details. During 1759 Miller supervised the building of the Temple of Theseus, designed by 'Athenian' Stuart. Hitchcox's son was the mason.

The new Hagley Hall, designed by Miller, was his biggest architectural commission. Initially he designed a Gothic edifice, but Lyttelton and his new wife decided to change their minds and have a Palladian design. Hagley Hall, built 1756-60, was the last of the great Palladian mansions. It owes much to the design of the 17th-century Wilton House, the plan of which had been supervised by Inigo Jones, whose work Miller had studied. It has also been compared to the original design for Houghton Hall, as designed by Colen Campbell, and illustrated in *Vitruvius Britannicus*, which has a similar rectangular plan with four corner towers. The south façade of Hagley, however, has a total of 11 windows on the piano nobile, including those in either tower, while at Houghton there are nine. Hagley, though it lacks a portico – George Lyttelton did consider adding one – has a slightly projecting central section with a pediment which copies the 'feel' of Campbell's design for Houghton with its central portico.[18] Hagley is also surprisingly similar to Lydiard House, in Wiltshire, built between 1743 and 1746 for John, 2nd Viscount St John, probably by Roger Morris. The similarity here extends to the skirted architraves to the principal windows in the end towers, discussed below, though the fenestration is different. The house itself, however, has only three towers, the design hiding older buildings to the rear.[19] Miller might not have visited Lydiard, but he would almost certainly have heard about it, for he knew Henry Hoare, of Stourhead, Lord Guilford of Wroxton Abbey was Lady St John's brother-in-law, and Henrietta, Lady Luxborough, who lived at Barrells Hall in Warwickshire, not far from Hagley, was Lord St John's sister. Hagley Hall also has many similarities with Lord Coventry's new mansion at Croome, thought to have been strongly influenced by Miller's ideas. The fenestration at Croome differs from that at Hagley, but the number of windows along the length of the piano nobile is the same, and the four corner towers with their pyramidal roofs are very similar. An interesting detail at Hagley is shown in the design of the main windows in the corner towers, which have triangular pediments and distinctive skirted architraves, the stone architrave being curved outwards at the base of the window. Skirted architraves to windows are found in an exactly similar position at Wilton House. This detail also occurs in the stone architrave to the door of Miller's extension to the south front at Farnborough Hall. Skirted architraves are not common in 18th-century designs, although another contemporary use is in Doctor John Wall's house at 43, Foregate Street in Worcester, where the window also has a balcony. Dr Wall was up at Oxford with Miller. In the 1730s, Lord Burlington used this design in his link building at Chiswick joining the old house to the new villa, and also in a design for Richmond House, Whitehall. A window with a skirted architrave and a balcony underneath (a 'pseudo balcony' is indicated in the design under the windows at Hagley) is, however, a recurring feature of Inigo Jones' work,[20] further underlining Miller's interest in and admiration for Jones.

Miller also designed the surrounding offices for the Hall. In 1747 the stables and coach house, surrounding a courtyard, were built, and in 1752 the Greenhouse and the Dairy were constructed in the walled garden. The greenhouse was probably built to house exotics during the winter, and is more like a house in appearance than would be expected today, with three very tall windows reaching to floor level in the south wall. The Dairy was a small rectangular building, eight yards by 12, built in stone in the classical style with four Tuscan pillars supporting a gable end in the manner of a pediment, forming a covered entrance or portico. This design is repeated at the opposite end of the building. Although a small building, this plan with a portico and four Tuscan pillars is quite similar to that of the east front of St Paul's church at Covent Garden, designed by Inigo Jones 1631-2. St Paul's has two rectangular pillars on the outside, and two inner round pillars supporting the portico, while the Dairy has four round Tuscan pillars supporting the portico and rectangular pilasters on the corners of the building at the back of the portico. The Tuscan order was recognised by Vitruvius as the most primitive of the five orders, and Palladio referred it as appropriate for country buildings.[21] Inigo Jones is said to have told his client, the Earl of Bedford, who wanted an inexpensive church 'not much better than a barn' for St Paul's in Covent Garden, that he should have the handsomest barn in England, so a design based on the Tuscan order was surely suitable for a rural dairy. With Miller's known interest in Jones' work, and his use of older buildings as basic models for his designs, the comparison between these two buildings is not too far-fetched. The main room in the Dairy could be used for simple entertaining, while the dairy itself was half underground, underneath the main room, where it would always be cool, and was reached by a small outer staircase leading down from the garden.

The parish church, which has 13th-century origins, is situated at the entrance to the park, behind the Hall. In 1754-6, Miller partly rebuilt it for George Lyttelton, though his work has now all gone. The church has several Lyttelton monuments, the finest being that carved by the Huguenot sculptor Roubiliac in memory of Lyttelton's first wife, Lucy.

In describing Miller's work at Hagley, no attempt has been made to include details of the park layout and the buildings with which he does not appear to be connected, such as Pope's Seat, Pope's Urn, Shenstone's Urn, Milton's Seat, the Palladian bridge, and Frederick, Prince of Wales's Column. Only remnants survive of the original designed landscape, and little water now flows down the valleys and the area of the cascades. The Grotto, and most of the buildings, including the Palladian bridge, have disappeared, yet the landscape at Hagley still retains a sense almost of fairyland. It is self-contained within its enfolding hills and woods, shutting out the proximity of modern Birmingham and its roads, and it still has a feeling of the 18th century Elysium that Lyttelton, Miller and their friends strove so assiduously to create.

Hagley, together with Enville and The Leasowes, was one of the most popular of the 18th-century landscaped estates for visitors. It was described by various writers, the series of letters published by Joseph Heely, *Letters on the Beauties of Hagley, Envil and The Leasowes*, in 1777 being one of the most detailed. Sir John Parnell, visiting in 1769, illustrated his tour of the grounds in his Journal with a series of drawings of the buildings.[22] In the 1770s Catherine the Great of Russia commissioned Josiah Wedgwood to make a dinner service for her, called the Frog Dinner Service. Each piece was to be decorated with a different English landscaped scene, one of which was a view of Hagley Park. The artists Anthony Devis and Samuel Stringer were responsible for most of the original views.

The poet James Thomson, who loved to wander in the park, wrote of Hagley and its master:

> O LYTTELTON, the Friend! Thy Passions thus
> And meditations vary, as at large,
> Courting the Muse, thro' HAGLEY-PARK you stray,
> Thy *British Tempe!* There along the Dale,
> With Woods o'er-hung, and shag'd with mossy Rocks,
> Whence on each hand the gushing Waters play,
> And down the rough cascade white-dashing fall,
> Or gleam in lengthen'd Vista thro' the Trees,
> You silent steal; or sit beneath the Shade
> Of solemn Oaks, that tuft the swelling Mounts
> Thrown graceful round by Nature's careless hand,
> And pensive listen to the various Voice
> Of rural peace … from these abstracted oft,
> You wander through the Philosophic World;
> Where in bright Train continual Wonders rise …[23]

It is still possible to sit 'beneath the Shade of solemn Oaks, and pensive listen to the various Voice of rural peace' at Hagley. The grounds have been carefully maintained as a private park, and the aura of Lord Lyttelton's achievement is still tangible, in spite of the fact that many of the more physical glories of his creation have now long gone.

Belhus

Belhus, or Belhouse, was a large estate near Aveley, in Essex. The estate was named after Nicholas de Belhouse, who was living there in 1339. His daughter married John Barrett, whose great-grandson, also John Barrett, built in 1526 the red brick mansion inherited by his descendant Thomas Lennard Barrett (1717-86). Barrett altered and Gothicised the house and landscaped the grounds extensively. Miller and Barrett (he transposed his two last names on coming into the title as 26th Baron Dacre on the death of his mother Lady Anne in 1755, henceforward being known as Barrett Lennard, but he will be referred to as 'Barrett' here) knew each other at least as early as 1744, when Miller was 28 and Barrett 27 years old. Both men were good amateur architects, and well versed in the management of land. They had many other interests in common, including academic tastes in literature, history and antiquities. They also shared a disposition to fits of depression, and several of Barrett's letters to Miller suggest ideas for combating 'the blew devils'. Between 1745 and 1747 Barrett rebuilt the west and south fronts of his house at Belhus and redecorated much of the interior in the Gothic style under Miller's direction, one of the earliest Gothic redecorations in the country. As well as these building operations, Barrett also turned his attention to the grounds. He pulled down the walls of the old-fashioned garden adjoining the house to open up the views to the south, constructed a new lake in the grounds and undertook extensive tree-planting. Miller visited Belhus in 1745, and perhaps in later years. Although it is not known to what extent Miller was responsible for the improvements to the grounds, it is likely that the two friends planned much of it together, with Barrett probably deferring to Miller's advice. In April 1744 Barrett wrote:

> You ask me how, upon so little acquaintance, I repose such trust in you? My answer to this shall be; the character Lords Deerhurst and Coventry gave of you and which I experienced, viz., that there is a certain simplicity and ingenuity in your Carriage and Discourse which in a week discovers your worth and goodness as much as if one had known you a year; and without any Compliment, from the first time I saw you I became so much prejudiced (if you may call it prejudice) in your favour that I from thenceforward desired nothing more than the happiness of your friendship.

In June 1744 Barrett thought that:

> I fancy that Lord North and you will be acquainted this summer; see if I am not a true prophet? I am sure he is happy to have you so near him. I wish it had been my good fortune to have been your neighbour, I should have valued my Place at two years purchase more for that advantage …

Barrett asked Miller's help in other ways. In September 1745, when expecting Miller's arrival, he wrote asking Miller if he could procure a suitable new horse for him – 'pray don't get me a prancing horse which is such a one as I know you Love' – and also enquiring if he knew of a suitable bailiff for Belhus, for 'I have now above 500 acres of land in my hands besides my Park and have no Steward or bailif to manage for me …'.

On 31 January 1748/9, Barrett reported to Miller about what he had been doing:

> I must tell you that I have made my River as wide as Ld. Norths and have open'd up Springs there so much that even before yᵉ Rains yᵉ waste water would have turned an overshot Mill. Besides this I have planted above 200 Elms yᵉ least of them above 20 foot high & many of them 30; these I have put in yᵉ grove behind my house where there were any spots thin of trees; and on yᵉ South lawn skirting along yᵉ west side of it, which will have a very good effect; another thing I have done (& a great piece of work it is) I have ploughed up all yᵉ ground round about my house (above 60 acres) which I do in order to clean it thoroughly and to lay it down quite smooth and fine; in order to which I am preparing a Dunghill of Chalk Marsh Earth and Dung; as Big as my House; to spread all over it.[24]

The detail and descriptions in this letter show that Miller must have known the grounds at Belhus well, and also have been familiar with Barrett's plans. From the reference to Lord North's 'river' it looks as if Miller had been advising Barrett on a similar scheme to that at Wroxton. Barrett's casual mention of the use of such large trees, and so many of them, suggests that this was not an unusual project; further, that he was fully expecting them all to grow. The moving of such large trees, although still considered difficult today, appears to have been something which 18th-century landowners undertook with reasonable expectations of success.

There was a later phase of building at Belhus in the 1750s, after the return of Barrett and his wife from a stay abroad following the death of their daughter. Miller was again much involved with the interior Gothic work, but it is probable that his visits to Essex became less frequent, for Barrett employed Capability Brown at Belhus from 1753-63, perhaps on Miller's own recommendation. In the early 1770s Richard Woods was employed, and probably gave the Long Pond its final form. Brown was employed at Belhus again in 1774.

Since the unfortunate sale of the property to London County Council and the subsequent demolition of the house, the grounds have been extensively redeveloped, and, as Dorothy Stroud remarks, 'nothing remains of the delectable scenes which had once been the apple of Lord Dacre's eye'.[25]

Packington

Packington Hall lies between Birmingham and Coventry. The predominantly light soil has many springs and a relatively high water table. In 1537 the manor was bought by John Fisher, the tenant of Kenilworth Abbey and Steward to the Earl of Warwick. Fisher built a new house, possibly the present Packington Old Hall, and his son enclosed land to make a park. Subsequent descendants all contributed to the beautification of the grounds. The first baronet made the Great Pool and 'much adorned this seat' c.1620s, and Sir Clement, the second baronet, laid out new gardens in 1666, and enlarged the park in 1674. Sir Clement's wife, Jane Lane, assisted Charles II to escape from England after the battle of Worcester. Their son, the third baronet, married the daughter of Humphrey Jennens, the Birmingham ironmaster, and his work is probably that described by the traveller John Macky, in 1732. Macky wrote that the Hall was 'new, and very beautiful; in the Middle of a spacious Park, with fine gardens, Fish-ponds, and a Decoy for Ducks; and may altogether vye with the best seats in England'. In 1729 the estate passed through marriage to Heneage Finch, the 2nd Earl of Aylesford.

Lord Guernsey, later the 3rd Earl, was part of the circle of Warwickshire gentry and nobility who were carrying out estate improvements. Evidence for Miller's involvement at Packington comes from a number of letters written to him from Lord Guernsey between 1746 and 1756. The two families used to visit each other regularly, and Guernsey was an enthusiastic supporter of the initiative to rebuild the Shire Hall at Warwick, designed by Miller and built 1752-8. He married the youngest daughter of the Duke of Somerset, whose dowry of £50,000 provided the finance for extensive improvements to the grounds, new stables (1756-8) and a new Palladian exterior for the Hall (1763-81).[26]

In July 1746 Guernsey wrote to Miller to say that he was expecting him with Sir Edward Turner at Packington, where he had been 'considering the proper place for a Gothic building, & flattered myself that the Foundation was laid by this time, & would be ready for the Reception of a white Ground & red knots by the end of the Year.' On the back of this letter there is a rough sketch of a crenellated castle tower, perhaps an octagon, with a wider defensive wall at its base which is also crenellated.[27] Is this Guernsey's

Gothic building? Did Packington ever have a mock castle designed by Miller? If so, no trace remains of it today. If it was actually built, it would have been the first mock castle tower to have been built by Miller for anyone other than himself.

In 1748 Guernsey wrote to Miller to say how disappointed he was at not being able to accompany him to Charles Jennens' estate at Gopsall. Packington being on Miller's way home, Guernsey hoped he would visit him, for 'I long to have some talk with you about my Pool and other Improvements, as well as of what has been done and is doing at Gopsall.' In a letter dated 20 January 1749/50 and written from London, Sir Edward Turner mentioned that 'Guernsey grumbles because he had no Opportunity of hearing your Lecture during the Holidays, upon intended stables at Packington.' Later that year, in April, Guernsey wrote to Miller to arrange a definite meeting at Packington 'as I should be glad of your advice in making some alterations.' In December Guernsey wrote to Miller, who was staying with Sir Roger Newdigate at Arbury:

> … Sr Roger and Ly Newdigate having promis'd us a visit for 3 or 4 days, I hope they will come with you, & as we shall return it soon after I shall then have an opportunity of considering Sr Roger's Improvements more fully than in a short visit. I want sadly the joynt opinion of yourself & Sr Roger, for placing the Cascade here, as my plantations depend on it.[28]

Guernsey hoped to pick up some hints on cascades, and if possible to obtain a promise of a visit from both men to come to Packington at the same time to advise him. In 1750, Capability Brown was commissioned to produce designs for the improvements at Packington. This was one of Brown's very earliest commissions after Lord Cobham's death in 1749, and Miller, who knew Brown's abilities, no doubt suggested to Guernsey that Brown was the man to put the plans for Packington into practice. Brown produced a sketch plan showing the proposed new Hall Pool, to be created from several old fishponds below the Hall. This plan required the felling of the greater part of the western avenue leading away from the Hall, the making of a new approach drive and extensive alterations to the woodlands. In Brown's finished plan of 1751 the new Hall Pool makes a dramatic long sheet of water, varying greatly in width. When the Hall Pool was drained recently, the outlines of the old fishponds could be seen clearly.

The creation of the Hall Pool is not suggested in any of the correspondence between Guernsey and Miller, so this may have been Brown's own idea. Brown's plans for a gently curving western end to the Great Pool were not put into effect, and the present shape of the Pool is slightly different from that on Brown's plan. Not all the belts and clumps appear to have been planted, and Brown also shows on his plan designs for 'My Lady's Lodge' and a Grotto, which were not actually built.

On 3 November 1756 Guernsey wrote hoping that he would have the pleasure of Miller's company for a day or two:

> I want much advice and shall not know what to do unless you will afford me a little assistance under the difficulties of building and planting. Besides, I long much to see you & I know the Christmas Holy Days are appropriated to another part of the Country [Miller used to go to Sir Edward Turner's for Christmas], & therefore unless you will in friendship take a dirty journey at this time I shall despair of seeing you before all mischief is done.[29]

The tone of Lord Guernsey's letters suggests that he felt quite dependent upon Miller's experience for his alterations, Miller's advice being of overriding importance to him before all Brown's suggestions were actually implemented on the ground.

Miller may well have designed the alterations to the Great Pool, to the east of the Hall, which were also carried out, probably by Brown, in the early 1750s. The Duck Decoy mentioned by Macky in 1732 was on this Pool, and quantities of fish from the Pool used to be sent regularly to the London markets. The outline of the Pool was made less formal, the dam was increased in size, and a cascade was made (as mentioned in Guernsey's letter of 1750) to take the water away to the lower fishponds, which eventually became the single Hall Pool. Dams, cascades and the informalising of pools were subjects where Miller's expertise had already been called into service, for example at Farnborough and Wroxton.

The stables at Packington (illus.79, pg. 123) were built in 1756-8 by the Hiorn brothers of Warwick, master masons who also built the Shire Hall to Miller's design. A country estate was totally dependent on a large number of horses; riding horses for the family and employees, carriage horses, at least double the number required to pull a chaise in case of lameness or other troubles, and heavy horses for work on the land. Twenty-five to thirty horses of various types would have been the minimum required for the smooth running of an estate. Stables demanded relatively simple architecture, being on 'the lowest rung of polite architecture'.[30] Their design, however, required good proportions, particularly since, as at Packington, they were usually adjacent to the house where the exterior architecture, at least, would be seen by all arrivals. The rebuilding of the stables at Packington was therefore an important commission. The stable building at Packington, a four-square Palladian plan enclosing a courtyard, with squat towers at each corner, is reminiscent of the quadrangle of the stables at Wilton, but the façades with their towers are like a simpler version of Hagley Hall, built at about the same time. The Tuscan portico, with its large overhanging pediment, is similar to Inigo Jones' design for St Paul's, Covent Garden. As with the Dairy at Hagley, the Tuscan order is used here for a rural building, as thought appropriate by Palladio. Miller has been suggested as the author of the stables,[31] although there is no definite evidence other than Sir Edward Turner's letter, in which despite his flippant manner he suggests that Miller had indeed provided the design.

Although it is clear that Miller was very much involved with the improvements at Packington, and that Guernsey had come to rely on his expertise, without more evidence it is not possible to assess the exact nature of Miller's total contribution.

In 1789 Joseph Bonomi designed the neo-classical church in the Park, which now contains Handel's organ, left by Charles Jennens to the family in his will. Bonomi also decorated the interiors of the new mansion, including the Pompeian Gallery. The 19th century saw further gardens and terraces, and a new conservatory. The Hall was restored after extensive fire damage in 1979, and the Hall and the estate remain the seat of the Earls of Aylesford. The property is kept in excellent repair, despite the proximity of two large urban conurbations.

Gopsall

Miller was called in to advise Charles Jennens at Gopsall, his estate in Leicestershire, in the autumn of 1748. The Gopsall estate is situated in open rolling farmland, about fifteen miles due east of Leicester. The site had no history as an estate prior to the purchase of the land in 1685 by the ironmaster Hugh Jennens (d.1689) from Erdington, Birmingham. His grandson Charles inherited the estate and a large fortune in 1747. He built a new Palladian mansion at a cost of more than £100,000, and greatly enlarged and landscaped the area of surrounding ornamental grounds.[32] Jennens (1700-73), a patron of the arts, himself wrote the words and chose the texts for several of Handel's oratorios, including the libretto for *Messiah* which was partly composed at Gopsall. Samuel Johnson gave Jennens the title of 'Solyman the Magnificent'.

The only positive evidence for Miller's involvement at Gopsall is to be found in a letter written by Lord Guernsey, of Packington Hall, in Warwickshire, to Miller on 7 October 1748:

> I am very much disappointed in not being able to meet you at M[r] Stratford's in order to attend you to Gopsall, but I have now Company with me & expect a gentleman to call on me to day, so that I am obliged to stay at home. M[r] Stratford (of Merevale Hall) I am told is not return'd yet out of Leicestershire, so that you will certainly be at Gopsall to night, where I hope you may be of great service to M[r] Jennens. Packington I believe you will find your nearest way home, where I hope Mudge will bring you tomorrow, for I long to have some talk with you about my Pool & other Improvements, as well as of what has been done & is doing at Gopsall.[33]

Charles Jennens' aunt had married into Lord Guernsey's family, so he and Jennens were cousins. Obviously Lord Guernsey had suggested to Jennens that Miller's talents would be useful to him at Gopsall. Jennens and Miller had many interests in common, including strong religious beliefs, a great interest in music and the arts, and a knowledge of classical languages.

Historical evidence for the landscaping of the new Hall is scanty, apart from some plans and drawings for Gopsall which are held in the Drawings Collection of the Royal Institute of British Architects (RIBA).[34] William and David Hiorn, the masons from Warwick whom Miller had used on previous projects, signed some of the plans of the ancillary buildings for the mansion, and also designs for the new gardens. Miller employed the Hiorns to prepare plans and execute his designs for other buildings, and it is probable, though not certain, that the same procedure was followed at Gopsall. There also exists an unsigned and undated painting of the new Hall and its landscape, showing a number of garden buildings and the Great Pond. Both mansion and landscape came to a sad end in the 20th century, when the 4th Earl Howe, a distant descendant of Jennens, overspent on new landscaping and lavish shooting parties arranged for King Edward VII. The estate was sold in 1919. Deterioration and army occupation during the Second World War spelled the final demise of both the mansion, which was demolished, and the designed landscape, which was returned to agriculture. It now requires imagination as well as a study of the few plans which remain, to reconstruct in the mind's eye the designed estate of which Charles Jennens was so proud.

In 1749, two years after Jennens had inherited Gopsall, he commissioned a plan of the house and immediate grounds by John Grundy junior, 1719-83. John Grundy senior had worked for Jennens' father, and both Grundys were surveyors and water engineers of note. The family had moved to Spalding in the 1730s, and between 1746 and 1748 Grundy

81 *Gopsall Park, Leicestershire, plan by John Grundy, for Charles Jennens, 1749. The unusual shape of the Great Pond, and the great length of the retaining dam, suggest that these features were not by Miller but by Grundy, who specialised in the engineering of dams. The Open Temple, most likely designed by Miller, was sited to the south of the Great Pond in the area marked 'Bilson Hill'.*

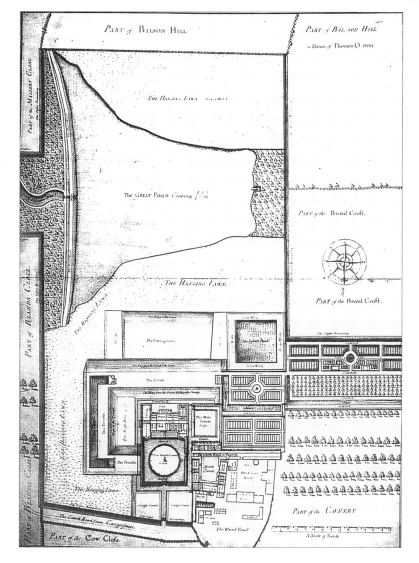

was working on a dam and the lake at Grimsthorpe, in Lincolnshire.[35] The Grundy plan illustrates a transitional period in landscaping style, with formal beds and water features, surrounded by sculpted grass slopes and terraces. Such sculpted terraces were already going out of fashion at this date, being more reminiscent of Bridgeman's work, or Burlington's early designs at Chiswick. Beyond the gardens on the south front a large irregularly shaped water feature known as the Great Pond was made, with an informally designed landscape partly enclosed with woods beyond the Pond. The plan was made the year after Miller's autumn visit. Two later plans in the RIBA archives show details of changes in the evolving landscape design, with which Miller may have been involved, since the writing on them suggests that they were by the Hiorns. Some of the formal beds have been replaced with areas of grass in between new wide beds marked 'flowering shrubs'.

The rather awkward shape of the Great Pond does not compare with the fluid and more natural outlines of Miller's pools at Farnborough, or the informalising of the

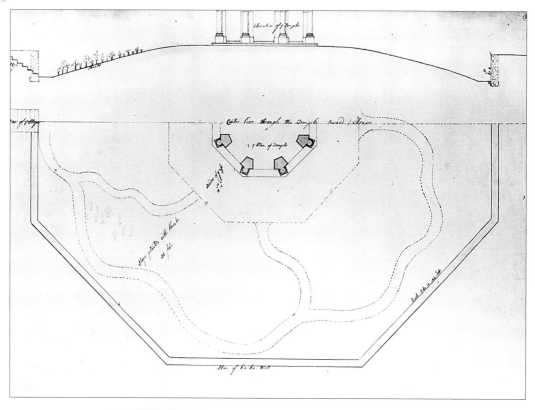

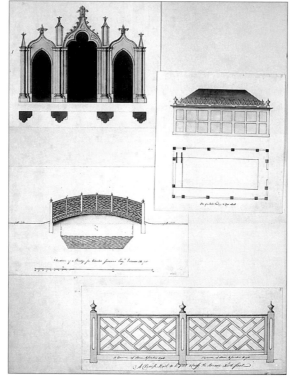

82   *Gopsall Park. The Open Temple, a section with plan of the sunken mound, showing access steps, paths, and ornamental shrubs graded for height.*

83   *Gopsall Park, designs, some in the Chinese manner, prepared for Charles Jennens for his landscape by the Hiorns brothers and ascribed to Miller.*

outline of the great Pool at Wroxton, and it seems probable that Grundy was the man responsible for the Great Pond at Gopsall. The dam here is of an extraordinary length, which must have greatly increased the chances of the dam failing somewhere, despite Grundy's advanced techniques in making his dams with clay cores. Whatever the reason, the Pond had gone by the late 19th century, for neither dam nor Pond is shown on the O.S. maps of this period. The Pond was definitely made, however, for the old clay lining still impedes modern ploughing along the exact line marked on Grundy's plan.

It is much more likely that Miller was concerned with the design of the outer landscape. Beyond the Great Pond was built a temple known as the Open Temple, the woods behind forming the skyline. In the Grundy plan this land is shown as tenanted. Perhaps Jennens took it back from his tenant to form the new landscape, for the high land forming the skyline beyond the Great Pond, Bilson Hill, was the obvious place for a distant eyecatcher. Woods along the crest of this hill were no doubt planted at this time. They provided the necessary backdrop for the Temple, and Miller's designs often included the clothing of hilltops with planting.

The Open Temple was the most important building in Jennens' designed landscape. It was dedicated to the memory of his friend the classical scholar Edward Holdsworth (1684-1746). Holdsworth and Jennens were both 'non-jurors' – they believed, on Biblical authority, that it was wrong to oppose a rightful ruler, and so would not swear allegiance to George I. Holdsworth lost a Fellowship at Magdalen College, Oxford, on account of his belief. Jennens gave financial support to 'non-jurors'. The Open Temple had within it an urn on a monument carrying a lengthy inscription to Holdsworth, and later a finely carved statue of 'Religion' was placed on the dome. This, an unusual subject for an 18th-century statue, was carved by Louis Francois Roubiliac in 1762. Roubiliac was probably introduced to Jennens by Handel, for in 1738 he had carved a statue of the composer for Vauxhall Gardens. The Greek inscription around the frieze of the Temple is taken from the first Epistle to the Corinthians, and reads: 'Thanks be to God who gives us the victory through Our Lord Jesus Christ. A Temple of Victory.'

There are elevations in the RIBA collection for the Open Temple both by James Paine and the Hiorns, the latter's drawing also illustrating a flat plan. Paine has been credited with the building, but enough of the ruins remain to see that the bases of the pillars accord with those on the Hiorns' plan, enabling a positive identification of the temple as that drawn by the Hiorns, probably actually designed by Miller. This is confirmed by the appearance of the Temple in the contemporary painting. There is also a plan by the Hiorns of the ha-ha encircling the mound on which The Open Temple was sited. The construction of the Temple and its mound is unusual. As is shown in the section drawing, the mount is sunk, with a ha-ha wall at the edge of the site. The Temple on its mound is therefore in a complete enclosure which could only be entered by steps leading through the brick ha-ha wall from the woodland behind. The section shows that the shrubs on the mound were graded, taller ones being planted on the lower slopes and smaller ones near the flattened top where the temple was built. This design is similar to that used on the mound of the Temple at Wroxton. From the Hall the eye was drawn across to the Temple with no visual interruption, and the design also gave the Temple and its mound protection from the animals in the parkland. The approach to the Temple may have been along the top of the long dam and through the woodland, with an unexpected view of the Temple as one emerged from the woods. Certainly the situation of the Temple on its sunken mound would have caused surprise when first seen at close quarters. From the Temple there were fine views, including that back to the Hall across the Pond. Part of the deer park could be seen to the west, and there was an extensive view north-east beyond the estate to distant higher ground. The whole design is consistent with Miller's ingenious approach to the siting of his buildings.

The Temple partly collapsed in 1835, and in 1857 the statue was given to the Leicestershire Museum by the then owner, Earl Howe. The urn remained at Gopsall until 1951, but now both are kept at the Belgrave Hall Museum, Leicester.

Other drawings in the RIBA collection include elevations for three structures in the Chinese style, and a plan for a Gothic façade. The drawings are all by the Hiorns with the exception of that for the Gothic façade. This is both unsigned and untitled. William Hawkes is of the opinion that some of the drawings in the RIBA collection are definitely by Miller, and this design has marked similarities with the Museum, a building which Miller

84 *The remains of The Temple at Gopsall. The nettles at the base are covering the mound, around which a small path once wound among flowering shrubs.*

designed for the grounds at Enville the following year. One of the drawings, entitled 'Plan of a Timber Building to Cover a Boat', shows an elegant long building with a decorative strip along the eaves, and other detailing suggesting Chinese influence. Another drawing depicts a small bridge with detailing matching that on the boathouse. These drawings seem to refer to a pool which was fed by the stream leaving the Great Pond. The old streamline is marked by land which floods easily and always lies wet, and ploughing still uncovers areas of the clay lining here, although the watercourse is now carried underground in drainage pipes. Miller's involvement in the landscaping associated with this pool was suggested by the site of a boathouse shown on the late 19th century O.S. map. A site visit revealed that around the pool the line of a small path could still be made out, encircling the pool and set among trees and shrubs on a definite raised bank. On a promontory some very old yews remain, together with other large trees nearby. The whole area is overgrown. The bridge may have been built to carry the path across the entry of the stream from the Great Pond into the pool. It is much too small to have been designed for any part of the Great Pond in front of the Hall, the only other likely situation for a bridge. The Chinese structures are contemporary with other Chinese buildings at both Honington and Wroxton. The design of the bridge, in particular, is very similar to the small Chinese bridge at Honington, where Miller was advising in 1749. Boating was very much a part of the contemporary landscape scene. A boat is shown on the Wroxton plan, and on one of the Honington paintings, and was used regularly on the river at Alscot and the canals at Arbury. At Gopsall the winding path along the raised bank around the pool is reminiscent of a pattern repeated in Miller's work elsewhere, where meandering paths run through narrow strips of open woodland alongside water. Such features were created at Farnborough, Honington and Wroxton, and also on Miller's own estate at Radway following the Radway Enclosure Act.

The Gopsall design represents an important halfway house in the development of the natural landscape style. The terraced and sloped lawns near the Hall are typical of the landscaping of 20-30 years earlier, such as that found at Claremont, at Castle Hill in Devon, and also at Stanway in Gloucestershire. All these sites have or had geometrically shaped and terraced lawns, those at Claremont being designed by Sir John Vanbrugh, at Castle Hill they are thought to be by the owner, Hugh, 1st. Lord Fortescue, Earl of Clinton, and at Stanway the work may have been by Bridgeman. Perhaps Jennens did not want to alter his father's designs completely, but just had the Great Pond made and the outer grounds laid out in the new informal manner. Did Miller plan the outer landscape? It is a matter for regret that both house and gardens have gone, and that there is not more archival evidence concerning Jennens' extensive and costly designs for his grounds.

Arbury

Arbury Hall and estate is situated in fairly flat and well-watered countryside about four miles south-west of Nuneaton, but despite its proximity to the town the estate remains remarkably rural. The site was originally monastic. In 1586, John Newdegate exchanged his estate at Harefield, in Essex, for that of the Elizabethan house at Arbury. The owner of Harefield, Edmund Anderson, had found that it was inconveniently far from London. John's lawyer grandson Richard purchased Astley Castle, adjoining Arbury, and also bought back the Harefield estate. He was created a baronet in 1677. Sir Richard's son, also Sir Richard, built the chapel within the house, which has carving by Grinling Gibbons and outstanding plasterwork by Edward Martin, of London. He also built the stable block, for which he commissioned an entrance design from Sir Christopher Wren, and was particularly interested in his formal gardens. In 1708 a drawing by Henry Beighton depicts the formal gardens, with ornamental gazebos fronting the entrance court.[36]

Sir Roger, Sir Richard's youngest grandson, eventually succeeded to the estate, aged 14, in 1733. During his long life he transformed the house into one of the finest Gothic mansions in the country, and also carried out extensive alterations to the grounds. Educated at Oxford during the same period as Miller, he developed major businesses in both coalmining and canal building, and was MP for Oxford for many years. Although Sir Roger was a firm Tory and many of Miller's friends were Whigs, they had much in common, including a love of history and the classics as well as a firm adherence to the Church of England and a paternalistic approach to their local communities. They remained on intimate terms, exchanging family visits at least as late as 1756. Sir Roger and his wife Sophia took a great interest in landscaping projects, taking their first tour in 1748 when Sir Roger sketched the buildings which they saw, and Sophia kept a journal, which included an entry on Farnborough and the Pentagon Temple.[37]

85 *Drawing of Arbury Hall. Miller designed the first Gothic bay window for the west end of the south front, built 1750-52, and a second matching window for the east end, shown here, was built in 1761 by Henry Keene.*

Although there is an extensive archive in the Warwickshire Record Office on Arbury, actual evidence for Miller's work at Arbury is limited to sketches made for Lady Newdigate's dressing room, in the Gothic style,[38] and references made to Miller's design for the new Gothic bow window for the south front of the mansion. The detailing, such as the crocketed spires above the angles of the bow, and the quatrefoil roundels above the lower windows, is typical of Miller's architectural work elsewhere, including that at Radway Grange in 1745-6 and at Adlestrop in the 1750s. The attribution of landscaping at Arbury to Miller is due to circumstantial and stylistic evidence, apart from one letter written by Lord Guernsey to Miller in 1750, quoted below.

The drive to the Hall, originally a straight approach from the Nuneaton road, was altered to a sinuous curve, approaching the gardens over a small canal and delaying a proper sight of the Hall until the entrance sweep in front of the stables had been passed. There is a family tradition at Arbury that Miller was consulted about this alteration. The round towers and lodges forming the entrance to the drive from the Nuneaton road were not designed by Miller, but were one of the last buildings to be erected by Sir Roger, probably as late as the beginning of the 19th century.[39]

The first mention of new buildings in the grounds at Arbury is in 1748, when David Hiorn was paid for building an Orangery, a Rotunda and a Teahouse. William Hiorn was paid two guineas for a plan of Arbury in the same year, but it is not known whether the plan was for the new work at the Hall or for landscape buildings.[40] The Rotunda has now gone. The Teahouse, which was in need of repair, is a small circular domed building hidden away in the woods, built especially for Sophia. It is of stonework in front with a brick service area hidden behind. The Teahouse has classical detailing, and inside has a coffered ceiling. Small niches around the wall were probably originally for statues or busts. It was finished with paintwork in two shades of blue. A pool was excavated in front of

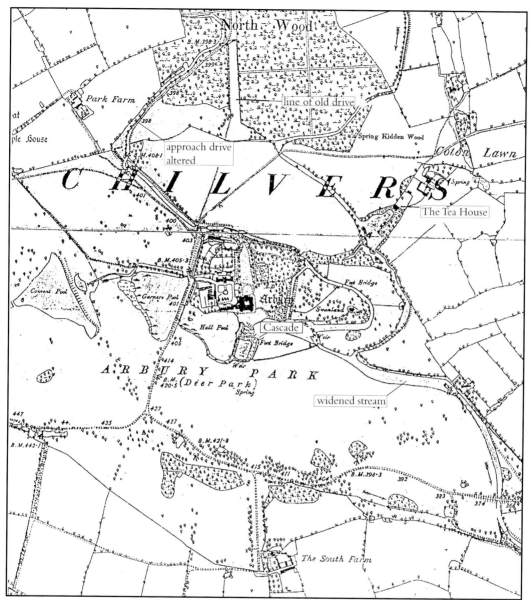

86 *Arbury, taken from the six-inch O.S. map, c.1880s, showing the newly landscaped grounds. The new drive curves in from the west, the Hall Pool has been formed from old fishponds, and the stream below the Hall to the east has been widened to form long, thin lakes typical of Miller's work elsewhere, such as those at Farnborough and Sudbury.*

the Teahouse, surrounded by a raised walkway. It must have made an attractive and tranquil summer retreat. A shaded walk around the pool could be enjoyed, or a boat ride could be taken from the canal surrounding the Hall gardens up to the Teahouse, where tea would be provided from the little room behind. David Hiorn worked regularly for Miller as a master mason, so it is likely that Miller was responsible for the design of these buildings, or at least that his was the guiding hand. In Miller's diary entry for 25 August 1750 he mentioned that he 'Wrote to Sr R.Newdig^{te} by Hitchcox'. This suggests that Hitchcox, Miller's own mason, was going over to Arbury, as normally Miller would have sent his letter by the post. Hitchcox may have been working under or with Hiorns.

In 1748 Sir Roger began to Gothicise the Hall, and in 1749 Miller recorded in his diary that he stayed at Arbury from 8 to 19 December. During his stay Miller was designing Sir Roger's new Gothic bow window, and teaching him how to draw Gothic arches. Sir Roger, on the other hand, showed Miller his drawings of Roman antiquities from his Grand Tour, and taught Miller perspective. The two men must also have walked the grounds discussing the planned 'improvements', although there are no specific references to work in the grounds. In 1750 Sir Roger was altering the lake and constructing the rockwork and cascade in front of the house. On 30 August, Miller recorded in his diary that Sir Roger came to stay at Radway and there was a discussion 'ab^t building &c.' – the writing is not completely clear. The following day they were again discussing 'building' at supper. On 2 December, Lord Guernsey wrote to Miller:

> On Saturday L^d and Lady Andover leave us which may possibly prevent my seeing you at Arbury, … but if I can I have some Intention of riding over on Wednesday to breakfast, as I shall be glad to see the Cascade and Bow window while you are there.[41]

From Lord Guernsey's letter it is obvious that Miller was again visiting Arbury at the beginning of December 1750, and the tone of the letter suggests strongly that Miller had been involved in the design of the cascade as well as the bow window. (Miller's diary for 1749/50 ends in September 1750.)

From a perusal of an Estate Plan of c.1680-1700 and the drawing by Henry Beighton of 1708,[42] it can be seen that prior to Sir Roger's improvements there was a series of fishponds, the stream from the lowest of these being led underground from the retaining dam into a rectangular narrow canal at the foot of the formal forecourt to the south of the Hall. In the Beighton drawing a carriage can be seen arriving at the gates to this forecourt, and it looks as if there are steps down to the canal on the right. Sir Roger altered the whole approach to the Hall, demolishing the garden gazebos and transforming the south forecourt and the formal gardens beyond. He also joined the two lowest fishponds to make one large pool in front of the Hall. Here there is a large retaining dam below which is a cascade designed in a romantic style, with massive boulders forming the drop, possibly to remind Sir Roger of those he had seen in his travels through the Italian mountains. Beyond the cascade is an overflow pool. This plan is reminiscent of that at Farnborough, made by Miller a few years earlier, although the waterfall there is more formal, being constructed of unevenly spaced steps of stone rather than boulders. At Farnborough it had been necessary to build up the ground considerably to provide the necessary height, and much smaller rocks were used than those at Arbury. From the pool below the cascade at Arbury the water was led down a retaining weir, beyond which the small stream from the Teahouse pool joined the main stream. This stream flowed on round the edge of the parkland to the mill some half a mile away. The stream was widened for a stretch, making a long narrow lake or 'river', which can be seen clearly in the 1880s O.S. map. Although canals were Sir Roger's speciality, the widening of small streams in this manner was a type of design which Miller used at Farnborough, Honington, Alscot and Sudbury, suggesting that this work was his. The informal gardens at Arbury are surrounded by paths and canals with bridges, the paths sometimes crossing the canals, sometimes each other. The stonework is solid and all of a similar age. There is an ice-house quite near the Hall, built within the ornamental planted mound which was probably made from the spoil following the excavation of the pool. There is also a boathouse, and it is known that Sir Roger enjoyed taking his wife and a boating party out on the small waterways surrounding his home; indeed, he is traditionally supposed to have been able to travel to London by boat from his home.

Miller recorded visiting Arbury once in his diary for 1756, on 29 November. He had been to Packington, where he had been walking with Lord Guernsey; then they went over to Arbury, where Miller again recorded walking with Sir Roger.

Although it is not possible to do more than suggest Miller's involvement with the alterations to the grounds at Arbury, it seems fairly clear that he had a hand in several aspects of the landscaping. The most important of these were the significant alteration to the approach road, the building of the Teahouse, and the creation of Hall Pool, the cascade and the lower stream system.

Today the Hall and the gardens are well maintained by the present Viscount Daventry.

Wimpole

The mock Ruined Castle at Wimpole was designed for Philip Yorke, Lord Chancellor and 1st Earl of Hardwicke, in 1749. The estate at Wimpole has always been strategically important due to its proximity both to Cambridge and to the Great North Road, the original Roman Ermine Street, and it was also mentioned in Domesday Book. The estate covered at least 11,000 acres during the heyday of the mid-18th century, and still comprises some 2,400 acres. The land is fairly flat, the soil being predominantly heavy Gault clay. In 1707 a Knyff and Kip engraving illustrated the great estate with its extensive formal gardens, then belonging to the

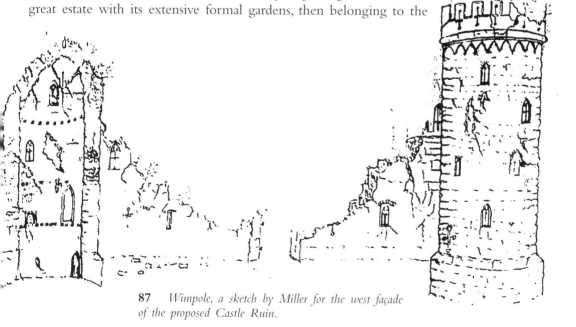

87 *Wimpole, a sketch by Miller for the west façade of the proposed Castle Ruin.*

88 *Wimpole, the*
Castle Ruin, finished
ink, wash and pencil
drawing by Miller.

2nd Earl of Radnor. Both the Earl of Radnor and the following owner, the 2nd Earl of Oxford, overspent and were forced to sell. When Lord Hardwicke bought the estate in 1739, he found a grand mansion recently extended by James Gibbs, with painted interiors by Thornhill. The grounds had been laid out between 1720 and 1725 for the Earl of Oxford by Charles Bridgeman, with new formal gardens and wildernesses with serpentine paths. Bridgeman's great south avenue extended for two miles and had a central vista 90 yards wide. This avenue survived until it fell victim to Dutch Elm disease in the 1970s.[43] When Hardwicke asked Miller to design him a mock ruin, Miller was being asked to follow in illustrious footsteps at one of the greatest estates in the east of the country. Miller must have been flattered by Lord Hardwicke's initial request to design a ruin for him at Wimpole, for Lord Hardwicke could have afforded to employ exactly whom he wished for his estate improvements.

On 1 June 1749 Miller received a letter from George Lyttelton asking him to design a ruined castle for the Lord Chancellor, who had both a suitable site and a quantity of old stone from his recent rebuilding of the parish church. Lyttelton wrote:

> Your great genius's in Architecture must expect to be importuned by your friends, of which I am going to give you a Proof. My Lord Chancellour told me, in a conversation I had with him lately, that he wanted to see the Plan of my Castle, having a mind to Build one at Wimple himself. Upon further Enquiry I found it would be better for him not to Copy mine, but have one upon something like the same Idea, but differing in many respects, particularly in this, that he wants no House or even room in it, but mearly the Walls and Semblence of an old castle to make an object from his House. At most he only desires to have a staircase carried up one of the Towers, and a leaded gallery half round it to stand in, and view the Prospect. It will have a fine Wood of Firrs for a backing behind it and will stand on an Eminence at a proper distance from His house ... With regard to the Dimensions ... you are not confined, but may make it of just what Height & Breadth you think fitt. He desired me to make his Compliments to you, and to say he would take it as a great Favour if you would sketch it out for him as soon as you conveniently can.

Miller replied at once to Hardwicke's request, for on 13 June Lyttelton wrote again to Miller:

> I have communicated your letter to my Ld. Chancellour and he desires me to Return you a great many thanks for it. The view of Wimple which you have seen will give you a pretty just Idea of the Place where he designs Building the Ruin. It is a Hill about half a mile from the House to which the Ground rises gently all the way. My Lord agrees to your notion of having some Firrs before part of the Walls. As the Back View will be immediately closed by the Wood there is no Regard to be had to it, nor to the Left side but only to the Front and Right side as you look from the House … As my Lord designs it meerly for an Object he would have no Staircase nor Leads in any of the Towers, but meerly the Walls so built as to have the appearance of a Ruined Castle. For Materials He has Freestone, or a mixture of Flint Pebbles and other stone, of which an Old Church in the Parish is built, and also Bricks in his neighbourhood.[44]

Hardwicke had already changed his ideas about having a staircase to enable visitors to go up the tower to see the view back to the Hall – perhaps on account of the extra expense. On 18 July Lyttelton wrote again to Miller : 'My Ld. Chancellour desires me to Return you his Thanks for the Castle. He seems mighty well satisfied with it, but says he shall Deferr the Building it till next year, and consider it upon the spot when he goes to Wimple this summer …'

In the spring Miller wrote to George Lyttelton suggesting that he should send his mason Hitchcox to Wimpole in preparation for building the castle. Hardwicke, however, was in no hurry to build. He asked instead that Miller meet him with the 'new Draught of the Plan' when he was next in Town. On 1 May Miller duly dined with the Lord Chancellor and his family in London, when he was invited to go to Wimpole the following September. He stayed at Wimpole from 11 to 14 August. On his first morning his diary entry records: '… rode out after bft with L^d C Mr Yorke to the clump. Surveyed Ground for Castle. & rode in ye Pk. 3h:.' The clump was on the top of Johnson's Hill, the chosen site for the Castle ruin half a mile to the north of the Hall. In the evening he was 'looking over' the Castle plans, then on 14 September he 'Came f^m Wimple at 7. after sketching out the Castle' before he left to visit Cambridge.

In the Wimpole archives there are four drawings which have traditionally been attributed to Miller. Three are elevations in pen and ink with pencil, and the fourth is a perspective drawing in pen and ink with coloured wash over pencil. They are done on similar paper, are contemporary with each other, and are almost certainly Miller's. In the drawings the central three-storeyed tower is similar to that in his design for Hagley, though it has the addition of cross arrow slits to the castellation. Both designs have the ruined remains of two other corner towers and a ruined joining curtain wall, but the Wimpole drawing has additional Gothic windows in a wall which looks as if it were part of a great hall.[45] The drawings give a good 'feel' of the proposed building, in particular the finished perspective of the romantic ruin, which obviously appealed to the Lord Chancellor. Miller was to oversee the work on the ground in due course.

From Cambridge, Miller went to visit Nugent at Gosfield, from where he wrote to Charles Lyttelton, George's half brother:

… In about four hours I arrived at Wimple where I met with the kindest reception
you can imagine. His Lordship, by dint of good sense has done every thing which
suits the character of the place. I find about half the plan I sent him will fit the place
very well, and if it is well executed it will be a great improvement … Staid at Wimple
Wednesday and Thursday. My Lord is extremely chearfull and easy, and has a noble
constitution. I walked with him six Hours one day …[46]

The following February Miller wrote to George Lyttelton about the necessity of
getting the materials ready and digging the stone if the Castle was to be built that year.
He also wanted to send Hitchcox down to Wimpole to 'see the matterials the Country
affords' so that he would be able to furnish Hardwicke with a better assessment of the
cost. Miller was probably at Wimpole again that autumn, and he was certainly there in
1752 and 1753. He was able to offer Hardwicke some glass with the Yorke arms upon
it, and Hardwicke in return appointed a friend of Miller's to the living of Radway with
Ratley. In September 1756 Miller mentioned in his diary visiting Wimpole again, and on
September 13 was 'Looking over Jones designs' there, but there was no further mention
of the Castle. Miller must have been disappointed not to have seen his design put into
execution, despite the friendly reception he always had at Wimpole.

Lord Hardwicke died in 1764, but the Castle was not actually built until the early
1770s, when the 2nd Earl employed Capability Brown to erect it, probably with the
assistance of James Essex, a Cambridge architect. By that time Miller's own health was not
good enough for him to supervise the work. Brown decided to make some alterations to
Miller's design, to the disappointment of the Earl's wife, Jemima, Marchioness Grey, who
wrote to her daughter in 1772:

> The Tower is better for being raised, but the additions Mr Brown has quite changed
> from our plan, though he undertook to follow it and said he liked it. That is, he has
> 'Unpicturesqued' it by making it a mere continuous solid object, instead of a Broken
> one. The wall – which is still going on – is continued *entire* at the bottom from the
> whole Tower to the Broken one, and is to be *fractured* only in the upper half of the
> Gateway, which is, I believe, to resemble our design. However, as it makes altogether
> a greater object it won't do ill, and the upper part of wall, if well done, may yet be
> sufficiently varied.[47]

In altering Miller's plan Brown increased the height of the main tower to four storeys,
decorated it with string courses, more regular windows and arrow slits, and removed the
arrow slits from the castellations. The details of the two side walls were also altered, the
windows on the east being reduced to one larger one, and the wall to the west being
extended. The walls were built two feet thick and more than 200 feet in length, while the
three towers were 20 feet across. The stone used was the local 'clunch', with some carved
stone, on top of a brick base. The whole composition looks 'flatter' and has a rather less
natural appearance than Miller's original, and it was not built with the cracks due to 'age'
which William Gilpin had felt were essential. Gilpin wrote in 1808 that 'to give the stone
its mouldering appearance – to make the widening chink run naturally through all the
joints – to mutilate the ornaments … are great efforts of art.'[48] Miller's castle drawing has
been described in the 20th century by Gervase Jackson-Stops as more believable (than the
building actually erected) as a medieval ruin, with overhanging machicolations, cracks in

the masonry rather than smooth ashlar, no string courses, and fewer windows and arrow-loops. Perhaps Capability Brown wished the building to appear more his own and have less of the stamp of Miller's hand on it.

Brief mention should be made here of the new library window put up by Lord Hardwicke, the design of which is attributed to Miller. William Cole, antiquary and friend of Horace Walpole, stated that Miller had advised removing the large Chimney-piece in the library and making a bow-window to the park. The arms put up in the window were those mentioned above, which Miller had had copied from an original given to him by his architect friend Thomas Prowse.

Although previously it has been assumed that Miller only designed the ruined Castle at Wimpole, it is obvious both from the correspondence that has survived and from Miller's diaries that he was also giving Hardwicke advice on his landscaping. On his first visit to Wimpole in 1750 Miller recorded in his diary that he and Lord Hardwicke 'rode in ye Pk 3h: …W [went] to the new Garden in the Even^g …' as well as visiting the site for the ruined castle etc. On the following day, 13 September, he 'w. with L^d C^r to see the C^{ch} Park &c. 8h. [hours]. Lady Gy [the Marchioness Grey] & Mr Yk. With us p^t of the time.' Writing to Charles Lyttelton (see above), Miller also remarked that he had been walking for six hours with Lord Hardwicke. In 1756 he was again walking in the park, and also visited the kitchen gardens. These brief comments do not specifically refer to discussions on the landscaping, although almost certainly that is what the two men were doing. Hardwicke, a busy man, would not have been passing such long periods of time simply showing his visitor the pleasure grounds.

Hardwicke greatly valued Miller's advice, as the following three extracts from his letters to Miller reveal:

> 16 June 1752, Powis-House:
>
> … The pleasure which I have already received by your good Company at Wimple makes me rejoice extremely to hear of your kind intentions to favour me with it again. I hope then to be able to shew you some Improvements, & to profit by your good Tast; for I am now actually putting in execution the Scheme you have heard me talk of by opening the West side of the Garden to the Park Hill. The Walls are now actually pulling down, & the Sunk-Fence digging …

> 1 September 1752, Wimpole:
>
> … I shall be happy in your company before I go to London … the sooner the greater will be the favour. I shall then be able to shew you that I have made some progress in altering my Garden, and make no doubt to profit by the Light which Your superior Skill and Taste will afford me …

> 9 September 1753, Wimple
>
> I expect Mr Yorke and Lady Grey here this week, who will be vastly glad of your good company, as well as my self … Besides, I want to Shew You my Alterations; to have the advantage of your Judgement upon them, & how to improve them; and You know long days & fine Weather are considerable Ingredients in such Business …[49]

When finally built, the Castle 'Ruin' at Wimpole drew many favourable comments from the family. In 1774 Agneta Yorke wrote to her sister-in-law Lady Grey: 'The ruins have a noble effect from every part where they meet the eye; and are of such a magnitude and so well executed that tho I saw them begun and finished yet I can scarce persuade myself that they are artificial.' Mary Yorke, Lady Grey's daughter, wrote in 1785: 'The ruin is beautiful and will grow every year more so, as the ivy comes up about it. The colour of the stone, however, already begins to mellow.'[50] The Hon. John Byng, travelling through Cambridgeshire in 1790, thought them 'foolish, fantastic, mock ruins, unlike every thing they wou'd wish to represent';[51] but his criticisms depended largely on his mood, and he had waited unsuccessfully to be admitted at Wimpole. Repton thought the Castle picturesque, and wished to widen the view of it from the house by removing or 'loosening' the clumps of trees which framed the view. He also suggested a practical use for the ruin as a gamekeeper's house, which it became until the First World War.

The fame of the Castle 'Ruin' spread abroad when two drawings of it made by Lady Grey's elder daughter Lady Amabel were chosen for Catherine the Great's Frog Dinner Service of 944 pieces. Perhaps the most interesting comment on the Castle 'Ruin' is the engraving which was published anonymously in 1777. The four stanzas printed on the engraving point to the contrast between the chivalrous past and 'the Patriot Baronet, the Courtier Lord' of the 18th century, but underline the Whig ideology which sought to reinstate 'the manly Virtues of the Norman Line' and join these with the 'true science and just Taste ... of these Modern days'.

The 2nd Earl, like his father, was an antiquarian, and both he and his wife Lady Grey were particularly interested in the new landscaping. He asked James 'Athenian' Stuart to design a modern Italian loggia in a neo-Palladian style for the park, to compare with the 'ruin', and serve as a direct 'contrast between ancient and modern times'. The Castle hilltop site at Hagley and the one at Johnson's Hill at Wimpole both had associations with the Saxons or with the ancient Britons. The 2nd Earl was mirroring those earlier Whig ideals of his father, George Lyttelton and Sanderson Miller, who were looking back to the chivalry of the ancients, embodied in mock Castle 'ruins', while looking forward to the true Science and just Taste they hoped to create in their own age.[52]

The formal gardens to the north of the house, looking towards Johnson's Hill and the site of the Ruined Castle, were altered to a new informal design, as described by Jemima, Marchioness Grey in 1753, writing to her friend Mary Talbot:

> I have found here quite a new place, my Lord having now completed his gardens, and nothing ever made a greater change or a more different scene. Instead of straight gravel walks with borders and cross plots surrounded by walls, and views into the park through iron gates, there is now a large green lawn behind the house, bounded by clumps of trees and flowering shrubs, a broad serpentine walk through them, and enclosed with a sunk fence that lets the park quite into the garden.

Robert Greening made a new plan for these gardens in 1752.[53] His father, the Royal gardener, had originally been a nurseryman, and Greening's own expertise lay particularly in the development of kitchen gardens. At Wimpole he designed a large kitchen garden, and installed a hot wall heated by flues for the ripening of fruit grown against it. It is possible that Miller's suggestions were incorporated in Greening's plan, for the new clumps of trees shown on the plan would have framed the views toward the Park Hill which Hardwicke mentioned in his letter of 16 June 1752.

As at Hagley, the Castle Ruin at Wimpole is the most important landscape building in the park. The Castle Ruin and the whole estate are well kept up today by the National Trust, who were bequeathed the property in 1976.

Ingestre

Miller's next commission, a castellated tower, was designed for Lord Chetwynd at Ingestre in south Staffordshire. At the beginning of the 17th century Sir Walter Chetwynd inherited the estate of Ingestre and built a new Jacobean Hall. Sir Walter's grandson, also named Walter, restored the Hall and built the church, 1673-6, which was designed by Sir Christopher Wren. In 1698, the extensive formal gardens, the walks and the 'wilderness' were much admired by Celia Fiennes on her visit, though she also commented that Ingestre lacked springs, and 'marle' (a heavy soil similar to a clay) for lining lakes.

In 1735 John Chetwynd, the 2nd Viscount, inherited the estate and began to landscape the grounds to the north and the west of the Hall. On 1 June 1749 George Lyttelton wrote to Miller on Chetwynd's behalf asking Miller to design a Gothic tower for Ingestre. Lyttelton and Chetwynd knew each other through their parliamentary duties in London. Lyttelton commented that he had engaged Miller in a great deal of business 'first for myself, then for Lord Chetwynd and … for my Lord Chancellor'. On 18 June he wrote again:

> I entirely approve the design you have sent for Lord Chetwynd, and only wish I could see it from Hagley Park. It will be a noble object, and everyway answer the purpose; so I daresay my lord will be highly pleased with it, and very thankful to you.[54]

The tower was castellated in a manner similar to that of Edgehill Tower, but it was in the shape of a pentagon rather than an octagon, and the hood-moulds to the windows were square, while at Edgehill the windows were of a pointed Gothic design. The Tower is illustrated in an undated drawing made c.1836-7 by T. Peploe Wood when he was tutor to the children at Ingestre Hall.[55] The drawing confirms the pentagon shape, since only a pentagon would provide the view of the Tower showing three sides as illustrated in the Peploe Wood drawing. However, it is not known exactly how much of Miller's design was built, for several years earlier two visitors had described a Pentagon Tower which obviously predates Miller's design. A Pentagon Tower on its 'artificial eminence' was described by William Freman, visiting Ingestre in 1743, who likened it to the Grecian marble Tower at Leghorn, Italy.[56] Inigo Jones had visited Leghorn, and the buildings and piazza there are thought to have influenced his designs for the Covent Garden church and piazza development for the Earl of Bedford in the 1630s. It would be interesting to be able to compare the earlier tower at Ingestre with Miller's later design, particularly with Miller's interest in Jones' work. Philip Yorke also commented on a tower – Gothic in design – after his visit in 1748. What is the explanation? Was there more than one tower? If there was only one, had it already been altered for Yorke to refer to it as Gothic? When Capability Brown was called in to landscape the park, he illustrated only one tower on his plan of 1756. It seems probable that Miller was asked to provide a design for a tower in the Gothic style so that Lord Chetwynd could alter the exterior of the existing tower along more fashionably Gothic 'medieval' lines.

The Tower was demolished in 1850, due to a series of murders carried out there by the gamekeeper, and the site is now overgrown and lies within recently planted woodland.

A site visit revealed pieces of stone, some of which were carved and may have been part of the square hood-moulds, among the undergrowth covering the site. The site itself is at the head of a sloping earth ramp, terminating in a wall of large sandstone ashlar blocks, the wall being about five feet high and constructed in the shape of four sides of a pentagon. The sandstone blocks matched those used on parts of the Hall. On the Brown map, a copy of which is held at Ingestre Hall, the Tower itself is clearly marked as a pentagon, and the ramp is also shown, with planting either side of it directing the eye down to the Rotunda in the park. From the top of the tower Ingestre Hall itself would have been visible, while in the opposite direction the outlook was over the neighbouring estate of Tixall. It is possible that Miller may have been responsible for the directional planting, and for raising the original height of the tower to obtain these views of the estate. He may also have been responsible for recommending Brown to Lord Chetwynd.

Other landscape structures at Ingestre included a Doric Rotundo on a bastion, a Pavilion, thought to be designed by Trubshaw in 1752, and a Triumphal Arch. The Rotundo has been moved to the estate at Tixall, but the Pavilion, which was also built on a mound and which closed the west end of a vista from the Hall, has recently been restored by the Landmark Trust. Much of the planting has gone, and modern woodland obscures some areas, but the outlines of the old park can still be seen to the north of the Hall, which is now owned by Sandwell Borough Council and used for teaching purposes.

Middleton Park

Miller's next commission was a request from Lord Jersey, of Middleton Park, in Oxfordshire, for a Gothic entrance lodge. Middleton Park occupies most of the parish of Middleton Stoney, nine miles north of Oxford, and part of the estate had been emparked since 1201. The original manor house had been close to the village, but in 1710 a large new house was built away from the village. The estate was owned by Lord Carleton, who used it as a hunting seat. In 1737 it was sold to William Villiers, 3rd Earl of Jersey, who made improvements to the park, and in the late 1750s replaced the house with a new mansion.

The attribution of the Oxford Lodge to Miller is based on its style, and more particularly on two letters written to Miller from William Villiers, Lord Jersey in 1749. The first of these, written from Bristol on 10 August, refers to two designs which Miller had completed.

> Being informed of your having been at Middleton & that you had finished the two designs you Were so good to promise me, I will take the liberty (as it is uncertain when I shall return home) to desire the favor of you to send them to me, in a letter to this place, which I hope will not deprive me the pleasure of seeing you at Middleton, & both will be adding to the obligations of
>
> Your Most Obliged Humble Servant, Jersey.

By 1 October, having received the drawings, Lord Jersey wrote concerning the two drawings:

> ... The One of which seems to be near the thing that I mean to build, but as it is too late in the Year to begin upon it I hope to have an occasion of talking it over with you. I am very apprehensive I have given you much trouble in this affair & am

equally at a loss to atone for it; I can only hope when you come into this Country that you will allow me the pleasure of your Company at Middleton … [57]

It is likely that Miller was introduced to Lord Jersey by mutual acquaintances, perhaps by George Lyttelton, since Lord Jersey's wife was the daughter of the 1st Duke of Bridgewater, and Miller mentioned in his diary entry for 12 August 1756, when he was visiting Hagley, that the Duchess of Bridgewater was there. Lord Jersey's younger brother had married into the Clarendon family, and thereby acquired the Kenilworth estates, so there is also a local Warwickshire connection.

The Oxford Lodge is at the south-east corner of the Park. From the Lodge the drive leads north-west to join the main drive near the house. The Lodge is a crenellated tower of grey stone built to an elongated octagonal plan, with a much smaller tower attached to it. The tower is constructed as part of a castellated wall flanking the entrance to the park, and the Lodge itself is built as part of the wall but projects into the park at an angle away from the drive. The entrance is through a Gothic arch in the wall, and the entrance to the tower itself is through a similar smaller arch. The windows are variously pointed, quatrefoil and round in shape. The effect is somehow rather like a toy fort, and the building appears not quite large enough to carry off the battlemented design, although the style is typical of Miller's other Gothic buildings. In designing a Gothic Lodge, Miller was reinforcing the undoubted antiquity of the Park and its medieval origins for Lord Jersey, who himself had only owned the estate for 12 years. If there were no actual medieval remains, then Miller's fashionable mock medieval Lodge was a good substitute. The mansion was converted to flats in the 20th century, but the Oxford Lodge appears to have survived in its original condition.

Enville

The date of the first recorded reference to Miller's work at Enville, the seat of the Earl of Stamford, is 23 October 1749. Miller's name is associated with several of the landscape buildings built at Enville by the 4th and 5th Earls of Stamford between about 1749 and 1770.

Enville is situated about four miles from Stourbridge and eight from Bridgnorth. The Hall itself is on low land, the park rising in the south west to over 600 feet, from where there are wide ranging views. The naturally attractive hilly landscape is intersected by steep valleys, with woodland on the ridges. The designed landscape today comprises about 750 acres. The present Hall was built in the 1530s, adjacent to an existing deer park. In the 17th century formal gardens existed, beyond and to the west of which there were pools. There were three main periods of garden design. An estate survey of c.1750 shows a typical early 18th-century design of allées forming a patte d'oie within the wooded hillside to the west of the Hall. The second phase took place between 1747 and 1760, when the 4th Earl, his head gardener, Sanderson Miller and William Shenstone all made contributions to the development of the designed landscape, with its lake, cascades and many landscape buildings. The medieval Shepherd's Lodge on the high sheep pastures was Gothicised in the 1750s. It was used as a summer retreat by the family. In 1768 the 5th Earl succeeded. The following year marked the final phase of the landscape design, with the building of the Gothic Boathouse and the construction of a cold bath in the woods.[58]

Miller's contribution to the landscaping at Enville is difficult to quantify because of the lack of precise information, and much of the attribution to him has been made on stylistic grounds and circumstantial evidence. Of Enville's many landscape buildings, the Gothic Greenhouse, referred to by 1777 as the Billiard Room and known today as the Museum from its 19th-century use, is the one building which was definitely attributed to Miller by contemporary writers. Miller would have met Lord Stamford through his friend George Lyttelton, for Enville is not very far from Hagley. In his diary for 23 October 1749, Miller, who was staying at Hagley, wrote that he was: 'with Hitchcox ab^t. L^d. Stamford's green House', as if this was a project which was already well underway. On 25 October he recorded that he was: 'Drawing L^d. Stamf^{d}s G^n.House' and again on 26 and 30 October, then the last such entry is on 23 November. In 1750 Miller referred to drawing a temple for Lord Stamford. Hitchcox, Miller's mason, visited Enville at the end of February, and Miller mentions in his diary that he was discussing Lord Stamford's 'building' with him in March and May. On 12 June Miller recorded in his diary that he sent his man Richard to Enville from Hagley, where he was staying with George Lyttelton. There is no comment as to why, or what Richard was doing, but it was probably something to do with the Gothic Greenhouse, for on the following day he went with Miss Lyttelton, daughter of Lyttelton's first wife Lucy, to Enville, where he: 'Saw the new GreenHouse Chinese h[ouse]: &c…'. These diary entries, although they are not specific, suggest that the Gothic Greenhouse was being built during the spring and early summer of 1750. The Chinese House was built before 1750, and is not thought to be by Miller.

The Gothic Greenhouse is built of ashlar cut stone, and has a large central bay with two smaller bays recessed beneath moulded ogee arches springing from clustered columns, with narrow side buttresses. The pattern of the arches is repeated in the central doorway and windows. Two Gothic windows appear in the smaller bays, and there are three rose windows within the ogee arches, the central one larger than those within the two side bays. The rose windows are divided into 16 segments, and not the more usual 12 of many Gothic rose windows. Sixteen was the classical 'perfect' number as advocated by the Roman architect Vitruvius. The interior shows the remains of delicate raised Gothic plasterwork and vaulting. There is an ornamental string course of repeated arches in the Gothic-style running across the building under the rose windows. This decoration is almost a Miller 'trademark'; it also occurs in the Boathouse here at Enville, in the chapel at Wroxton Abbey, in the design for the Bath House at Walton and at Lacock Abbey, where Miller designed a Great Hall and a new entrance court in 1754-5. On the Enville estate map dated 1750 the site of the 'elegant Gothick summer house' is marked, and is in the same position as that known today as The Museum.

Contemporary support for Miller's authorship of the Gothic Greenhouse comes from two letters written by William Shenstone, and from the descriptive travel writings of Bishop Pococke. On 4 February 1750 Shenstone wrote to Lady Luxborough, who lived at 'Barrells', not far from Henley-in-Arden, and with whom he shared his interests in landscape gardening, about the Gothic Greenhouse. Later, on 15 March, he wrote to Richard Jago, to whom he also mentioned the Gothic Greenhouse. Shenstone was a little envious of Miller, as is apparent from the wording of his letter to Jago: '… By the way, he [Lord Stamford] is now building a Gothic green-house by Mr Miller's direction, and intends to build castles, and God-knows-what. By all accounts the place is well worth seeing

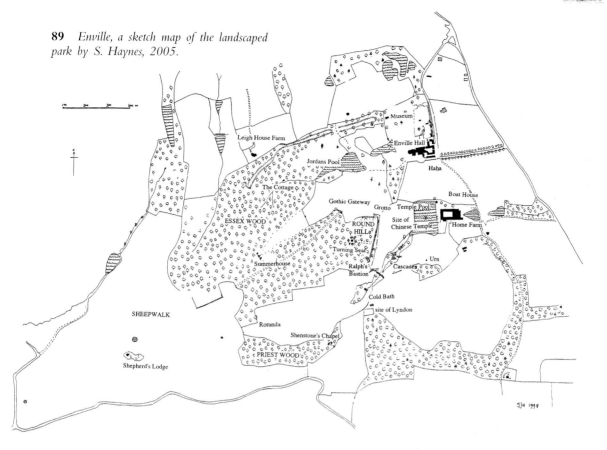

89 *Enville, a sketch map of the landscaped park by S. Haynes, 2005.*

when you come into the country, which I hope you will not fail to do this spring …'.[59] Bishop Pococke, a friend of Miller's, gave a detailed description of his walk around the Enville estate in 1756, describing the approach to the Gothic Greenhouse, described as the 'Gothick' summer house, thus:

> Behind the house is a gravel and lawn on each side of it, and from the end of it is a walk up to an elegant Gothick summer house of Mr Miller's design; from this there is a winding walk through shrubberies, which leads to a lawn, at the upper end of which is a Gothic seat which commands a fine view of the vale towards Bridgenorth … Hagley, and the country to the south. We then went along the top of the hill to a gateway that appears like a castle, and to a string of ponds which extend down to the lawn behind the house.[60]

Joseph Heely, visiting Enville in 1777, wrote:

> The BILLIARD ROOM … is a stately gothic edifice and does much credit to the designer. Its inside is curiously and richly adorned with stucco: the ceiling remarkably so. At one end in a niche is a bust of Homer; at the other a Cicero. A billiard table and a small organ are the furniture of this superb room; and you have from the windows a lively view … Don't you think it is much to be regretted that this elegant building is visible from no other point in these grounds, than at the gothic gateway?[61]

Modern writers have suggested both Henry Keene (1726-76) and Thomas Farnolls Pritchard (1723-77), a Shrewsbury architect, as possible designers of the Museum, though contemporary evidence in favour of Miller seems reasonably conclusive. Henry Keene was, in any case, a protegé of Miller's, and he had initially employed him to oversee his architectural alterations at Nelm, near Hornchurch, in Essex, when Keene was a young unknown architect. Keene may well have been involved in the building of the Museum, since in 1749 and 1750 he was designing the alterations to the chapel for Miller's friend Bishop Maddox at Hartlebury, near Worcester, less than two hours' ride from Enville, where Miller was also involved. The fan vaulted ceilings in both buildings are stylistically quite similar. Earlier in 1749, Miller had been employing Keene to make the Gothic furniture for the Ruined Castle at Hagley. Pritchard has also been suggested as a possible author of the Museum, but the style of the building does not accord with his other known works.[62] The Museum, which had suffered considerable decay and been invaded by ivy and elder, has recently been restored.

The Museum has a satisfying solidity in spite of its unusual design, and the strong columns tie the romantic ogee curves of the roofline effectively to the base. The three arched bays have similarities with the three windows of New College Chapel, Oxford. There is also a similarity between the unusual design of the ogee arches and the single ogee arch of The Red House in the Painswick Rococo Garden in Gloucestershire, although the Museum is a much larger and more impressive building. In both buildings the ogee arches stand proud of the building, and both have three arches in their design, together with side towers.

It is quite possible that Miller had visited Painswick, for he had relatives in Siston, a village between Bath and Bristol. Benjamin Hyatt created the garden in the 1740s, and Thomas Robins painted it in 1748, so in 1749/50 it would have been a modern garden of great interest.

Bishop Pococke's 'gateway that appears like a castle' is known as the Gothic Gateway. It acts as the entrance to the woods on Round Hill, to the south west of the Hall, and was intended as an eyecatcher, the light colour of the stone standing out well against the dark woodland behind. Neither the name of the designer nor the date of its construction is known, Pococke being the first to mention it, but the Gothic Gateway is typical of Miller's work. Not a mock ruin, nor yet a gateway in the ordinary sense of the term, it is designed specially for its position as an eyecatcher and also a place where visitors, having climbed the hill, can pause to look at the view. In appearance it looks, as Pococke remarked, very like part of a castle. It has a main arch, forming the actual gateway, over which is a castellated gable, and low crenellated walls link this with flanking pavilions which have open arches and crenellated parapets. The side arches, which are blind and at an angle to the main arch, each shelter seats from which the extensive views in two directions may be admired. Joseph Heely, writing in 1777, remarked that the views 'slide together into a landscape that cannot but give every spectator the highest gratification ...'. He also notes that the 'billiard room' (the Gothic Greenhouse, or the Museum) which can be seen in the distance, 'rises, remarkably scenical, among groups of delicate trees and knots of flowering shrubs'. The fact that this building was visible from the Gothic Gateway may add a further point in favour of Miller's authorship of the latter. The Gothic Gateway is still in good condition.

90 *Enville, the Boathouse on Temple Pool, a photograph taken prior to 1970 when a tree fell on the building and demolished it. Although it was not built until 1769, Miller is credited with the design. Both the combination of geometric shapes in the construction (an octagon inner room on a square base), and the distinctive repeated Gothic arch ornamental line on the exterior lend support to this attribution.*

The Doric Temple, known in addition as the Portico and the Summerhouse, has also been attributed to Miller. It may have been the unidentified 'temple' that he was drawing for Lord Stamford and which he referred to in his diary entry for 29 January, 1750. It is rectangular in shape, with a pediment supported on four square rusticated columns, and is marked on the 1750 estate map. The Temple must also have been intended for an eyecatcher, for it is built in light coloured stone, and situated at the head of a narrow dry valley, with dark hanging woods behind – which are carpeted with bluebells in May. It provides a sheltered spot from which to appreciate the extensive view over the Black Country with the spire of Sedgley church on the distant horizon. The Temple has recently been restored.

The Gothic Seat only occurs in one description, by Pococke. It is not mentioned either by Miller or by other contemporary visitors to Enville, but it is on the Enville map of *c*.1750, and the site has been located in the grounds. It may have been Miller's 'fine Gothick design' which was seen by John Ivory Talbot in 1754, who wrote to Miller saying: 'At Enville we saw an Horrid Massacre of a fine Gothick design of yours: committed by the Hands of some Shrewsbury man, we were very angry, and would not let the gardiner give us the Particulars of the misfortune'.[63] Whoever the 'Shrewsbury man' was, it is unlikely to have been Pritchard, a well respected architect in his own right. If the building had been vandalised in some way it may have been completely pulled down at this time.

The Boathouse was built on the north-east corner of Temple Pool during 1769, the year after the 5th Earl of Stamford inherited the estate. Although the Boathouse was built some years after the other buildings at Enville with which Miller is associated, the unusual combination of geometric shapes in the construction of the building, and the ornamental detailing are both typical of his work. It has traditionally been ascribed to Miller.[64] It may be that the design was prepared in the 1750s, and was not built until later. The square base of the Boathouse was of stone with an arch for boats to enter from the water. Above this was a brick and wooden structure. The façade facing the Pool, which was of stone, had three Gothic arches supported on narrow pillars. The two side arches were blind, and within the central one, which was also the largest, there was a sliding window of painted glass, which opened on to the Pool. Beneath and within the triangular pediment there was the simple repeated small Gothic arch ornamental course which Miller used in other buildings. The upper interior room was octagonal in shape. It was decorated with medallions and festoons which may have been of papier maché, as there are bills in the archives for work of this kind carried out at the Boathouse.[65] The whole impression is of a romantic, almost fairytale building.

Visitors to the Boathouse were brought inside, and while they were admiring the glass window a servant was sent to release the water held back by a dam and sluices above the cascades on the opposite side of the Pool. The window was then flung open, revealing the cascade as it entered the Pool in full flow. Heely, writing in 1777, enthused about the hidden site of the Boathouse, so that you came upon it unexpectedly. He goes on to describe it as: 'an octagon, prettily ornamented within by festoons of flowers, and medallions in stucco. A curious sliding window, that opens to the water, adorned with painted glass in whimsical groups of grotesque figures, is certainly very ornamental…' William Marshall, who visited Enville in 1801, wrote of the view of the cascades from the window as:

> A Shenstonian Cascade in full flow and fury; foaming and bellowing, as if the mountain were enraged, pouring down a river of water as white as snow, and apparently so copious, as to render our situation alarming; less the house and its contents be hurried away with the torrent.[66]

The flow of water was not normally sufficient to produce this spectacle. In 1769/70 the Chinese Temple (in the middle of Temple Pool) and the bridge leading to it were taken down. The Temple had been repaired several times during its existence and was in any case out of fashion by this time. It was also right in the line of view from the Boathouse to the cascades across the Pool. From the Boathouse site the Gothic Gateway is visible on the hill, and other features, such as a small Grotto, Ralph's Bastion and Shenstone's Chapel, would have been visible before the growth of the surrounding trees obscured the views. Unfortunately a tree fell on the Boathouse in the 1970s, and only a pile of rubble and stone blocks now remains.

The design of the Boathouse has marked similarities with that of the Bath House at Walton, built by Miller in 1749. Both buildings had a stone base, with a central entrance arch, over which there is an elegant octagonal room for receiving visitors, decorated with ornate raised swags. The windows and detailing of the Bath House are classical, while those of the Boathouse are Gothic. Painted glass windows were an enthusiasm of Miller's, and of several of his friends, including George Lyttelton and Lord Hardwicke, though a sliding window was obviously unusual. Miller also used sliding fittings on the Temple on the Mount at Wroxton.

The rotunda, in another prominent position at the head of a valley near the sheepwalks, had open sides, and contained a seat over which there was a domed roof supported by six Ionic columns. It was mentioned by Shenstone as a new feature in 1750, but has now gone except for the foundations and the earth bastion on which it was built, and there is nothing in the archives or Miller's diary to connect him with this building. The Cascades drop down over about 1,200 feet through a narrow strip of woodland from a spring half way down the valley which has the Rotunda at its head, the water finally entering Temple Pool. The upper cascade is stepped, and is similar to those designed by Miller at Farnborough and Wroxton. The lower cascades are thought to have been designed by

91   *Enville, a view of Temple Pool, the Boathouse, and the Hall, c.1800.*

Shenstone, who actually caught the chill which led to his untimely death after a visit to the estate. The design of these is more naturalistic and the drops vary in height. There is a winding path the length of the cascades, originally planted with woodland shrubs and climbers. The 1750 estate survey shows pencilled lines suggesting informal outlines for planting by the cascades and on the adjacent hillside to the south. These are thought to have been drawn in by Shenstone.

As in the description of Hagley, no attempt has been made to give a complete description of all the features of the Enville landscape, but the discussion has covered those features which are more directly associated with Miller. Even from a description of these, it can be appreciated how attractive was the designed landscape in the 18th century. Enville, together with Hagley and The Leasowes, became one of the most visited places in the Midlands. Arriving from Hagley, when the road crossed through 'wild heath, nearly barren', the change was dramatic as one approached Enville's verdant wooded hills, its waters and its many landscape buildings. The landscape had some affinity with the Rococo style, with its emphasis on surprises, and ingenious design, but the whole estate, with its sweeping vistas was on a larger scale than much of the Rococo. The design was natural and informal, apart perhaps from the outline of Hall Pool, and the general topography played a major part in the siting of the various buildings.

During Victorian times great changes were made to the gardens around the Hall, and a very large glasshouse, the Great Conservatory, was built. In the second half of the 19th century, crowds of up to 6,000 people a week came to visit these gardens with their fountains and carpet bedding, such was their popularity. The landscaped estate remained almost untouched, however, and today, apart from the loss of some of the buildings, and the silting up of much of the cascade system, it can still be seen much as it was in the 18th century. There are plans to begin a restoration programme, with the cascades as one of the primary objectives.

Hartlebury

The Castle and its grounds at Hartlebury, ten miles north of Worcester, date from the 13th century. In Henry VIII's time the estate was described by Leland as having 'a parke and deere, a warren for coneys, and fayre pooles; but the soyle about the castle is barren'.

The Castle was a Royalist stronghold; in 1646 the garrison surrendered to Cromwell, and the Castle was left in ruins. After the restoration in 1675-7 the Castle became the seat of the Bishops of Worcester. Bishop Maddox, Bishop of Worcester from 1743 until his death in 1759, spent £1,200 on the reconstruction of the chapel at Hartlebury, the interior of which was refurnished in the Gothic style with fan vaulting by Henry Keene in the late 1740s to early 1750s. The situation of the Castle at Hartlebury was described in 1782 as:

> extremely pleasing; placed on a rising hill, or knoll, it has to the south a most extensive prospect over the vale of Severn; and it occupies a very extended space on the level of the park … It has altogether an air of grandeur when seen through the breaks in the surrounding woods, which are not, however, very extensive.' … The road from Kidderminster to Worcester goes close by the park-paling; and the 'pooles', or fish-ponds spoken of by Leland , still remain.[67]

Letters from Maddox to Miller from 1750 onwards testify to the friendship between the two men. Maddox was able to accede to Miller's requests for posts for clergy or to augment their stipends, and Miller approved of Maddox's scheme for increasing the stipend of poor clergy in the diocese of Worcester. Miller recorded several visits to Hartlebury in his diary for 1749/50. On Thursday, 26 October, 1749 Miller arrived from Hagley in one hour and five minutes for breakfast with the Bishop. He then wrote: 'walk^d with him 2hr. in ye Park &c. Bps. Chapl very near finished & very handsome. Dined at Hagley.' Later in the year Miller visited Maddox again. On 15 June 1750 he went to prayers in the new chapel, then: 'drew pl: of Seat for Chap. Rode with the B^p. Came to Hagley …' This entry in Miller's diary is the only reference to Miller actually contributing a design for the chapel. In August Miller rode over from Hagley to Hartlebury with his mason, Hitchcox. There does not seem to be any reason for the mason to accompany Miller on this visit unless he was involved in stonework for the refurbishment of the chapel. Miller's diary entry for 21 August reads: '… walked with his Lordsh^p. Bfd. & went for p^{rs}. W again in ye Pk. With the B^p. Mr Keene & Mr Rowel there…' Maddox appreciated Miller's opinion about his chapel, for when the work was nearly completed he wrote to Miller: '… shall think myself happy if it [the chapel] does not displease a Gentleman of your judgement and elegant Taste'.[68] Keene was responsible for the refurnishing and interior design of the chapel. Keene's association with Miller has already been mentioned. J. Rowel prepared the glass for the chapel. The windows had been designed by Dr John Wall of Worcester, who with others was to establish the Worcester Porcelain Manufactory in 1751. Although Miller, as is usual in his diary entries, does not actually mention discussing the Bishop's improvements, his brief entries, such as 'walked 2 hr. in ye Park', are the same as similar entries made when he visited the gardens at Stowe, Wimpole and other estates where he was giving advice. The park is not very large at Hartlebury, and the amount of time during his short visits which Miller spent walking in it with the Bishop strongly suggest that Miller was advising him on its landscaping, although no actual archival evidence has yet been found supporting this conclusion.

There is now one lake, in the valley, formed from the earlier fishponds. This lies immediately below the Castle. The hillside beyond the lake is crowned with woodland.

There are still walks planted with trees and shrubs leading down to the valley today. There is a recognisable similarity between these features and designs including walks, lakes and hilltop belts of trees at other sites where Miller worked, such as Farnborough and Honington.

The hand-lettered historical panels on display in the Great Hall at Hartlebury, which give details of all the Bishops since the creation of the diocese of Worcester in A.D. 680, give the following lengthy description of Bishop Isaac Maddox's achievements at Hartlebury:

> Founder of Worcester Royal Infirmary. Lived at Hartlebury Castle (except in winter). Completely refurnished the Chapel, employing as architect Henry Keene, surveyor to Westminster Abbey. Placed cupola over Great Hall roof. Greatly developed the grounds, planting many trees and making walks around the moat & pool, with bastions at each end of the South wall, above the sunken garden 'to contain each its mulberry tree'. Crenellated the roofs of the 'little lodges', also the garden walls. Planted shrubberies along the moat bank to the West, where had been a kitchen garden, & raised the boggy ground to the North to Form a new kitchen garden.'

The Castle moat has been converted into gardens, but otherwise the grounds and the view over the park from the Castle must be little different from their appearance in the mid-18th century. The Castle now houses the Worcester County Museum as well as the Bishop's house, and the State Rooms are used for public functions.

Walton

October 1749 was a busy month for Miller, for he was working on landscape designs for Enville, advising Bishop Maddox at Hartlebury on his improvements to the grounds, and on 31 October he mentioned in his diary that he was 'Setling ac^{ts}. with Hitchcox ab^t. S^r. Charles Bath &c – and with Heritage and Hands'. The Bath House at Walton had probably been under construction for most of the preceding year, but this is the first mention of it in contemporary literature, and the earliest diary that we have of Miller's begins in October 1749.

The manor of Walton is situated about five miles west of Stratford-upon-Avon, in a shallow valley with low hills rising to either side. The estate is mentioned in Domesday Book, and was owned by the Earls of Warwick after the Conquest. In the 16th century Walton was acquired through marriage by Robert Mordaunt, whose grandson L'Estrange Mordaunt was created a baronet in 1611. By the beginning of the 18th century the land had already been enclosed. In 1721, Sir Charles Mordaunt (1698-1778) 6th Baronet, succeeded to the title. He was M.P. for Warwickshire for 40 years. Sir Charles was twice widowed, with a teenage family, when in 1750 he embarked on rebuilding the old manor house in a simple classical style with two projecting wings. At the same time he built the Bath House in the woods adjacent to the house.[69]

The attribution of the Bath House to Miller is said to be 'almost certain' by Hawkes, who was the architect for the restoration of the building in the late 1980s.[70] Hawkes remarks that Hitchcox rarely worked for anyone other than Miller. Heritage and Hands were also men employed by Miller.

Sir Charles wanted an elegant summerhouse, for taking tea, and also a cold plunge bath. Miller would have used his knowledge of springs from his experience at Radway in choosing the site, for the cold spring which fills the bath itself rarely fails. To take a cold bath was considered good for the health, and was also used in the treatment for gout, from which Sir Charles suffered. Miller probably had his own cold bath, for at Radway Grange there is an outside entrance with a wrought-iron gate leading down steps to a plunge pool below ground level, which may well date from the 18th century. On Bowles' map of Warwickshire, dated 1785, a spring of petrifying water is marked on the high ground near where the Bath House is situated. The water in the Bath House spring may well have had restorative properties due to the dissolved salts in it. There are a number of small restorative springs known locally, such as that near Bishopton, just north of Stratford-upon-Avon, besides the well-known curative springs at the Royal Pump Rooms at Leamington Spa.

Neither Gothic nor classical, the Bath House is a mix of styles. The lower part of the building is made of rough-hewn stone, with an arched entrance where a wrought-iron gate allows access to the spring-fed unheated Roman-style plunge bath. The building is set into the hill, with the main entrance at the level of the upper room, at the back. The upper room, built of ashlar cut stone, is an elegant octagonal shape which contrasts with the rough stone of the base. It has a wide view across the valley to the rising land beyond. The tiled, octagonal pointed roof is finished with a small chimney. Inside the upper room, the walls are decorated with swags of exotic shells, and the ceiling with lines of small 'icicles'. The decoration was almost certainly the inspiration of Mrs Delany. In 1754 Mrs Delany sent a barrel of shells to Walton, and she remarked that:

92   *Walton, the Bath House. Designed by Miller for Sir Charles Mordaunt, it has an octagonal upper room built on a rectangular base of rough hewn stone enclosing a spring-fed plunge bath in the Roman style. The building was restored in the 1990s.*

93 *Walton, the Bath House, seen on the hillside in its woodland setting. Yews planted behind the building provide an evergreen backdrop to the light grey stone.*

the stucco … is meant to represent a wall worn by water drops, with icicles sticking to it. The festoons of shells are additional ornaments; or how could they come in that form unless some invisible sea nymph or triton placed them there for their private amusement? I should not wonder, indeed, that so pretty a place allured them.[71]

Mary Delany's sister, Anne Dewes, lived only a mile or so away at Wellesbourne Hall, and Mrs Delany and the Dewes family were regular visitors both at Walton and Radway. As well as her fine paper collages of flowers, Mrs Delany was also expert in decorating with shells, which she often obtained from mariners back from the West Indies. She had decorated her own home near Dublin with shellwork.[72] The decoration of the upper room was probably carried out with her sister and niece together with Sir Charles' daughters.

The interior decoration of the salon, which continues the watery theme established by the lower room, may have been inspired by the grotto at Wilton House, designed by Isaac de Caux *c.*1647, which has stylised cornices and ceiling decorations of icicles. De Caux' inspiration may have been his elder brother Salomon's publication in Paris in 1624, *Les Raisons des Forces mouvantes*. In this volume there was an engraving of the Grotto of Orpheus at St Germain-en-Laye (late 16th-century), which also had decorative icicles hanging from the roof.[73] Miller was no doubt familiar with the design of the Wilton grotto.

The Bath House is situated in woods known as the Bath Woods, which run from behind the Hall along the eastern side of the valley to the Kineton road. The Bath House itself has an attractive westerly outlook across the little valley of the river Dene to the

94 *Wilton House, Wiltshire, the Grotto, taken from a drawing by Isaac de Caux in Hortus Pembrochianus, c.1647. The lines of 'icicles' are reminiscent of those used in 1749 to decorate the interior of the Bath House at Walton.*

rising land beyond. The view is directed by banks of planting either side of a clear grassy area directly in front of the building. A map of Sir Charles' lands in Walton in 1762 show a path leading from the House up to the Bath House, with a little figure, presumably Sir Charles himself, walking towards it.[74] Visible on this map is an enclosed and planted space around the Bath House, within the woods, and a photograph taken before the 1940-45 war showing planting here suggests that there was always a small garden in front of the building. Miller's characteristic planting of yews provides an evergreen background to the Bath House. Although there are Victorian plantings within the woods, including Wellingtonias, the planting shown on the 1762 map was probably designed by Miller with Sir Charles. The woods run along a ridge of land, a feature which echoes Miller's ridgetop plantings at Farnborough, Radway and Honington.

Miller recorded taking breakfast with Sir Charles at the Bath House, and tea taken in the woods was a favourite family pastime. It was remembered with pleasure by John Dobson, Sir Charles' nephew, writing home to his cousin Mary from Naples and imagining himself back at Walton by rubbing a magic ring:

> … Gently alighting on ye Pavement of ye Bath Room I become an invisible guest at ye Tea-Table, and enjoy that Conversation in which you maintain so bright a Part. Sir Charles complains the Tea is weak, Miss Mordaunt says the Kettle never boil'd, but I have drain'd the Pot.[75]

In constructing the so called 'Roman' cold bath, and the salon with its classical outlines, Miller was indulging in the current fantasy for buildings which purported to be from antiquity but actually had a modern and fashionable use. The building fits its purpose admirably, and in its woodland setting is as attractive today as it must have been when newly built.

8

The Decade from 1750 to 1760

෨·෧

The year 1750 saw Miller working on several new projects. Miller's diary entries reveal that in April he was preparing a plan at Alscot Park, near Stratford-upon-Avon; in June he was at Coughton Court, near Alcester; in July at Upton House near Banbury, drawing a design for Mr Vernon of Sudbury Hall in Derbyshire in August and in September he was at Gosfield, in Essex for a week. These all represented fresh commissions, with the exception of Gosfield Hall, where Miller had known Robert Nugent since at least 1736.

These projects were in addition to the ongoing work at Hagley, Enville, Wroxton, Honington and Ambrosden, and a busy social life. On Edgehill there was still much work to be done at the Tower, where Miller was putting up the adjacent small gatehouse tower, and there was always the work on the estate at Radway to organise. The majority of his income was derived from his estate, so Miller could not afford to neglect it, and he himself always did a certain amount of the work as his time allowed. Entries in his diary show that he was cutting trees on 6 May and with the haymakers on 22 June, a Saturday afternoon, for at that date the working week was a full six days. The number of extensive visits Miller undertook during the year is surprising, considering how much work he was undertaking for others, how long it took to travel anywhere, and how restricted travel was not only by the weather but by the state of the roads, particularly during the winter and early spring months. At the end of April Miller recorded spending a week in London, socialising and visiting Ranelagh and Vauxhall pleasure gardens, and in June he visited George Lyttelton at Hagley, going to Enville and Hartlebury during his stay and going home by way of Coughton Court, near Alcester, and Stratford-upon-Avon. In August he was at Hagley again, then in September he journeyed to Wimpole. He visited Cambridge while staying with Lord Hardwicke, then left Wimpole for his friend Robert Nugent's mansion at Gosfield, where he stayed for a week. From Gosfield Miller visited William Pitt at Enfield Chase, went on to Cassiobury, to see the unusual 'forest garden' created in the mid-17th century, then to visit Colonel Conway (Horace Walpole's cousin) to see his newly acquired estate at Henley on Thames before returning home by way of Stowe.

Alscot Park

A few days before his spring visit to London, Miller went to stay at Alscot Park. Alscot Park lies mainly in the parish of Preston-on-Stour, about three miles south of Stratford-upon-Avon. The estate was in Gloucestershire until it was moved into Warwickshire in 1931. The land, which is predominantly loam, varies from about 130 feet to 250 feet in height. The river Stour runs through the park, with the manor house on the south bank.

Land at 'Sture' is first mentioned in 804, when it belonged to the monastery of Deerhurst, in Gloucestershire. Alscot Park was established to the north east of the Stour by 1401, and in the early 1500s was held by George Catesby, whose widow Elizabeth married Sir Thomas Lucy of Charlecote. In the late 17th century Thomas Mariett, of the neighbouring estate of Whitchurch, married the heiress to the Alscot Park estate. Their grandson Richard altered the house in the 1720s and was probably responsible for the formal layout of the gardens and the grand avenues laid out in the park during this period.[1] In 1747 the land was sold to James West, M.P., whose family roots were in Banbury but who was at that time joint secretary to the Exchequer, and a noted antiquarian. James West Gothicised the manor house, laid out extensive informal designs in the grounds, and rebuilt the local church.[2] Sanderson Miller is thought to have had a hand in the alterations to both house and grounds. Our knowledge of Miller's activities at Alscot is limited to Miller's diary entries made in April, 1750. On Friday, 20 April, Miller 'Went after breakfast with B. [Mr and Mrs Bowes were staying at Radway] to Mr West in 1h:2/1[one and a half hours] on horseb. Mr Lytt^n ... by us. .... Walk^g at Mr W. abt [about] the P^k. [Park]. Seeing Painted Glass drawing Plan for Mr W. Staid all night'. On Saturday: 'Catched a bad cold. H^d ached. Walking with Mr West Mr Lytt^n &c — came to R^y. [Radway] in 2.2/1[two and a half hours] with B [Bowes]'.

Miller and West had many interests in common besides their liking for Gothic architecture and landscaping, both men being interested in religion and in antiquarian pursuits, and both having unusually extensive libraries.[3] Miller had invited West to Radway the previous year,[4] and West would have known of Miller's expertise in laying out grounds from their mutual friend George Lyttelton. There is no clue in Miller's diary entries as to what he was designing for West. From the repeated references to walking in the park it is very probable that it was the landscape improvements that the men were discussing, particularly since Miller and Lyttelton were making improvements to the park at Hagley at this time. The 'Plan' which Miller was drawing out may have been for the landscaping, but it is also possible that Miller was drawing out designs for the initial Gothic alterations to the house, begun in 1750. The new north wing, built around the old house, had battlements and projecting bays with pointed Gothic windows. John Phillips and George Shakespear, two London master builders, drew the plans, and the Woodwards, expert local masons from Chipping Campden, carried out the work.

James West (1703-72) began to take the grounds in hand immediately following his purchase of the estate. His memorandum book gives meticulous measurements for various areas, for de-silting the pond — probably the largest fishpond on the approach to the house, for making new stairs down through the garden to the river Stour and for clearing trees from the far bank to improve the view.[5] In a letter to her brother Mrs West describes the estate:

> [it] really is a sweet place & we have a river which winds very beautifully through the park ... & close to one part of it is a very quick rising hill upon which is the finest growth of tall firs I ever saw; besides the river we have 3 very fine pieces of water

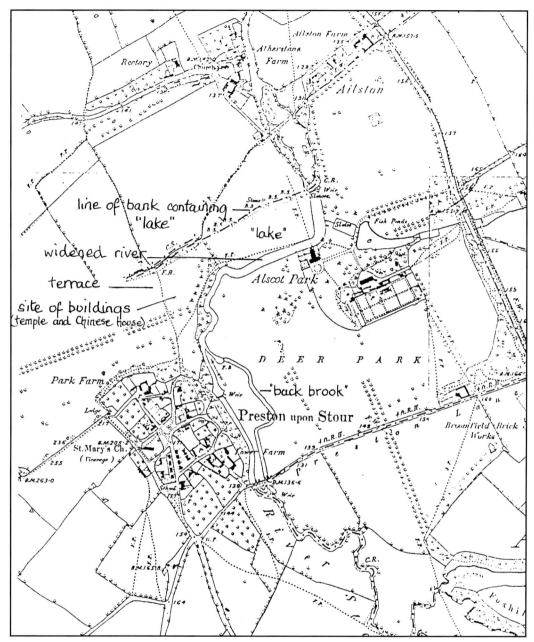

95   *Alscot Park, a map adapted from the six-inch O.S. map for 1884, showing the widened river upstream from James West's 'penstock' or weir, and the designed landscape and park. The size of the mid-18th-century 'lake' formed from the river is delineated on the map by the parish boundary (marked by a dashed and dotted line) which runs along a bank, still visible today, in the water meadow to the north of the widened river.*

in the park which fat the finest carp, tench, perch and pike. The house is a very bad one, but if I get a good prize in the Lottery we are to build in the spring …[6]

History does not relate if Mrs West won a good prize in the lottery or not, but her husband certainly found enough money to make extensive alterations to the house and the park, and also to rebuild the chancel and the tower of the church at Preston-on-Stour, the village on the opposite bank of the Stour and adjacent to the park on the west.

Landscaping carried out in about 1750 included a new design for the higher ground by the village beyond the river, and the widening of the Stour by the house to create a more impressive sheet of water, the latter being obvious from the detail shown in the 1883 O.S. map. Beyond the river, on the higher ground, a rotunda, an obelisk and a Chinese house were erected. Behind these buildings a terrace was constructed. From here the views were far reaching, and West lists them in his memorandum book. Also in the book is a small sketch plan, with dimensions, of William Holbech's terrace at Farnborough, which West is known to have visited in 1760, although he would certainly have known about it before then. West's memorandum book gives great importance to the creation of a 'penstock', a device or weir for retaining and regulating the flow of the river, which he sited to the north of the river bend on which the house is situated. There is still a weir here.

A contemporary map in the Alscot archives revealed unexpected information. At the top of the map were tiny drawings of the Chinese house, with its concave roof, and the Rotunda. A plan exists in the archives for a hexagonal Chinese house, dated 1757. On the contemporary map the lower half of the water meadow adjacent to the river to the north of the house is marked as 'Lake', although there is no lake here today. The remains of an otherwise unexplained retaining earth bank running lengthways down this meadow and parallel with the river show the original extent of the 'lake'. The drawings of the buildings and the marking of the 'lake' had been forgotten over the years. The 'lake' would have made a dramatic setting to the house, and would not have been seen until the visitor actually went into the garden running down from the north side of the house to the river. This was a fine Rococo touch, for the entrance to the house, which is built on a bank above a bend in the river, is approached from the east through the park, and the river itself is not seen from the drive.

The appearance of the buildings on the map matches a description of the park written in 1896 by J. Harvey Bloom, rector of Whitchurch, a village which was part of the Alscot estate in the 18th century:

> Mr West, after the purchase of Alscot, erected various buildings in his park in accordance with the taste of the age, but all have been demolished.
>
> There was an obelisk, designed by Woodward in 1757. A 'Chinese temple', surmounted by an acorn, which stood at the top of a flight of steps leading up from the river, not far south of the rotunda mound, and a lofty erection (the Rotunda) erected on a mound of earth still remaining to the east of the footpath across the park leading to Atherstone. It had an octagonal tower with domed roof; the alternate sides of the octagon were pierced with arches, the other four being filled in. In the second storey were round-headed windows, and the total height from floor to dome was 50 feet. The rotunda was standing within the memory of the traditional 'oldest inhabitant', one Widow Gaden, who has told the author that she and her companions used to creep

96 *Alscot Park, the mound on which the Octagonal Rotunda stood. From this higher land, north of the village of Preston on Stour, there was a wide view of the river, the house and park, and most of the estate. The terrace was to the left. The wood is recent.*

under the chains which fenced it in, to dance on its marble floor, delighted with the echo of their footsteps. Children in her day called it the 'sounding house'.[7]

Bloom was particularly interested in local history, and his description gives a good idea of the appearance of these buildings. The land rises quite steeply from the river bank at this point, allowing a good view of the buildings from the park. From the terrace, the outlines of which can still be seen, the view in the opposite direction is of the house and its park and on towards higher land in the distance.

Other improvements to the park included a cascade, an ice-house, and, on 4 July, West recorded in his memorandum book: the 'surpentine in the Back Brook will be done by the Middle of Next Week: and has a very good effect'. This may be where the Stour has been divided into two streams over a short distance between the park and the village. There is a footbridge here leading from the park to a small area of land between the two streams, and access to the village and the church was probably over an adjacent weir. Was this another of Miller's areas where one could walk under trees, surrounded by water on two sides? It is possible, despite the fact that there are no trees marked on the 1883 O.S. map, for after 150 years any trees originally planted here may have been cut down or washed away in floods. In 1758 a new single-span stone bridge was built over the Stour, taking the road to the village, and later a smaller one was erected over the 'back brook'. In the park surrounding the house there was a Chinese bench in a wooded area by the Stratford road, and trees of many different varieties were planted, some sent from Hampton Court. West also noted that he had received seeds of several varieties from the Duke of Argyll, including seeds of some North American species. Argyll was known for his interest in trees, particularly the new introductions from North America. Large mature trees still growing in the park at Alscot include cedars, sweet chestnuts and limes, and a tulip tree. In 1753 a handsome orangery was built adjacent to stables of the same date. No further visits to Alscot are recorded in Miller's diaries, nor are West's improvements referred to in any of Miller's letters.

There are a number of features in the Alscot design which have similarities with those at Farnborough, Wroxton and Honington, where the attribution of the work to Miller is more definite. The creation of a lake formed by the penstock or weir, allowing the river level to rise and flood an adjacent water meadow, is similar in technical approach to the work carried out at Honington, but on a larger scale. The terrace and the serpentine have similarities with the work at Farnborough, though the terrace is much smaller and simpler in construction. The buildings can be compared with those at Wroxton and Farnborough. The Chinese building is in the form of a hexagon, unusual for a Chinese garden building of this period, but a shape which Miller himself had used before in the Game Larder at Farnborough. There are several similarities between the Rotunda and the Temple on the Mount at Wroxton. Both were octagons, both had arched openings, the Rotunda at Alscot having the alternate sides filled in, and both had domed roofs. The Rotunda is similar to the Pentagon Temple at Farnborough in that it had an upper storey. If the ground floor was open, perhaps the upper room was used for refreshments, as we know the upper room in the Pentagon Temple was at Farnborough. The siting of the buildings at Alscot on mounds to improve the views from them is similar to the positioning of many of Miller's buildings, for example at Gopsall, Honington and Wotton Underwood. Other men, such as William Kent, had used large, purpose-built mounds to position eyecatchers or other buildings, but Miller habitually used smaller mounds, only up to two yards in height, with gradually sloping sides, on which to site his buildings. These mounds produced a much more natural appearance in the landscape, but still provided sufficient elevation to improve the views from them.

The landscaped grounds at Alscot were well known by 1767, when Richard Jago, writing in his narrative poem 'Edgehill' in that year, described the Stour by Alscot:

> Boasting as he flows of growing fame,
> And wondrous beauties on his banks display'd –
> Of Alscot's swelling lawns, and fretted spires,
> Of fairest model, Gothic or Chinese.[8]

Alscot's beautifully preserved Rococo-Gothic House was extended again in 1762-6 when West retired to live there, with Palladian proportions but a Gothic exterior to match the north wing. The same craftsmen were employed. On the south front there are two semi-octagonal bay windows carried up as lanterns beyond the parapet. Lanterns are a device used by Miller on some of his designs, for example at Lacock Abbey, and also on the Gothic Temple at Stowe, which has been attributed to him. The larger projecting Gothic bay windows are also reminiscent of Miller's work both at Arbury and Radway. The interior of the south wing in particular is richly decorated in Gothic plasterwork. Some of the work rivals that at Arbury in its magnificence, and is thought to be by the same craftsman, Robert Moore.

Coughton Court

On 16 June, Miller paid a visit to Coughton Court, near Alcester, the seat of Sir Robert Throckmorton. The Throckmortons had held the Court and estate at Coughton since the 15th century. The family were staunch Roman Catholics, and were implicated in the Gunpowder Plot. Miller visited Coughton after a visit to Hagley, just mentioning in his diary entry for 16 June 1750: 'rode to Stratford and saw Coughton: 5h.1/2'. On 2 July he was 'd.(drawing) Sr R. Th. Plan'. On 27 June Miller referred again to drawing 'S^r. R Throckmorton's H', and also on 28 June 'S^r. R. Throgm: build^g before bft.' There is no further mention of the Plan, and nothing further has come to light in the Coughton

XXI   *The cascade at Honington. Originally there was a reclining statue of a river god on the stone plinths on either side of the cascade, one of which is shown below.*

XXII   *One of the two reclining river gods from the cascade. The two statues have been moved nearer the Hall because of fear of vandalism.*

XXIII   *Wimpole, the Castle Ruin. The original design was carried out by Miller in 1750, when he and Lord Chancellor Hardwicke surveyed the site, a small hill facing south towards the distant garden front of Wimpole Hall. The ruin was not built until 1772-6, when the design was somewhat altered and erected by Capability Brown for Hardwicke's son, the 2nd Earl.*

XXIV   *The western façade of the Castle ruin at Wimpole, altered and enlarged from Miller's original drawing. The path from the Hall approaches the ruin from the west.*

XXV *Arbury Hall, the landscaped pool below the cascade. The excavated earth has been used to create the mound, on which are planted a mix of trees including Scots pine. Within the mound is situated the ice-house, conveniently near both pool and house.*

XXVI *The Oxford Lodge, Middleton Stoney. The lodge has Gothic windows and quatrefoil openings, and is a solid and sturdy building, with a second small tower behind the main tower. The main tower is an octagon, Miller's favourite shape.*

XXVII *Enville, the Gothic Gate. This building stands on the top of the hill leading into woods behind Enville Hall. Seats were provided within the shady recesses of the side arches. There are extensive views from here over the estate lands and towards Hagley Hall and the Clent Hills.*

XXVIII *The Museum at Enville. This building is Gothic in design but has classical detailing in the rose windows. It also had extensive plaster tracery work and fan vaulting inside, but much of the interior work has decayed over the years. The exterior has recently been restored.*

XXIX *Walton, the elegant interior of the upper room (restored 1990s). The shells for the swags were given by Mrs Delany, and she and her nieces from Wellesbourne Manor are thought to have decorated the room themselves. The 'icicle' ceiling decorations are similar to those used in the Grotto at Wilton House, c.1640.*

xxx *View of the north façade of Alscot Park, with the river Stour. The weir made by James West in the 1750s (behind the position from which the photograph was taken) held the river back and flooded the water meadow to the right, making a 'lake' through which the river flowed. A boat ferried people across from the house to the terrace and pleasure grounds, and the church. The house was Gothicised at this time, probably also by Miller.*

xxxi *The Upton Estate. View down the line of the old cascades (underneath bushes) towards the lake. Miller's temple, now gone, was at the nearer end. A later temple stands at the further end. A clump of pines and oaks can be seen on the hillside beyond the lake. Similar ancient clumps are situated on the hill behind the cascades.*

XXXII The Deercote at Sudbury Hall. When built in the 1720s it had ogee domes on the corner towers, and no gatehouse. It was altered c.1750, when the gatehouse with its sham entrance was also inserted in the centre of the south wall.

XXXIII The Octagon Seat at Wotton Underwood. This building stands on a small mound opposite the Grotto Island. Composed views across the lake are visible through six of the arches. Restored by Mrs Brunner, the floor is the original but the superstructure is new.

XXXIV Wotton Underwood, the restored Five Arch Bridge. Behind the bridge is the dam to the long narrow south end of the main lake. To the right, the retaining wall meets the southerly arm of The Warrells, the water level of which is some six feet below the main lake.

XXXV *Miller's design at Lacock Abbey, showing the Hall with its carriage sweep, which was approached from the left through a large Gothic stone arch. The ha-ha, just visible in front, separated the carriage sweep from the park. The Gothic Hall, with its solidity, its attractive ogee detailing over the windows and its side towers, is typical of Miller's architectural style, as is the repeated Gothic arch line of ornamentation above the windows.*

XXXVI *Sham Castle, Bath, 1762. Built for Ralph Allen, to be seen from his town house. Miller's plan was probably adapted by the builder, Richard Jones. The number of blank openings, and their size in relation to the building, are not typical of Miller's work.*

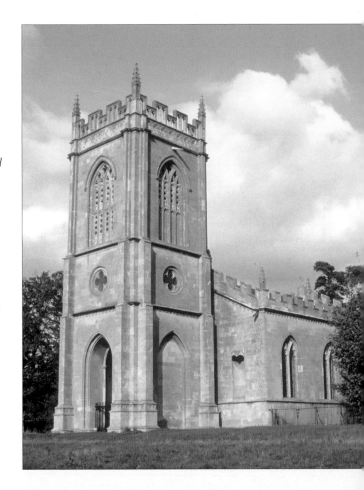

XXXVII above: *Stowe, the interior of the Gothic Temple, showing the arms of the Saxon Heptarchy. This design is attributed to Miller, who had used it earlier in his own Tower at Edgehill.*

XXXVIII above right: *Stowe, the Gothic Temple or the Temple of Liberty. Designed as the climax to Lord Cobham's politically inspired gardens, it was built to a plan of James Gibbs between 1744 and 1748. The two turrets and the pinnacles to the tower are attributed to Miller and were added later.*

XXXIX right: *Croome church, built between 1758 and 1763 by Capability Brown. The Gothic detailing and the likeness of various parts of the design to both Wroxton church and some medieval Oxford college chapels suggest Miller's hand in the exterior design.*

archives or elsewhere, so it is not known exactly what Miller was designing, though 'H' suggests the house rather than a landscape building. The west range of the Court was remodelled in 1780, and the Gothic ogee headed windows and quatrefoil decorations are similar in style to Miller's own Gothic work, though there is apparently nothing to connect his name with these alterations.

Upton

Later in July, Miller paid several visits to Upton, a mile or so south of Edgehill, an estate which had been bought by William Bumsted in 1732. The manor of Upton was originally a hamlet within the parish of Ratley, and is situated about five miles from Banbury at an elevation of about 600 feet just to the east of the Edgehill scarp. The village was depopulated and the open fields enclosed to make sheep walks before 1518, although Ratley itself was not enclosed until nearly 300 years later. In 1688 the estate was bought by Sir Rushout Cullen, a successful London merchant who, although the son of immigrants from the low countries, had purchased a baronetcy at the restoration. He rebuilt the house and made formal gardens. Early records of Upton are sparse, but there is a detailed estate map of 1774 which shows the formal gardens and the wilderness around the house, and a quarter of a mile away, to the south, a large pool. William Bumsted, also a London merchant, owned Upton from 1732 to his death in 1757, when the estate was sold to the banker Francis Child. Bumsted enlarged the house, and is thought to have been responsible for landscaping the grounds to the south, beyond the gardens.[9]

Miller's diary for 1749-50 includes brief notes of several visits to Upton. On July 20, 1750, Miller recorded that he: 'Went to ye Wkn. [workmen] & with Mr Willes to Upt^n & to L N [Lord North] to bft. [breakfast]. Drawing floor for ye Build^g & Mr Child's plans …', and the day before he and his wife had taken breakfast at Upton. The first diary entry suggests that Miller went with workmen to supervise a project at Upton before continuing on to Wroxton, a further two miles away, to breakfast with Lord North. Miller may have been supervising work at the pool prior to going on with his plans for the design of the building, or temple, with which his name has traditionally been associated. The reference to Child is interesting. Perhaps Miller was designing a plan for Child which was quite separate from his work at Upton. Bumsted seems, however, to have forecast that Miller would have to sell Radway because of his expenditure on the Tower. Letters written to Miller by his university friend Deane Swift, and also from William Henry Lyttelton cite Bumsted variously as a rascal, being Miller's enemy without cause, and as having an 'unrelenting soul'. In 1748 Deane Swift wrote: 'I am Governor of the Castle (Edgehill Tower) by your own deputation, which shall never be surrendered, like Fort Augustus, into the hands of Bumsted or any such rascal…'. Probably Bumsted was envious of Miller and was hoping to buy him out. In 1750, just before the opening Ball at the Tower, Miller's great friend Sir Edward Turner wrote: '… But could you find no other person as a purchaser of Radway than Mr Bumshead? I little thought his prophecy wou'd so soon have been completed.'[10] In the event, Miller managed to put off the impending catastrophe by one means or another. On 5 September 1750 Miller referred in his diary to going to Bumstead's pond in the postchaise, probably with Sir Edward Turner and Mr Leigh of Adlestrop who had both stayed on at Radway after Miller's opening ball two days previously at

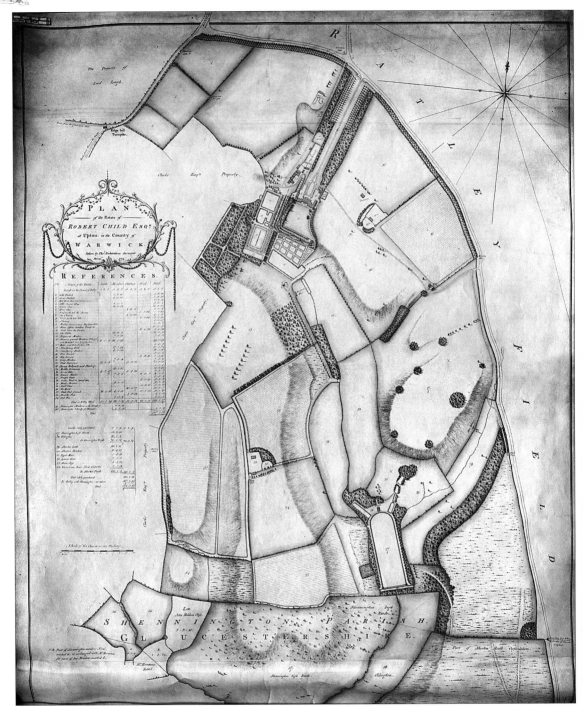

97   *Upton, the estate map of 1774 by T. Richardson, surveyor. Upton House with its formal gardens and wilderness is to the north, and the formal shape of the lake can be seen to the south. The cascades are at the head of the lake, on the eastern side. Seven round ornamental clumps of trees crown the hillside above. Some of the Scots pines and oaks in these clumps are still there today, the largest clump being protected by a ha-ha.*

Edgehill Tower. On 7 September Miller went again, this time with Colonel Conway and Lord Aylesford, obviously showing his guests the pool. Six years later, in his diary entry for 8 October he refers to riding round 'Mr Bumsted's Pool to ye theatre and red Horse &c finest d (day)…'. The Red Horse was a figure cut into the reddish soil of the hill above Tysoe, a village below the scarp south of Edgehill. Probably Anglo Saxon in origin, the Horse used to be scoured out regularly on Palm Sunday, but now no longer exists. In 1756, on 10 and 11 October Miller referred to riding round 'Mr Bumpstead's pool'. There are no further details given in the diaries, either concerning work at Upton or visits to Temple Pool.

The estate design of 1774 provides a picture of what the landscaped area south of the big house might have looked like in the 1750s.[11] The plan shows the formal gardens, pools and a wilderness area surrounding the house. A stream leaving the lowest pool within the gardens empties into a canal-shaped narrow pool in the adjacent field. The stream then continues south through woodland and another field before entering a formally shaped large pool with various associated features, including another small formal feeder pool, a temple, and, on the eastern side, a series of four small pools and cascades leading down the hillside. Above, on a spur of the hill, there are eight round clumps of various sizes, planted to overlook the valley. On the crest of the hillside across the valley from the main house there is a short and wide avenue of trees, and there are lines of double hedging in places on the boundaries of the fields on the undulating landscape to the west.

In Upton House there is an undated painting by Anthony Devis, which is thought to have been painted for the Child family in about 1784. This painting shows a winter skating scene on Temple Pool. On the bank there is a small temple, which has five pillars supporting a low triangular pediment. The design is not dissimilar from the Ionic temple at Farnborough. On the hill above there is a clump of oaks and pines, and Upton House can be seen on the distant hillside. A rider with hounds is visible beyond the pool. The Child family used Upton mainly as a hunting seat, which explains the season and subjects chosen by Devis. In the estate map of 1774 the same landscape details are shown, with the addition of a small ornamental construction in front of the temple, and also a series of four 'pools' or cascades on the hillside to the north east leading down to the main pool. Devis did not show these cascades, though of course it is always possible that he left them out to simplify the painting.

The large pool at Upton is not connected to the designed gardens and the house today, though slight earthworks suggest that the shallow valley watered by the stream which leaves the gardens might once have been landscaped. A substantial dam was formed to allow the stream to form Temple Pool. There is now no temple on the north bank, as illustrated on the 1774 map, but instead there is another temple, of a different design, on the dam at the southern end, shown on a later map of 1819. Both this map and the O.S. map for 1886 show Temple Pool, the later temple and the cascades much as they are shown in 1774.

When the small hillside pools illustrated on the 1774 map were investigated, the ground above the top 'pool' had obviously been made up, as had the edge of the hill in front of the adjacent clump of pines which are shown in the painting. Although the area is very overgrown, it was possible to make out the remains of the dams and the lower pools. The slope is steep, and there is no water now where the top two cascades must have been, only rough ground and shrubs, with a path between the top 'pool' and the second. Within the undergrowth in the area of the third 'pool' there is a rectangular concrete pond which still holds some water, and below this another grassy track crosses the site, supported by a wall of rough local Hornton stone, faced with plaster now green with age. Harts-tongue ferns grow in the cracks. At the base a small cave or grotto has been made, which now has small stalactites of limestone in the roof. The wall is about 11 feet high by 24 feet across, and the cave itself is only 18 inches high by about 2½ feet. Below the grotto wall are the remains of the lowest pool, now only fed by a spring or two, leading into the lake. The presence of a 19th-century hydraulic ram here suggests that the flow of water used to be much greater than it is today. At the site of the temple at the north end of the pool, some of the stone foundations can still be found under the weed growth. The hilltop clumps remain today much as shown on the 1774 map, the biggest clump being surrounded by a wall with a drop on the field side, making a ha-ha. From the hilltop the views are extensive; over the estate to the south west, and to Upton House to the north west. Adjacent to Temple Pool, there is a small wood known as Hiron's covert. The Hiorn brothers often worked as masons for Miller, the name being spelt in a variety of different ways, and it is possible that they were the masons responsible for the first and perhaps both temples, and that the name of the covert commemorates this fact.

The 1774 map shows interesting and extensive planting on the hills of the estate as well as that round Temple Pool. Remains of the planting and most of the tracks with their ancient hedges alongside can still be seen. Some of these tracks run within double hedges, reminiscent of Miller's own double hedges at Radway. The hedges kept stock in, and the tracks across the rolling hilly landscape would have made excellent exercising rides for horses. The avenue of ancient sweet chestnuts, planted only on the hilltop, must have been designed to be seen from the upper gardens at Upton House. The valley bottom was not visible from the house or upper gardens, but looking across from here to the hill rising on the other side one would have automatically assumed that the avenue continued down to the valley bottom, at the end of the garden grounds. Two outer lines of new trees have been planted to form an eventual replacement for the old avenue.

Although it is not certain that Miller actually worked at Upton, the temple and some of the landscaping shown on the 1774 map is typical of his work. The ingenious use of the hillside springs forming the cascades, and the small grotto with its petrifying drip, can be compared with Miller's own work at Radway. The hilltop clumps of mixed pine and oak are similar to those at Farnborough and Honington, and are similarly used on hilltop positions. The earlier temple may be by Miller, but there is insufficient evidence to ascribe it to him. The formal outline of the main pool suggests that it was not designed by Miller, and was possibly of an earlier date than Miller's work. Taken together, the evidence indicates a reasonably strong attribution to Miller for the design of the cascades and the hilltop clumps, but not for the formal lake and the later temple.

Sudbury

On 4 August 1750 Miller recorded in his diary: 'drawing a design for Mʳ Vernon of Sidbury'. No further mention of the design is made in the diary for this year, but Miller's diary references to his designs are often very brief. Although no further evidence of Miller's work for George Vernon, or indeed any note of Miller ever having visited Sudbury, has

98 *Sudbury, a map adapted from the six-inch O.S. map, 1890, showing the Deercote in the park, and the stream to the east of it, which has been widened to form ornamental long narrow pools.*

come to light, Miller did several designs for other men without visiting their properties, and a visit to Sudbury revealed several aspects of the mid-18th-century landscaping which strongly suggest Miller's hand.

The Vernon family acquired the manor of Sudbury, in Derbyshire, through marriage in the reign of Henry VIII, when there was a medieval deer park of 65 acres to the west of the church. The first manor house was built in 1613, and in 1614 a new deer park was made to the north of the estate. As the steward relates:

> When sixtene hundred and the fourtenthe yeare
> Of Christ our Lord almost accomplish'd were …
> The olde Blakmore (enlarged with some more ground)
> Was with a strong high pale encompaste round.
> The purpose was (as shortly did appeare)
> To make a Parke for redd and fallowe deere.

The park pale was three miles around, and the work, carried out by one man, took almost two years to complete. A square fishpond in the new park, still there and shown on the O.S. map for 1890, probably dates from this period.[12]

A new and larger house was built *c.*1659, with formal gardens and avenues, and a series of ponds created from original fishponds. George's grandson, also George (1709-80), was created Baron in 1762. He had inherited in 1718 as a minor and the Hall was let during his childhood. In 1723 a Deercote was built. In appearance it was three-sided, with plastered walls and four towers capped with ogee domes. A painting hanging in the stone passage at the Hall illustrates a distant view from the Hall of the towers rising above trees, looking rather elegant and French in appearance. The Deercote obviously had a dual function, to aid in corralling or feeding the deer, and also to give the appearance in the distance of an old castle in the grounds. During the middle part of the 18th century Vernon made sweeping changes to the grounds. The formal avenues were thinned to leave fashionable clumps, the formal gardens were altered and one large lake was made in front of the house from the linked ponds, terminated by a sham bridge over the dam. The Deercote now looked old fashioned, and in 1750 it was Gothicised and the surrounding walls were thatched. It now has repeated capped crenellations along the length of the walls. These may have been added later in the century.[13] It is the major alterations to the Deercote, and the landscaping associated with this building in the deer park, with which Miller is associated.

The alterations included a new sham gatehouse, with no actual opening, which was inserted in the centre of the south-facing wall. The castellated walls joining the towers were lowered at this time by perhaps a third. This alteration would have provided the bricks for the new gatehouse, so that it matched the original work. The gatehouse has two tall towers on either side of a pointed, castellated Gothic-arched centre wall. The towers in cross section are an exact copy of those forming the gatehouse at Warwick Castle, as viewed from the courtyard, with longer sides facing outwards and inwards and shorter sides on the corners. The sham windows in the Deercote are rectangular, however, as compared with the arched windows in the Castle gatehouse, and the Deercote towers have repeated stringcourses up their length. The Deercote gatehouse is of brick, originally plastered to look like stone, while at Warwick the gatehouse is of real stone; nevertheless, the two are remarkably similar. At this time the domes were also removed from the four corner towers and the arrow slits were replaced by quatrefoil windows with stone surrounds. Gothic pointed open arched entrances leading into the towers, also with stone surrounds, would have provided shelter for the deer in bad weather. Similar open archways are repeated along the length of the south wall. The whole structure is built of brick except for the decorative stonework, and there are remnants of white plaster still adhering to the brickwork. In the painting in the Hall the Deercote is shown as a light stone coloured building, but as only the towers are illustrated, rising above the surrounding trees, a direct comparison with the present building is not possible. These Gothic alterations would have given the old Deercote the satisfactory and fashionable appearance of an old medieval castle when seen across George Vernon's park from the Hall.

Bishop Pococke visited Sudbury between 1751 and 1765, and commented:

> ... a serpentine river runs through the lawn behind the house, and in the park is a square arcade, with a turret at each corner, and trees being planted about it, through which it is seen, has a very fine effect.[14]

The effect is now lost, at least at close quarters, for the park has been turned over to agriculture and the Deercote, although still in good condition, stands marooned in the middle of crops.

The six-inch O.S. map for Derbyshire (1890) shows further details which probably relate to the mid–18th-century landscaping. The stream flowing south along the field boundary to the east of the Deercote has been artificially widened to form four long narrow pools. The levels in these pools used to be held up by two weirs, and a site investigation showed the old dams still clearly visible, although the pools are now largely weed filled. The ruinous weirs revealed evidence of large stone blocks which are probably of 18th century origin. Although there are no trees here now, the 1890 O.S. map shows that when it was parkland there were individual trees and groups of trees scattered in the park and planted around the Deercote. There are footpaths leading across the park towards the pools, and the pools appear to have been part of ornamental landscape work in the vicinity of the Deercote, which visitors would have been taken across the park to see. The alteration of a length of a small stream in this manner, with long, narrow pools with controlled water levels, is a distinctive feature of Miller's work at Farnborough, at Wroxton and at Arbury.

The alterations to the Deercote, with the strong resemblance of the gatehouse to that of Warwick Castle, and the typical long narrow pools on the nearby stream, again with a strong resemblance to Miller's work elsewhere, make it almost certain that the work at Sudbury is his.

Gosfield

In September 1750, after his visit to Wimpole, Miller went to stay for a week with Robert Nugent at Gosfield Hall, near Braintree. The estate is situated on fairly level ground with a slight slope from west to east. Dominating the landscape to the south is the large lake, which was originally formed by damming the Bourne brook in the 16th century. The fine church is an integral part of the grounds, standing alone to the south of the Hall.

Gosfield Hall was built as a defensible mansion around a central courtyard in about 1545 by Sir John Wentworth. During the 1560s Queen Elizabeth visited Gosfield twice to see Lady Maltravers, Sir John's only daughter. The property was later bought by Sir Thomas Millington, First Physician to both William and Mary, and Queen Anne, who added a new Grand Salon. In 1715 the property was bought by John Knight, whose widow married as her third husband Robert Nugent, later Earl Nugent and Viscount Clare.

Nugent had money and personal charm, and although his reputation was dubious he was a popular M.P. for 50 years and was friendly with the Prince of Wales. Horace Walpole, the poet Pope and the dramatist Goldsmith all visited Gosfield. Walpole thought Gosfield 'extremely in fashion, but did not answer to me, though there are fine things about it …'. Nugent married in succession three rich widows, and to his friends 'to Nugentise' became to marry a rich widow. Nugent enlarged the Hall, and carried out extensive improvements to the park. In 1788 Nugent died, and the estate was inherited by his daughter Mary, the wife of George Grenville, who became the 1st Marquis of Buckingham in 1784. Gosfield therefore became part of the vast Grenville-Temple estates. In 1807-9 the Hall was rented to Louis XVIII of France, who planted several groups of elms in the park, one of which, near the church, was known as the King's Clump.[15]

Miller had known Robert Nugent since at least 1736, when Miller obtained an alabaster chimneypiece for Mrs Nugent from a farmhouse in Essex, the farmer happening to be storing his corn in the room at the time.[16] Letters from Nugent to Miller from the

1740s testify to Miller visiting Gosfield regularly. Miller has traditionally been credited with the Gothic alterations to the Hall, both inside and out. Nugent liked to have everything in the first fashion, not only with his house but also on the estate, and was particularly interested in landscaping improvements. On October 15, 1746, Nugent wrote referring to '… great Alterations which I hope will please you. This week concluded the new Head to my *Lake* …', and two years later, in June 1748, he wrote to Miller saying:

> I wish heartily to see you here; the place is greatly altered, the Lawns are greater, the water is greater, the Plantations are much greater and the House indoors is hardly to be known again. Why may you not come some time before the middle of August …[17]

In 1750 Miller stayed at Gosfield from 15 to 24 September. On Sunday, 16 September Miller recorded in his diary that he walked down to the lake with other guests. On Monday he was walking with Nugent, then on Tuesday Miller wrote: 'w. with Mr Nugent, laying out the valley near the Lake.' In the evening they were out walking again. On Thursday Miller and Nugent went again 'to the Lake & etc.' – presumably again discussing the laying out of the park near the lake. Later that day Miller and Nugent rode out to look at the site of a farmhouse, and in the evening they both went down to the lake again with a Mr Dickens, who was also staying at Gosfield. On Friday, as well as going to the lake once more, Miller drew a plan of the proposed farmhouse for Nugent and then on Saturday he drew out the 'Ground Plot of ye Farm'. Nugent and Miller were also interested in the current books on country seats and their pleasure grounds. While at Gosfield Miller recorded reading Vitruvius Britannicus and looking at drawings by Buck, both of which must have been in Nugent's library. Miller left Gosfield on Monday, 24 September, on his way to visit Mr Pitt at Enfield Chase. Pitt, who besides his many other talents was an able landscape designer, was carrying out many improvements to the grounds at Enfield Chase which he was leasing. In 1753 Miller visited Gosfield again, but no details of this visit are known.

Eighteenth-century maps show that the parkland surrounding the Hall was quite extensive, and also that in 1769 the grassland came right up to the Hall itself.[18] There was a ha–ha about 70 yards south of the Hall. Clumps of trees and single specimens were planted in the park both within the 'lawns' running down to the lake from the Hall, and also on the rising ground beyond the lake which led to Parkhall wood on the skyline. Some of these fine trees still exist today, including Weymouth or Eastern White pines, Scotch pines and one remaining Tulip tree in the Menagerie plantation. Those to the south west beyond the lake have largely disappeared under modern agriculture. The lake, which was nearly a mile long, was terminated by a long dam, and a bridge which gave the impression that the lake extended the far side of it. Nearby was an ice-house in a small plantation. The enlargement of the lake was the most important visual improvement to the landscape. It was an impressive sight from the Hall, and was used for boating in the summer. On the lakeside there was both a boathouse and a landing stage.

No other designer is known to have been involved at Gosfield, so the conclusion must be drawn that the landscape here was designed primarily by Miller, together with Nugent. He had probably been assisting Nugent with the laying out of his grounds for some years, as the content of the letter written by Nugent in 1748 would suggest. It is more than likely that Miller had had a hand in the enlargement of the lake, and perhaps had suggested that the stream which fed it, though small, would provide an adequate flow for the job. The harnessing of comparatively small streams to make effective landscape features was typical of Miller's work. The comment in Nugent's letter suggests that the damming of the lake had already been carried out, and that the water was slowly filling up behind the dam.

An important point to make about Miller's work at Gosfield is that it is almost the only time when he makes a direct reference in his diary entries – or for that matter in his letters – to the actual *laying out of ground*. Typically, the diary entries do not give much detail, and even with the entry cited above no more description is given than 'laying out the valley near the Lake'. It is not certain, therefore, whether this phrase refers to planting plans pegged out on the ground, choice of trees, actual planting (although it would have been rather early in the year for this) or even earth-moving and reshaping. Normally Miller only says that he was walking in the garden or grounds at a given venue, perhaps giving the time taken, which may suggest that discussions were taking place. At Gosfield he was definitely involved with the actual designing of the landscape.

Kirtlington

Some time during 1750, Miller prepared a plan of a landscape building for the estate at Kirtlington Park, about eight miles north of Oxford, the seat of Sir James Dashwood, brother to Sir Francis Dashwood of West Wycombe. Sir James was a great friend of Sir Edward Turner of Ambrosden, who lived only six miles away to the east, and it was probably through the latter that Miller was introduced to him. Sir James went on the Grand Tour with Sir Roger Newdigate, for whom Miller designed the first Gothic alterations at Arbury. Between 1741 and 1746 Sir James built a new Palladian mansion at Kirtlington, designed by John Sanderson and built by him together with William Smith of Warwick.

During this period Sir James had commissioned a plan for the improvement of the grounds by Thomas Greening, the Royal Gardener, only part of which was carried out. In an undated letter from Sir James to Miller, written from Sir Edward Turner's house, he apologised for having to delay his visit to Radway due to illness, and mentioned renewing 'our scheme'.[19] No further information has come to light concerning the scheme, but it is obvious that discussions were quite advanced. The 'scheme' may well have been have been carried out by Capability Brown, who signed a contract with Sir James to landscape the grounds in 1751, one of Brown's first commissions in private practice. Brown was probably recommended to Sir James by Miller, who had connections with most of the owners of the estates where Brown worked during the early years of his private practice. There exists a plan for the grounds at Kirtlington on which is written: 'Greening's plan totally changed by Brown', showing Greening's Switzer-like plan of clearings and rather tortuous paths.[20] Some of Brown's ideas on a further plan, in Brown's hand, seem also to have been scored through by Sir James. The scenario is similar to that at Wimpole, where Miller gave advice on the grounds and where plans drawn up by Robert Greening, Thomas' son, were later superseded by those of Brown.

Adlestrop

Following the dissolution of the monasteries, Sir Thomas Leigh acquired the manor of Adlestrop in the 1530s, and the family first began to live there in 1632. In 1725, William Leigh inherited the property, and in 1750 his son James, who knew both Sir Edward Turner and Sanderson Miller through their Oxford connections, asked Miller to design a two-storey extension to Adlestrop House. James Leigh inherited the property in 1757, and in 1759 Miller was asked to provide a further design, this time for the south-west front. This new front has two Gothic bow windows on each side, and a matching central Gothic façade with three windows above and two windows either side of the door below. All are surmounted by crocketed finials and have typical Gothic detailing. The design is among Miller's finest Gothic work. Investigations have failed to uncover anything to suggest Miller's hand in the actual landscaping there, other than a single instruction to order plants from Thomas Bincks in 1752-3.[21] Samuel Driver, in the employ of Sir Edward Turner, James' brother-in-law, provided plants in the 1750s, and in 1759 prepared a simple plan for Adlestrop of serpentine curves, water features and a mount, totally unlike Miller's work.[22]

In 1796-9 James' son, James Henry, added a further wing on the east side of the house in a Gothic style similar to Miller's earlier work. The grounds were extensively redesigned by Humphry Repton in the late 18th century. Jane Austen was staying at Adlestrop with her uncle, the Reverend Thomas Leigh, rector of Adlestrop, when he unexpectedly inherited Stoneleigh Abbey, in Warwickshire, in 1806. Stoneleigh Abbey subsequently became the family's principal residence, but the Leigh family still own the freehold of Adlestrop House (now known as Adlestrop Park) and grounds, which are let on a long lease.

Chart Park

During 1751 Miller was asked to design a Gothic Greenhouse for Henry Talbot at Chart Park, just south of Dorking in Surrey, and a building, or buildings, for the grounds at Eythrope, in Buckinghamshire. Henry Talbot (1700-84) was a wealthy businessman who had been on several trading voyages to China for the East India Company. After his return from his last voyage, in 1746, he bought the property known as The Vineyard, renaming the estate Chart Park. He made an elegant Gothic mansion out of the original house, enlarged the estate by additional purchases of land, and 'improved' the gardens and grounds. In February 1751 Lord North asked Miller on behalf of Talbot to design a plan for him:

> Mr Henry Talbot my neighbour wishes extreamly to obtain a favour of you, & does not know how to ask it but thro me. He is to build a Green House, & wishes to have the front Gothick if he could have the sanction of your taste; without which he dares not venture upon it. The experience I have had of your goodness has engaged me to undertake being his advocate, & send you the dimensions of the building he proposes; which if you will be so good as to take under your consideration, & make your report by way of plan, you will oblige us both extreamly. Mr Talbot proposes to make the front of wood, and desires to set about the building as soon as he may …

Probably on Miller's advice, the Talbots asked Henry Keene to carry out the work. On 9 March Mrs Talbot wrote to Lord North, not to Miller himself, as follows:

> My Lord, The inimitable plan y[r]. Lord[p]. Was so good to send me from Mr Miller has charm'd both Mr Talbot and myself so much that we have sent after Mr Keene and propose setting out tomorrow morning for surry in order to carry it into immediate execution, therefore I fear we must trouble Mr Millar again by accepting of his obliging offer to drawing out the middle windows and mouldings etc. by a larger scale.

No plan has come to light, but mention is made of a Gothic Greenhouse in the sale of the house in 1813. Not content with the Greenhouse, Mrs Talbot then asked Lord North if he would 'drop a hint' to Miller about a plan for a Gothic arch she wanted. This was to be quarter of a mile from the house, large enough for a coach to drive under. She wrote: 'I should fancy something of a bitt of a wall on each side (of the Arch) in the nature of a ruin for the paling to join to would make the enclosure look prettier … which Arch and walls I propose to build of flint.' Lord North, enclosing her letter to Miller, wrote: 'I doubt when you see her farther views, you will think Ladys are a little craving; but that will happen to men whose abilities for satisfying them are so well known …'.[23] It is not known if Miller continued to oblige her, or if he ever visited Chart Park, but the work may have stood him in good stead, for Henry Talbot's relation John Ivory Talbot was to ask Miller to design much more substantial and interesting Gothic buildings for him at Lacock a year or two later.

The estate was described in the 1813 Sale Particulars as 'abundantly supplied with fine Spring and Soft Water, Walled gardens, Hot House, Green House, Ice House, extensive Park, Pleasure Grounds, Woods, Groves, Plantations, Terrace Sheet of Water … Orchard …'. In 1754 Henry Talbot married as his second wife Katharine, daughter of Sir Hugh Clopton of Stratford-upon-Avon. The property came into the hands of Thomas Hope, owner of the adjacent property, who demolished the house as he had no use for a second mansion.

Eythrope

Eythrope was one of two seats in Buckinghamshire owned by Sir William Stanhope, who was friendly with the Prince of Wales and also Sir Francis Dashwood. Eythrope was only about five miles from Wotton Underwood, where George Grenville lived, and it was probably through the Grenvilles that Miller met Sir William. Sir William was laying out his grounds between 1738 and 1751, when he was said to have been expending 'large sums in the improvement and decoration of the house and grounds …The imitation of ruins of an amphitheatre, castles and turretted buildings, erected … on the neighbouring eminences, gave an air of extent and magnificence to the grounds.'[24] Miller certainly designed a plan for Sir William, who referred to it in a letter to Miller, dated 7 September, but with no year, in which he says:

> I approve extremely of y^r Plan for my farm wch I receiv'd yesterday, but as I am now very Deep in Mortar wth my kitchen Garden walls, I cannot begin any Building this year. Early in the next Spring, if you will favour me with y^r Company & advice, you will lay a very Great Obligation upon
>
> Sr, yr. Most Obedient & Obliged
> Hum. Ser^t.
> W. Stanhope.[25]

On the back of the letter there are some interesting sketches of a Gothic window and the head of a Gothic door or window. The word 'farm' may have been used to indicate an actual farmhouse, or ornamental grounds which were also used for general agriculture, or at least for grazing animals – both Enville and The Leasowes have been described as farms.

There are two drawings in the British Museum showing different designs of a turreted Gothic gateway. Neither of these drawings is signed. The earlier drawing, showing the gateway with three flanking bays, is entitled; '27 June 1751: Design approved by Sir Wm Stanhope at Twittenham for Ethrupe: shortened two windows at each end'. The second drawing shows two of the bays at each end removed, and corner buttresses and pinnacles added to the gateway. It is entitled 'July 3rd. 1751: Sir W.Stanhope's Ethrupe'.[26] The architect Isaac Ware was employed at Eythrope, where he designed the stables. These were in the Palladian style on the east side but on the west were in the Gothic style to match the house. The drawings held in the British Museum may have been by Ware, but Ware did not like the Gothic style, and the drawings look rather like a design for a toy castle. In a description of Stanhope's follies by William Robertson of Kilkenny in 1797, some of the follies are described as 'poor imitations of ruins' but 'those of castles upon others [other hillsides] nearly perfect – with a Gateway in the centre and two towers at each side.'[27] A further drawing of this Gateway, which was erected as a façade to a farmhouse known as Eythrope Park Farm on a hill overlooking the park to the south, is entitled 'Wichendon Castle' and shows the building, as described by Robertson, with additional Gothic roundels in the second towers. It looks as if the second 1751 drawing was altered again before being built finally as 'Wichendon Castle', the additional towers making the whole look much more like a genuine old castle. This final plan is more likely to have been by Miller. The Eythrope Gateway, or Wichendon Castle, as built, is similar to 'Sham Castle' at Prior Park. Bishop Pococke, visiting in 1751, commented on a fine bridge over the river Tame 'at which the river is stop'd to raise it' so that it could be seen from Stanhope's house.[27] This produced the effect of a lake, similar to that produced by Miller's work at Honington and Alscot, raising the question as to whether Miller had advised Stanhope on how to achieve this feature. Neither Sir William nor Eythrope is mentioned in either of Miller's two diaries, for 1749/50 and 1756, but this is not surprising if Miller's particular association with Sir William over his 'plan' was only in the years 1751 and 1752. The house was demolished in 1810–11, and little remains of a once extensive landscaped property with a large lake and several landscape buildings.

Stoke Gifford

In 1752, Miller was asked to advise at Stoke Gifford. The extensive designed landscape at Stoke Gifford was created from an agricultural estate by Norborne Berkeley from the 1740s to 1768. In 1749 he called in Thomas Wright to assist him. A great viewing terrace around Sims Hill was constructed, and Wright designed several landscape buildings, as well as a series of woodland gardens connected by paths within the plantations for which Stoke became most well known. Bishop Pococke noted in 1764 that it was 'reckon'd among the finest things in England'. At Badminton House the Beaufort archives contain a reference to Norborne Berkeley contacting Miller through George Lyttelton, asking Miller to advise on landscaping and waterworks.[28] Lyttelton often conveyed such requests to Miller, who usually acted on them quite promptly. However, the date when Miller was asked to advise, 1752, is between the years of Miller's two diaries, and there is nothing in the Miller correspondence relating to Stoke.

No more details have come to light concerning Berkeley's request, but it is interesting to note that Wright is not thought to have been involved with the creation of the lake at

Stoke, which was the focal point of the landscape. Miller's wife had relations living only about five miles away at Siston Court in the village of Siston east of Bristol, so Miller could well have combined a visit to Stoke Gifford with a visit to Siston Court. In 1768 Berkeley left to become Governor of Virginia, and the estate was taken over by his sister, the 4th Duchess of Beaufort.

In the 20th century the landscape became vandalised and semi-derelict, and the lake was filled in when the motorway was built, but recently efforts have been made to restore parts of the landscape.

The Shire Hall, Warwick

The new Shire Hall, designed by Miller *c.*1753, is a dignified and well proportioned building, well suited to its main purpose as a judicial court. In 1752, at a meeting of the county gentry, it had been decided that a new Shire Hall was to be built, since the deteriorating condition of the old Hall was causing concern. On 25 September 1752, Sir Roger Newdigate wrote in his diary: 'To Warwick with Mr Stratford [of Merevale Hall] meeting for re-building Town Hall subscribed 10gs [a guinea was 21 shillings] – all the Lawyers there declared the Trustees have no power to interfere in any determination of a general meeting to repair or rebuild Mr Miller to receive and spend at his discretion'.[29] The members of the meeting had not the power to levy a rate; Miller, therefore, was vested with the authority to collect voluntary subscriptions. The county of Warwickshire was not alone in this situation, but Miller and his friends were to find it difficult to obtain enough money by subscription, those living in Birmingham, although then the richest part of the county, being particularly set against contributing. Despite opening an account

99 *The Shire Hall, Warwick, an engraving by Edward Rooker after a plan and elevation by Francis Hiorn, 1768, showing Miller's design for the new Shire Hall, c.1753. The decorative swags between the capitals were finally put in place c.1762.*

at Hoare's bank in London, and advertising in the London papers, insufficient funds were raised. Having stayed overnight on 24 June 1756 at David Hiorn's, Miller's diary entry for 25 June reads as follows:

> Settling Mr Hiorn's Acct. &c. bfd [breakfasted] at Mr Hiorn's....w.w. [went with] M^{r}H to Ld Brooke's. Con^n [conversation] with Ld B. and Mr Wise ab^t ye Hall &c. W.[went] to the Swan. Sr C. Mord^t, [Sir Charles Mordaunt of Walton Hall] Mr Craven, Mordaunt, Wise, Wheeler, Stratford, Geest, Bird, Talbot, Dewes [from Wellesbourne Hall], Hutsford, Bromley, Beardesley, S^r R Newdigate &c. 20 in all – when it was thought best to have an Act of P. [Parliament] to raise a sum not exceed^g £4000 the Subscript^{ns} not amounting to much above 1250 – W^t. [went] to the Hall with S^r C, S^r R &c.

The Act of Parliament 'for the Rebuilding and Keeping in repair the Shire Hall of the County of Warwick' (30 GeoII.c.56) was duly passed in 1757. This allowed the Quarter Sessions to make a special rate for the money deemed necessary (£4,000) to complete the project. Despite the continuing financial problems, Miller had immediately begun to design the new building on being appointed architect in charge, and by 1753 estimates had been received for the work by the Hiorn brothers and also from Job Collins together with John Polton, both Warwick men. Miller had employed the Hiorns on other projects, but decided to employ all four men, possibly because Collins had been working for Lord Brooke at Warwick Castle, and Lord Brooke's subscription had been the largest. In the event, David Hiorns took over the management of the whole project, while William Hiorn, with Job Collins, worked on the masonry. Polton's name does not appear again. Although the Hiorns drew up the plans, and Miller, in his usual way, did not take any payment for his work, it seems quite certain that the design of the Hall was his. The interior design was for two octagons of free-standing pillars, open to the main hall, to form the Nisi Prius Court and the Crown Court respectively. Later, additional walls were added to close the courts off from the main hall. The central room under the grand jury chambers was also an octagon, the main hall itself being a rectangle. Miller's design was discussed by other informed amateurs, including Sir Roger Newdigate and Thomas Prowse, who were both critical of the octagons. Prowse, who had property in Somerset and at Wicken in Northamptonshire, was a good architect himself and also a friend of Miller's. He was concerned about the choice of Corinthian columns, and was convinced that a round court would be better than the octagon shape, but finally Miller's design prevailed. Besides those mentioned, other specialists involved in the practical work included Richard Newman, mason, David Sanders, a local carpenter, the Warwick carver Benjamin King, and the plasterer Robert Moore. Newman, who also worked elsewhere in the south Midlands, had worked on at least one of the pavilions at Farnborough Hall. In 1748/9, Miller had himself employed Moore at Radway. Moore also worked on Miller's designs at Hagley, and at Belhus, in Essex, and both King and Moore had been employed at Arbury on the initial Gothicising of the Hall in the 1750s.

The Palladian exterior of the Shire Hall was composed of a central pedimented façade with four Corinthian demi-columns. Three windows on either side of the central façade are separated by Corinthian pilasters, with double pilasters at either end. Between the capitals with their acanthus leaves were swags of leaves and flowers, beautifully designed, with no two flowers alike. Miller may well have taken the ideas for the flowers from

100 *Siston Court, Gloucestershire, one of two octagonal Gothic gate lodges built for Samuel Trotman, Miller's brother-in-law. The lodges are similar in design to the square garden pavilions of an earlier date at Arlescote House, near Radway.*

the superb plasterwork on the ceiling of the 16th-century chapel at Arbury, carried out by the English plasterer Edward Martin. The expense of carving the swags meant that cube sandstone blocks were substituted for ashlar until such time as the money could be found to complete the work, which did not take place until *c.*1762.[30] The Corinthian columns together with the finished ornamental swags give a rich and decorated air to the whole stately edifice. Hawkes has drawn attention to the striking resemblance of the elevation of the front of the Shire Hall to the upper storey for Somerset House as drawn by Inigo Jones, and to a further similarity in a drawing by Jones for Whitehall Palace. Miller's classical architectural work seems to have been inspired largely by the work of this 17th-century master designer, the first Englishman to introduce Palladian concepts to the world of English architecture.

Siston

Siston Court is a magnificent stone Elizabethan house in the tiny village of Siston to the east of Bristol. In 1252 the new deer park was licensed at Siston, the licence allowing the owner, Robert Walerand, to keep any deer that entered from Kingswood Chase, which was nearer Bristol. The house itself was probably built by Sir Richard Denys 1572-98. Kip's engraving of 1712 shows extensive formal gardens. Siston Court belonged in the mid-18th century to Samuel Trotman, uncle to Miller's wife, Susannah.

During this period new Gothic building work was carried out, including a Gothic garden pavilion and new gate lodges. The gate lodges are octagonal, with pointed roofs finished with a stone finial and ball on top. In 1754 Miller advised on unspecified work for Samuel Trotman, almost certainly including the lodges and possibly other Gothic building work. The lodges are octagonal, a favourite shape of Miller's, and are similar in design to the garden pavilions at Arlescote House, only a mile or two from Radway, but for the shape being octagonal instead of square. In 1759 Miller produced a sketch for a 'Poor's House' at Siston with two corner towers and a central spinning room. Its design was not unlike a miniature Hagley Hall.[31]

An engraving done in 1805 by Fiennes Trotman shows a view of a house rising above shrubs and trees. It has two Gothic pointed towers, and a castellated lower roofline over a Gothic entrance. The part of the garden building shown in the foreground repeats this style, with Gothic windows and a repeated Gothic-arched motif at roof height, and may be by Miller.[32] In the grounds adjacent to the Court and on the line of the higher ground to the west, groups of large trees, now well past their prime, look as if they were part of a mid-18th-century landscaping scheme similar to those Miller carried out at Radway, Honington and Farnborough. There are limes, chestnuts, and groups of mixed hardwoods and Scots pines. At the bottom of the hill, adjacent to the road leaving Siston to the south, an old wall now half submerged in undergrowth may have been designed to dam the stream and form a permanent ornamental small lake upstream of the road. It also has the effect of containing the water in times of high rainfall, and preventing the road below from flooding. There is a path running near the stream in an adjacent small piece of woodland. From the dam the stream falls over a small waterfall and under a narrow attractive stone bridge which carries the modern road, and from this point it is only a short walk up to the groups of large trees adjacent to the Court.

Although there is no specific archival evidence to attribute the gate lodges and the landscaping at Siston to Miller, the similarity of both the design of the gate lodges and the landscaping to Miller's work elsewhere, together with the close family connection, suggests strongly that the work was his.

Lacock Abbey

Lacock Abbey, founded in 1232, was originally an Augustinian nunnery. In 1539 at the dissolution, the property was bought by Sir William Sharington, who converted the buildings into a private house. The property descended through the female line and in the 17th century Sharington Talbot married Jane Lyttelton. John Ivory Talbot, who inherited Lacock in 1714, was their great-grandson. In 1753 Talbot, an M.P. and a Doctor of Law from Oxford, approached Miller to replace his Tudor Hall with a Gothic Hall, and a new forecourt. Talbot had been experimenting with Gothic additions to his house for at least twenty years, and was in his 60s when he decided to embark on rebuilding his great hall in the 'Gothick Taste'. An earlier scheme by Francis Price, the surveyor of Salisbury Cathedral, had not pleased Talbot, and Miller was recommended to him and asked if he could spare the time to design what Talbot required. Talbot was well pleased with his designs, writing to Miller 'I return many thanks for the sight of the Plans, which please me extreamly …' and later 'I return'd to this Place last night, and found my Hall in such forwardness that its Roof will begin Rearing on Monday: it still advances in beauty, and I long to see it compleat'.[33]

The Hall demanded a new entrance to the building. Miller made a double staircase approach to a new Gothic door, the design showing details which are typical of Miller's work elsewhere, particularly the angled buttresses with crocketted caps, similar to those on his own house at Radway. He designed a new gravel sweep in front, beyond which a ha-ha was created to carry the eye over into the parkland beyond. Talbot had ashlar left over from the Hall, and he next asked Miller 'Could not a Gothick Gateway be contrived in the Middle of the Wall wide enough to admit a Coach?' The wall ran alongside the old drive, which led into the stable yard. Talbot wished visitors arriving by coach to enter through a fine arched gateway in this wall and on to the gravel sweep before his new entrance and Hall. Miller duly designed an impressive Gothic arch with pinnacles at either end.[34] Talbot commented on the 'compleat Finish both of the Hall, Staircase and Gateway, each of which do honour to their Architect and reflect some on their Workmen …'. During the course of Talbot's building, he and Miller became good friends, despite the gap of thirty years or so in their ages. Talbot decorated the ceiling of his new hall with the arms of his friends, as Miller had done at Edgehill, and Miller was asked for his own arms to put up.

In an estate plan for 1764 illustrating the grounds around the Hall, the gardens show a geometric layout of straight paths, and also a large 'L' shaped formal canal and a circular pool.[35] This layout is reminiscent of the ideas of Switzer, and suggests that Talbot laid this area out soon after he succeeded to the property in 1714. In the gardens there is a rock construction over a stream which has always been referred to by the family and the villagers as 'the rockworks'. It was never a traditional grotto shape. No details concerning either the making of the rockworks or its designer have been found, and the only historical description of 'the rockworks' seems to be in Witham's History of Lacock Abbey, written in 1806: 'the shrubbery grounds are beautifully laid out, ornamented by the river Avon in serpentine directions. The cascade resembling a ruin is well executed and very appropriate to its situation'. In 2000, the rockworks area was the subject of an archaeological and archival investigation by the National Trust, to whom the Lacock estate was gifted in 1944. The remains are difficult to date, but the rockworks, in some form, appear to have been in place before Miller's arrival, and may be 18th-century overlaid by 19th-century alterations. There are still some interesting remains of the rockworks where the brook enters the gardens along the north boundary, including tufa-like rocks which look similar to those in other grottoes known to have been constructed in the mid-18th century, such as the remains of that at Honington. Water appears to have come through the rockwork wall from behind. If so, this design had similarities with Miller's grander grotto at Honington, and alterations to an existing cascade to create a 'cascade resembling a ruin' would have been very much in Miller's line of work, though without further evidence it is impossible to do more than speculate.

In 1755 Capability Brown visited Lacock and was paid a total of £250, but it is not now known what work he carried out.

Sham Castle, Bath

In 1755, Miller was asked by William Pitt to prepare a Gothic design for Ralph Allen, to be seen on the hill from Allen's town house in Bath. Allen had come to Bath from Cornwall in 1710, and made his fortune firstly from reorganising the postal system, and then from quarrying and selling Bath stone. Allen owned a considerable estate outside Bath, and had built himself a mansion on the upper slopes of a deep valley running down towards the city. The mansion, known as Prior Park, was built in 1734 by John Wood, and the poet Pope, among others, assisted Allen with the creation of the landscaped garden below the mansion.[36]

On 30 October 1755, William Pitt wrote to his friend Miller:

> … I shall then have one call upon your Imagination for a very considerable Gothic
> Object which is to stand in a very fine situation on the Hills near Bath. It is for Mr
> Allen, the idea I will explain to you when we meet. The name of that excellent man

will render my desires to you to do your best unnecessary. I shall have a particular pleasure in procuring to him the help of the Great Master of Gothick …[37]

There is no reason to suspect that the design was not carried out. Miller and Allen had many friends in common, but it is not known if Miller ever visited Allen at Bath, and the Sham Castle was not built until 1762. It was erected on a hill outside the city which was part of Allen's extensive estate, the site being chosen so that the Sham Castle could be seen from Allen's town house. The site was known as The Warren, and Allen had previously carried out extensive plantings here. Although not actually visible from Prior Park itself, the Castle was linked to it by a carriage drive through the estate.

A plan and elevation of the 'Castle at the Warren' is shown on Thorpe and Overton's estate plan of Prior Park, which although not dated was probably drawn up between 1761 and 1762. This plan also shows the landscape garden, the sham bridge at the end of the 'serpentine river' which is attributed to Pope, the Palladian bridge and other garden buildings and features.

The Castle is built as a stone façade, with a crenellated wall joining two central towers either side of a Gothic doorway. Two smaller towers are connected by further walls on either side. It is symmetrical, and is not built as a ruin. Both the Thorpe and Overton plan[38] and a drawing by Samuel Grimm in 1788 show the Castle in detail, showing that it has survived from when it was built without alterations.[39] Allen's Clerk of Works, Richard Jones, supervised the construction of Sham Castle in 1762, when Jones claimed the design as his own. However, it has been suggested that Jones probably carried out some alterations to Miller's original plan. Jones also built the Palladian Bridge spanning the lake in the Prior Park gardens in 1755. It is also possible that Capability Brown had a hand in the building, since Brown carried out further landscaping to the grounds at Prior Park in the early 1760s.[40] The general plan of Sham Castle is reminiscent of Miller's other Gothic designs, and the arrow slits and Gothic windows are typical of his castle 'ruins', but it is unlike Miller, and certainly not historically accurate, to cram so many windows into a tower or wall. It seems that the most likely explanation is that Miller's initial design was altered by Jones, who then took the credit for the building.

Allen died in 1764, and from 1769 his daughter leased the mansion. The building is now used as a school, and the 18th-century landscape garden in the valley below the house is being restored by the National Trust.

Mr Goodwin's 'Terras', near Warmington

On 16 October Miller recorded in his diary that he 'rode w. Grenville [George] to Mr. Goodwin's Terras & Warmington'. Mr. Goodwin lived at Arlescote, a mile or so from Radway Grange, and Warmington is about two miles further on. Along the steep hillside across the road from Warmington church, there is a single long, levelled stretch of grass, with a few old trees, beyond the farm buildings and just below the brow of the hill. There is an extensive view from here across the valley and north-east towards Farnborough, with its great hillside terrace facing south-west. Situated so near Warmington, this levelled area must be Mr Goodwin's terrace, no doubt created with Miller's advice. Miller and Grenville probably rode along the top road from Edgehill, then admired the view before going for a canter along the terrace, on to Warmington, and home via Arlescote along the valley road.

Stowe

The only actual reference to any positive contribution by Miller to the on-going designs for the gardens is limited to his diary entry for 15 July 1756, when he had visited the gardens with Mr Pitt and Earl Temple. The entry reads: 'W^g. in Garden w Mr Pitt & L^d.T contriv^g. a finish^g. to Gibbs build^g.' In the evening they were singing at the Grecian Temple, and on 19 July: 'walking in the evening … The Grotto etc. illuminated. W^g. till 10. fine Even^g.' Miller's grandfather had owned land at Boycott, adjacent to the Stowe estates, and Miller had been visiting Stowe since he was an undergraduate at Oxford. Entries in Miller's two diaries for 1750 and 1756 show that he visited Stowe several times a year, spending several hours at a time walking round the grounds with his host and other guests. Capability Brown was a member of the party on at least one occasion, Miller mentioning him by name in his diary entry for Tuesday, 7 November 1749.

To set Gibbs' Building, or the Temple of Liberty, in context, it is necessary to give some details of the history and development of the gardens at Stowe. The gardens are too well known to warrant a full explanation; this description will provide only a brief outline. Stowe is situated on a south-facing slope amid the gently rolling countryside to the north of Buckingham. The landscaped grounds, originally part of an extensive estate, cover about 400 acres. The Temple family had acquired the estate at Stowe in the 16th century. In the 1680s the third baronet, Sir Richard Temple, rebuilt the old Tudor house and created formal gardens. His son Richard, later Viscount Cobham, greatly enlarged the gardens to suit his position as both an important military commander and one of the foremost Whig politicians. A cultured man, he commanded the assistance of those most skilled in architecture, the arts and the laying-out of grounds in the pioneering development of his garden; men such as John Vanbrugh, Charles Bridgeman, James Gibbs, the poet Alexander Pope, and William Kent. Under Bridgeman the formal designs of the gardens were softened, although vistas and long diagonal walks and avenues were retained. Ha-has enabled sweeping views to be appreciated well beyond the garden limits. The designed area was greatly extended, including a forest park with axial rides. In 1724 Lord Perceval described the new designs: '…Nothing is more irregular in the whole, nothing more regular in the parts, which totally differ, one from the other …'[41]

After Cobham's political quarrel with the Prime Minister in 1733, he began to develop new areas of the gardens as a political statement against modern corruption and in praise of the historic English virtues of freedom, liberty and patriotism. With William Kent as designer, the Elysian Fields were created, including the Temples of Ancient Virtue, Modern Virtue, which was designed as a ruin, and British Worthies. Hawkwell Field was laid out with three large temples and the Palladian bridge, the Gothic Temple or Temple of Liberty being the ideological climax to the whole design. Built of ironstone in 1744-8, on a commanding hilltop setting, the Temple commemorated the importance of the ancient Saxon liberties, and was dedicated to Liberty, Enlightenment and the Constitution. Cobham's last venture was his creation of the informal Grecian Valley, carried out by Capability Brown. On Cobham's death in 1749, Richard Grenville, Cobham's nephew, inherited Stowe and added the name of Temple to his own, later becoming Earl Temple. He enlarged the whole concept of the gardens at Stowe, employing the best European architects. The political vision became imperial, monuments were erected to Wolfe and Captain Cook, and the Grecian Temple

was renamed the Temple of Concord and
Victory after the triumphant conclusion of
the Seven Years' War in 1763. The reputation
of the gardens became international. The
descendants of Earl Temple dissipated their
great wealth, and finally in 1921 the whole
estate was sold up, the house becoming Stowe
School. In 1989 the National Trust took
over a large part of the historic landscape,
implementing an on-going programme of
research and restoration.

Between about 1750 and 1756 the
Gothic Temple underwent several additions
and alterations. The original design by James
Gibbs, a triangular ground plan with three
pentagon-shaped towers, may be considered
more Elizabethan than Gothic. It was
possibly based on Sir Thomas Tresham's
unfinished Triangular Lodge of 1594-7, in the
neighbouring county of Northamptonshire,
for it is almost identical in size. Gibbs was
a Catholic, and Sir Thomas Tresham had
been imprisoned for his adherence to the
Catholic faith. His Triangular Lodge had
definite religious associations with the Blessed
Trinity.

Miller, who had known Lord Temple for
many years and was only five years younger,
appears to have been asked by him to add
further Gothic details to the Gothic Temple.
Engravings of the Gothic Temple by Bickham
and Seeley, both dated 1750, show that by
this date two lanterns had been added to
the tops of the two lower towers of Gibbs'
original building.[42] The ceilings of the two
ground-floor circular chapels were decorated
with the arms of the Temple family, including
those of Countess Temple. This work was not
completed until 1750 or later, since Countess

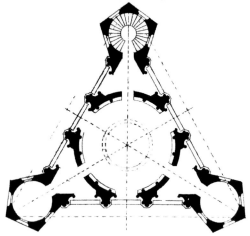

101 *Stowe, elevation and plan of the Temple of
Liberty, by James Gibbs (1682-1754). The Temple
of Liberty, or the Gothic Temple, was built between
1744 and 1748, as shown in this drawing. By
1750, engravings by both Bickham and Seeley
show the addition of a small cupola to each of the
two lower towers, and c.1752 crocketed pinnacles
were added to the central tower. These additions
are typical of Miller's work elsewhere, and it is
very likely that they are by him.*

Temple, Lord Cobham's sister Hester, did not receive her elevation until this year. In 1756
crocketed pinnacles were added to the corners of the highest tower, and the vaulted ceilings
inside the two first-floor chapels were decorated with the arms of the Saxon heptarchy.
It is quite possible that Miller was responsible for both the lanterns, reminiscent of those
at Lacock, and also the crocketed pinnacles, for both are very much in his style.[43] The
internal decoration of the Saxon heptarchy is similar to that which Miller had used in his

own decoration of the interior of the Tower at Edgehill six years previously. The exterior was originally decorated with statues of the seven Saxon Gods who gave their names to the days of the week. Horace Walpole wrote about the Gothic Temple in August 1753, reporting that 'the windows are throughout consecrated with painted glass; most of it from the Priory at Warwick'.[44] Miller knew the Wises at the Priory well. Henry Wise, the royal gardener, purchased the Priory as a house for his retirement. He died in 1738, and his son John was involved with the deliberations concerning the new Shire Hall in Warwick. Miller had used painted glass himself on numerous occasions, so it is likely that he obtained the painted glass for the Gothic Temple at Stowe from John Wise.

Gibbs' original design for the Gothic Temple had a formal simplicity and a regularity which was quite altered by the Gothic additions. Further decoration was added to the Gothic windows in the towers to match those in the main body of the Temple, as well as the additions of the two lanterns and the decorated pinnacles. The finished appearance of the Gothic Temple is far more like an asymmetrical Gothic church, with a hint of fantasy about it, perhaps harking back to the asymmetry and fantasy of Vanbrugh's own Castle in Greenwich. Miller often based his designs on parts of buildings in Oxford, and the additions give the Gothic temple something of the appearance of 'Oxford Gothic'. There are several lanterns or cupolas on Oxford buildings which could have served as models for Miller, including the old cupola on Wren's Sheldonian, and the large cupola above the entrance to All Souls which has decorated lines joining the segments of the dome. At Lacock, where Miller began work in 1753, the two lanterns at either end of the entrance façade to the new Great Hall are similar to those on the Gothic Temple, although they are much smaller.

It has been suggested, though there is no known archival or stylistic evidence to prove it, that Miller may have designed other buildings at Stowe. One possibility is the design

102   *A copy of the print of the Gothic Temple at Stowe by Benton Seeley, from 'Views of Temples and other Ornamental Buildings in the Gardens at Stow', 1750. Note the cupolas on the lower towers of the Gothic Temple, but as yet no pinnacles on the highest tower. Miller listed in his diary under expenses for 10 July, 1750, that he paid two shillings and sixpence for 'Seely's prints of Stow'.*

103 *Park Place, the Grotto exit and the arches at the head of Happy Valley. Miller worked at Park Place, and noted in his diary walking in the Garden and setting out a building with General Conway, but the extent of his contribution to the landscaping is not known.*

for Stowe Castle, built as an eyecatcher to be seen from the gardens *c.*1738. It does not seem typical of Miller's work in comparison with his other mock 'castles', however; for it is too massive and too regular in outline. It is perhaps Lord Cobham's own design, for it is not unlike the gaol he erected in the town of Buckingham in 1748.

With Miller's own sentiments (as evidenced by his buildings) according so well with the ideals which inspired the Temple, and the stylistic likenesses in the Gothic additions to his own work elsewhere, it seems certain that his 'finishing' in 1756 must have been for the Gothic Temple. On stylistic grounds it is also likely that he was responsible for the exterior Gothic lanterns added *c.*1750.

Park Place

In his diary for 1756, Miller recorded being at Park Place, General Conway's estate, in September and again in December. He was both drawing plans for the interior of the house and assisting Conway in the gardens. The estate of Park Place lies just east of Henley-on-Thames. It is bounded to the south west by the Henley to Wargrave road, beyond which is the river Thames. The land, part of the southern Chilterns, rises steeply to the east of the river, and there are fine views overlooking the river and to the south. In the early 18th century Lord Archibald Hamilton bought the land at Park's Place and built a Palladian mansion. In 1738 Park Place was sold to Frederick, Prince of Wales, and following his death in 1751 the estate was bought by General the Hon. Henry Seymour Conway (1720-95). Conway was Horace Walpole's cousin and went on the Grand Tour together with him and the poet Thomas Gray. With Walpole's enthusiastic encouragement

Conway enlarged the estate, creating an extensive landscaped park, and planting many of the new species of trees which were being introduced at the time. The estate was sold on Conway's death. Much of the landscaped park still remains today, though there are now two golf courses on the site.

Miller's diary for 1750 mentions Henry Conway, then Colonel Conway, as both a visitor to Radway and also as a fellow guest during a visit to Hagley. At Radway, Conway and Miller walked up the hill to visit the Castle, and in the evening they played duets. At Hagley, when the Lytteltons had musical evenings, Miller and Conway both contributed. They walked round the park with the company, and also visited Shenstone at The Leasowes with the Lytteltons and Lord Aylesbury. It is not surprising, therefore, to find Miller intimately concerned with the improvements at Park Place after Conway had bought the estate in 1751.

In Miller's diary for 1756, he recorded dining with Conway, now General Conway, at the *Queen's Head*, Brackley, on 3 September on their way to Stowe. Four days later, on 7 September, Miller stopped at Park Place on his way up to London, and walked with Conway in the garden. On 10 December Miller was at Park Place again, Lord Lyttelton also being of the party. On this occasion Miller was 'dr^g. [drawing] Plan for Lib^y [library] &c'. On 11 December in the morning he was 'dr^g. fair Copy of Plan' then he was 'w^g rnd. [round] Garden & setting out y^e Build$g$ w. Genl Conw^{y}'. Miller used the word 'garden' on different occasions to mean either garden in the modern sense, or the landscaped park, so it is not clear to which he was referring, but it seems likely that he meant the latter. Later that day he left for London with Lord Lyttelton. In the new year of 1757 Miller was again drawing plans for Conway. From 6 to 7 January he was staying with his old friend Sir Edward Turner. On 7 January he was 'dr^g Gen Con=way's Hse [house]' and the next day 'dr^g Hse' again. After visiting Lord Saye 'by Wooton', on 8 January he returned home on 9 January, and the next day he was again drawing Conway's house. No details are given as to what the 'Hse' was, whether it was a building for the grounds, or was part of General Conway's mansion. The last entry for the diary is on 11 January.

South-east of the mansion there was an area of caves, and an underground tunnel about 170 metres in length was made, opening out at an arched grotto with a view looking down an area known as Happy Valley. The bottom of the valley is closed by a bridge of huge boulders carrying the Wargrave road, hidden from view underneath which the river can be glimpsed. There was also a Tuscan Villa, built to house a chemistry professor who extracted oil from Conway's lavender plantation, a Gothic Cottage and a conservatory. Following his appointment as Governor of the island of Jersey, the inhabitants presented Conway with 45 granite megalithic stones, which he re-erected in 1787 at Park Place as the circular Druidic Temple.[45]

Judging from Miller's brief diary entries, it looks as though he was considerably involved with the designs at Park Place, both in alterations to the mansion and in the grounds. In 1791 van Biljoen, a Dutchman, visited Park Place and referred to a Gothic pavilion which was glazed and which overlooked the view of the river and Henley from Happy Valley.[46] The building for which Miller was marking out the site with Conway could have been this Gothic pavilion. It could also have been the Gothic cottage, now gone, which was built near the grotto exit at the top of Happy Valley.[47] The references to walking round the gardens are reminiscent of Miller's diary entries for his visits to Stowe, and suggest

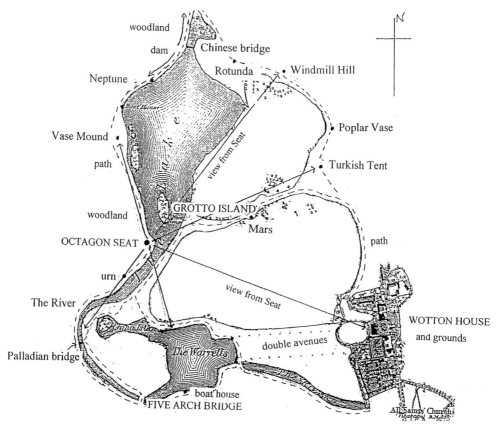

104 *Wotton Underwood, a plan taken from the six-inch O.S. map c.1880s, showing the new landscape with the extensive lake system, and the carefully contrived views from the Octagon Seat, designed by Miller in 1758. (See pp.190-6.)*

that he and Conway were walking round with a critical eye assessing the landscaping. No more diaries have come to light, so no more is known of Miller's doings at Park Place. There are no letters from Conway in the collection in the Warwick Record Office, and no further references have been found.

Conway, of course, also used designs by other friends and acquaintances. The group of people involved seems to have been similar to those involved in the creation of the landscape at Hagley. Near the site of the old house there are large cedars of Lebanon reputed to have been planted by Frederick, Prince of Wales. The dramatic bridge at the end of Happy Valley was designed by Thomas Pitt, 1st Lord Camelford. Either side of the opening in the grotto on the hillside above the valley, brick and flint 'Grecian' ruins were constructed, reputed to be by James 'Athenian' Stuart. Both men also designed park buildings for George Lyttelton at Hagley.

In 1763, the year of the construction of the bridge, Horace Walpole wrote approvingly:

> The works at Park Place go on bravely; the cottage will be very pretty, the bridge sublime, composed of loose rocks that appear to have been tumbled together there, the very wreck of a deluge.[48]

If Walpole approved, Park Place must certainly have met the fashionable criteria of the mid-18th-century cognoscenti.

Shrub Hill

In the spring of 1758, Miller was asked by Henry Grenville (1717-84), Lord Temple's brother, to assist him with the design for the grounds of their new house at Shrub Hill, Dorking. Henry became an M.P., then in 1755 was made Governor of Barbados. On his return in 1757 he married Margaret (Peggy) Banks, and settled at Shrub Hill. Miller had known all the Grenvilles from his university days, but was particularly friendly with Henry, and admired Peggy, whom he had also known for some years. Miller had provided Henry with plans for a new house at Beechley Mount in 1755, and Grenville had provided Miller with much needed financial assistance by buying his Moreton Morrell property from him. Miller continued to assist Grenville by overseeing and managing the property and its enclosure until at least 1759. In 1756 Grenville had intended to build a temple at another property, St Leonard's Hill, writing to Miller to say: 'but without my Friend, my Adviser, my Architect what can I do?' However, his appointment to the Governorship of Barbados 'will unfortunately put a Stop to the Execution of any Design which you and Mr Hitchcox may have planned for me …'.[49] It is not known whether any plans were actually prepared.

After his return to England and his marriage in 1757, Henry wrote to Miller inviting him to their new residence at Shrub Hill, 'a place, which I should think, unless you are extremely changed, the name itself would alone be sufficient to tempt you to come and see, but when you remember that no inconsiderable part of the Beauty of Stowe is transplanted hither, I think (at least I hope) you will not be able to withstand the Temptation …' Miss Banks often used to stay at Stowe. Miller duly went to visit the Grenvilles, advised them on their plantings, and drew out a plan for their new grotto. On 1 February 1758, Mrs Grenville wrote to Miller in the third person:

> … she is very desirous of receiving some information from him, with respect to the New Grotto in the Wall; neither Mr Grenville, nor her self can well comprehend how the water, which is contain'd in the Bank, is to be carry'd off, if it should rise from below; or how it is to be convey'd into the Bason, if it should descend from the top of the Rock: we should therefore be very much oblig'd to Mr Miller, if he would send us his Idea about it, together with a Plan, & ample directions how to proceed upon that plan: he may remember that he drew a rough sketch of it, upon the table in the House=keepers room; but as that is quite effac'd, & they can receive no assistance from it, they are therefore obliged to trouble him upon this important occasion: the Bricklayer begins tomorrow morning with taking out the bricks in the wall, six foot wide, & afterwards to dig out the sand, six foot deep; but when Mr Grenville has proceeded this far, he will be oblig'd to stop, until he has receiv'd instructions from Mr Miller, which will be a great satisfaction to him in his distress …

On 14 April Grenville wrote to say that the frost was retarding the progress of the plantings, and that the Grotto was still causing problems:

> Our Grotto remains in a very imperfect, unfinished State, the Water distils from it, by very plentiful droppings, in 6 or 8 different places, but how to collect them into one main channel, is a matter that puzzles all the Wit & Abilities that Shrubhill, or

105 *Wotton House, from the double avenues. The house, enlarged in the 1700s and redesigned by Sir John Soane in 1820, was saved from destruction in the 1950s by Mrs Elaine Brunner, who subsequently restored both house and landscape.*

Dorking, can boast of, and is an Operation reserv'd for you, & for the happy hour when we shall see you here again: may that soon arrive …'.[50]

Presumably Miller arrived and solved the problem, for there are no more references to any other projects at Shrub Hill in Grenville's many letters to Miller during the next three years. These are full of the on-going work at Moreton Morrell, mainly relating to tithes, mortgages, and rent collection[51]. The letters quoted above show that Miller's friends wanted more than just plans from him; they were quite confident in his practical abilities and anxious that he should advise on all the details. Between 1761 and 1765 Henry Grenville was British ambassador at Constantinople. Between 1767 and 1771 he lived at Eastbury, in Dorset, which was offered to him by his brother Richard, Earl Temple, so his occupancy of Shrub Hill was limited. Shrub Hill is shown on the O.S. map for 1873, but the site had been built over by 1896.

Wotton Underwood

Although Miller had probably visited Wotton House many times since his undergraduate years, given his friendship with the Grenville family, the existing correspondence between George Grenville and Miller suggests that Miller's main involvement with the improvements at Wotton was in the year 1758. Wotton House and estate lie on level, well timbered land in the parish of Wotton Underwood, some eight miles west of Aylesbury. The history of the estate dates from the 11th century, when the Norman ancestors of the Grenville family first came to Wotton. In 1618 a new manor house was built, and this was enlarged in the early 1700s by the 6th Richard Grenville. The new mansion had connecting pavilions and was similar to Buckingham House, later Buckingham Palace. Between 1704 and 1714 George London designed a new formal garden at Wotton, together with five avenues radiating out from the mansion. Richard Grenville's son married Lord Cobham of Stowe's sister, Hester. When their eldest son inherited Stowe in 1749, subsequently becoming Earl Temple, he took the head gardener, Woodward, with him from Wotton to Stowe. Capability Brown was also at Wotton, firstly in the 1740s, probably visiting from Stowe, and later, in 1757-8, after he had set up his own private practice. When his eldest brother moved to Stowe, George Grenville, the second eldest, came into the family home at Wotton.

In 1820, after a disastrous fire, Sir John Soane was commissioned to redesign the house. In the 1920s the estate was sold. The house was finally left as a shell without even the lead on the roof, when it was bought in the 1950s from the County Council by Mrs Elaine Brunner, for £6,000. From 1958 onwards Mrs Brunner restored the house, recreating the Soane interior, and gradually buying back the estate from various owners. Before she died, in 1998, Mrs Brunner had restored or rebuilt most of the landscape buildings, and had replanted the avenues in front of the house.

The first record of Miller visiting Wotton was in 1750. His diary entry for 3 July 1750, mentioned that he went over to Wotton from Stowe and stayed till 10.30p.m. George Grenville was a prominent politician, and was to become Prime Minister in 1763, so the development of the estate at Wotton was of importance to him socially, particularly with Stowe so close. In 1756 Miller recorded in his diary correspondence between himself and 'Mr Grenville',[52] and on 7 October of that year 'Mr Grenville' came to Radway. He stayed till 17 October, visiting Wroxton, Upton House, the Bath House at Walton, Warwick Castle and Birmingham. In the following year three letters are known to have been written to Miller from the Grenvilles, two from George and one from his wife, Elizabeth.

106 *Wotton Underwood, the restored Turkish Tent, which can be seen across the Lake from the Octagon Seat.*

Grenville wrote from Upper Brook Street on 11 March 1758:

> Our future prospects too of fine walks and perpetual verdure are not so promising
> as those you paint & yet most people think that we are as much in the mud as you
> can be. To leave allegory which I have not sufficient time for at present I will in
> plain English give you a thousand thanks & those very sincerely for your obliging
> attention in drawing out the plan of the bridge & for your more obliging letter to
> me & yet there is a circumstance in your letter still kinder than either of the former
> which is your promise to come & see me at Wotton in the Easter Holydays, which
> I depend upon the performance of. I shall go thither about the 22nd. or 23rd. of
> this month …

On 20 June 1758 Grenville wrote from Wotton to remind Miller of his promise to
come and visit them, although he makes allowances for Miller's many commitments. He
is expecting both Miller and his wife to:

> … give us the pleasure of your company here and see how our works go on. I must
> put you in mind too of our Octagon Seat upon the mount which calls for dispatch,
> and which if you have time to send me the exact plan I shall be much obliged to
> you as soon as it is convenient to you …

The rest of the letter says that if virtue and friendship bring their own reward Miller
must be the richest man in England. The last letter is written in the third person, as if
from Mrs Grenville, but probably by Grenville himself, from Wotton, on 14 September.
No year is given:

> Mrs Grenville presents her comp[n] to Mr Miller & begs he will cast his Eye over the
> very imperfect sketch here inclos'd & let her know whether there is anything very
> absurd and contrary Rule in it. the meaning of it is for a Grotto upon the new Island
> with four Ionick Pillars before it with the entire entablature upon it. the Grotto is to
> be decorated with shells and the pillars with flints and shells (preserving the appearance
> of the real architectural ornaments) like some that are at Stowe. Mr Grenville having
> no Draughtsman at hand has emply'd Mrs Grenville to scratch it out who professes
> herself totally unable and unskillfull & implores Mr Millers assistance to correct her
> errors and to return it when done … the sooner it can conveniently be done the
> better because no time sh[d] be lost in getting up the Building.[53]

These letters are the basis for attributing to Miller the design for a bridge and the
Octagon Seat, and also for advising on the design of the grotto.

Because the land at Wotton is comparatively level, the interest in the designed landscape
had to be created by the introduction of man-made features. Altogether there are 72 acres
of water, forming two lakes and two 'rivers'. The water feeding the larger lake flows in
from three different directions, and is thought to be supplied by springs within the lake.[54]
The whole concept at Wotton is built around the idea of creating views to be seen from
different stations around a circular walk, much of the paths being alongside the lakes.
Fourteen garden buildings were constructed, and statues, urns or vases also occupied
strategic positions. Of the main buildings, Miller is associated with the Five Arch Bridge,
the Octagon Seat and the Grotto. Other mid-18th-century constructions of importance

107 *Wotton Underwood, a fossil inserted in the stonework of the Five Arch Bridge, the bridge almost certainly designed by Miller in 1758. It has been restored by Mrs Brunner. (See colour plate XXXIV for a view of the bridge.)*

were the Turkish Tent, the Rotunda, the Chinese Bridge, the small Palladian Bridge and the two Tuscan Temples on either side of the eastern end of the Warrells.

The improvements continued from about the late 1740s to the late 1760s. There was already an existing small lake at some distance from the west front of the house. This lake was later enlarged, and is known as the Warrells. The eastern part of the main lake, known simply as the Lake, was dug first. The 'River', on the west, which nearly, but not quite, joins the Lake to the southern arm of the Warrells, was probably excavated by 1752. The Five Arch Bridge, at this junction, was built between 1758 and 1760. The 'New River', east of the Warrells, was probably the last feature to be made, thought to have been constructed by Brown *c*.1767.[55]

The organisation of the Wotton landscape appears to have been co-ordinated from an early date, despite the later excavations of the 'River' and the 'New River'. The views are all important, and to achieve the best effects planting was used to direct the eye, and mounds were used to elevate the position of the viewer. From Wotton House there is a fine view to the west, towards the Warrells and beyond to Muswell Hill in the distance, the eye directed by double avenues, which have been replanted. Another view towards the main Lake was punctuated by a statue of Mars, originally a very pale colour, in the middle distance. Going along the track northwards from the House, the first building to be seen is the Turkish Tent, which has been recently restored. Both from here, and further on from Windmill Hill, there are good views across the Lake. Windmill Hill is a medieval mound which was taken as the centre for several radiating avenues. It has no windmill on it now, but the mound, useful in the new landscape for aesthetic reasons, was a practical solution to the problem of obtaining sufficient wind on this level site to work a mill. Around the northern end of the Lake there is a view from the Rotunda across to the Grotto on Grotto Island. The grotto is at present derelict, though following some clearance of vegetation the remains of the Ionic pillars and the entrance to the grotto are now visible from the banks of the lake. It seems reasonable to suppose that Miller approved of Mrs Grenville's design and that it was probably built as described in the letter sent to Miller. From the north end of the Lake, and framed by the dramatic curve of the Chinese Bridge (recently rebuilt), there is a view down the length of the water.

Following the path southwards, past the site of Neptune, and the Vase Mound, the path reaches the Octagon Seat, which has been restored, leaving the original floor in place. It is thought to have been built as designed by Miller. Under its pointed roof the building has eight arches, and through each arch, except the two facing towards the trees at the back of the building, there is a carefully designed view framed by the uprights of the arches and the distant landscaping. To the south, through the first arch, the view is along the river, past an urn and towards the Palladian Bridge in the distance. To the south east there is a view of a mound near the north bank of the Warrells. Using a cardboard cut-out, it has been discovered that a vase or urn placed on the top of this mound would be visible exactly through the middle of the next arch. Through the third arch, the House can be seen in the distance. Through the fourth arch, the Turkish Tent can be seen back across the Lake, and through the fifth, Windmill Hill. From the sixth arch, there is a view north along the bank of the lake towards the Vase Mound. The organisation of these various views has obviously been carefully thought out.[56] It is difficult to avoid the conclusion that Miller's was the guiding hand behind both the plan of the Seat and the views to be obtained from it (see map on page 188). Further round the 'river', the views from the Five Arch Bridge and the Boathouse, concealed under its mound on the south bank of the Warrells, are all of a more rural nature.

At Wotton there are many distinct raised mounds. These mounds, not usually more than six feet or so at their highest point, blend seamlessly into the landscape. They may all have had features, such as vases or urns, on them originally. Such mounds are particularly useful in such flat terrain for improving the views, and the undulations so formed add interest. Miller may well have introduced the idea of mounds to improve the views generally at Wotton, for he had used mounds at Honington, in 1749-50, for the temple in Ray Wood, and for the buildings at Alscot Park, in 1750. His temples at Wroxton and Gopsall are also both built on mounds.

Continuing south, the Lake narrows into the 'River', crossed by the small Palladian Bridge. Water is retained here by a long dam which carries the carriage drive, following the 'River' and proceeding to the Five Arch Bridge, where there is a drop in the water levels of about 12 feet. The bridge mentioned in Grenville's letter is most likely to be this bridge, since it has been suggested that the Palladian Bridge, which marked the original end of the Lake, was built in 1752. The latter was probably rebuilt two years later when the water was allowed to continue beyond it. The Five Arch Bridge, which has been carefully restored, is superficially like the Shell bridge at Stowe. Both have affinities with the Sham Bridge designed by Pope for Ralph Allen at Prior Park. There is a second 'bridge', or dam, below the first, over which runs the grassy perimeter track. The whole edifice cunningly conceals the fact that the upper body of water, the 'River', is actually terminated by an earth dam, the main bridge itself being just an ornament with the bridge arches forming the openings to tunnels which are set on the skew. These openings are circular at one end and elliptical on the other. The second dam, although looking as if it is part of the main bridge, actually marks the end of the southerly arm of the smaller lake, a totally separate body of water the level of which is a good six feet lower than that of the larger lake. The whole design is built on a wide-angled plan, to accommodate the fact that the lower body of water is at an angle to the upper. The layout of the Five Arch Bridge was designed specifically to suit its unusual situation. It is an ingenious design to cope with the problems of joining the different water levels so that, unless one looks closely, the whole just appears to be one simple bridge. Thomas Whately, visiting in 1771, while omitting to comment at all on the bridge itself, says of the joining of the different water levels:

> a real junction is however impossible, from the difference of the levels, but the terminations are so artfully concealed, that the deception is never suspected; and when known, is not easily explained.[57]

It seems certain that the design is by Miller. The technical solution to the problem of the two lakes and their differing water levels is consistent with Miller's known abilities in the management of water, and it is characteristic of Miller to take another older building as his model, but for his final design to be an individualistic adaptation. On 19 July 1759, Hester Grenville wrote to William Pitt:

> I went Last night in the chaise to the New Bridge, which is built after That in the Elysian Fields at Stowe, and conceals the joining of the new river. It is Glorious to Look from it, and pleases me more than any Thing George has yet done Here.[58]

Another point of particular interest with reference to the extent of Miller's involvement at Wotton are the great dams which, though all but invisible on a casual walk around the site, are vital to the retention of the water in the two lakes. At the north end of the Lake there is an extensive dam. At the northernmost point there is a drop of about 10 feet and a sluice which takes any overflow down to the ditch at the bottom. The main track, which was wide enough for a carriage to pass along it, continues south along this dam. Beyond the Chinese bridge the drop below the dam increases for some 50 yards to about 40 feet at its maximum, making a large and impressive structure. Tree growth over the top of the dam and the drop results in the dam itself remaining almost undetected. The other dams have already been described in the discussion on the Five Arch Bridge and the River which leads to it. The organisation of the water sources and the creation of these large bodies of water at different levels required both ingenuity and a knowledge of hydrology. The use of dams, one of a considerable height, to create lakes is similar to the work at Farnborough. At Wotton the large dams are equally crucial to the retention of the large body of water in Wotton's lakes. The dams are still in good order today, as are those at Farnborough.

The planting in the grounds is distinctive; groups of box and oak, or yew and elm gave a mix of large and stately deciduous trees with smaller evergreen trees or shrubs which would give colour and cover in the winter. The native species used are comparable with Miller's work elsewhere. This planting of native trees complemented the existing woodland at Wotton, which lies adjacent to the ancient Bernewood forest.

From the evidence on site, and the stylistic comparisons with Miller's previous work, together with his friendship of long standing with George Grenville and other members of the family, Miller's involvement with the fundamental design at Wotton looks certain. This conclusion is reinforced by the recent work on the identification of the views created on the site, in particular those to be seen from the Octagon Seat.

The only other likely candidate for the design of the dams and the lakes is Capability Brown, who received two payments of £100 from George Grenville for work done at Wotton in 1750 and 1757. In 1758, when 'water works' were in progress at Wotton, and

Miller had completed his design for the Five Arch Bridge in the spring, Brown was paid a further £200.[59] In 1757/8 Miller was experiencing more trouble with those disabling headaches which had led to his first seizure in 1756. Having discussed the work at Wotton with Grenville, Miller may well have recommended that Brown carry out the extensive practical work involved and make further changes if necessary.

Barrowby

In 1759 James Stuart Menteath was given the living of Barrowby, in Lincolnshire. Miller recorded in his Memoir to Menteath that he and his family visited Menteath at Barrowby several times. Miller is credited with Gothicising the rectory, and he reported in the Memoir that he 'planned his two Stables and Coach House'. Menteath was a close friend of Miller's from university days, and Menteath's visits to Radway are mentioned in Miller's diaries.

The village of Barrowby lies on a ridge of land just west of Grantham. Menteath was given the living by his employer, the Earl of Thanet, and was rector there from 1759-1802, dates which are commemorated in the list of rectors inside the church. The rectory garden looks down the slope north-north-east towards Lincoln, the cathedral just being visible on the horizon, with a wide prospect over the intervening vale. Miller wrote following a visit in March, 1759: 'Barrowby is a Charming Situation, and enough to Tempt any Man to lay out much money upon it.' A site visit revealed that the garden itself has an overgrown yew walk on the west side leading from the site of the stables to the edge of the lawn, from where a grass field slopes down to the Grantham to Nottingham road at the lower end. This field appears to have been parkland in the past. On a visit to see Grimsthorpe when staying with Menteath, Miller recorded in the Memoir that Menteath was anxious to return home to see the surveyor who was measuring the field.[60] A few large mature trees, including some yews and other evergreens, still stand, and there is a sunken area with trees either side leading up to the present garden from the road. This may well indicate a previous private drive to the rectory. Yews were trees which Miller used in many designs, and at Farnborough there is a yew walk. At Barrowby the 'drive' and its avenue was sited well to the east of the view of distant Lincoln from the garden. Part of the rectory garden has been lost to enlarge the grounds of the local modern school, and housing now abuts the yew walk, so it is difficult to visualise what the garden may have looked like in past times. The house, probably 17th-century or even earlier, has pointed Gothic windows and decorations typical of Miller's Gothic work. It has recently been restored, but the stables and Coach House have gone, and a new building adjacent to the house probably occupies their site. Barrowby is interesting in view of Miller's close connection with Menteath. Miller obviously carried out considerable work on the buildings here, and would have naturally advised on the landscaping of the grounds, but unfortunately there is little to substantiate what he did.

9

Sanderson Miller and Capability Brown

❧·❧

anderson Miller and Lancelot Brown were both born in 1716, but followed very different paths before their first meeting, some time in the 1740s, at Stowe. Miller was born into a family with a small estate and reasonable means, though not one that was socially particularly important. He attended Oxford University, was influenced by the architecture there, and made friendships with upper-class students who would later request assistance from him with their estate improvements. In contrast, Brown was born in the village of Kirkharle in Northumberland, attended the local grammar school at Cambo, two miles away, then left when he was 16 to start work in the gardens of Sir William Loraine, the principal landowner in the parish. In 1737 Miller inherited Radway and started landscaping his own estate, following this with work at Farnborough, begun *c*.1740. In 1739 Brown moved south to work in the Midlands, and then in 1741 started work as head gardener for Lord Cobham at Stowe. Brown did not start out in business on his own until after Lord Cobham's death in 1749. Many plans and accounts exist covering Brown's numerous commissions over the following thirty years,[1] and several books have been written on him and his work, which is in direct contrast to the relative lack of archival evidence, and the very limited discussion in the modern literature that exists on Miller's work.

Brown and Miller first became acquainted through Miller's visits to Stowe. The following brief facts are known concerning their relationship. On Tuesday, 7 November 1749, when Miller was at Stowe, he recorded in his diary: 'Walking in the Garden – with the Comp^y [company] & Mr Brown & Dorrel 5h [hours].' Dorrel was a local clergyman. On Friday, 9 August 1750, Miller recorded at Radway the following entry in his diary: 'Wet. Mr Brown came w. [went] with him to Castle &c. he dined here – rode with him cross ye Valley &c'. Farnborough was 'across the valley', and was the estate which Miller had been laying out for William Holbech over the previous ten years or more.

In 1756, when Brown was working for the Earl of Exeter at Burghley, Lord Dacre, whom Miller had assisted with his improvements at Belhus, in Essex, wrote to Miller concerning a discussion he had had with Brown about Miller's abilities:

> … he [Brown] says he would give the world you should see his designs; having the highest opinion of your skill in this way; I asked him why he did not send them to you; that I knew your good nature; but his answer was that the Drawings were so large it was impossible. He wanted much to know whether there was any chance of

July 18-1748

*I was in hopes my Dear Miller to have seen you here long ago, where I much want your Assistance; independent of the pleasure your Company always affords me. I will not suppose I am to go without, like the Middle of August, but should that be the Case I shall beat up your Quarters at Radway about that time when I have discharg'd a Visit long since promised to Warwick. I saw Mr C Mordaunt a few days ago at Cheltenham who could give me no account of you so that this is only a search Letter, & where it may find you the Lord knows, but wheresoever it does it will bring you the sincere Wishes of — Your Affect: Friend
Comp.ts to Talbot.   D.*

Croome, July 18. 1748.

108   *A letter written to Miller by Lord Deerhurst, later the 6th Earl Coventry, from Croome on 18 July 1748.*

seeing you soon in this part of the world ...[2]

From Lord Dacre's letter it is apparent that Brown not only appreciated Miller's skills but also valued his advice.

Although a reasonable proportion of Miller's landscape work had been completed by 1750, there is no evidence that Brown had actually seen any of Miller's work before his visit to Radway in the summer of 1750. At Stowe, the creation of the Grecian Valley, Lord Cobham's last plan, was the only completely informal design based on actual landscaping in the whole extent of the gardens. Brown had carried out the practical work in making the Grecian Valley, although it appears from the following letter that it was Cobham who was responsible for the design. On 24 February 1746, Brown wrote to Cobham: 'I had never formed any other idea on it [the Valley] than what your Lordship gave me which was to Forme the Laurell Plantation with the sweep under it and Concave to the Ovall ...'.[3] Lord Cobham has been described as having had 'a rare ability to move forward in garden design', and it has been suggested that 'if anyone should be called the Father of English Landscape Gardening it is he'.[4] So it would seem that at Stowe Brown had not originated any completely informal designs himself.

When Brown visited Miller, the works at Radway and Farnborough had already had time in which to mature. The creation of Farnborough's lakes and great terraces had involved moving a large amount of earth, and Brown's recent work in creating the Grecian Valley, in contrast to the other areas at Stowe, had also involved a considerable amount of earth moving. Brown would have been particularly interested to see the maturing landscape at Farnborough.

Although Miller's involvement at Croome is definite, as will be seen from the quotes from his correspondence with George Coventry, Lord Deerhurst, later the 6th Earl of Coventry (1722-1809), it is difficult to quantify exactly what he did. Correspondence between 1744 and 1756 shows that Miller was George Coventry's confidant following the death of his elder brother in 1744, when he had unexpectedly become Lord Deerhurst and stood to inherit the estate at Croome. The moving letters written to Miller immediately after this unhappy event show Deerhurst's extreme grief at losing his brother, and his difficulties in coming to terms with his loss. Deerhurst very much appreciated Miller's frequent letters to him at this time.[5] After the death of his eldest son, the 5th Earl lost much of his interest in the estate, the affairs of which were gradually assumed by the new Lord Deerhurst.

Deerhurst's letters to Miller tell of ongoing advice requested for the estate. In July 1747, Lord Deerhurst first wrote to Miller mentioning various projects for Croome: 'I … must insist upon your Anniversary visit here having various Projects in my head to embellish this untoward place which I wou'd not execute without your Taste ….' He also mentioned having acquired some painted glass from a priory for Miller.[6] On 3 August 1747, Miller wrote to Deerhurst:

> As Mr Talbot [of Lacock] tells me your Lordship's spirit in improvement begins to exert itself, I have no Idea how you can live within a day's ride to such places as Wroxton and Hagley and not see either of them. Was you to see them that once you would return with Ideas as much enlarged as Poet would be the first time he reads Homer or Virgil. If you cannot possibly see Wroxton this month but you may come to Hagley while I am there and let me have the pleasure of walking with you round the most enchanting spot of Ground in England, I will attend you back again to Croome and stay a day or two while my little woman is left at Hagley. I hope to be there about the 20th and meet Mr Lyttelton and Mr Pitt.[7]

In July 1748, Deerhurst wrote: 'I was in hopes my Dear Miller to have seen you here long ago, where I much want your Assistance, independent of the pleasure your Company always affords me …' On 13 December 1748, Deerhurst wrote from London: 'I shall be glad to hear you are coming to Town, having some things of importance to confer with you upon relating to my Water'.[8]

In Miller's diary for 1749/50, there are several brief references to correspondence with Lord Deerhurst in early spring, then on Friday, 2 March, and again on Saturday he was drawing a plan for Lord Deerhurst. On Monday he was again 'draw^g Plan for Lord Deerhurst 2h [two hours]', and on Tuesday he 'finished L^d D Plan. & wr^{te} [wrote] to him'. Miller worked on this plan over four days. He gives no further details, nor does the correspondence reveal more, but it may well have been for the new mansion, for Miller rarely refers to taking so long over completing a plan. On 27 August 1750, Miller noted in his diary 'd [drew] Stables &c. for L^d. D'. In the Croome archives there is a drawing of the stables in a plain classical design inscribed in what appears to be Miller's own handwriting. The two-storey building, erected in the 1750s, is constructed on three sides of a square, each with a central stone-faced portico. The main entrance is through the arch in the west-facing portico. The old house at Croome was to form the foundation for a new Palladian design. In February 1750, before the new mansion was built, Deerhurst referred to a request for a further plan from Miller for a Gothic lodge, for which he wanted the ground plan at least, although he was not in a hurry: '…it will give me frequent opportunity of speaking of the Architect [i.e. Miller] in other parts of his character besides his Vitruvian'. Vitruvius was the Roman architect on whose works Palladio, then, later, Inigo Jones had based their own designs. This comment may be interpreted as yet a further indication that the original design for the new mansion at Croome, which was Palladian in style, was by Miller. In February 1756, Deerhurst, now Lord Coventry, wrote: '…The Water is brought up to the garden Wall I hope for your approbation next summer …'. A further letter in the same month was sent to Miller reminding him that Coventry had hopes of '… seeing a plan of my Lodge … I have some reason to think it finished'.[9] Capability Brown finally built the Lodge in 1760.

The Croome estate stretched from the Lias ridge to the east, across a low-lying shallow valley (now, sadly, bisected by the M5 motorway) to rising ground in the west, beyond which can be seen the Malverns. The house itself was low-lying. Much of the valley land was heavy clay marl. This lay wet and undrained, and was described in the estate inventory of 1719 as 'unfit'.[10] How best to drain the site was the main problem, and if the ground could be successfully drained then the old house could be made dry enough to countenance Lord Deerhurst's building plans.

The formal gardens were removed, and the problem of the boggy land around the old house was solved by the construction of large drains feeding into the stream below the house. The water was led into a long narrow lake created from the existing small stream in the valley bottom, so forming a new 'river'. The shape was very similar to that of the widened Stour at both Honington and Alscot. The term 'river' was often used by 18th-century landscapists to denote a long narrow piece of water, usually man-made, whether or not it was part of a flowing stream. This work, finished by 1748, follows the familiar pattern in Miller's own work of making advantageous use of unproductive poorly drained land and small streams. In August 1748, Sir Edward Turner wrote complimenting Deerhurst on the work, and on 20 September Nugent, of Gosfield, wrote giving practical advice on making the river watertight. In April 1750 Lord Bateman wrote, 'I dare say Croomb is in great beauty …, You have made a River where no water ever ran before …' – suggesting that an actual new channel had been made to receive the drainage water.[11] In 1751 Lord Deerhurst inherited Croome as the 6th Earl of Coventry, and engaged Brown in the same year to assist him. Were Miller's ideas behind the early improvements, as well as the design for the new mansion? Miller had many other calls on his time at this period, and was committed to building the new Shire Hall in Warwick, and the new mansion at Hagley, the latter having a strong resemblance to that at Croome. Knowing Brown and the quality of his work at Stowe, did Miller provide the plans and the expertise, and recommend Brown, hitherto unknown as an architect but skilled in carrying out landscaping and the construction of landscape buildings, to Lord Coventry to carry out all the work? It is almost certain that such was the case.

Lord Coventry, described by Horace Walpole as 'a grave young Lord of the remains of the Patriot Breed', was an M.P., and also had many local interests. He was Lord Lieutenant of Worcestershire for many years. A well educated man, his interests extended to architecture and the arts, as well as both landscaping and agriculture. Beside the ornamental aspects of the landscaping, which were due in no small part to Coventry himself over his long life, he was concerned that his tenants should benefit from agricultural improvements. He kept pedigree cattle, including Shorthorns, which were to become the leading dairy breed in the 19th century, and also carried out cross-breeding of Cotswold sheep with Leicesters to combine the best features of both types.[12]

Brown, Robert Adam and James Wyatt all contributed to the later improvements, though Brown's was the guiding hand. An ornamental lake was formed at the western end of the 'river', which had a large grotto at one end. Two bridges led across the water to an island on which was a small classical temple, designed by Robert Adam in 1776-8. A dry arch bridge designed by James Wyatt took the old carriage drive over the private lakeside walk used by the family. An imposing Temple Greenhouse or Orangery was designed by Robert Adam in 1760. At the far end of the gardens, on the lias ridge, a Rotunda was

109   *George William, 6th Earl of Coventry,*
1722-1809, painted by Allan Ramsay c.1765.

110   *Croome Court, a painting made by*
Richard Wilson in 1758.

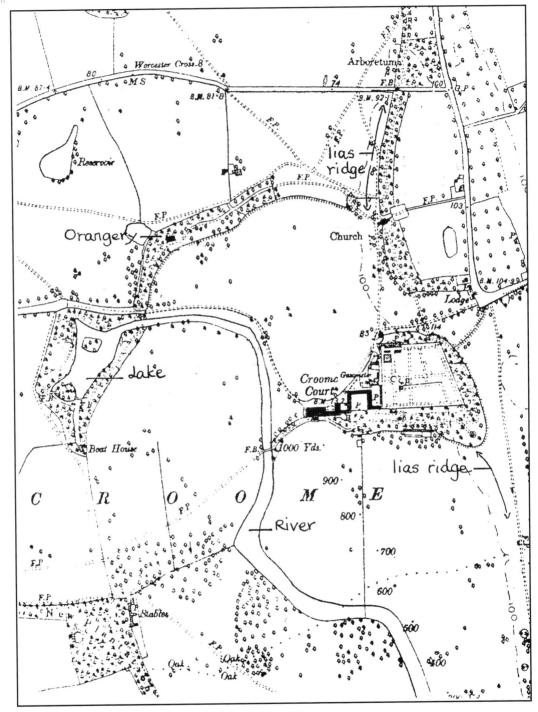

111 *A map of the Croome landscape, taken from the six-inch O.S. map for 1905 (2nd edition)*

112   *Croome, the Rotunda in the garden area above the Court. There are good views across the estate from here. Miller's name has occasionally been associated with the design.*

built between 1754-7. From it are fine views across the valley. Beyond the gardens on the lias ridge, Adam designed both the Owl's Nest Alcove Seat, 1766 and, further away to the south, the mock ruins of 'Dunstall Castle', built 1766-7. The latter, although it has also been ascribed to Miller, is stylistically dissimilar to Miller's work, and the towers are taller and narrower in appearance than most of his own mock ruined towers. A menagerie, 1768, was built in the valley, and there was an arboretum, stocked mainly between 1760 and 1780. At the beginning of the 19th century other buildings were erected, including another mock ruin to the north of the site, known as Pirton Castle, and across the valley, James Wyatt's Panorama Tower. Both of these were built in 1801. From the Panorama Tower there are fine views to the Malverns, and across the valley back to the house and the church on the ridge.[13]

The commission to improve the landscape at Croome, and to be entrusted with the building of the new mansion, were significant steps of great importance to Brown in the early years of his private practice. Many features of the overall plan at Croome are similar to those which Miller had used in his own work. The drainage scheme and the formation of a long narrow 'river' out of the stream into which the waters fed is the most important similarity in the design of the new landscape. The detailed treatment of the large ditches and the 'river' banks is thought to have been carried out by Brown. These ditches have shallow turfed slopes, to facilitate animals approaching them to drink. The original 'river' was later given a more serpentine outline, and the edge of the banks lowered slightly so that rushes and other vegetation did not impede the sight lines.[14] The siting of the buildings in the landscape is particularly important in relation to the views to be obtained from their situations, both from the ornamental valley grounds up towards the higher land, and from points on the higher land back across the site. Views have a comparable importance in Miller's own work. Other similarities include the extensive planting on the hills to beautify the landscape and emphasise the topography over the wider estate. As at Farnborough in the early 1740s, the ridge of land behind the house at Croome was used to good effect, with a new belt of trees and several landscape buildings at or near the top of the ridge.

The most important of the buildings along the lias ridge was the new parish church of St Mary Magdalen, which makes a fine eyecatcher, particularly when caught by the evening sunlight from across the valley. It was consecrated in 1763. Brown constructed the building, and the interior is largely by Robert Adam, but it is not known who designed the exterior, though Adam, Brown and Miller have all been put forward as possible candidates.[15] Several aspects of the exterior suggest that the design was by Miller. The tower is divided unequally into three sections, with a single long Gothic window in the largest section, a design which has similarities to Wroxton church tower, rebuilt by Miller in 1748. These Gothic windows are large for a rural church. The battlemented gable end of the nave of Croome church, where it joins the tower, is also unusual for a local parish church. The impact of Oxford architecture and its decorative features on Miller has been

113 *Croome, the mock ruin known as Dunstall Castle, by Robert Adam. Built in 1766-7, one mile east of Croome Court on Dunstall common, it was originally clearly visible from the Court.*

114   *Croome Court seen across the parkland.*

mentioned before, and there are several precedents in the design of Oxford college chapels for both the distinctive gable end and the Gothic windows. A battlemented gable end can be seen in Magdalen College Chapel and that at All Souls College, and the Gothic windows could have been copied from several buildings, for example the windows in New College Chapel. These features in Oxford college chapels may well have served as patterns for Miller. Finally, the church has Gothic details and simple, clean lines. It also has the repeated small Gothic arch line under the first string course which is so typical of Miller's work, occurring, for example, in the Wroxton Chapel, at Lacock, and on the Gothic Greenhouse (Museum) and the Boathouse at Enville.

Brown continued to work for Lord Coventry until his death in 1783. In 1797 Lord Coventry erected a Coade stone casket beside the lake which he had made in praise of Brown's work. The inscription on the pedestal reads: 'to the Memory of Lancelot Brown Who by the powers of His inimitable and creative genius formed this garden scene Out of a morass'.[16] The extensive works at Croome also testify to Lord Coventry's own abilities over his long life in improving his estate, as well as those who assisted him, and much of the credit for the landscaping achievements at Croome must be given to the energy and enthusiasm of Lord Coventry himself.

How indebted Brown may have been to Miller's ideas and recommendations is not known, but Brown's overall work at Croome not only made Croome into one of the outstanding estates laid out in the new informal landscape style, but also set Brown himself firmly on the ladder to success. Gordon, in her book on the Coventrys of Croome, states that 'the introduction, by Sanderson Miller, of Brown to Lord Coventry was momentous. At Croome, Brown rose to the notice of men whose power and means could ensure that his new landscape style flourished, changing forever the scale and extent of landscape design'.[17] The link between Brown's commission and subsequent work at Croome, and Miller's undoubted influence on the whole improvements, pointed up by the stylistic likenesses between Miller's work and Brown's, must be looked at in terms of Coventry's comment to Miller, made in 1752: 'Whatever merit Croomb may in future time boast, it will be ungrateful not to acknowledge you the primary Author … It was to your assurance that Nature had been more liberal to me than I apprehended'.[18]

A look at the important features of Miller's plans and those of Brown's other designs in the first decade or two of his private practice will serve to compare and contrast different aspects of their work, with a view to elucidating Miller's possible influence on Brown. Both Miller and Brown were concerned to produce a natural effect in their work. Miller's approach was more pioneering in this respect, since his work was carried out earlier in the century than Brown's. The impact of Miller's designs on open unenclosed country, and the comparison with existing formal, or semi-formal landscapes has already been discussed. This approach by Miller is one of the most important reasons, together with the fact that Brown actually saw Miller's own designs in their semi-maturity, for suggesting that his work had a major influence on that of Brown. The idea of a *natural* estate landscape was gaining in popularity, and Miller's naturalistic and informal approach to the improvement of the estate landscape is particularly evident in his work. The natural appearance of Brown's landscapes was eventually to be recognised as the pinnacle of achievement in this, the English landscape style.

In his approach to making a 'natural' landscape, Miller handled large earth-moving projects with skill in the creation of both lakes and terraces. Brown certainly went on to move large quantities of earth in his projects. He had, of course, gained experience under Lord Cobham's tutelage.

Views were of great importance in the designs of both men. Both used planting to direct the eye towards views or features of importance, setting eyecatching clumps of trees on hills, and introducing belts of indigenous trees, particularly along ridges, as at Farnborough and Croome. Both men sited buildings in the landscape to take advantage of the best views. Earth mounding was used in specific ways. Mounds were used by Miller to elevate his buildings to improve the views from them, as at the Chinese Seat at Wroxton, late 1740s, the Chinese House at Alscot, c.1750, and the Octagon Seat at Wotton Underwood, 1756. Sometimes the mounds were themselves significant features, as at Wroxton and at the Open Temple at Gopsall, in Leicestershire. Decorative shrubs were planted on the mount of the Temple on the Mount at Wroxton, c.1749, and, in an ascending spiral beside a path leading up to the temple, at Gopsall also c.1749, where the mound was sunk to preserve the level appearance of the parkland. Brown used a similar design with shrubs at Badminton for a small temple in 1752, although he did not use the sunken enclosure

115 *Croome, a view west from the Panorama Tower (James Wyatt, 1801) towards the Malverns.*

device.[19] He also used shrubs in a mounting spiral to ornament the large and ancient Ethelfleda's mount at Warwick Castle, illustrated in 1753 by Mrs Delany.[20] Brown used shallow earth mounding very effectively to conceal undesirable features, for example at Croome, where the banks of the river were designed with a slightly lower edge to conceal riverside vegetation, and at Himley Hall, in Staffordshire. Here he concealed the carriage drive by a low bank along its length as it crossed the parkland, providing a view of an uninterrupted sweep of grass,[21] a device not used by Miller.

116 *Badminton, Gloucestershire. An unexecuted design by Capability Brown, 1752, for a temple on a mound with ornamental planting and a path winding up to the top.*

Both Brown and Miller were adept at handling water in the landscape, and both men used inventive means of solving problems connected with water. If Miller's most inventive solution to problems was his creation of the system of pools at Farnborough, and his handling of the water levels at Wotton Underwood, then Brown's, on a larger scale, must be the decision to build a dam at Blenheim and then to flood the valley and the lower half of Vanbrugh's bridge to create the great lake there. Miller's ability in the handling of water and poorly drained land has already been described, as has also Brown's initial work along the same lines at Croome. Miller undertook the successful widening of the River Stour at both Honington and Alscot. Later, Brown also widened rivers, for example at Charlecote, at Burghley and at Chatsworth.[22]

Miller created new lakes, sometimes using a bridge over a dam to further the illusion that the water actually continued beyond the dam, as at Wotton Underwood and Gosfield. Brown also used methods of hiding the dams he had made to give the impression that the water continued beyond them.[23] The positioning of a lake so that it can be viewed from the house, or alternatively moving earth to create a sight line making it possible to see water from the house, was practised by both men. Miller positioned the lakes at Farnborough so that the water could be seen from the Hall. Brown carried out the same exercise at Kirtlington, *c.*1751, and also at Chatsworth, *c.*1761, where the sight line right down to the river was created by considerable earth moving.[24] Other 18th-century practitioners also used this device, in particular William Emes, at Hawkstone Park, Shropshire, *c.*1786, and at other properties.[25] Brown's name has come to be associated with the large lakes which he introduced into his schemes; that at Blenheim, on a significantly larger scale than any of Miller's lakes, being perhaps his most famous creation.

Miller used old fishponds in his schemes at Radway (*c.*1739), Farnborough (1739-early 1740s) and at Wroxton (1744-50). One of Brown's early designs was at Packington, where in 1751 he created the large lake by joining up several old fishponds in front of Packington Hall for Lord Guernsey. On 3 November 1756, after Brown's arrival, Guernsey wrote to Miller asking him to come over to advise him for otherwise he would despair of seeing him 'before all the mischief is done'.[26] Despite having secured the services of Brown, Guernsey still considered Miller's help and advice vital to the success of his schemes.

Miller's work differed from Brown's in his use of comparatively small streams to create features which are unlike any designs created by Brown. Miller's 'double waterways', a diagnostic feature of his work, are intimately connected with his small-scale landscapes. Examples are at Wroxton, with the 'canal' constructed from the 'Sor' brook, at Farnborough, where the stream leaves the 'River', and at Honington, by the Grotto area. A further diagnostic feature of Miller's work with small streams is his use of a system of dams and sluices to create small 'serpentine rivers' composed of several long narrow pools. This feature is found at Farnborough, Alscot, Arbury and Sudbury. These small but inventive water features can be contrasted with Brown's large-scale schemes.

Miller's work always included a variety of small-scale designs within his overall plan: areas such as the small streamside walks and the narrow serpentine pools at Farnborough, the riverside walk at Honington, the valley landscape at Wroxton, and the small cascades at Upton. Brown used small paths around the lake and onto the island at Croome, where the likely connection with Miller has already been discussed. Otherwise, Brown's use of small paths is largely restricted to paths in and around ornamental grounds near the house, particularly within shrubberies, rather than in the larger landscape of the park or alongside streams. Typical examples can be seen in his plans for Petworth, and for Tottenham Park, Wiltshire. In his proposal plan for Petworth in 1752, Brown used meandering paths in the garden shrubbery, and around the old wilderness, although he retained the intersecting straight paths within the wilderness itself. In 1765, Brown worked to a similar pattern in

117 *Warwick Castle, Ethelfleda's Mound. A drawing by Mrs Delany entitled 'Part of Warwick Castle & Church', dated 29 August 1753, showing Capability Brown's ornamental planting, the path winding up to the summit, and also steps – the medieval mound is quite high. The church is St Mary's.*

the redesign of the pleasure grounds near the house for Lord Bruce at Tottenham Park. Serpentine paths were introduced within the new shrubberies, but the old paths laid to a geometric pattern in the wilderness were retained.[27]

Discussing Brown's landscaping, Hinde remarks that one of the important new features in Brown's work was the idea that the house became important to the garden or park, rather than the other way round.[28] This point is also true of Miller's work of an earlier date, particularly at Farnborough, where the views of the Hall from both the terraces and the lakes are important. The house was seen in Brown's plans as the main feature on the approach drive, and also provided the centrepiece of the changing views visible from a new carriageway running through belts of trees on the estate boundary. Such carriage drives are present in many of Brown's plans, for example, that for Temple Newsham, 1762, and Bowood, 1763. At Warwick Castle, where Brown began work in 1749, when he was still head gardener to Lord Cobham, Lord Brooke and his friends were able to enjoy the park from a new circuit drive as well as from the castle. The circuit drive crossed a new bridge over the Avon, and emerged from an avenue by Spiers Lodge, past a fine view back towards the Castle across the park, newly ornamented with clumps of trees.[29] Circuit drives were not a particular feature of Miller's designs.

Landscape buildings were constructed by both men in different forms, although Miller had a well justified reputation for 'mock' ruined castles with a genuine 'medieval' appearance. Miller's smaller Gothic buildings may reasonably be compared with Brown's early Gothic work, which was, on the whole, practical but more prosaic, more regular in its outlines and less inventive in its detail. When he first went into private practice, Brown was not well known for his architecture, and Brown's early Gothic essays may have been due to his appreciation of Miller's success in this regard. At Blenheim, Brown remodelled High Lodge in the early 1760s, and designed Park Farm Granary in a similar castellated style in 1765. At Burghley, from 1756, he designed both a Gothic orangery, and stables with a castellated roofline, using a simple repeated pattern of Gothic fenestration in both buildings. In the late 1760s, when Brown's successful career was bringing great demands for his services, he showed more confidence in his plan for a summerhouse at Burghley which is designed in a more sophisticated and ornamental style.[30]

This chapter has shown that Brown used many of the same features and techniques that Miller had used, but that after these beginnings Brown went on to alter his approach as he gained experience. As Brown's style matured, his sweeping plantings and great belts of trees, often almost encircling the estate, the newly constructed lakes which were a large and dominant feature in his landscapes, and the carriage drives which wound in and out of the perimeter belts were all on a larger scale than Miller's work. Brown's use of smaller, more intimate designs such as those which were a typical part of Miller's schemes became confined to those sites where the owner required a flower garden or wished to utilise a former wilderness. The single belt of hilltop trees became the belt of trees around the whole estate, and Miller's landscape, designed predominantly for enjoyment on foot, became the great landscape of the park with the encircling carriage drive. Despite the few marked differences which these comparisons have pointed up between the work of the two men, Miller's naturalistic designs do appear to have had a direct effect on much of Brown's early work. These similarities are naturally to be expected, as gradually Brown gained confidence from his initial successes to develop his own style.

118 *A view of Warwick Castle from Spiers Lodge, showing the river Avon and the designed parkland. Aquatint by Paul Sandby, 1776.*

P. Sandby Fecit.

Magnificent CASTLE, are Humbly Inscribed,
Obedient and most Humble Servant. Paul Sandby R. A.

In the decade following his appointment at Croome, when his career had scarcely begun, many, though not all, of Brown's commissions have connections with Miller or Miller's circle of friends. At Warwick Castle, where Brown began work in 1749, Lord Brooke and Miller met both socially and through Miller's work on the new Shire Hall in Warwick. At Ingestre, Lord Chetwynd had asked Miller, through George Lyttelton, to design a Gothic Tower for him in 1749. Brown prepared a design for the park in 1756.[31] At Packington, where Brown started work in 1750, mention has already been made concerning Lord Guernsey's requests for help with his landscaping from Miller. At Kirtlington, Sir James Dashwood, with whom Miller was on friendly visiting terms, initially commissioned a plan by Robert Greening, who had also worked at Wimpole. Brown signed a contract with Sir James to landscape the grounds at Kirtlington in 1751.[32]

In 1752, Brown prepared a contract for his design for the estate at Petworth. Petworth was the seat of Lord Egremont, whose sister was George Grenville's wife. Both Miller and Brown worked on the estate at Wotton Underwood for Grenville, and Miller was a long-standing friend of Grenville's. At Belhus, in Essex, Miller, who had known Lord Dacre since at least 1744, had advised on both the Gothicising of Lord Dacre's house, and on his new 'river' and extensive plantings. Essex was a long journey from Warwickshire, so it is not surprising to find that Brown was again asked to take over Miller's initial plans, particularly since he was by then based in London. Brown worked intermittently at Belhus from 1753 to 1774.[33] Some of the associations between Miller, Brown and Brown's early clients have been remarked upon by other writers. Stroud suggests that Miller was responsible for recommending Brown at Croome, at Kirtlington, and at Belhus, and discusses the relationship between

Miller and Lord Hardwicke at Wimpole, giving the impression that Miller might also have suggested Brown to Philip Yorke, the 2nd Earl Hardwicke, who finally instructed Brown to build Miller's castle ruin in 1768.[34] Hinde indicates that Miller recommended Brown to Lord Coventry and Sir John Dashwood,[35] and Gordon discusses Miller's likely involvement with Brown's commission at Croome. Although no conclusive archival evidence has come to light, other than that cited above, the contacts between Miller, Brown and Brown's clients suggest strongly that Miller must have been instrumental in recommending Brown to many clients, and that Miller himself had often provided the initial advice on their estate improvements. After these successes in the early years of his private practice, Brown's own abilities and his businesslike approach to his work ensured an increasing and eventually a countrywide demand for his services.

On Brown's death, three years after Miller's, Walpole pasted into his notebook an anonymous obituary on Brown, which read: 'Such, however, was the effect of his genius that when he was the happiest man, he will be least remembered; so closely did he copy nature that his works will be mistaken'.[36] Two hundred and fifty years on, the natural appearance of Miller's schemes, particularly that at Farnborough, which is his only work to have survived virtually unscathed by the passage of time, is quite the equal of those of his better known contemporary, whose designs had such a natural appearance that this has become the trademark of a 'Brown' landscape.

10

Miller's 'Stylistic Signature'
and his contribution to the natural landscape movement

❧·❧

M
iller's approach to landscaping was both an intellectual concept conceived within the contemporary movement away from formal garden design, and also a response to the treeless appearance of the working countryside around him. His plans were also influenced by his experience of newly designed gardens and estates, in particular that of the modern ideas being put into practice at Stowe.

In 1712, Addison wrote that to open a man's thoughts and to enlarge the imagination it was necessary to 'gain a due Relish of the Works of Nature, and be thoroughly conversant in the various Scenary of a Country Life'. Addison thought that a man ought also to know about Art, Architecture and Ruins, and have studied the works of the ancient Roman and Greek writers.[1] Miller's upbringing and education and his own developing interests fulfilled this wide range of criteria. He continued to study the classics long after he had left Oxford, his reading material, noted down daily in his diaries, including the writings of Horace, Euclid and Plato.

The idea that Nature leads to Beauty, and that the Arts are founded on an understanding of Nature as revealed by direct experience, had existed since the teachings of Aristotle (384-322 B.C.). Both Pliny (A.D. 61?-115) and Horace (65-8 B.C.) admired and observed Nature. Horace praised the simplicity of life at his farm among the Sabine hills. His satires, odes and epistles testify to his love of the natural beauty of these peaceful rural surroundings, and his enjoyment of the leisure in which to study away from the pressures of Roman city life. Perhaps something of Horace's attitude to life touched the young Oxford student who built Egge Cottage on Edgehill for his studies. Pliny, more cosmopolitan than Horace, described his villas at Tuscany and Laurentum in letters of elegant prose. In his villa gardens he preferred a semi-formal plan, with that part furthest from the house designed to appear as if it was simple countryside. Pliny took great pleasure in waterfalls, both the sound of the water falling and the actual sight of the cascades, which he liked to have near his residence. Cascades were a feature which Miller used repeatedly in his schemes. Pliny's ideas may well have provided Miller with inspiration.[2]

Joseph Addison, in his suggestion that a whole estate may be 'thrown into a kind of garden', was not advocating turning a whole estate into pleasure grounds. That concept would 'alienate so much ground from Pasturage and the Plow' that it might be unprofitable or of 'ill consequence to the Publick'. Addison, on the contrary, was of the opinion that a working landscape might be beautified and still remain agriculturally profitable. He suggested that 'a Marsh overgrown with Willows, or a Mountain shaded with Oaks are not only more beautiful, but more beneficial (in that both are thus producing timber), than when they lie bare and unadorned.' He thought that 'the natural embroidery of the Meadows' might be 'helpt and improved by some small additions of Art' ...[3] Miller's planting plans added immeasurably to the beauty of the landscapes he designed without detracting from their agricultural value. The crowning of hilltops with clumps of oaks and pines is an effective ornamental device, and Miller's belts of trees, particularly at Radway and Farnborough, underline his ability to create a beautiful wooded skyline. Miller was looking at how a whole estate could be planned to create a pleasurable scene with water and trees, and he was also improving it from an agricultural point of view, creating shelter for stock and timber for future income. He was carrying out Addison's suggestions, and shading his 'mountains' with oaks, almost to the letter.

Miller's approach seems to have been to walk or ride round an estate with the owner, discussing the possibilities of the site and suggesting situations and designs for buildings, but rarely writing down more than a note in his diary to say that he had been there. On those estates where there is, perhaps, only a single mention in his diary or his correspondence of his having given advice, it is only through an awareness of his style that Miller's hand can be tentatively identified in the subsequent improvements, suggesting that his influence was probably much more extensive than has been shown.

The achievement of a 'natural' appearance in a landscape is clearly the aim behind Miller's designs, although it is never mentioned in Miller's own writings. The only reference to this aim is given in Oswald's letter, quoted previously, concerning the water gushing through the Grotto wall at Honington, in which there was an actual discussion about how to create as natural a scene as possible. The fact that to the modern eye the Honington landscape appears somewhat contrived is immaterial. When contrasted with the rectilinear formal terraced plan which had preceded it, the new design would have been strikingly 'natural' in appearance to any onlooker.

The informal outlines of Miller's new lakes, and in particular his constant use of the designation 'serpentine river' for his long, narrow pools formed on winding small streams, accords with William Hogarth's serpentine Line of Beauty. Hogarth's ideas were a central part of the mid-18th-century approach to culture and aesthetics, and the Line of Beauty has since become associated with the principle underlying Capability Brown's landscape work. Miller does not record reading Hogarth's book, *The Analysis of Beauty*, published in 1753, or meeting Hogarth (1697-1764), yet his introduction of a 'serpentine river' into at least three of his sites – Farnborough, Wroxton, and Alscot – underlines his appreciation of Hogarth's description: 'the serpentine line, by its waving and winding at the same time different ways, leads the eye in a pleasing manner along the continuity of its variety'.[4]

Miller's mock castle ruins, so genuine in their appearance, became almost legendary in his lifetime. Despite the blatant make-believe aspect of such buildings, they struck a chord with his contemporaries. This was not only because they stood for the liberties and the constitution of old England as embodied in the ideals of our Saxon forbears, a politically fashionable concept with Lord Cobham and his Whig adherents. The increasing popularity of mock Gothic seems also to have been in no small way because in the 18th century the gentry enjoyed their pleasures, and a mock ruined castle was all part of the scene; it looked fine, it perhaps suggested that the owner was 'old' nobility, and it certainly provided somewhere faintly exotic to entertain and be entertained. One has only to read Horace Walpole's amusing description in 1770 of an 'Arcadian entertainment' for Princess Amelia, sister of George III, who had been invited to Stowe to see the Doric Arch built in her honour, to appreciate to what lengths the gentry went to provide entertainment. The local populace was invited into the grounds, the moon, luckily, was shining, the Grotto was lit up, the whole company from Stowe House ate supper within the Grotto, and 'an ancient militia-man who played cruelly on a squeaking tabor and pipe' provided the music. The fact that Walpole thought that to sup in the Grotto was as suitable in the English climate, even in mid-July, as 'a sea-coal fire would be in the dog-days at Tivoli', is neither here nor there.[5]

Having discussed Miller's work, and the particular attributes of his landscaping in previous chapters, it has become apparent that he has a definite style, a 'stylistic signature'. This stylistic signature has been of great use in confirming, or on occasion denying, the suggestion that a given design was actually by Miller, since there is such a lack of detailed archival information on his work. In general these design attributes are not individually diagnostic of Miller's work, apart from his use of double water features. Together, however, they create a picture which is identifiable as Miller's work, though not all the attributes are necessarily to be found at one site. The examples discussed below are all taken from sites which have already been discussed, and it will now be assumed that attributions to Miller of the works referred to are very likely to be accurate, in some cases because of tradition handed down within the family.

Miller followed a similar approach in all his designs. His designs were informal, and topography was used as the basis from which to create a new landscape picture of a natural, uncontrived appearance. This was a radical change from the previously accepted approach, in which ground was first levelled or terraced to take an intricate plan based on geometrical designs. Miller's plans were conceived around the views which could be obtained either within the estate or beyond it; buildings were set on mounds or in elevated positions, and the siting of water features and groups of trees was thought out to make the most of the available views. Since the views associated with a site were anyway considered important during this period, the fact that they were also important to Miller is not, by itself, diagnostic of his work. However, in all his plans special attention is paid to views. His diary entries refer several times to visiting a site to decide upon the best position for a building, for example at Wimpole, for the position of the Castle Ruin, and at Hagley, where Miller marked the exact position for the Gothic seat with stakes.

The importance of views in the newly laid out landscapes is clear at Farnborough, at Wotton Underwood, and also at Honington. The sites of the Temple on the Mount and the Dovecote at Wroxton, those of the Gothic Gateway and the Boathouse at Enville, the Tower at Ingestre, the Bath House at Walton and the buildings on the terrace at Alscot all reflect the importance of the positions chosen in relation to the views to be obtained from them.

The value of a view from a garden has been appreciated at least since Tudor times, when mounts were constructed within walled gardens to allow the landscape beyond to be seen and enjoyed without the need to risk confronting possible danger outside. During the first half of the 18th century, views had gradually come to be considered as an indispensable feature of any designed landscape of merit. The poets Pope and James

119   *Radway Tower and 'ruins', with two gentlemen using a camera obscura to view the prospect over Radway and the Vale of the Red Horse. The illustration is taken from the narrative poem 'Edge-Hill, or the Rural Prospect delineated and moralised' by Richard Jago, 1767. Jago was a friend of Miller's, and doubtless intended Miller to be identified as one of the two men.*

Thomson both eulogised views. 'Heavens! What a goodly Prospect spreads around', wrote Thomson about the famous view from Richmond Hill, in his poem *The Seasons*, written in 1727. Pope, Thomson, Horace Walpole, the Shakespearean actor David Garrick, Richard Owen Cambridge and Henrietta Howard, Countess of Suffolk, mistress to the Prince of Wales (later George II) all had homes by the Thames at Twickenham, where they could plan their grounds and planting to frame and enhance the river views.[6] Describing a visit to Stowe in 1738, an anonymous writer referred repeatedly to the views, which included a 'Fine Visto of Part of the Lake, an Obelisque, the Meadow and the Temple of Venus …'[7] The importance of views in this period might be due, in part, to the featureless agricultural landscape seen by travellers; strips in large open fields, with no hedges and only a few pollarded trees, before enclosure became common towards the end of the century. Bishop Pococke, who visited Miller and reported on Radway and Farnborough during his travels in 1756, frequently remarked on the views he had seen. He mentioned, among many others, views at The Leasowes, where he described 'a glorious view of the country and of Dudley, as well as the town of Halesowen', Hagley, which 'commands very extensive and beautiful prospects to the west, north-west and south-west', and Enville, where he noted Miller's Gothic Seat 'which commands a fine view of the vale towards Bridgnorth, of the country beyond Wolverhampton, of Lord Ward's house, of Dudley Castle, Hagley and of the country to the south'.[8]

Miller had a camera obscura, which he took great delight in using. At Hagley, looking through this device from the Castle Ruin, he was able in fine weather to see the tower at Radway, more than twenty miles away. In August 1750 he was at Hagley, and mentioned in his diary for the evening of 15 August, after playing duets with Colonel Conway, that he was 'mending Cam. Obsc.'. He was obviously successful, for the following day, after 'writing des:ign for the History of Architecture in Britain', he 'w. [walked] in Pk. [Park] Cam. Obsc.'. The camera obscura provided the possibility of seeing views and appreciating the detail in the distance without the need for a telescope. Miller does not give any details of how the projection of the image was managed, but presumably it would have been projected onto a flat surface of some kind which he and his friends would have taken out to the park with them. The History of Architecture, which his friends had asked him to write, was never completed due to the illness which he developed in later years.

The frequent use of small mounds to elevate landscape buildings is a definite feature of Miller's work, although other designers besides Miller set their buildings on mounds, occasionally of several feet in height. William Kent, for example, often used natural undulations for the site of a temple, or set buildings part way up a hill in his designs. Kent also used purpose-built mounds such as the large mound in Kensington Gardens, constructed in 1733, for the summit of which he designed a summerhouse.[9] Mounds such as this echoed the use of mounds within Elizabethan gardens, which were built high enough for a view of the countryside outside to be obtained from the top. By the mid-18th century, security within a fenced garden against the possible dangers outside had long since ceased to be important.

Miller used clumps and woodland to draw attention to high ridges, or the tops of hills, throughout his work. At both Radway and Honington, belts of trees along high ground defined the property boundaries. Planting directed the eye and defined the view. Miller often used yews to provide an evergreen background against which his buildings could stand out. The presence of these features, while adding weight to the attribution of a site to Miller, since he used them frequently, are not specific to his work. Capability Brown, in particular, used belts of trees and clumps in a similar way.

The inventive use of water, and an ability to find successful technical solutions to intractable drainage problems together form a major component of Miller's 'stylistic signature'. The technical solutions to the problems of poor drainage, and the creation of lakes on such sites often involved both the harnessing of suitable streams and the making of large dams. The actual building of a dam, and ensuring that the finished dam was completely watertight and safe, was a skilled undertaking and one at which Miller excelled. Examples are the creation and the specific siting of the lakes at Farnborough, the work at Wotton Underwood, and the management of lakes and dams at Arbury and Packington. Miller's use of an informal outline for lakes was a comparatively new idea, despite the informal lake created by Lord Bathurst at Cirencester in 1736. The construction of an informal lake in the mid-18th century is described by Roberts as the most extensive and demanding of all the operations undertaken in realising a landscape design. There was a very necessary balance to be achieved between what was technically possible and the most aesthetically pleasing result to be obtained. The work involved the penning of a large and heavy body of water, the level of which had to be maintained throughout the year. Roberts uses as an illustration the technical solution to the problems at Croome Court, where the extensive drainage system channelled the water from boggy ground into a small stream to form a 'river'.[10]

Rivers were artificially widened to form lakes through the use of weirs, as at Honington and Alscot. This was, again, a major technical undertaking, with the consequences of insufficient water downstream for mills or other uses, or the possibility of disastrous flooding after a period of heavy rainfall, if the levels of the weirs were not calculated correctly. Cascades were introduced in varying forms and at many sites; single, as on small streams, stepped, as at Honington, or as an informally broken fall, as at the artificial cliff by the 'River' at Farnborough. The introduction of a series of small waterfalls interspersed with long, narrow pools along a length of a brook, usually with retaining stone sluices, was a specific feature of Miller's schemes. Examples can be found at Farnborough, Arbury and Sudbury. The only comparable type of contemporary design which has been located in the south Midlands area is that at Heythrop, in Oxfordshire, where a series of falls was created on the stream below the bridge on the north approach to the mansion (finished in 1716). A plaque on the bridge dates it to 1750, but the date of the stream system is not known, nor the designer, despite recent investigative work on the site.[11] Miller would have known of the estate, since he travelled near it on his way to Oxford.

The creation of double waterways, or streams running more or less parallel with each other, is a further unusual feature which seems to be quite specific to Miller. Double waterways were created at Farnborough, at Wroxton and at Honington. At Farnborough, an isthmus of land planted with trees was created between the eastern end of what is known today as Rookery Pool, and the stream or 'serpentine river' taking the overflow from this pool southwards. At Wroxton, the stream entering the site from the north was divided, the new parallel stream taking the form of a canal wide enough to take a small rowing boat. A path shaded with trees led along the length of the land between the two streams. At Honington an isthmus was again created and planted with trees, with the main river on the east and the diverted section of the river to the west. No two schemes were alike; at each site Miller created a different double feature of interest.

Miller's schemes reveal a particular interest in the pleasurable sound made by moving water. His work on small streams where he created pools connected by waterfalls, his introduction of shady paths beside streams, and the numerous cascades of different designs all contribute to this idea. Even his grotto at Honington, where there was already the sound of the river, was designed to produce an extra rushing sound of water where part of the secondary stream from the river was led through a hole in the grotto wall, spurting out in a gush to drop into the pool below. Miller's repeated series of cascades at Upton, complete with tiny fairy-tale grotto, also show his interest in the sound of falling water, for the hillside itself is not very high. It would have been far simpler – but nothing like so interesting – to have made just one waterfall here.

Miller's small-scale water features, devised from modest sources, are his own individualistic solution to the problem of providing extra and unexpected interest. In all of Miller's landscapes where there is an appreciable part of his original plan still remaining there are small, winding, shaded paths beside water. Sometimes the paths could also accommodate riders on horseback, but they were never intended as carriage drives, which only appear occasionally in Miller's designs. These paths were intended as footpaths, to be followed in a leisurely manner, with time to appreciate the sound of the nearby water.

Miller himself often walked with his friends around their respective properties. The fact that in the middle decades of the century walking was a popular pursuit, either purely for pleasure, or to admire the new landscape improvements, is often ignored. When walking, small features, such as a new sluice and waterfall on a stream, can appear as interesting as a large expansive view – which is not the case when passing swiftly by in a carriage, an activity particularly associated with Brown's larger parks of the 1760s and 1770s.

A comparison can be made between the paths which Miller introduced in his landscapes, and those of his contemporaries. Perhaps the best examples of paths in early informal landscapes are those of the *ferme ornée*. Two well known examples are Philip Southcote's Woburn Farm, in Surrey, *c.*1737,[12] and Shenstone's The Leasowes. Although it was a farm, Southcote's paths were far from simple farm paths, being carefully designed with shrub and flower borders running alongside them. Shenstone also used flowering plants, but the paths were principally laid out to show visitors the correct way to appreciate his designs and the poetical allusions he attached to his seats and groves. Kent, at Rousham, and Henry Hoare, at Stourhead, both used the path as a device to lead the visitor around their iconographic designs. The smaller 'Rococo' gardens, such as the Painswick Rococo Garden, were also laid out with small winding footpaths and, naturally enough, without carriage drives.[13] Most designers used a path to lead visitors along a particular route. In contrast, Miller's shady waterside paths beckoned simply for pleasure rather than for instruction.

Several of Miller's contemporaries experimented with the harnessing of sources of water to create special features in their landscapes. A particularly inventive use of water was undertaken by Charles Hamilton at Painshill, who used an engine and large wheel system to raise sufficient water from the river Mole to feed his system of lakes, which were at a higher level than that of the river. In the early 1760s Hamilton also made an extensive and decorative grotto giving on to one of the lakes.[14] Miller only created one grotto of any size, that at Honington. William Kent dealt with water in a simple but effective way, using small ornamental bridges combined with waterfalls, a design repeated, with variations, at Chiswick, Stowe and at Rousham, among others. The ideas influencing Kent's design in, for example, Venus' Vale at Rousham differed from what appears to be Miller's rationale. Hunt describes how Venus presides over a series of descending pools and cascades that are likened to the rustic cascades at the Villa Aldobrandini in Italy, or perhaps the pools at the villa at Pratolino, both well known to Kent from his Italian travels. Rather than becoming involved with the mechanics of creating lakes, Kent's use of water was 'pictorial', as a necessary component of a bridge scene, or as part of the edge of a lake in a drawing.[15] Miller's bridge at Wotton did not, as far as can be ascertained, relate to any specific myth or design from antiquity, but he may have used Kent's design as a basis either because the design was aesthetically pleasing, or simply because George Grenville wished to have one similar to that at Stowe, which his elder brother had inherited from their uncle. Again, pleasure rather than instruction by means of artifice characterises Miller's work.

In the middle decades of the century, years when Miller carried out most of his work, all designed grounds had ornamental buildings in various styles, so his attitude to architectural design was important to his 'clients'. Miller's buildings in the landscape are a definite part of his 'stylistic signature'. His mock castle ruins speak eloquently of him as author, but his other buildings also show his individualistic style. The most important building in many of the designed landscapes where Miller was involved is the presence of a mock castle ruin, or a castellated façade as a dominant feature. Miller designed these buildings in a variety of styles, yet each one had a genuinely medieval appearance, and so solidly were they built that many are still standing today.

In Miller's time there was no-one creating mock ruins as a focal point on the estate in the manner of his Tower and ruins at Edgehill, apart from Lord Bathurst's ruined castle known as Alfred's Hall (completed in 1734) at Cirencester, harking back to the Saxon period, and Lord Cobham's mock castle façade built at Stowe, c.1737, again with overtones of the ancient Saxon liberties associated with Gothic castles. After 1750, the development of an enthusiasm for ruins saw the construction of many more mock Gothic ruins in landscaped parks and gardens across the country. An early construction of sham ruins was the fragment of castle wall and window on the hillside overlooking Plymouth Sound at Mount Edgecumbe, built in the park in 1747, two years after Miller had begun his Tower. Around 1750, Thomas Wright built the Ragged Castle, a small castle ruin, and added crenellations to a barn subsequently known as Castle Barn for the 4th Duke of Beaufort at Badminton, in Gloucestershire. Later in the century, Robert Adam also designed mock 'ruins', including ruinous towers for the bridge at Culzean Castle, Ayrshire in 1789, which were thought to have been constructed with a poor stone to aid picturesque ageing.[16]

Both Miller's own books on classical architecture and his diary entries illustrate his interest in Palladian or classical architecture and the works of Inigo Jones. All architects of the day studied Palladio's architecture, which was based on that of the Roman architect Vitruvius (1st century B.C.). In Vitruvian architecture, 'perfect' numbers are to be found in 'ideal' human proportions, and the ancient measures of the finger, the foot, the forearm etc. are dominated by the two 'perfect' numbers of six and ten. The most perfect of all is the number sixteen.[17] These perfect numbers, or multiples and combinations of them, were used by Palladio, by Inigo Jones, and also by English architects using the classical style in the early 18th century.

The influence of Palladian design has been discussed in Miller's various buildings in the classical style, both in larger buildings, such as Hagley Hall, the Shire Hall in Warwick and the stable block at Packington, and in his many landscape buildings, such as the Ionic Temple and the Oval Pavilion at Farnborough, and the Open Temple at Gopsall. Miller often took older buildings as a model, or incorporated details from older buildings in his designs, and a list of the models he used in this way is given in the back of this book.

Not everyone was won over to the new enthusiasm for classicism. In the city of Oxford, Miller's architectural Bible, both Gothic and classical buildings continued to be built. In 1715, Hawksmoor had produced designs in both styles for the Fellows at All Souls College in central Oxford. The Fellows decided upon Hawksmoor's Gothic design. Although Gothic in appearance, however, Hawksmoor had actually based his measurements on the classical precepts of proportion and symmetry, even extending these to the fenestration.[18] Miller used a similar combination of styles in several of his landscape buildings. In the design for The Museum, at Enville, Miller has used classical numbers in an essentially Gothic design. The exterior façade has three Gothic arches, but the rose windows underneath the arches are not divided into the more usual 12 decorated segments, but into the classically correct sixteen. This leaves no room for decoration, so Miller left the divisions plain. The large lower windows are also a mixture of Gothic and classical, while the small windows either side of the doorway in the central section are made up of repeated Gothic quatrefoil shapes. Between the upper rose windows and the lower windows there is a simple ornamental line consisting of a small repeated Gothic arch, the Miller 'signature'. This ornamental line of repeated Gothic arches is also seen on the Boathouse at Enville, on the entrance façade and the interior of the hall at Lacock, and on the Castle Ruin at Wimpole. It may have been inspired by Hawksmoor's line of Gothic arches between the towers at All Souls (see illustration on p.31). Both the Temple on the Mount at Wroxton and the entrance façade at Lacock show aspects of the mix of Gothic and classical styles. The Temple on the Mount was a classical design, yet between the pillars were arches of a Gothic shape. At Lacock, the design is in the Gothic idiom, yet the building with its Palladian styled staircase and its symmetry has a decidedly classical 'feel'. The influence of Oxford's architecture can thus be seen in much of Miller's architectural work.

Miller's use of many different geometric shapes in his landscape buildings is an unusual feature of his architecture, resulting in added interest and, often, a picturesque appearance to their forms. Miller's fascination with polygons and geometrical designs in his buildings may be traced back to the works of the Greek classical arithmetician Euclid (323-285 B.C.). Miller noted in his diary for 19 January 1750 that he had 'r [read] Euclid Ih', and again on 8, 9 and 10 February that he was reading Euclid, though he does not comment further. In the fourth book of 13 books entitled 'The Elements', Euclid discussed the relationship between circles and straight-sided figures such as triangles, squares, and certain regular polygons. He described figures which could be drawn inside a circle, and figures which could be drawn outside a circle. Different books in Euclid's 'The Elements' describe other aspects of geometry, and also the theory of proportion, all important in the practice of architecture. New mathematical advances in these ancient arithmetical concepts would only be made at the end of the 18th century. Miller's design for the Pentagon Temple at Farnborough illustrates the application of this geometry, for the temple is, as Lady Newdigate recorded, 'in ye form of a Pentagon without and a Rotunda within the diamr. 16 foot and 1/2 the height about ye same.' The Pentagon Temple is a further example of Miller's ability to combine different styles; the body of the temple is classical, with a diameter of 16 feet, the 'perfect' classical number, but it had a roof in the Chinese style. The Tower at Ingestre is another pentagon. Miller used different polygonal figures in other garden buildings, and he was intrigued by combinations of geometric shapes. The Game Larder at Farnborough is a hexagon. The so called Octagon Seat at Hagley is actually a half-hexagon shape to the front, overlooking the valley, built on to a rectilinear back. The octagon was, however, Miller's

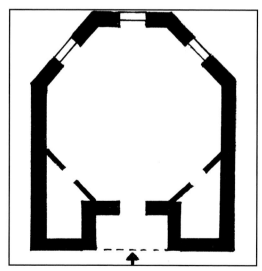

120 *Walton, the Bath House, a plan showing the octagon room within the overall structure. The building was set into the hillside, the entrance to the octagon room being behind, but the outer door to the plunge pool room being at the front, or downhill side. The Bath House was restored 1987-91.*

120   *Corpus Christi College, Oxford, the castellated roofline, c.1741 and, below, a repeated Gothic arch line of ornamentation similar to that used by Miller on several of his buildings. Miller would have seen Corpus Christi regularly when returning to Oxford, for the College is adjacent to Oriel College and St Mary Hall.*

favourite shape. Both Miller's own Tower at Edgehill, and the Dovecote at Wroxton were octagons. There is the Octagon Seat at Wotton Underwood, the Temple on the Mount at Wroxton is eight-sided, and both the Open Temple at Gopsall and the Oxford Lodge at Middleton Stoney are octagons. The designs for the Bath House at Walton and the Boathouse at Enville show variations on the theme of constructing an octagon on top of or within a square; in the Bath House the exterior of the upper room is an octagon, in the Boathouse it was only the interior of the upper room which was an octagon. The octagon shape was also the basis of the design for the interior of the Shire Hall in Warwick, a complicated layout where the two Courts are a part octagon on a rectangle, while the central room under the Grand Jury Chambers is a full octagon. The entrance Hall is a rectangle.[19] This particular interest in a variety of geometric forms and differing combinations of forms is clear to see in Miller's plans.

To summarise, those characteristic elements in Miller's landscape work which form Miller's 'stylistic signature' include firstly, an informal approach to design in which the views in and out of the site are particularly important, and the topography is enhanced with features to support this concept; secondly, the construction of new lakes on unpromising and often boggy sites, or the manipulation of the flow of rivers so that water is held back to make ornamental 'lakes' or other features; and thirdly, the introduction of specific small-scale water features such as double waterways, and small rectilinear pools on streams. Fourthly, his designs always have small-scale areas which could be called Rococo in their conception, with pleasant paths, views, small pools or cascades, and a summer house or two for outdoor meals.

Miller's buildings constitute an important part of his 'stylistic signature', reflecting his personal architectural flair. His mock castle ruins stand apart for their idiosyncratic character. His other landscape buildings, designed in a manner which is both attractive to the eye and often unusual in plan, are also interesting for the varied geometric forms and combination of forms which they exhibit.

Miller's work has been shown to be in the forefront of the development of the natural landscape style during the period immediately preceding the middle of the 18th century. Social requirements fuelled much of the 18th century's preoccupation with 'improvements'; on the one hand the need to entertain guests, and on the other to show those guests just how extensive and well laid out the estate was, and how refined a 'taste' could be displayed in the different architectural styles of the landscape buildings. There is a certain lightheartedness and pleasure about the more intimate areas of Miller's designs which accorded well with the 18th-century fashion for entertainments in the fresh air.

Miller's interest in the development of the wider landscape beyond the immediate ornamental grounds around a mansion was an innovative design concept which only began to be used by others after Capability Brown had used the same design concept in the development of the Croome landscape. Following Brown's successes, other landscape designers such as Richard Woods, whose initial work was in Essex and the eastern counties, William Emes, whose work was largely in the north Midlands, and Richard White, who worked mainly in the north of England, all used this pattern in their plans for estates.

It is not possible to present a complete assessment of the impact that Miller's work had on others, though his designs had far-reaching effects. They can certainly be said to have influenced Brown, who first used, then altered and significantly expanded these ideas. Other landscape designers followed, thus creating the English landscape style, which spread abroad to Russia, to the landscape gardens of Catherine the Great (1762-96); to Germany, where Prince Franz of Anhalt-Dessau's design for his landscape park in the English style, laid out from 1765 at Wörlitz, became famous,[20] and to the landscape gardens of France with their 'fabriques' copied in spirit from the landscape buildings of the English parks.[21]

When Miller was working in the years before the middle of the century, the tide of fashion for naturalistic landscaped grounds was growing and would certainly have developed, with the genius of Capability Brown. Miller's contribution, while not responsible for the whole subsequent development of the movement, was important at the outset and in moving it forward. Miller's work predated most of Brown's work, and Miller's designs probably inspired Brown to be more adventurous than he might otherwise have been with his creation of lakes and his drainage projects, at least in the early years of his private practice. The lines of Miller's influence can clearly be seen in the evidence which has been presented. Miller's informal plans, built around the importance of views and the inventive use of water resources, and his emphasis on beauty and pleasure, as well as utility in design, showed what it was possible to achieve and left the way open for Brown to enlarge his own work on similar lines as opportunity arose. Brown became the pre-eminent figure in English landscape gardening; nevertheless, Miller's own work holds an important place in the initiation and development of the natural landscape style, which is one of England's greatest claims to artistic fame.

Appendix 1
Models for Miller's Landscape Buildings

ॐ·ॐ

Unless otherwise identified, buildings used as models are located in Oxford. Miller generally used only particular parts or aspects of a building in his own design, the model serving as his inspiration. This list is assembled from personal observation (apart from two buildings*), and makes no claim to be complete.

Croome, Church	Wroxton church, Magdalen College chapel.
Enville, Museum	New College chapel, All Souls, repeated Gothic arch line between towers
Boathouse	Façade similar to Museum, also All Souls, Gothic arch line
Farnborough, Ionic Pavilion	Pediment from the Clarendon Building.
Oval Pavilion*	Oval Pavilion, Ecton, attributed to Inigo Jones.
Stepped Cascade	The narrow cascade on the Glyme at Heythrop.
Gopsall, The Open Temple	The Rotunda at Stowe, by Sir John Vanbrugh.
The Gothic Façade	New College chapel.
Hagley, The Castle Ruin	Corpus Christi College towers.
Honington Hall, Grotto	Cheddar, exit of the Axe river from the limestone.
Chinese Seat	Similar to Chinese seat at Wroxton.
Lacock Abbey, entrance façade	Divinity School doorway arch, All Souls, Gothic arch line
Middleton Park, lodge	Corpus Christi College towers.
Radway, The Castle Ruin*	Guy's Tower, Warwick Castle.
Stowe, The Gothic Temple	The Sheldonian, Wren's original cupolas, also large Cupola above entrance to All Souls College.
Siston Court, entrance lodges	Garden gazebos at Arlescote House, near Radway.
Sudbury, The Deercote	The gatehouse entrance, Warwick Castle.
Walton, The Bath House	The grotto, Wilton House, Isaac de Caux c.1647. Arched entrance similar to crypt windows in old Saxon churches.
Wimpole, The Castle Ruin	All Souls, Gothic arch line
Wroxton, The Dovecote	The monastic tower at Idlicote.
The Chinese Seat	Similar to that at Honington.

* The models for these buildings have already been identified by William Hawkes in his thesis.

Taken from *The Diaries of Sanderson Miller*, ed William Hawkes.

Adlestrop House, Gloucestershire, for James Leigh. New Gothic front to house, including bay windows, two periods of building: 1750-4, 1759.
   Church of St Mary Magdalene: new south transept to form family pew, re-roofing and new west gallery. Work carried out 1758-9.

All Souls College, Oxford, for the College Council. Gothic alterations to library, 1751.

Ambrosden House, Oxfordshire, for Sir Edward Turner. Recasing of old house in classical style, 1745-56. Demolished *c*.1779. Design for farmhouse and offices, 1749.
   Church of St Mary: west gallery with Tuscan columns, now demolished.

Arbury Hall, Warwickshire, for Sir Roger Newdigate. Gothic bay window to exterior, Gothic alterations to interior, 1749-55.

Arlington Street, London, for Henrietta Fermor, Countess of Pomfret. 'Pomfret Castle', Gothic, designed with Sir Roger Newdigate. Built 1757-61, demolished

Astrop Wells, Northamptonshire, for Dr Grey and Mr Herbert. Advice on new card room at Spa, 1756. Now demolished.

Barrowby Rectory, for James Menteath, Rector. Stables and coach house, classical, 1759. Demolished *c*.1962.

Bath, Somerset, for Walter Wiltshire. Advice on ventilation of assembly rooms, 1758.

Beckett House, Shrivenham, Berkshire, for William, Viscount Barrington. Alterations to interior of house, 1757-8. Stables, classical, 1762-6. The latter have been much altered.

Belhus, Essex, for Thomas Barrett Lennard, Lord Dacre. Gothic alterations to west and south fronts of house, also alterations to interior, 1745-58. House demolished 1956.

Burton Dassett, All Saints Church, Warwickshire for Richard, Earl Temple (of Stowe). Renovation of John Temple's monument (1603), 1751-2.

Carlisle Cathedral, Cumbria, for Charles Lyttelton, Bishop of Carlisle. Design for stone screen and choir arcading, 1764.

Mr Child's plan, for Francis Child. Plan for an alcove, 17 April 1750. No further details given; Hawkes suggests it may have been for Osterley Park, Middlesex.

Cricket St Thomas, Somerset, for Alexander Hood. New house designed in the 'Farm stile', 1774.

Croome Court, Worcestershire, for Lord Coventry. Miller recorded in his diary that he was drawing Lord Coventry's plan over four days from 2 March 1750. This probably refers to a plan for the new mansion. Stables, classical. Hawkes has identified a drawing for the stables in Miller's hand in the archives at Croome.
   Church of St Mary Magdalene, Croome d'Abitot: probable design for exterior, built 1761-3.

Durham Castle, for Joseph Butler, Bishop of Durham. Internal alterations, classical and Gothic, 1751-2.

Edgeworth House, Clewer, Windsor, Berkshire for Mrs Sarah Stanley. New bay window and kitchen alterations, 1755-6.

Farnborough Hall, for William Holbech. Remodelling and enlarging of Hall, including new south front and new interior work.

Frankley, Church of St Leonard's, Worcestershire, for Charles Lyttelton. Advice on alterations, 1749, probably including the rebuilding of the tower.

Gosfield Hall, Essex, for Robert, Lord Nugent. New quadrant wing to west front, to match existing, 1754. Demolished *c*.1812.

Hagley Hall, for George, Lord Lyttelton. Stables, 1750. Gothic design for new Hall rejected, 1752. Monument to Sir Thomas Lyttelton in church of St John the Baptist.

Classical design for Hall 1753, built 1754-63. Grotto built within Hall 1754-5. Alterations to interior of church, 1756, swept away in Victorian period.

Hanworth Park, Middlesex, for Lord Vere Beauclerk, stable block, 1749.

Hartlebury Castle, Worcestershire, for Isaac Maddox, Bishop of Worcester. Advice on new interior for chapel, work carried out by Henry Keene 1749-50. Design for Bishop's seat in chapel.

Hillingdon House, Little Hillingdon, Middlesex, for the Hon. John Talbot, advice on stables.

Honington Hall, Warwickshire, for Joseph Townsend. Advised John Freeman on his design and detail for the new octagonal saloon, 1751.

Kilkenny Cathedral, Ireland, for Bishop Richard Pococke. Redesign of chancel and choir, chapter house and bishop's court in south transept, Gothic/classical, 1756-63. Miller had carved wooden sample patterns prepared and sent to Ireland. Work swept away in Victorian period.

Kineton, Church of St Peter, Warwickshire, for the Rev. Willliam Talbot. Rebuilding of nave with gallery and transepts, Gothic, built 1756. Work all swept away in Victorian period, except chancel east window.

Mongewell, Oxon, for Shute Barrington, later Bishop of Llandaff. Advice on alterations to vicarage, 1776; now demolished.

The Nelmes (now the Manor House), Hornchurch, Essex, for Godfrey Webster. Design for house restoration; work carried out by Henry Keene, who was given the job as a young man by Miller who was anxious to encourage him.

Packington Hall, Warwickshire, for Lord Guernsey. Stables in classical style, built 1749.

Park Place, for Henry Seymour, General Conway. Design for library, 1756-7, demolished 1867.

Place House, later Ealing Park, Little Ealing, Middlesex, for Colonel Richard Lyttelton. Miller spent part of two days, 17 and 18 August, 1750 on a design for the Gothicising of the old house, now demolished.

Preston, Lancashire, for James, Lord Strange, later Earl of Derby. Design for Gothic cock-pit, 1749.

Radway Grange, Gothic dining room, 1744-5. Gothic exterior alterations: new south-east front to house, 1745-6, south-west bay windows, 1746, further interior improvements, 1749.

Rockingham Hall, Hagley, Worcestershire, for Admiral Thomas Smith. Garden front in Gothic style, and other alterations, 1750.

Ross on Wye, Church of St Mary, Hereford for the Rev. John Egerton. Alterations to chancel, 1754, removed 1878. Advice on alterations to rectory.

Sandywell Park, Gloucestershire, for Thomas Tracy. Design for a room at the house, 1750.

Swalcliffe Park, Oxon, for Richard Wykeham. New kitchen, 1750.

Swerford Park, Oxon, for John Travel. Design for stables, 1750.

Shire Hall, Warwick, for the County. Crown and Nisi Prius courts, 1752-8.

Siston Court, Gloucestershire, for Samuel Trotman. Alterations to Court, built 1754-5. Design for 'Poor's House', 1759.

Temple Guiting House, Temple Guiting, Gloucestershire, for the Rev. George Talbot. Design for a 'Chinese rail', 1750.

Teston House, Kent, for Sir Philip Boteler. Advice on alterations, 1753.

Wellesbourne Hall, Wellesbourne, Warwickshire for Mr Dewes (brother-in-law to Mrs Delany). Advice on alterations.

Wimpole Hall, Cambridgeshire, for Lord Hardwicke. Library alterations and new bay window, classical, 1754.

Wroxton Abbey, Oxfordshire, for Francis, Lord North. Alterations to window and interior design of chapel, 1747. New lantern top for parish church, 1747-8. Hall ceiling and pendant, Gothic, c.1751.

---

* Works listed are those unconnected with Miller's landscapes. Less likely attributions are not included; for these, and further details, see *The Diaries* ... pp.391-408.

Gazetteer

❧ ⋅ ❧

Alscot Park

Site details:

Estate:	Alscot Park
County:	Warwickshire
Grid reference:	SP 2050
Listing:	Grade II
Owner:	Mrs Emma Holman-West

Miller's involvement:

Date:	1750
Owner at this period:	James West
Certainty:	Definite
Design:	'Plan' – details not known
Survival of design:	Landscape buildings gone; designed areas beyond river reverted to agriculture. Gardens and park well maintained.

The house, Gothicised in the mid-18th century, stands in its own parkland and estate. It is not open to the general public, though visits by parties or societies may be arranged by private appointment. The gardens are open occasionally in support of the National Gardens Scheme.

Ambrosden

Site details:

Estate:	Ambrosden
County:	Oxfordshire
Grid reference:	SP 6019
Listing:	not listed
Owner:	estate broken up and in multiple ownership

Miller's involvement:

Date:	1745-1760s
Owner at this period:	Sir Edward Turner
Certainty:	Definite
Designs:	Gothic Barn 1747, Gate and entrance lodge 1748-9. Ruins, prior to 1750. Also advised on new mansion from at least 1743, and designed new farmhouse for estate 1758.
Survival of designs:	Landscape buildings and mansion now demolished, latter soon after Sir Edward's death in 1766.

Few remnants of this site survive. The church, which has monuments to members of the Turner family, and the village pub, the *Turner Arms*, provide the only record of the 18th-century Turner estate.

Arbury Hall

Site details:

Estate:	Arbury
County:	Warwickshire
Grid reference:	SP 3389
Listing:	Grade II★
Owner:	Viscount Daventry

Miller's involvement:

Date:	c.1750
Owner at this period:	Sir Roger Newdigate, 5th Baronet
Certainty:	Very probable
Design:	Dam and cascade, new drive, rotunda and teahouse etc
Survival of design:	Landscape survives, buildings gone or semi-derelict

Arbury Hall is probably the finest 18th-century Gothic revival house in the country, with 17th-century stables, ornamental lakes and pleasant gardens. Visits by parties or societies may be arranged by private appointment. The house and gardens are open occasionally, but not the estate grounds, which are private.

Croome Court

Site details:

Estate:	Croome Court
County:	Worcestershire
Grid reference:	SO 8844
Listing:	Grade I
Owner:	Multiple ownership. The National Trust owns 667 acres (270ha) comprising the designed parkland, the Sun Alliance Insurance Group owns the rest of the agricultural estate.

Miller's involvement:

Date:	c.1748-early 1750s
Owner at this period:	George William, Lord Deerhurst, later (1751) 6th Lord Coventry
Certainty:	Definite
Design:	Details are not known with certainty. Advice on landscaping definite. Design for Croome church likely, for Rotunda possible.
Survival of design:	Landscape being restored. Church in good repair, Rotunda needs restoration.

One of the most important 18th-century designed landscapes. Landscaped area around house restored and open regularly. Outer landscape buildings have public access via footpaths. House and walled garden in private ownership.

Enville

Site details:

Estate:	Enville
County:	Staffordshire
Grid reference:	SO 8387
Listing:	Grade II★
Owner:	Mr and Mrs P.B. Williams

Miller's involvement:

Date:	1749–*c*.1760
Owner at this period:	Harry, 4th Earl of Stamford
Certainty:	Definite, but extent of involvement not certain
Designs:	The Museum and the Gothic Gateway, both Grade II The Boat House. Possibly the Doric temple, Grade II,
Survival of designs :	Graded structures: excellent or restored, except for the Boat House, which is ruinous.

One of the most important 18th-century designed landscapes, with extensive 19th-century additions. The Hall is private, the gardens and grounds are not open to the general public, though visits by parties or societies may be arranged by private appointment. The gardens are open occasionally.

Farnborough

Site details:

Estate:	Farnborough Hall
County:	Warwickshire
Grid reference:	SP 4349
Listing:	Grade I
Owner:	The National Trust hold the Hall and part of the estate on a long lease by Mr and Mrs Geoffrey Holbech, the remainder is privately farmed.

Miller's involvement:

Date:	Late 1730's(?) to 1748 and perhaps later
Owner at this period:	William Holbech
Certainty:	Traditional
Design:	Landscaping of whole estate, including terrace and lakes.
Buildings:	Ionic Temple, Oval Pavilion, Obelisk, Pentagon Temple, Game Larder.
Survival of design:	Landscaping largely intact, though some water features derelict. Buildings survive except for Pentagon Temple, now gone.

Important mid-18th century designed landscape of which part only, including the main terrace and the lakes, is regularly open to the public. The Hall is also open to the public. The northern terrace area, now on private farmland, can be viewed from a public footpath which leaves the village of Farnborough down a small lane opposite *The Butcher's Arms*.

Gopsall Park

Site details:

Estate:	Gopsall Park
County:	Leicestershire
Grid reference:	SK 3707
Listing:	not listed
Owner:	the Crown

Miller's involvement:

Date:	1748 onwards
Owner at this period:	Charles Jennens
Certainty:	Definite
Design:	Advice on grounds, possibly also on temple, Gothic façade and Boathouse.
Survival of design:	House demolished; pleasure grounds and

lake gone, few outlines remain. Land restored to agriculture, though ruins of Temple exist, also vestigial landscaping around fishpond to east of drive.

Privately farmed, no public access.

Gosfield Hall

Site details:

Estate:	Gosfield Hall
County:	Essex
Grid reference:	TL 7729
Listing:	Hall and landscape both Grade II
Owner:	Country Houses Association Ltd., estate: divided ownership

Miller's involvement:

Date:	At least from 1750 onwards
Owner at this period:	Robert, later Earl Nugent
Certainty:	Definite
Design:	Advice on laying out of grounds 1750. House Gothicised in 1755.
Survival of design:	Hall survives. Parkland part golf course, rest farmed. Lake still exists, also some groups of old trees.

Privately owned, no public access.

Hagley

Site details:

Estate:	Hagley Hall
County:	West Midlands (was Worcestershire)
Grid reference:	SP 9282
Listing:	Grade I
Owner:	John Lyttelton, 11th Viscount Cobham.

Miller's involvement:

Date:	1747-60
Owner at this period:	George, later 1st Lord Lyttelton
Certainty:	Definite. Extent of involvement in landscape not certain
Designs:	Ruined Castle, Grotto, Gothic seats, advice given on rotundo and landscaping.
Architectural designs:	Hagley Hall, cottage, stables, dairy, greenhouse, redesign of church.
Survival of designs :	Landscape designs: Castle restored and now lived in. Rotundo survives, part derelict. Park well maintained, but most of landscape buildings gone. Grotto area derelict and overgrown.

House available for corporate entertaining etc, otherwise open occasionally to the public. Garden private. Landscaped park not open to the public, though visits by parties or societies may occasionally be arranged by special appointment.

Honington

Site details:

Estate:	Honington Hall
County:	Warwickshire
Grid reference:	SP 2642
Listing:	Grade II★
Owner:	Benjamin Wiggins

Miller's involvement:

Date:	*c*.1749
Owner at this period:	Joseph Townsend
Certainty:	Definite, though extent of involvement not certain.

| Design: | Landscaping, waterscape, grotto and cascade. |
| Survival of design: | Outlines still present, but largely overgrown and semi-derelict. Cascade in good working order. |

House and immediate gardens open regularly, also adjacent parish church. Mid-18th-century gardens overlaid by 19th-century additions. Landscaped grounds to the west of the river and north of the house now largely derelict, with no public access.

Ingestre

Site details:

Estate:	Ingestre Hall
County:	Staffordshire
Grid reference:	SJ 9724
Listing:	Miller's building demolished
Owner:	Sandwell Borough Council

Miller's involvement:

Date:	1749
Owner at this period:	John, 2nd Viscount Chetwynd
Certainty:	Definite
Design:	Pentagonal Gothic Tower
Survival of design:	Demolished 1850

House now used as an institution. Gardens kept up, but no general public access. No public access to landscaped grounds. Both adjacent parish church and large 19th-century stables (now a riding school) are of interest.

Lacock Abbey

Site Details:

Estate:	Lacock
County:	Wiltshire
Grid reference:	ST 9168
Listing:	Landscape: Grade II
Owner:	The National Trust (The family still live in the house.)

Miller's involvement:

Date:	1754-55
Owner at this period:	John Ivory Talbot
Certainty:	Definite
Designs:	Gothic Hall, entrance, and Gothic arch to forecourt. Possibly grotto.
Survival of designs:	Buildings survive as designed.

Abbey and gardens both open regularly, with some access to grounds beyond the gardens.

Middleton Park

Site details:

Estate:	Middleton Park, Middleton Stoney
County:	Oxfordshire
Grid reference::	SP 5223
Listing:	Oxford Lodge, Grade II
Owner :	House split into flats

Miller's involvement:

Date:	1749
Owner at this period:	William Villiers, 3rd Earl of Jersey
Certainty:	Very probable
Design:	Oxford Lodge
Survival of design:	Survives and appears to be complete

House and grounds private. The Oxford Lodge is also private, but can easily be seen from the road at the south-east entrance to the park, south of the village of Middleton Stoney.

Packington Hall

Site details:

Estate:	Packington Hall
County:	Warwickshire
Grid reference:	SP 2283
Listing:	Landscaped park and lakes grade II
Owner:	The Right Hon. The Earl of Aylesford

Miller's involvement:

Date:	1746-56.
Owner at this period:	Heneage Finch, Lord Guernsey, later 3rd Earl of Aylesford
Certainty:	Definite
Design:	Miller definitely gave advice on landscape improvements, and probably designed the stables, 1756-8.
Survival of design:	Stables and parkland survive in good condition.

House and grounds private. Landscaped park not open to the public, though visits by parties or societies may occasionally be arranged by special appointment.

Park Place

Site details:

Estate:	Park Place
County:	Berkshire
Grid reference:	GD 1578
Listing:	Main house and various garden buildings, Grade II
Owner:	Divided ownership, house privately owned, two golf courses in park

Miller's involvement:

Date:	after 1751, when Gen. Conway bought the estate
Owner at this period:	General the Hon. Henry Seymour Conway (1720-95)
Certainty:	Miller both designed and set out a building (possibly more than one) in the park
Design:	Simply described as 'Buildg.' or 'Hse.' in Miller's diary.
Survival of design:	Park with some of the buildings survives, with the overlay of two modern golf courses.

Estate private, with no public access, though the main road following the river south of Henley–on-Thames goes over the great rock arch ascribed to Thomas Pitt.

Sham Castle, Prior Park

Site details:

Estate:	Prior Park
County:	North Somerset
Grid reference:	ST 7864
Listing:	
Owner:	City of Bath

Miller's involvement:

Date:	1755
Owner at this period:	Ralph Allen
Certainty:	Design almost definite
Design:	Sham Castle, built 1762
Survival of design:	In good state of preservation

There is public access to Sham Castle, which is some distance from the house at Prior Park and its associated designed landscape. The house is private, the landscaped park has been restored by the National Trust and is open regularly to the public.

Stowe

Site details:

Estate:	Stowe Landscape Gardens
County:	Buckinghamshire
Grid reference:	SP 6737
Listing:	Grade I
Owner:	The National Trust

Miller's involvement:

Date:	1756
Owner at this period:	Richard Grenville-Temple, Earl Temple
Certainty:	Definite
Design:	The later additions to James Gibbs' Gothic Temple, 1744-48
Survival of design:	Restored. Now let by Landmark Trust for holidays

The gardens constitute the most important 18th-century designed landscape in Britain. They are open regularly and have been extensively restored by the National Trust. The restored Gothic Temple can be rented for holidays from the Landmark Trust. The house can sometimes be seen by prior appointment and when Stowe School is not in residence.

Sudbury Hall

Site details:

Estate:	Sudbury Hall
County:	Derbyshire
Grid reference:	SK 1532
Listing:	Grade II
Owner:	The National Trust

Miller's involvement:

Date:	1750
Owner at this period:	George Vernon, 1709-80, became Baron Vernon 1762
Certainty:	Very probable
Design:	Alterations to Deercote, c.1750. Tree planting. Creation of several long narrow pools on an adjacent stream.
Survival of design:	Trees now gone, Deercote, in good condition, left isolated in an arable field. Remains of pools and sluices still visible.

House and immediate gardens open regularly. Deercote and remains of deerpark not open to the public.

Upton

Site details:

Estate:	Upton House
County:	Warwickshire
Grid reference:	SP 3746
Listing:	Grade II★ (Gardens and landscaped parkland together.)
Owner:	House and gardens: the National Trust Landscaped parkland: Mr and Mrs R.B. Waley-Cohen

Miller's involvement:

Date:	Probably during the 1750s
Owner at this period:	W. Bumpstead, d.1757 Francis Child bought estate in 1758.
Certainty:	Uncertain but probable.
Design:	Temple pool, and Temple at N. end. Cascades down hillside, and clump planting on hill.
Survival of design:	Pool and clumps existing. Temple gone. Cascades partly gone, partly overgrown.

Upton House and gardens regularly open to the public. The estate grounds are private, though there is a public footpath which runs from the Wroxton road south past the lake, though the lake and its immediate surrounds are private.

Walton Hall

Site details:

Estate:	Walton Hall
County:	Warwickshire.
Grid reference:	SP 2854
Listing:	Bath House grade II
Owner:	Sir John Hamilton; inherited from mother, Irene née Mordaunt

Miller's involvement:

Date:	1748/9 onwards, probably until 1754(?)
Owner at this period:	Sir Charles Mordaunt, 6th Baronet, 1698-1778
Certainty:	Definite
Design:	Bath House, built 1748/9
Survival of design:	Restored by Landmark Trust, 1987/91, let for holidays

The Bath House, in Bath Woods close to the Hall, has been restored by the Landmark Trust, and can be rented for holidays. The immediate surrounds to the Bath House have been newly landscaped to return the area to its 18th-century appearance. The Hall is now a hotel, and timeshare houses have been built in the walled garden. The simple 18th-century church adjacent to the Hall is worth a visit.

Wimpole

Site details:

Estate:	Wimpole Hall
County:	Cambridgeshire
Grid reference:	TL3351
Listing:	Grade I
Owner:	The National Trust

Miller's involvement:

Date:	1749 to at least 1756
Owner at this period:	Philip Yorke, Lord Chancellor and 1st Earl of Hardwicke
Certainty:	Definite
Design:	Ruined castle. Advice on landscaping.
Survival of design:	As finally built (1772-6) the Castle was altered somewhat from Miller's original. The ruin still stands, in very good condition, but the landscaping has since been altered.

Castle ruin, landscaped grounds, gardens and Hall are all open regularly to the public.

Wotton House

Site details:

Estate:	Wotton Underwood
County:	Buckinghamshire
Grid Reference:	SP 6817
Listing:	Landscape: Grade II★ Buildings: Grade II.
Owner:	Mr and Mrs David Gladstone

Miller's involvement:

Date:	1758 definitely, probably both before and after this date
Owner at this period:	George Grenville
Certainty:	Definite
Designs:	Plan of 'the bridge', Octagon Seat, and assistance with design for Grotto. Possibly responsible for ideas behind landscaping.
Survival of designs:	Bridge and Octagon Seat restored since 1958. Grotto semi-derelict.

An important mid-18th-century landscape, restored but otherwise virtually unaltered since its inception. Both house, also restored, and grounds are private, though visits by parties or societies may be arranged by private appointment.

Wroxton Abbey

Site details:

Estate:	Wroxton Abbey
County:	Oxfordshire
Grid reference:	SP 4141
Listing:	Grade II★
Owner:	Fairleigh Dickinson University

Miller's involvement:

Date:	late 1740s to mid 1750s
Owner at this period:	Francis, Lord North
Certainty:	Temple on the Mount: definite Other garden structures and extensive landscaping: almost certain, but evidence lacking.
Design:	Temple on the Mount, cascade and serpentine river, creation of double 'river' with path. Dovecote, Drayton Arch.
Survival of design:	Temple gone, Mount remains, dam of great pool and serpentine river below it now restored. Double 'river' system derelict. Dovecote restored. Drayton Arch remains.

Grounds open regularly, but the lower landscape is not now accessible from the upper grounds. The lower valley may be accessed from a public footpath leading along the stream from the bridge taking the main road between Wroxton and Drayton. The Abbey is used as a university campus, hence is not open to the public, though visits by parties or societies may be arranged by private appointment.

Lesser Sites

Adlestrop Park, Gloucestershire
O.S. grid reference: SP 2427
Present owner: Trustees of the Leighs of Stoneleigh Abbey. House and gardens held on long lease by Dominic Collins.
Mid-18th century: Miller designed the additions to the house; one of his best architectural works. He probably also advised on the grounds.
Owner at this period: William Leigh and son James Leigh.
Grounds and house private. Parsonage once visited regularly by Jane Austen, whose uncle the Rev. Thomas Leigh inherited Stoneleigh Abbey in Warwickshire in 1806. Part of the estate can be seen from a public footpath which runs between the grounds of the parsonage and Adlestrop Park.

Barrowby Rectory, Lincolnshire
O.S. grid reference: SK 8736
Mid-18th century: Miller Gothicised the house, designed two stables and a coach house. Grounds landscaped at same period.
Owner at this period: James Menteath, Miller's friend and the rector of the parish.
Grounds and house private; stables and coach house demolished, gardens and grounds have been negelected and parts sold.

Belhus, Aveley, Essex
O.S. grid reference: TQ 5680
Present owner: London County Council
Mid-18th century: Miller designed Gothic alterations to mansion and probably advised on early landscaping.

Owner at this period: Thomas Lennard Barrett, 26th Baron Dacre
House demolished mid-20th century, grounds extensively redeveloped as public parkland. Virtually nothing remains of 18th-century landscape.

Chart Park, Dorking
O.S. grid reference: TQ 1768
Mid-18th century: Miller provided a plan of a Greenhouse, and possibly a plan of a mock ruined arch.
Owner at this period: Henry Talbot
House demolished, grounds became part of adjacent mansion, no public access.

Coughton Court, Warwickshire
O.S. grid reference: SP 0760
Present owner: The National Trust; the Throckmorton family live at Coughton and manage the property.
Mid-18th century: Miller visited Coughton and prepared a plan; no further details are known.
Owner at this period: Sir Robert Throckmorton
House and gardens regularly open. Nothing remains of the 18th-century gardens, extensive new gardens having been made toward the end of the 20th century. Riverside walk with bluebells.

Eythrope, Buckinghamshire
O.S. grid reference: SP 7714
Mid-18th century: Plan designed by Miller, but no further details

known.
Owner at this period: Sir William Stanhope
House demolished early 19th century; little remains of landscaped grounds

Hartlebury Castle, The Bishop's Palace, Worcestershire
O.S. grid reference: SO 8470
Present owner: the Diocese of Worcester
Mid-18th century: Miller very probably involved in landscaping
Owner at this period: the Diocese of Worcester; property lived in by Bishop Maddox, Bishop of Worcester, 1743-1759
Castle and grounds open to the public. Eighteenth-century landscaping still exists in the parkland. The castle moat has been made into gardens.

Holkham, Norfolk
O.S. Grid reference: TF 8944
Present owner: Earl of Leicester
Mid-18th century: Miller was asked by George Lyttelton to prepare a plan of a Gothic Castle for Lord Leicester, but no Gothic Castle was built.
Owner at this period: Thomas Coke, 1st Earl of Leicester
Hall, gardens, and National Nature Reserve open regularly to the public.
Nursery Gardens closed 2006. Estate covers c.3000 acres.

Kirtlington, Oxfordshire
O.S. grid reference: SP 4919
Mid-18th century: Miller prepared a plan, Brown later called in.
Owner at this period: Sir James Dashwood
House and grounds private

Portsmouth
O.S. grid reference: SU 6501
Mid-18th century: Miller was asked to draw a plan for an 'eye trap'
Owner at this period: friend of Robert Eddowes, Miller's wife's uncle
Site unidentified.

Shrub Hill, Dorking
O.S. grid reference: TQ 1649
Mid-18th century: Miller advised on landscaping and designed a grotto.
Owner at this period: Henry Grenville
Site built over by end of 19th century.

Siston Court, Siston, near Bristol
O.S. grid reference: ST 6875
Mid-18th century: Miller designed octagonal gate lodges and almost certainly advised on landscaping.
Owner at this period: Samuel Trotman, uncle to Miller's wife.
House now in multiple ownership, house and grounds private.

Stoke Gifford, Bristol
O.S. grid reference: ST 6280
Mid-18th century: Miller's advice on landscape sought through George Lyttelton.
Owner at this period: Norborne Berkeley
In 20th century house in institutional use. Estate now bisected by motorway, but some restoration has been carried out by the Avon Gardens Trust, the Stoke Park Restoration Trust and Avon County Council. Public access to some areas.

References

꙾·꙾

Chapter 1: Introduction, pp.1-6

1. Meir, J. (2002), 'Development of a natural style in designed landscapes between 1730 and 1760: the English Midlands and the work of Sanderson Miller and Lancelot Brown', *Garden History* 30 (1), 24-48.

2. The gardens at Shotover contain the first Gothic revival garden building, the Gothic Temple, *c.*1720, designed probably by Townesend, the Oxford master mason, for Lt General James Tyrrell. Behind the house there is a temple by William Kent. Hartwell is of interest because the gardens were still markedly formal as late as 1738, when they were illustrated in eight large paintings by Balthazar Nebot (now held in the Buckinghamshire County Museum, Aylesbury). Both Wroxton Abbey and Wotton Underwood are estates where Miller worked, and both were homes of 18th-century Prime Ministers, Lord North at Wroxton and George Grenville at Wotton.

3. See Chapter 3 for a discussion on the historical and romantic trends influencing Miller in his decision to build a mock ruin on Edgehill.

4. Hawkes, W. (1983), 'The Gothic Architectural Work of Sanderson Miller', *A Gothic Symposium.* Georgian Group. A symposium held at the Victoria and Albert Museum.

5. There are two architectural sketches held in the Warwickshire County Record Office (WCRO), Arbury archives, CR764/214, and several sketches of the Castle Ruin at Wimpole, Cambridgeshire, held in the National Trust collections at Wimpole Hall. None is signed by Miller, or dated.

6. Diaries: Diary 1, October 1749-September 1750, WCRO CR1382/1. Diary 2, April 1756-January 1757, WCRO, CR1382/32. Miller's letters are nearly all held in WCRO CR125B/. The *Memoir to James Stuart Menteath,* 1774, is held in WCRO CR1382/2.

7. Letter from Lord Guernsey to Miller, 7 October, 1748. WCRO CR125B/908. See Chapter 7 for further details of Miller's work at Gopsall.

8. Royal Institute of British Architects (RIBA), Drawings Collection, Folder K10.

9. Details of Miller's work for Lord North at Wroxton are discussed in Chapter 6. The Castle Ruin at Hagley is discussed in Chapter 7, the Gothic Pentagon Tower at Ingestre and Sham Castle at Bath are discussed in Chapter 8.

10. Letter from William Pitt to Miller, 1755, WCRO CR125B/584.

11. This letter, held in WCRO CR125C/1, is one of the few not held in the main archive WCRO CR125B/. For a discussion on the Honington landscape, see Chapter 6.

12. The house at Wotton was saved from demolition by Mrs Brunner in the 1950s. She restored the house, and some of the park buildings. Her work has been continued by the family, and most of the landscape and buildings have been restored. For details of Miller's work here see Chapter 8.

13. Diary 1, WCRO CR1382/1.

14. Dickins, L. and Stanton, M. (1910), *An Eighteenth Century Correspondence.* London: John Murray.

15. Edwards, P. (1986), 'The Gardens at Wroxton Abbey, Oxfordshire', *Garden History* 14 (1), 50-60.
Hawkes, W. (1969), 'Miller's Work at Wroxton', *Cake and Cockhorse* 4 (6), 99-107. *Cake and Cockhorse* is the magazine of the Banbury Historical Society. For Miller's work at Wroxton, see Chapter 6.
Wood, A. (1969), 'Sanderson Miller of Radway', *Cake and Cockhorse* 4 (6),79-98.
Wood, A. and Hawkes, W. (1987), 'Radway, Warwickshire: the making of a landscape', *Journal of Garden History,* 7 (2), 103-30.

16. Batey, M. (1989), *The Historic Gardens of Oxford and Cambridge.* London: Macmillan. See also Batey and Lambert (1990), and Symes (1991) in the Bibliography.

17. For Cousins (papers published in *Follies,* the magazine of The Folly Fellowship), Williamson (1995) and Mowl (2000) see Bibliography.

18. The association between Brown and Miller is discussed fully in Chapter 9. See also the paper cited in reference 1, above.

Chapter 2: A Biographical Account, pp.7-18

1. Details concerning Miller's early life have been taken from the following article: Wood, A. (1969), 'Sanderson Miller of Radway', *Cake and Cockhorse* 4 (6), 79-98. A copy is held in the WCRO. Details of Miller senior's history is given in Miller, G. (1900), *Rambles round the Edge hills*, 26.

2. A copy of the articles of agreement between Thomas Goodwin the elder and the younger and Sanderson Miller of Banbury for the subsequent conveyance of the estate, dated '12 Oct GeoI, 1715', is held in the Miller papers, WCRO, CR1264/1, 105.

3. A map illustrating the battlefield of 1642, which shows the extent of the old park above Radway Grange, is shown in Miller, G. (1900), opposite page 123.

4. Warwickshire County Book, Warwickshire County Council (1959), 334.

5. Mentioned in Menteath's introduction to Sanderson Miller's *Memoir to James Stuart Menteath*, WCRO, CR1382/2.

6. *Alumni Oxoniensis*, Foster.

7. The Rev. Walter Harte (1709-74) became Vice-Principal of St Mary Hall in 1740. *Dictionary of National Biography*.

8. Dickins, L. and Stanton, M. (1910), *An Eighteenth Century Correspondence*, 6-7. King, Principal of St Mary Hall from 1718-63, is described as a lover of the classics, especially Ovid, and a genial and philosophical man. He was a Jacobite sympathiser, and a friend of Pope and Swift.

9. Tyack, G. (1998), *Oxford an Architectural Guide*. Details concerning the architecture of buildings in Oxford have been taken from this source.

10. Miller, S.M., *Memoir to James Stuart Menteath*, WCRO, CR1382/2, 48-9.

11. Mentioned in Menteath's introduction to Miller's *Memoir to James Stuart Menteath*.

12. Wood, A. (1969), 'Sanderson Miller of Radway', *Cake and Cockhorse* 4 (6), 79, 88.

13. Entries in Miller's Diary for 1749/50. Reference to Lord North asking Miller to bring his flute when he came to Wroxton: correspondence, WCRO CR125B/940.

14. An urn commemorating this event exists in the garden at Radway Grange.

15. Correspondence, WCRO CR125B/122-155, 735, 861.

16. Entries in Miller's Diary for 1749/50. Miller used his own special shorthand for references in his diaries.

17. Part of Menteath's introduction to Miller's *Memoir to James Stuart Menteath*.

18. Correspondence, WCRO CR125B/410.

19. Dickins, L. and Stanton, M., 453.

20. Radway Parish Register, WCRO DR47/4.

21. Correspondence, WCRO CR125B/302.

22. Miller, G. (1900), *Rambles Round the Edge Hills*, 30.

23. Wood, A. (1969), 'Sanderson Miller of Radway', *Cake and Cockhorse*, 4 (6), 89.

24. Miller's library was sold in two parts; the first in 1863, the remainder in 1910. Copies of both catalogues are held in WCRO CR1264/7 and CRFilms 866iii reel 28.

25. Miller archives, WCRO CR1264/1, 52.

26. Correspondence with Henry Grenville. A number of letters mention the ongoing work at Moreton Morrell, WCRO CR125B/590-613.

27. Miller, G. (1900), *Rambles Round the Edge Hills*, 29.

28. For a discussion on the design of Hagley and Croome, see Summerson, J. (1990), *The Unromantic Castle*, 100.

29. For further details on Miller's architectural work, see Appendix 1 and 2, and Hawkes, W., 'Sanderson Miller of Radway, 1716-1780,' unpublished thesis. A copy of the thesis is held in the WCRO.

30. Wood, A. (1969), 'Sanderson Miller of Radway', *Cake and Cockhorse*, 4 (6), 83.

31. Dickens, L. and Stanton, M., 439.

32. Correspondence, WCRO CR611/725/9.

33. Miller, S.M., *Memoir to James Stuart Menteath*, 137.

34. Correspondence between Miller and his wife, sent from Becket, WCRO CR125B/825, 826, 827.

35. *The Gentleman's Magazine*, April 1780, 203.

Chapter 3: The Historical Background, pp.19-34

1. Brewer, J. (1997), *The Pleasures of the Imagination*, 3-6.

2. Russell, B. (2004), *History of Western Philosophy*, 550.

3. Russell, B. (2004), 453-6.

4. Batey, M. (1982), *Oxford's Gardens*, 31-47.

5. Hutchinson, H. (1976), *Sir Christopher Wren: a biography*, 41-2.

6. Russell, B. (2004), 523-4.

7. Dalrymple, W. (2003), *White Mughals*. Although chiefly biographical, the detailed background information is carefully researched and gives a good picture of the increasing importance and power of the East India Company.

8. Hampson, N. (1990), *The Enlightenment*, 97-9, 154-5.

9. Hampson, N. (1990), 157-61.

10. Spencer, C. (2004), *Blenheim, Battle for Europe*.

11. Summerson, J. (1990), *The Unromantic Castle*, 82.

12. Harris, J. (1995), *The Palladian Revival, Lord Burlington, His Villa and Garden at Chiswick*, 2.

13. Watkin, D. (2001), *English Architecture*, 101-02.

14. Godber, J. (1968), 'The Travel Journal of Philip Yorke, 1744-6', in *The Marchioness Grey of Wrest Park*. Publications of the Bedfordshire Historical Records Society, XLVII.

15. Lewis, M. (2002), *The Gothic Revival*, 7-8.

16. Tyack, G. (1998), *Oxford an Architectural Guide*. Details concerning buildings in Oxford are taken from this source.

17. Summerson, J. (1993), *Architecture in Britain 1530-1830*, 292.

18. Hart, V. (2002), *Nicholas Hawksmoor*, 158.

19. Lewis, M. (2002), 13.

20. Swift, J. (1897-1908), 'Abstract of the History of

England', Prose works of Jonathan Swift, 225.

21. Sweet, R. (2004), *Antiquaries: The Discovery of the Past: Eighteenth-Century Britain*, 190.
22. Langley, B. (1742), *Gothic Architecture, Improved by Rules and Proportion*, 1.
23. Kliger, S. (1972), *The Goths in England*, 20.
24. Clark, K. (1995), *The Gothic Revival*, 26-7.
25. Clark, K. (1995), 22.
26. Baridon, M. (1985), 'Ruins as a mental construct', *Journal of Garden History* 5 (1), 84-9.
27. Lewis, M. (2002), 13.

Chapter 4: Developments in Garden Design between 1700 and 1740, pp.35-54

1. Hinde, T. (1986), *Capability Brown, the story of a Master Gardener*, 8.
2. Strong, R. (1992), *Royal Gardens*, 28, 33.
3. Strong, R. (1992), 34.
4. Addison, J. (1712), *The Spectator*, 25 June, 6 September.
5. Batey, M. (1999), *Alexander Pope, the Poet and the Landscape*, 33.
6. Pope, A. (1995), *The Works of Alexander Pope*, 261.
7. Batey, M. (1999), 63.
8. Pope, A. (1995), 345.
9. Dickens, L. and Stanton, M. (1910), *An Eighteenth Century Correspondence*, 150.
10. Switzer, S. (1718), *Ichnographia Rustica or the Nobleman, Gentleman and Gardener's Recreation*, 5.
11. Eyres, P. (1989-90), 'Landscape as Political Manifesto' in P. Eyres (ed), *Castle Howard, Landscape of Epic Poetry*, 49.
12. For the possible influences of Rome and antique architecture on the Castle Howard landscape and elsewhere see Worsley, G., Chapter 8, 140-53, in Ridgway, C. and Williams, R. (eds) (2000), *Sir John Vanbrugh and Landscape Architecture in Baroque England, 1690-1730*.
13. Hart, V. (2002), *Nicholas Hawksmoor*, 114.
14. Williams, R. (2000), Chapter 4, 53-69 in C. Ridgway and R. Williams (eds), *Sir John Vanbrugh and Landscape Architecture in Baroque England 1690-1730*, 54-69.
15. Memoir to Menteath, WCRO, CR1382/2, 168.
16. Stembridge, P. (1996), *Thomas Goldney's Garden: the creation of an eighteenth-century garden*.
17. Correspondence, WCRO, CR125B/589.
18. Strong, R. (1992), *Royal Gardens*, 42.
19. Walpole, H. (1995), *The History of the Modern Taste in Gardening*, 42.
20. Mowl, T. (2000), *Gentlemen and Players*, 74.
21. Watkin, D. (1983), *The English Vision: The Picturesque in Architecture, Landscape and Garden Design*, 45-6.
22. Personal communication, Lord Bathurst.
23. Batey, M. and Lambert, D. (1990), *The English Garden Tour: a View into the Past*, 155.
24. Batey, M. and Lambert (1990), 155, and Mowl, T. (2000), 101.
25. Hayden, R. (1980), *Mrs Delany, her Life and her Flowers*, 98.

26. Historic Manuscripts Commission Report, 1897, 143-4.
27. Mowl, T. (2000), 118.
28. Wilson, M. (1984), *William Kent, Architect, Designer, Painter, Gardener, 1685-1748*, 214-5.
29. Laird, M. (1999), *The Flowering of the Landscape Garden, English Pleasure Grounds 1720-1800*, 3-23, for a discussion on this subject. Mark Laird worked on the restoration of Hamilton's landscape at Painshill, and has carried out extensive research into 18th-century planting plans.
30. Laird, M. (1999), 7.
31. Correspondence, WCRO, 125B/622.
32. Rorschach, K. (1983), *The Early Georgian Landscape Garden*, 76.
33. Clarke, G. (ed) (1990), *Descriptions of Lord Cobham's Gardens at Stowe 1700-1750*, 21, and fig.4.
34. Walpole, H. (1995), *The History of the Modern Taste in Gardening*, 42-3.
35. Jackson-Stops, G. (1992), *An English Arcadia 1600-1990*, 64.
36. Brooks, C. (1999), *The Gothic Revival*, 54.
37. Watkin, D. (1983), 23.
38. Mowl, T. (2000), 136.
39. Mowl, T. (2000), 136.
40. Walpole, H. (1995), *The History of the Modern Taste in Gardening*, 38-9.
41. Watkin, D. (1983), 31.
42. Tait, A. (1980), *The Landscape Garden in Scotland*, 94.
43. Gallagher, C. (1996), 'The Leasowes: A History of the Landscape', *Garden History* 24, no.2, 201-20. This article gives a history of the landscaping developments at the Leasowes, including Shenstone's approach to his work, dating from before Shenstone inherited the estate to the present day.
44. Allen, R. (1992), *Enclosure and the Yeoman, the Agricultural Development of the South Midlands 1450-1850*, 30-1.
45. Tait, W. (1943-44), 'Enclosure Acts and Awards Relating to Warwickshire', *Transactions of the Birmingham Archaeological Society*, LXV, 45, 78-9.
46. Williamson T. and Bellamy, L. (1987), *Property and Landscape*, 10, 140.
47. Anon (1789), *A Companion to Hagley, The Leasowes and Enville*.
48. *Lady Newdigate's Tour in the South of England* (1748), WCRO, CR1841/7. The memorandum book of Sir Roger and Lady Newdigate's tour, written by Lady Newdigate.
49. Miller, G. (1900), *Rambles Round the Edge Hills*, 119.
50. Linnell, E. (1772). Estate map prepared for William Holbech the third, on the latter inheriting the estate of Farnborough from his uncle William Holbech II in 1770. WCRO, Z403, v.

Chapter 5: Miller's Approach to Landscaping, pp.55-80

NB. Miller's accounts are not referenced individually

in the text. They are held in WCRO CR125B/5, and WCRO CR 125/1. The holdings are incomplete, as not all of Miller's accounts have survived.

1. When a stretch of road was 'turnpiked', a toll was collected from everyone who used it, which paid for the maintenance of the surface. In February 1753, Lord North was discussing the turnpiking of the Stratford to Banbury road, which went through the hamlet of Edgehill. The road was in a bad condition, for Lord North was asking if the road might soon be made passable for a coach. It was to be turnpiked past Wroxton, but Lord North preferred it to go through the village of Drayton rather than through his park, which latter route was 'the handsomest and most convenient way to my house'. The main road now goes through Drayton, and the old road through the park is only a footpath. Correspondence, WCRO CR125B/962.

2. Hawkes, W. (1983), 'The Gothic Architectural Work of Sanderson Miller', unpaginated. A Gothic Symposium, Georgian Group, a symposium held at the Victoria and Albert Museum.

3. Correspondence, WCRO, CR125B/419.

4. Salmon, G. (1756), Pre-enclosure map of the parish of Radway, commissioned by Miller. WCRO CR1596.

5. Deane Swift, correspondence WCRO CR 125B/302; William Pitt, correspondence WCRO CR125B/583, quote, 30 October 1755 CR125B/584, and Henry Grenville, correspondence WCRO CR125B/589, 590, 592.

6. Wood, A. and Hawkes, W. (1987), 'Radway, Warwickshire: the making of a landscape', Journal of Garden History 7 (2), 103-30, also Hawkes, W. (1983). The article by Wood and Hawkes discusses the Radway landscape up to the Enclosure Act of 1757, but not later.

7. Batey, M. and Lambert, D. (1990), The English Garden Tour: a View into the Past, 56.

8. Williamson, T. (1995), Polite Landscapes, Gardens and Society in Eighteenth-century England, 19. For a detailed discussion on this subject see pp. 19–75.

9. Williamson, T. and Bellamy, L. (1987), Property and Landscape, 71.

10. Jacques, D. (1990), Georgian Gardens: The Reign of Nature, Holkham, 42; Painshill, 63-4.

11. Arbury Hall: Beighton, 1708, WCRO, CR 1199/70, a copy; Castle Bromwich: Beighton, 1726, engraving, illustrated in Batey and Lambert, 1990, 101; Charlecote Park: Beighton, 1722, engraving, illustration in Dugdale, 1730, I, 507; Compton Verney: Fish, 1736, estate map, Shakespeare Birthplace Trust Record Office, DR 98/1819; Edgbaston Hall: Dugdale, 1730, illustration; Honington Hall: Buck and Buck, 1731, engraving, WCRO CR351/11BR; Newnham Paddox: Kip and Knyff, 1708, RIBA Drawings Collection; Croome Court: Beighton, 1714, illustration in Gordon 2000, 76; Wroxton Abbey: Anon, 1729, plan of gardens, copy held at Wroxton Abbey.

12. For Stowe, see Rigaud, 1739, illustration in Robinson, J. (1990), Temples of Delight, Stowe Landscape Gardens, 61. For Blenheim, see Green, D. (1987), 'The Palace and Gardens under Vanbrugh, Hawksmoor and Wise', 67-79, in Bond, J. and Tiller, K. (eds), Blenheim, Landscape for a Palace. For a map of Col. Armstrong's canal, see Green, D. and Bond J. (1987), 'Blenheim after Vanbrugh: The Second Phase', 80-9, in Bond, J. and Tiller, K. (eds), Blenheim, Landscape for a Palace. For Lodge Park, Sherborne, see Willis, P. (2002), Charles Bridgeman and the English Landscape Garden, 209. For Cirencester, see Batey, M. and Lambert, D. (1990), 153-4.

13. Miller, G. (1900), Rambles Round the Edge Hills, 123.

14. Williams, M. (ed) (1939), The Letters of William Shenstone, 252.

15. Miller's accounts, WCRO CR125/5, f3.

16. Miller, G. (1900), 20-1. A grange was the name given to a farm run by a monastic settlement but away from the main monastery.

17. Correspondence, WCRO CR125B/302.

18. Williams, M. (ed) (1939), 252.

19. Miller, G. (1900), 31.

20. Williams, M. (ed) (1939), 252-3.

21. Hunt, J. (1987), William Kent, Landscape Garden Designer, 87.

22. Williams, M. (1939), 253.

23. See Salmon, G. (1756), Pre-enclosure map of Radway.

24. Miller's accounts, WCRO CR125B/5.

25. The first reference to Egge Cottage in Miller's accounts is in 1744, WCRO, CR125/5, f6; and his friend Deane Swift also mentioned the cottage in a letter to Miller in the same year, WCRO CR125/B307.

26. Dickens, L. and Stanton, M. (1910), An Eighteenth Century Correspondence, 267.

27. One example is found in the correspondence, WCRO CR125B/924.

28. Miller's papers, WCRO, CR1052/bundle 11.

29. Miller, G. (1900), 24-5.

30. Bodleian Library, Ballard MS, 40, f108.

31. Miller, G. (1900), 25.

32. Greening Lamborn, E. (1943), 'The Shields in Ratley Roundhouse', Notes and Queries, 13 March.

33. Williams, M. (ed) (1939), 253.

34. Dr Richard Pococke became Bishop of Ossory in 1756, then subsequently Bishop of Meath. He will be referred to throughout as Bishop Pococke.

35. Dr Richard Pococke, The Travels through England of Dr Richard Pococke … during 1750, 1751 and later Years, ed. J.J. Cartwright. Vol.II, p.240, 1756. 1888-89 (London, Camden Society).

36. Correspondence, WCRO CR125B/216.

37. Accounts, WCRO CR125, f92. Entry for 14 January 1756.

38. Oswald, A. (1946), 'Radway Grange, Warwickshire, I', Country Life, 6 Sept, pp.440-1.

39. Fielding, H. (1749), *Tom Jones*, Penguin Classics edition, 1966, pp.58-9.
40. Correspondence, WCRO CR1680/43.
41. Correspondence, WCRO CR125B/512.
42. Salmon, G. (1756), pre-enclosure map.
43. Wallsgrove, S. (1997), Map of the Radway Inclosure Award, 1757, WCRO Z939/2 L. This map was originally undertaken to ascertain the line of historic tracks and footpaths, but has proved a very useful tool in the analysis of Miller's post-enclosure landscaping of his estate.
44. Dickens, L. and Stanton, M. (1910), 348-9. Pope, A. (1995), 344. First published *c.*1738.
45. Miller refers to Sir Roger Newdigate, of Arbury Hall in the poem. Sir Roger was Gothicising both the exterior and interior of the Hall, which was to become the showpiece of the 18th-century Gothic revival. One of his first alterations had been to add a Gothic bow window to his hall designed by Miller, similar to Miller's own work at the Grange. Miller had also designed Gothic improvements to his house for Lord Dacre at Belhus, in Essex, who carried out one of the earliest Gothic redecorations in the country. In his own house Miller had designed some fine stone Gothic fireplaces, and these modest interior alterations suited the Grange far more than Gothic columns would have done. The paymaster referred to is William Pitt, who had been given the governmental office of Paymaster General in 1746.
46. WCRO CR1052/box E/bundle 7c, box F/bundle 1, also Cr1052/box F/bundle 1.
47. Correspondence: letters from Henry Grenville concerning Moreton Morrell, WCRO CR125B/590-2, 598-600, 611-12; letter from Miller to Clement Newsham, his sister Anne's son, who was serving with the army in Germany, WCRO CR611/725/2. The increase in rental of Miller's land after enclosure is given in Miller, G. (1900), 29.
48. Wood, A. and Hawkes, W. (1987), 121.
49. Dickens, L. and Stanton, M. (1910), 325. The authors say that the poem (not now with the Miller papers) was written in Miller's handwriting, but was probably composed by his friend Sir Edward Turner.
50. Correspondence, WCRO CR125B/589.
51. Jago, R. (1767), *Edge-Hill, or the Rural Prospect Delineated and Moralised*, 3. A long poem eulogising the beauties of the local seats of the gentry. Jago was a clergyman friend of Miller's, and lived locally.

Chapter 6: Farnborough, Wroxton and Honington, pp.81-112
1. See Gazetteer for complete list.
2. Miller, G. (1900), *Rambles round the Edge Hills*, 60-1.
3. Markham, S. (1984), *John Loveday of Caversham, 1711-1789*, 342.
4. Land Use Consultants, unpublished report,

National Trust, 1995, 9. A summary provided by William Hawkes formed the basis for this report.
5. Diary for 1749/50. Lord and Lady Cobham stayed at Radway from Friday to Sunday.
6. WCRO, Z403v.
7. Markham, S. (1984), *John Loveday of Caversham, 1711-1789*, 342.
8. The laurels were allowed to grow up to screen the M40, which bisects the valley, but this negates the whole idea of the view across the valley towards Edgehill which was the principal reason for the construction of the terrace.
9. Jackson-Stops, G. (1984), *Farnborough Hall*, 20, and Haworth, J. (1999), *Farnborough Hall*, 20, both give Miller as the likely architect in their respective booklets on Farnborough Hall prepared for the National Trust. Haworth acknowledges information from Hawkes, and both authors cite the Warwick mason William Hiorns as the mason responsible. Miller used Hiorns at the Tower at Radway, and at various other sites, for example the Shire Hall at Warwick, the landscape buildings at Hagley, and the new Gothic work at Adlestrop Park, Gloucestershire. Cornforth, J. (1996), 'Farnborough Hall, Warwickshire − 1', *Country Life* 11 July 1954 has queried Miller's authorship of the buildings (but not the landscaping), doubting whether Miller was designing in the classical style in the 1740s, but provides no archival evidence to support his alternatives. Miller was actually designing Ambrosden House in the classical style in the 1740s.
10. Jackson-Stops, G. (1984), *Farnborough Hall*, 20.
11. Jackson-Stops, G. (1984), *Farnborough Hall*, 23.
12. 'Lady Newdigate's Tour in the South of England', 1748. Memorandum book written by Lady Newdigate describing the various estates she and Sir Roger visited. It includes Farnborough and Stowe among many others. WCRO CR1841/7.
13. Summerson, J. (2000), *Inigo Jones*, 79-80.
14. Pococke, R. (1756), *The Travels through England of Dr Richard Pococke … during 1750, 1751 and later years* ed. J.J. Cartwright (1888-89), v.II, 260.
15. Laird, M. (1999), *The Flowering of the Landscape Garden, English Pleasure Grounds 1720-1800,* 30-3.
16. Batey, M. (1989), *The Historic gardens of Oxford & Cambridge*, 107. Quotes taken from Philander's Essay No. 414 in *The Spectator*. The Magdalen Walks are illustrated in a section of the Loggan map in Batey, M. (1982), *Oxford Gardens*, 95.
17. Jago, R. (1767), *Edge-Hill, or the rural prospect delineated and moralised, 1767*. Excerpt from this poem.
18. Mentioned in the unpublished report by Land Use Consultants, National Trust, 1995.
19. *The Victoria History of the Counties of England, A History of the County of Oxfordshire* (1969),v.9, 171-3.
20. Batey, M. and Lambert, D. (1990), *The English Garden Tour, a View into the Past*, 204-6.
21. Correspondence, WCRO CR125B/426.

22. Hawkes, W. (1969), 'Miller's Work at Wroxton', *Cake and Cockhorse*, v.4, no.6, 99-105. This article covers Miller's architectural works at Wroxton for Lord North, as well as discussing the garden improvements.
23. Correspondence, WCRO CR125B/771.
24. Correspondence, WCRO CR125B/941-947, 950, 951. The quote is from /942.
25. Correspondence, WCRO CR125B/745, 927, 929, 930. The quote is from CR125B/942.
26. Markham, S. (1984), *John Loveday of Caversham, 1711-1789*, 374.
27. Pococke, R. (1756), *The Travels through England of Dr Richard Pococke ... during 1750, 1751 and later years*, ed. J.J. Cartwright (1888-89), v.II, 240.
28. Hawkes, W. (1969), 'Miller's Work at Wroxton', *Cake and Cockhorse*, v.4, no.6, 107. Quoted from North MSS, c56, held in the Bodleian Library.
29. Hawkes, W. (1969), 102.
30. Greatheed, B. (1822). Berie Greatheed's Journal, entry for 19 June 1822. WCRO CR1707/124.
31. Batey, M. and Lambert, D. (1990), *The English Garden Tour, a View into the Past*, 208. Quote Walpole, H. (1753), *Horace Walpole's Correspondence*, ed. Lewis, W, 359.
32. Correspondence, WCRO, CR125B/939.
33. Desmond, R. (1995), *Kew, the history of the Royal Botanic Gardens*, 45.
34. Symes, M. (1991), *The English Rococo Garden*, 45.
35 Cousins, M. (2005), 'Wroxton Abbey, Oxfordshire: an eighteenth century estate', *The Follies Journal*, no.5, 39-72, 68.
36. Scott, S. (1995), *The Follies of Boughton Park*, 50.
37. Markham, S. (1984), *John Loveday of Caversham, 1711-1789*, 374.
38. Salmon, T. (1748), *The Foreigner's Companion through the Universities of Cambridge and Oxford*, p.11.
39. Godber, J. (1968), 'The Marchioness Grey of Wrest Park', the *Travel Journal of Philip Yorke, 1744-6*. Publications of the Bedfordshire Historical Society, XLVII, 139.
40. Correspondence, WCRO CR125B/429.
41. Correspondence, WCRO CR125B/943.
42. Correspondence, letters referring to the Temple on the Mount: WCRO CR125B/943, 946, 951, 953.
43. Correspondence, WCRO CR125B/954.
44. Pococke, R. (1756), *The Travels through England of Dr Richard Pococke ... during 1750, 1751 and later years*, ed. J.J. Cartwright (1888-89), v.II, 240.
45. Godber, J. (1968), 'The Marchioness Grey of Wrest Park', the *Travel Journal of Philip Yorke, 1744-6*. Publications of the Bedfordshire Historical Society, XLVII, 139.
46. Bodleian Library, MS North d14, fol.209.
47. Correspondence, WCRO CR125B/582.
48. Details of the history of Honington are taken from *The Victoria History of the County of Warwick*, 1949, Vol 5, 93-4.
49. WCRO CR351/11BR.
50. Correspondence, WCRO CR125C/1.
51. Gatacre, E., Stanton, W. and Winsor, D. (1980), *Wookey Hole*, 34.
52. WCRO, PV HON HAL 1.
53. Miller, N. (1982), *Heavenly Caves* 36. Ovid's *Metamorphoses* 3, 157-62.
54. Dickens, L. and Stanton, M. (1910), *An Eighteenth Century Correspondence*, 447.
55. Thomas Robins (d.c.1770), is the only known artist to have painted the newly landscaped gardens of the mid-18th century. His paintings date from 1747-70, and have a free and romantic style.

Chapter 7: Landscapes and Architecture, pp.113-158

1. In 1756, Miller was preoccupied with his coming Enclosure Act for Radway, and in this same year he had begun to experience increasing attacks of severe headaches, which eventually compromised his work and resulted in fits of 'madness' in 1759.
2. Hawkes, W. (1964), 'Sanderson Miller of Radway, 1716-1780'. Unpublished thesis, 58. A copy is held in the WCRO.
3. Correspondence, WCRO CR125B/ the Barn: /494; the Gate: /504.
4. Correspondence, WCRO CR125B/508.
5 Correspondence, WCRO CR125B/510.
6. Nares, G. (1957). 'Hagley Hall, Worcestershire', *Country Life*, 19 September 546.
7. Cousins, M. (2004), 'Athenian Stuart's Doric Porticoes', *The Georgian Group Journal*, XIV, 48.
8. Unpublished work on Hagley, courtesy of Peter Goodchild.
9. Batey, M. and Lambert, D. (1990), *The English Garden Tour: a View into the Past*, 210. A description of the landscape works carried out by Hugh, 1st Lord Fortescue, at Castle Hill between 1733 and 1751.
10. For the Gothic chairs, correspondence, WCRO CR125B/653; for the inventory of the goods and chattels, Hagley Hall, Barrel Room, ref.7H7
11. B.M.Add.MSS 28958. The letter is also printed in Williams, M., ed. (1939), *The Letters of William Shenstone*, 147/8.
12. Williams, M., ed. (1939), 157.
13. Heely, Joseph (1777), 'A Walk through the Grounds of Hagley, Enville and the Leasowes'.
14. Horace Walpole in a letter to Richard Bentley, September 1753, quoted in Hunt, J. Dixon and Willis, P. eds. (1990), *The Genius of the Place, The English Landscape Garden 1620-1820*, 313.
15. Correspondence, WCRO CR125B/671.
16. Pococke, R. (1888-9), *The Travels through England of Dr Richard Pococke*, volumes I and II, ed. J. Cartwright, 1888-9, Vol 1, 226. (First published 1757.) Dr Pococke became Bishop of Ossory in 1756.
17. Correspondence, WCRO CR125B/351.
18. For a comparison of Wilton and Campbell's design for Houghton, see Summerson, J. (1990), *The Unromantic Castle*, 99.
19. Fry, C. (2004), 'An Architect for Lydiard House',

The Georgian Group Journal, v.XIV, 2004, 26-32. The following article in the same journal is also of interest: Hewlings, R., 'Roger Morris and Lydiard Tregoze'.

20. For Lord Burlington's designs and a drawing of the link building at Chiswick, see Harris, J. (1995), *The Palladian Revival, Lord Burlington, His Villa and Garden at Chiswick*, 182. This catalogue was published for the exhibition of the same name. For drawings by Jones, see Harris, J. and Higgott, G. (1989), *Inigo Jones Complete Architectural Drawings*. Of particular interest is Cat 22, the presentation design for a town house façade, ascribed to Sir Fulke Greville's house, 151. Sir Fulke Greville, later Lord Brooke, owned Warwick Castle.

21. Summerson, J. (2000), *Inigo Jones*, 79-80.

22. Parnell, J. (1769), *Journal of a Tour through England and Wales*.

23. Thomson, J. (1730), *The Seasons*. An extract from this poem is quoted in Hunt, J. Dixon and Willis, P. eds. (1990), *The Genius of the Place, The English Landscape Garden 1620-1820*, 194.

24. Correspondence, WCRO CR125B/410, 426, 415, 429. References given in order of letters quoted in text.

25. Stroud, D. (1975), *Capability Brown*, 74

26. Tyack, G. (1994), *Warwickshire Country Houses*, 152-3.

27. Correspondence, WCRO 125B/904.

28. Correspondence, WCRO CR125B/ Gopsall letter:/908, the intended stables:/509, advice in making alterations: /909, Arbury visit:/911.

29. Correspondence, WCRO 125C/3.

30. Worsley, G. (2003), 'Courtly stables and their implications for 17th-century English architecture', *The Georgian Group Journal*, vXIII, 137.

31. Worsley, G. (2004), *The British Stable*, 138.

32. Nichols, J. (1811), Vol IV, part ii, 857. *History and Antiquities of the County of Leicestershire*, vIV, part ii, 857.

33. Correspondence, WCRO CR125B/908.

34. RIBA Drawings Collection, Folder K10/11, /13, /14, /15.

35. Wright, N. (undated), *John Grundy of Spalding Engineer, 1718-1783; his Life and Times*.

36. Tyack, G. (1994), 9-11.

37. Lady Newdigate's Tour in the South of England, 1748. WCRO CR1841/7.

38. One of these drawings shows two Gothic bookcases either side of a Gothic fireplace. On the drawing is written, in Sir Roger's hand, 'Miller's drawing for Arbury L[ys] [Lady's] dressing room', WCRO CR764/214.

39. Tyack, G. (1994), 15.

40. Hawkes, W. (1964), 20.

41. Correspondence, WCRO CR125B/911.

42. Estate plan *c.*1680-1700, WCRO CR1199/69. Drawing, *c.*1708, probably by Henry Beighton, WCRO CR1199/70.

43. Souden, D. (1991), *Wimpole Hall*, National Trust publication. Details on the history of the site are taken from this publication.

44. Correspondence, WCRO CR125B/348 349.

45. Bambridge Collection, Wimpole Hall, Cambridgeshire, held by the National Trust.

46. British Library, Stowe MS 753, fol.146v.

47. Bedfordshire Record Office, L30/21/2/8.

48. Adshead, D. (1998), *The design and building of the Gothic Folly at Wimpole, Cambridgeshire*, 81.

49. Correspondence, WCRO CR125B/, 16 June:/792, 1 September:/794, 9 September:/772.

50. Bedfordshire Record Office, letter from Agneta Yorke, L/30/9/97/32; letter from Mary Yorke, L/30/9/111/138.

51. Byng, J. (1935), 'Tour in the Midlands, 1790', *The Torrington Diaries II*, 239.

52. Adshead, D. (1998), 84.

53. Plan held at Wimpole Hall by the National Trust. Illustrated in Souden, D. (1991), 82.

54. Correspondence, WCRO CR125B/348, 350.

55. Staffordshire Record Office, D240/17/26, Album of sketches 1836-7 by T. Peploe Woods.

56. Rowe, A. (ed) (2001), *Garden making and the Freman Family: A Memoir of Hamels 1713-1733*, 75.

57. Correspondence, WCRO CR125B /722, 723.

58. Details concerning the history of Enville courtesy of Sandy Haynes, Archivist at Enville.

59. Shenstone, W. (1939), *The Letters of William Shenstone*, ed. Williams, M., 262.

60. Pococke, R. (1888-9), *The Travels through England of Dr Richard Pococke volumes I and II*, ed. J. Cartwright, vol.II, 231. Dr Pococke became Bishop of Ossory in 1756.

61. Heely, J. (1777), *Letters on the Beauties of Hagley, Envil and the Leasowes, II*, 82.

62. Mowl, T. (1982), 'The Case of the Enville Museum', *Garden History* 3, no.2, 134-43. Julia Ionides, author of *Thomas Farnolls Pritchard of Shrewsbury, Architect and 'Inventor of Cast Iron Bridges* (1999), is of the opinion that the Museum is not by Pritchard, since the architecture is not typical of his other work (personal communication).

63. Correspondence, WCRO CR125B/401.

64. Hawkes, W. (1964), 61.

65. The Enville Accounts, 1769/70, information supplied courtesy of Sandy Haynes, Archivist.

66. Marshall, W. (1785), *Planting and Rural Ornament*, 328-9.

67. Nash, J. (1782), *The History and Antiquities of Worcestershire*, vol I, 250-1.

68. Correspondence, WCRO CR125B/809.

69. Hamilton, E. (1988), *The Old House at Walton*, 9-16.

70. Hawkes, W. (2001), *The Walton Bath House, Warwickshire*, 29-34.

71. Hawkes, W. (2001), 29-33.

72. Hayden, R. (1980), *Mrs Delany, her Life and her Flowers*, 56.

73. Miller, N. (1982), *Heavenly Caves*, 61-5.

74. Map of Walton estate, 1762, by Richard Overton, WCRO CR750/3.

75. Hamilton, E. (1988), 15-16.

Chapter 8: The Decade from 1750 to 1760, pp.159-196

1. *Victoria History of the County of Gloucestershire, 1968*, Vol 8, 83-5.
2. Tyack, G. (1994), *Warwickshire Country Houses* 1-3.
3. Tyack, G. (1994), 1.
4. Correspondence, WCRO CR125B/679.
5. James West's Memorandum Book is held in the private archives at Alscot Park.
6. Tyack, G. (1994), 1.
7. Bloom, J. (1896), *A History of Preston-upon-Stour in the County of Gloucester*, 12-13.
8. Jago, R. (1767), *Edge-Hill, or the Rural Prospect Delineated and Moralised.*
9. Berger, R. and Hodgetts, C. (1999), *Upton House, Warwickshire*, 2. Leaflet printed for the Warwickshire Gardens Trust, based on original research.
10. Correspondence, WCRO CR125B/, Deane Swift:/313; Sir Edward Turner:/512.
11. Richardson, T. (1774), *Plan of the Upton Estate*, WCRO Z85/u.
12. Hallam, W. (1989), *Sudbury Derbyshire, the history of the village, church and Hall*, 12.
13. Hallam, W. (1989), 22.
14. Pococke, R. (1888-9), *The Travels through England of Dr Richard Pococke volumes I and II* ed. J Cartwright, 1888-9 Vol 1, 219. (First published 1757).
15. Preston, C. (undated), 'Gosfield Hall the Building and its History', printed report held in the Essex County Record Office. G1, 'History and Description, Gosfield Hall'. Historical details taken from this source.
16. Letter held in the Essex County Record Office, D/DL C52. It can also be found in Dickens, L. and Stanton M. (1910), *An Eighteenth Century Correspondence*, 434.
17. Correspondence, WCRO CR125B/164, /165.
18. Essex County Record Office: Map of Essex, Chapman and André, 1777. Estate Plan, 1772, revised 1793, T/M 297.
19. Correspondence, CR135B/675.
20. Stroud, D. (1975), *Capability Brown*, 69.
21. Shakespeare Birthplace Trust Record Office (SBTRO) D18/8/7/2.
22. SBTRO, D18/25/Bn1a.
23. Mercer, D. and Mercer, E. (1993), *Chart Park: Dorking – A vanished Surrey mansion*. Details concerning Chart Park are taken from this publication. The letters are quoted on 27 and 29.
24. Lipscomb, G. (1831), *History of Buckinghamshire, I*, 483.
25. Correspondence, WCRO CR125B/725.
26. British Museum, Kings Maps, XXX, 19, u-v.
27. Robertson, William (1797), *Journal of William Robertson of Kilkenny*, National Library of Ireland, MS.248, 164; Pococke, R. (1888-9), *The Travels through England of Dr Richard Pococke*, volume I, ed. J. Cartwright, 161-2.
28. Beaufort MSS, Badminton House, Gloucestershire.
29. WCRO CR136/A583.
30. Wood, A. (1983), *The Shire Hall, Warwick. Its Rebuilding in the mid-eighteenth century*. Details concerning the building of the Shire Hall have been taken from this booklet. William Hawkes wrote an architectural supplement which is printed in the back of the booklet.
31. Correspondence, WCRO CR125B/678. Plan drawn on the back of this letter.
32. Harding, S. and Lambert, D. (eds) (1994), *Parks and Gardens of Avon*, 43-4.
33. Miller was asked to design for Talbot by Richard Goddard of Swindon, who wrote to Miller that, when he last met Talbot, the latter had decided to fit the new Great Hall up 'in the Gothick Taste… You will not be surprised that I mentioned your name on the occasion … He was much pleased at the thoughts of having it under your direction …' Hawkes, W. (1964), 'Sanderson Miller of Radway, 1716-1780', unpublished thesis, 48. A copy is held in the WCRO. Further details concerning the building of the Hall can be found in Dickens, L. and Stanton, M. (1910) *An Eighteenth Century Correspondence*, 301-10, also in correspondence held in the WCRO; CR125B/387, 392-7, 400-4.
34. Some sketches for the Gothic Gateway can be found on the back of Talbot's letter written in January 1755. Correspondence, WCRO CR125B/403.
35. Lacock Estate Plan of the whole Parish and part of the parish of Pewsham, 1764.
36. Clarke, Gillian (1987), *Prior Park, A Compleat Landscape*. Details of the history of Ralph Allen and Prior Park are taken from this publication. For the development of the landscape at Prior Park see chapters 4 and 5.
37. Correspondence, WCRO CR125B/584.
38. The Plan and Elevation of the Sham Castle, as shown on the Thorpe and Overton Survey *c.*1758, is illustrated in Clarke, G. (1987), 58.
39. The drawing of the castle by Samuel Grimm, 1788, is held in the British Museum: BM Add MSS 15, 546, no.116.
40. Sales, J. (1994), *Report on Prior Park for the National Trust*, 19, 2.63.
41. John, Viscount Perceval, from letter to Daniel Dering, 14 August, 1724. BL.Add MS 47030, ff. 156-9.
42. Bevington, M. (1990), 9 illustration by Bickham; Clarke, G. (ed) (1990), *Descriptions of Lord Cobham's Gardens at Stowe 1700-1750*, 156 illustration by Seeley.
43. Hawkes (2006), pp.64-5, suggests that an entry in Miller's diary for 6 November 1749 may refer to Miller advising the stonemason about the lanterns.
44. Bevington, M. (1990), *Templa Quam Dilecta, Stowe, The Gothic Temple*, Number VI. Details concerning the size and building of the Gothic Temple, including Walpole's report that the painted glass used in the windows came from the Priory at Warwick, are taken from this publication, 9-11.

45. Rutherford, S., 'Park Place and Temple Combe', English Heritage draft register (1998), also entry for Park Place in the *Oxford Companion to Gardens* (eds Jellicoe et al.) (1986) by Mavis Batey, 422. Details of the landscape at Park Place are taken from these two sources.

46. van Biljoen, J. (1791), 'A Dutchman's Visits to some English Gardens in 1791', extracts from the unpublished journal.

47. Rutherford, S. (1998), 3.

48. Walpole, H. (1845), *Walpole's memoirs of the Reign of George III*, vol III, quoted in Jacques, D. (1990) *Georgian Gardens, The Reign of Nature*, 92.

49. Correspondence, WCRO CR125B/380.

50. Correspondence, WCRO CR125B/, invitation to Shrub Hill:/593, details concerning the grotto construction: /597 and /594.

51. Correspondence, WCRO CR125B/603, 604, 610-613, 616.

52. Richard Grenville and Hester Temple had five sons: Richard, later Earl Temple, b.1711, George, b.1712, James, b.1715, Henry, b.1717, and Thomas, b.1719 but killed in action in 1747. Their daughter, Hester, b.1720, married William Pitt the elder. References in Miller's diaries and correspondence to 'Mr Grenville' are assumed to be to George, since Miller referred to Richard by his title, to Henry as Governor Grenville (he became Governor of Barbados), and to James as J. Grenville.

53. Correspondence, WCRO CR125B, 11 March 1758: /595, 20 June 1758: /601, 14 September (no year given): 587.

54. Hinde, T. (1986), *Capability Brown, the story of a Master Gardener*, 72.

55. Phibbs, J., personal communication.

56. I am indebted to Michael Harrison, the Estate Manager at Wotton, for pointing out to me the significance of the views in the landscape, and the importance of the figures, urns etc. in specific situations.

57. Whateley, T. (1771), *Observations on Modern Gardening*, 84–8.

58. Letter quoted by Phibbs J., personal communication.

59. Temple-Grenville Muniments, Henry E. Huntington Library, San Marino, California.

60. Miller's *Memoir to Menteath* (1774), WCRO CR1382/2. Barrowby 'a Charming Situation', 127; Menteath wishing to return from Grimsthorpe to see the surveyor, 168.

Chapter 9: Sanderson Miller and Capability Brown, pp. 197–212

1. Stroud, D. (1975), *Capability Brown,* Brown's early years, 38; list of his commissions, 214-47.

2. Correspondence, WCRO CR125B/473.

3. Stroud, D. (1975), *Capability Brown,* 53.

4. Mowl, T. (2000), *Gentlemen and Players*, 150.

5. Correspondence, WCRO CR125B/132.

6. Correspondence, WCRO CR125B/147.

7. Croome Estate Archives, Family Box 5, F32/37.

8. Correspondence, WCRO CR125B/149 (July 1748), CR125B/150 (December 1748).

9. Correspondence, WCRO CR125B/152 (Gothic Lodge, 1750), CR125B/156 (Gothic Lodge, 1756).

10. Wyatt, H. (2001), 'The 18th Century Landscape Park: its Functional Use and Management,' MA in Architectural Conservation, de Montfort University, Vol 1, 18.

11. These letters can be found in the Croome Estate Archives, F28:1/1, also Family Box 2 F15/20.

12. Wyatt, H. (2001), Vol 1, 37.

13. Gordon, C. (2000), *The Coventrys of Croome,* details of the landscaping and its buildings, 116-31.

14. Wyatt, H. (2001), Vol 1, 27.

15. Colvin, H. (1998), 'Croome Church and its Architect', *Georgian Group Journal,* VIII, 28-32.

16. Gordon, C. (2000), *The Coventrys of Croome*, 105, 127.

17. Gordon, C. (2000), 100.

18. Correspondence, WCRO CR125B/153.

19. Brown, D. (2001), 'Lancelot Brown and his Associates', *Garden History*, 29 (1), 5.

20. Jacques, D. (2001), 'Warwick Castle Grounds and Park, 1743-60', *Garden History*, 29 (1), 56.

21. Phibbs, J., personal communication.

22. Williamson, T. (2001), 'Chatsworth, Derbyshire', *Garden History*, 29 (1), 88.

23. Hussey, C., in the introduction to Stroud, D. (1975), *Capability Brown*, 33.

24. Williamson, T. (2001), 'Chatsworth, Derbyshire', *Garden History*, 29 (1), 85.

25. Goodway, K., personal communication.

26. Correspondence, WCRO CR125B/921.

27. Laird, M. (1999), *The Flowering of the Landscape Garden English Pleasure Grounds 1720-1800*, 137 (Petworth), 276-7 (Tottenham Park).

28. Hinde, T. (1986), *Capability Brown, the story of a Master Gardener*, 45.

29. Jacques, D. (2001), 'Warwick Castle Grounds and Park, 1743-60', *Garden History*, 29 (1), 58, 59.

30. Stroud, D. (1975), *Capability Brown*. Blenheim: illustrations 29b, 30b; Burghley: illustrations 13a, 13b, 14a.

31. Stroud, D. (1975), *Capability Brown*, 146.

32. Correspondence, WCRO, CR125B/675. See also Stroud, D. (1975), *Capability Brown*, 69, and Hinde, T. (1986), *Capability Brown, the story of a Master Gardener*, 46-8.

33. Stroud, D. (1975), *Capability Brown*, 68-9, 72-4.

34. Stroud, D. (1975), *Capability Brown*, 57, 69, 72-3.

35. Hinde, T. (1986), *Capability Brown, the story of a Master Gardener*, 40, 47.

36. Stroud, D. (1975), *Capability Brown*, 202.

Chapter 10: Miller's 'stylistic signature', pp.213-224

1. Addison, J. (1712), *The Spectator*, no. 417, 28 June.

2. Farrar, L. (1998), *Ancient Roman Gardens*. For characteristics of Roman gardens, and the attitudes of Roman writers to nature and the countryside,

see Chapter 10, 187-93. Pliny and Horace are referred to throughout the text.

3. Addison, J. (1712), *The Spectator*, no.414, 25 June.
4. Hogarth, W. (1997), *The Analysis of Beauty*. First published 1753. Paulson, in his introduction, explains Hogarth's ideas and his 'Line of Beauty', xii, li. For Hogarth's own description, see 42.
5. A letter from Horace Walpole to George Montagu, written from Strawberry Hill on Saturday, 7 July 1770. Quoted in Robinson, J. (1990), *Temples of Delight, Stowe Landscape Gardens*, 134-40.
6. Batey, M., Buttery, H., Lambert, D., Wilkie, K. (1994), *Arcadian Thames, the River Landscape from Hampton to Kew*, 59-72, 95-100.
7. Clarke, G. (ed.) (1990), *Descriptions of Lord Cobham's Gardens at Stowe 1700-1750*. Buckinghamshire Record Society 26, MCMXC, 68-73.
8. Pococke, R. (1888-9), *The Travels through England of Dr Richard Pococke volumes I and II*, ed. J Cartwright, London: Camden Society. First published 1757.
9. Hunt, J. Dixon (1987), *William Kent, Landscape Garden Designer*, 118, 137, 141. For Kensington Gardens, see Strong, R. (1992), *Royal Gardens*, 40-2.
10. Roberts, J. (2001), 'Well Temper'd Clay: Constructing Water Features in the Landscape Park', *Garden History*, 29 (1), 14.
11. Phibbs, J., personal communication.
12. Jacques, D. (1990), *Georgian Gardens, The Reign of Nature*, 25.
13. Mowl, T. (2000), *Gentlemen and Players*, 161.
14. Batey, M. and Lambert, D. (1990), *The English Garden Tour, a View into the Past*, 189.
15. Hunt, J. Dixon (1987), *William Kent, Landscape Garden Designer*, drawings 117, 118, 119.
16. Astley, S. (2000), *Robert Adam's Castles*, 20. Exhibition catalogue.
17. Tavernor, R. (1991), *Palladio and Palladianism*, 37.
18. Tyack, G. (1998), *Oxford an Architectural Guide*, 161.
19. Wood, A. (1983), *The Shire Hall, Warwick. Its Rebuilding in the Mid-Eighteenth Century*, 16-17.
20. Trauzettel, L. (1996), 'Worlitz, England in Germany', *Garden History*, 24 (2), 221-36.
21. Mosset, M. and Teyssot, G. (2000), *The History of Garden Design, The Western Tradition from the Renaissance to the Present Day*, 263, 302, 333.

Bibliography

❧'❧

Addison, J. (1712), *The Spectator,* 25 June, 26 September. London

Adshead, D. (1998), 'The design and building of the Gothic Folly at Wimpole, Cambridgeshire', *The Burlington Magazine*, pp.76-84

Aldrich, M. (1994), *Gothic Revival,* London: Phaidon Press

Allen, R. (1992), *Enclosure and the Yeoman, the Agricultural Development of the South Midlands 1450-1850,* Oxford: Clarendon Press

Anon (1789), *A Companion to Hagley, The Leasowes and Enville*, London

Anon (1746), *Hypomnemata,* BL Add. Ms. 6230

Aslet, C. (1983), 'Why Farnborough's views must be saved', *Country Life*, 22 December 1983, pp.1856-7

Astley, S. (2000), *Robert Adam's Castles.* The Soane Gallery, Sir John Soane's Museum. Nottingham: The Sherwood Press

Baridon, M. (1985), 'Ruins as a mental construct', *Journal of Garden History*, 5 (1), 84-96

Batey, M. (1977), 'An Early Naturalistic Garden, Shotover, Oxfordshire', *Country Life*, 22 December, 1912-1914

Batey, M. (1982), *Oxford's Gardens*, Aldershot: Scolar Press, 1986

Batey, M. (1989), *The Historic Gardens of Oxford and Cambridge*, London: Macmillan

Batey, M. (1999), *Alexander Pope, the Poet and the Landscape*, London: Barn Elms Publishing

Batey, M. and Lambert, D. (1990), *The English Garden Tour, a View into the Past*, London: John Murray

Batey, M., Buttery, H., Lambert, D., Wilkie, K. (1994), *Arcadian Thames, the River Landscape from Hampton to Kew*, London: Barn Elms Publishing

Berger, R. (1997), 'Kitty Lloyd Jones: Lady Gardener and Nurserywoman', *Garden History*, 25 (1), 107-116

Berger, R. and Hodgetts, C. (1999), *Upton House, Warwickshire*, Leaflet printed for the Warwickshire Gardens Trust, based on original research

Bettey, J. (1993), *Estates and the English Countryside*, London: B.T. Batsford

Bevington, M. (1990), *Templa Quam Dilecta, Stowe, The Gothic Temple, VI*, Buckingham: Capability Books, Stowe

Bloom, J. Harvey (1896), *A History of Preston-upon-Stour in the County of Gloucester*, Hemsworth: C.E. Turner. Only 25 copies were printed; Warwick Library has no.1, held in Local Studies, Reserve Stock 942.41

Bond, J. and Tiller, K. (eds) (1987), *Blenheim, Landscape for a Palace*, Gloucester: Alan Sutton Publishing Limited and the Oxford University Department for External Studies

Brewer, J. (1997), *The Pleasures of the Imagination*, London: Harper Collins Publishers

Brooks, C. (1999), *The Gothic Revival*, London: Phaidon Press

Brown, D. (2001), 'Lancelot Brown and his Associates', *Garden History*, 29 (1), 2-11

Byng, J. (1935), 'Tour in the Midlands, 1790', *The Torrington Diaries, II*, ed. Andrews, C., London

Campbell, C. (1715), *Vitruvius Britannicus*, I. London

Carte, T. (1750), *General History of England*, London (1-4, 1747-55, 1:1747, 2:1750, 3:1752, 4:1755)

Castell, R. (1728), *The Villas of the Ancients*, London

Clark, K. (1995), *The Gothic Revival*, London: John Murray (First edition, 1962)

Clarke, Gillian (1987), *Prior Park, A Compleat Landscape*, Bath: Millstream Books

Clarke, G. (1973), 'Grecian taste and Gothic Virtue', *Apollo*, 97, 566-71

Clarke, G. (ed) (1990), *Descriptions of Lord Cobham's Gardens at Stowe 1700-1750* Buckinghamshire Record Society

26, MCMXC. Dorchester: Henry Ling

Coffin, D. (1994), *The English Garden, Meditation and Memorial*, New Jersey and Chichester: Princeton University Press

Collins, E. and Jones E. (1967), 'Sectorial advance in English agriculture', *Agricultural History Review* XV, 65-81

Colvin, H. (1948), 'Gothic Survival and Gothic Revival', *Architectural Review*, 103, 645, 91-8

Colvin, H. (1998), 'Croome Church and its Architect', *Georgian Group Journal*, VIII, 28-32

Colvin, H., Foreword in Summerson, J. (2000), *Inigo Jones*, New Haven and London: Yale University Press. First published in 1966

Cornforth, J. (1981), 'Wroxton Abbey', Oxfordshire II', *Country Life*, vol. 170, pp.854-7

Cornforth, J. (1996), 'Farnborough Hall, Warwickshire, I', *Country Life*, 11 July 1996, 52-5

Cousins, M. (1995), 'Farnborough Hall, Warwickshire', *Follies*, 7(2), 9-11

Cousins, M. (1998), 'The Sham Ruin, Hagley, Hereford and Worcester', *Follies*, 10 (1), 3-4

Cousins, M. (1998), 'Did You Know?' *Follies*, 10 (1), 18

Cousins, M. (2002), 'The Garden Buildings at Enville Hall, Staffordshire', *The Follies Journal*, 2 (Winter), 65-98

Cousins, M. (2005), 'Wroxton Abbey, Oxfordshire: an eighteenth century estate', *The Follies Journal*, 5, Winter 2005, 39-72

Cowell, F. (1986), 'Richard Woods (?1716-93): A Preliminary Account, Part I, 'Woods Surveyer at Chertsey in Surry' and at London Stile', *Garden History*, 14 (2), 89

Cowell, F. (1987), 'Richard Woods (?1716-93): A Preliminary Account, Part II, 'Mr Wood of Essex', *Garden History*, 15 (1), 20

Dalrymple, W. (2003), *White Mughals*, London: Flamingo, Harper Collins Publishers

Davis, T. (1974), *The Gothic Taste*, Norwich: David and Charles

Desmond, R. (1998), *The Bibliography of British and Irish Gardens*

Dickens, L. and Stanton, M. (1910), *An Eighteenth Century Correspondence*, London: John Murray

Dugdale, W. and Dodsworth, R. (1655), *Monasticon Anglicanum*

Dugdale, W. (1656), *History of Warwickshire*, Illustrations by Beighton, H. in 1730 edition

Edwards, P. (1986), 'The Gardens at Wroxton Abbey, Oxfordshire', *Garden History*, 14 (1), 50-60

Evelyn, J. (1664), *Sylva, or a Discourse on Forest Trees*, London

Everett, N. (1994), *The Tory View of Landscape*, New Haven: Yale University Press

Eyres, P. (1989-90), 'Landscape as Political Manifesto' in P. Eyres (ed), *Castle Howard, Landscape of Epic Poetry*, 32-65. Leeds: New Arcadian Press

Farrar, L. (1998), *Ancient Roman Gardens*, Stroud, Gloucestershire: Sutton Publishing Limited

Fielding, H. (1749), *Tom Jones*, Penguin Classics edition, 1985. London: Penguin Books

Fiennes, C. (1995), *The Illustrated Journeys of Celia Fiennes 1685-c.1712*, Ed. Morris, C. Stroud: Alan Sutton Publishing Ltd. (First published 1982 by Webb and Bower (publishers) Ltd)

Fox, M. (1985), *The Church of St John the Baptist and the Parish of Hagley in the Diocese of Worcester*, Revised with additional material by Pritchard, J. (First published 1979, no publisher recorded)

Fry, C. (2004), 'An Architect for Lydiard House', *The Georgian Group Journal*, v.XIV, 2004, 26-32

Gatacre, E., Stanton, W. and Winsor, D. (1980), *Wookey Hole*, published by Wookey Hole Caves Ltd

Gallagher, C. (1996), 'The Leasowes: a History of the Landscape', *Garden History*, 24 (2), 201-20

Garnett, O. (1998), *Sudbury Hall*. London: Centurion Press Ltd. for National Trust Enterprises. (First published 1982, revised 1998)

Gentleman's Magazine (1780), Issue for April 1780, containing Sanderson Miller's obituary notice

Godber, J. (1968), 'The Travel Journal of Philip Yorke, 1744-6', in *The Marchioness Grey of Wrest Park*. Publications of the Bedfordshire Historical Records Society, XLVII

Gordon, C. (2000), *The Coventrys of Croome*. Chichester: Phillimore

Green, D. (1987), 'The Palace and Gardens under Vanbrugh, Hawksmoor and Wise', 67-79, in Bond, J. and Tiller, K. (eds), *Blenheim, Landscape for a Palace*, Gloucester: Sutton and Oxford University Department for External Studies

Green, D. and Bond J., (1987), 'Blenheim after Vanbrugh: The Second Phase', 80-9, in Bond, J. and Tiller, K. (eds), *Blenheim, Landscape for a Palace*, Gloucester: Sutton and Oxford University Department for External Studies

Greening Lamborn, E. (1943), 'The Shields in Ratley Roundhouse', *Notes and Queries*, 13 March

Hallam, W. (1989), *Sudbury, Derbyshire, the History of the Village, Church and Hall*. Derby: Derbyshire Countryside Ltd. First published 1972

Hamilton, E. (1988), *The Old House at Walton*. Salisbury: Michael Russell Publishing

Hamilton, E. (1965), *The Mordaunts, an Eighteenth-century Family*, London: Heinemann

Hamilton, E. (1991), *Life on a Country Estate in the mid-nineteenth century*, Dugdale Society Occasional Papers No. 34. Hertford: Stephen Austin and Sons Ltd

Hampson, N. (1968), *The Enlightenment*. London: Penguin Books, 1990

Harding, S. and Lambert, D. (eds) (1994), *Parks and Gardens of Avon*, Avon Gardens Trust. Wells: Open Books Publishing Ltd

Harris, J. (1995), *The Palladian Revival, Lord Burlington, His Villa and Garden at Chiswick,* New Haven and London: Royal Academy of Arts in association with Yale University Press

Harris, J. (1998), *William Kent 1685-1748, A Poet on Paper*, London: The Soane Gallery

Harris, J. and Higgott, G. (1989), *Inigo Jones Complete Architectural Drawings*, New York: The Drawing Centre, also Philip Wilson Publishers. A catalogue published to accompany the exhibition at The Drawing Centre

Hart, V. (2002), *Nicholas Hawksmoor*, New Haven and London: Yale University Press

Harvey, J. (1988), *The Availability of Hardy Plants of the Late Eighteenth Century*, Garden History Society. Direct Offset, Glastonbury

Hawkes, W. (1969), 'Miller's Work at Wroxton', *Cake and Cockhorse*, 4 (6) 99-107, Magazine of the Banbury Historical Society

Hawkes, W. (1983), 'The Gothic Architectural Work of Sanderson Miller', *A Gothic Symposium*, Georgian Group. A symposium held at the Victoria and Albert Museum

Hawkes, W. (2001), 'The Walton Bath House, Warwickshire', *The Follies Journal*, 1, 29-34

Hawkes, W. ed. (2006), *The Diaries of Sanderson Miller of Radway*, Bristol: J.W. Arrowsmith, Ltd for The Dugdale Society

Haworth, J. (1999), *Farnborough Hall*, London: Centurion Press for National Trust Enterprises Ltd

Hayden, R. (1980), *Mrs Delany, her Life and her Flowers*, London: British Museum Publications

Heely, J. (1777), *Letters on the Beauties of Hagley, Envil and the Leasowes*, London

Hey, C. (1991), *The Warwickshire Coterie, an Eighteenth Century Interlude*, Shipston-on-Stour: Colin Hey, printed by Avon Litho Ltd, Stratford-upon-Avon

Hinde, T. (1986), *Capability Brown, the story of a Master Gardener*, New York, London: W.W. Norton and Co

Historic Manuscripts Commission Report (1897), Carlisle, in Harris, J. (1995), see above

Hogarth, W. (1997), *The Analysis of Beauty*, New Haven and London: Paul Mellon Centre for British Art, Yale University Press. First published 1753

Hunt, J. Dixon (1987), *William Kent, Landscape Garden Designer*, New York: A. Zwemmer.

Hunt, J. Dixon and Willis, P. eds. (1990) *The Genius of the Place, The English Landscape Garden 1620-1820*, Cambridge, Massachusetts and London, England: The MIT Press

Hutchinson, H. (1976), *Sir Christopher Wren a biography*, Exeter: A.Wheaton and Co

Hussey C. (1967), *English Gardens and Landscapes 1700-1750*, London: Country Life

Hussey, C. in Stroud, D. (1975), *Capability Brown*, London: Faber and Faber

Jackson Stops, G. (1984), *Farnborough Hall*, London: Stellar Press for The National Trust

Jackson-Stops, G. (1992), *An English Arcadia 1600-1990*, London: National Trust Enterprises

Jacques, D. (1990), *Georgian Gardens, The Reign of Nature*, London: B.T. Batsford. (First published 1983)

Jacques, D. (2001) 'Warwick Castle Grounds and Park, 1743-60', *Garden History*, 29 (1), 48-63

Jago, R. (1767), *Edge-Hill, or the Rural Prospect Delineated and Moralised*, London

Jellicoe, G., Jellicoe, S., Goode, P., Lancaster, M. eds. (1986), *The Oxford Companion to Gardens*. Oxford, New York: Oxford University Press

Kliger, S. (1972), *The Goths in England*, 1972, New York: Octagon Books (First edition, 1952) (Mason's quote taken from 'Poems' London, 1764, p.121

Laird, M. (1999), *The Flowering of the Landscape Garden, English Pleasure Grounds 1720-1800*, Philadelphia: University of Pennsylvania Press

Lang, S. (1966), 'The Principles of the Gothic Revival in England', *Journal of the Society of Architectural Historians*, XXV, 240-67

Langley, B. (1728), *New Principals of Gardening*, London

Langley, B. (1742), *Gothic Architecture, Improved by Rules and Proportions*, London

Lewis, M. (2002), *The Gothic Revival*, London: Thames and Hudson

Lipscomb, G. (1831), *History of Buckinghamshire*, London

Markham, S. (1984), *John Loveday of Caversham, 1711-1789*, Wilton: Michael Russell

Marshall, W. (1785), *Planting and Rural Ornament*, 328-9, London

Martins, S. (2002), *The English Model Farm*, Macclesfield: Windgather Press

McCarthy, M. (1987), *The Origins of the Gothic Revival*, New Haven and London: Yale University Press

Meir, J. (1994), *Arbury Hall, A Brief History of the Site*, Warwickshire Gardens Trust. ISSN 1469-0276

Meir, J. (1995), *Farnborough Hall, Warwickshire, A brief history of the estate*, Warwickshire Gardens Trust. ISSN 1469-0276

Meir, J. (1996), *Croome Court, Worcester. A brief history of the estate*, Warwickshire Gardens Trust. ISSN 1469-0276

Meir, J. (1997), 'Sanderson Miller and the landscaping of Wroxton Abbey, Farnborough Hall and Honington Hall', *Garden History* 25 (1) 81-106

Meir, J. (1998), *Wroxton Abbey, Oxfordshire, a brief history of the estate*, Warwickshire Gardens Trust. ISSN 1469-0276

Meir, J. (1999), *Alscot park, Warwickshire, a brief history of the estate*, Warwickshire Gardens Trust. ISSN 1469-0276

Meir, J. (2002), 'Development of a natural style in designed landscapes between 1730 and 1760: the English Midlands and the work of Sanderson Miller and Lancelot Brown', *Garden History* 30 (1) 24-48

Meir, J. (2002), 'The Great Terrace at Farnborough', *Journal of the Warwickshire Gardens Trust Journal*, Warwickshire Gardens Trust. ISSN 1469-0276

Meir, J. (2003), *Radway Grange Estate and Sanderson Miller, a brief history of the landscaping of Radway*, Warwickshire Gardens Trust. ISSN 1469-0276

Meir, J., Fryer, H. and Lovie, J. (1994), *Honington Hall, Warwickshire, a brief historical survey: 1995*, Warwickshire Gardens Trust

Mercer, D. and Mercer, E. (1993), *Chart Park: Dorking, A Vanished Surrey Mansion*, Dorking: Rayment Printers Ltd. Printed for the Dorking Local History Group

Midgley, G. (1996), *University Life in Eighteenth-Century Oxford*, New Haven and London: Guildford and King's Lynn: Biddles Ltd for Yale University Press

Miller, G. (1900), *Rambles Round the Edge Hills*, London: Elliot Stock, also 1896 edition, Banbury: William Potts

Miller, N. (1982), *Heavenly Caves*, New York: George Braziller, Inc

Miller, P. (1731), *The Gardeners Dictionary*, first edition. London

Mosset, M. and Teyssot, G. (2000), *The History of Garden Design, The Western Tradition from the Renaissance to the Present Day*, London: Thames and Hudson

Mowl, T. (1983), 'The Case of the Enville Museum', *Journal of Garden History*, 3 (2), 134-43

Mowl, T. (2000), *Gentlemen and Players*, Stroud: Sutton

Mowl, T. (2002), *Historic Gardens of Gloucestershire*, Stroud: Tempus Publishing Ltd

Nares, G. (1957), 'Hagley Hall, Worcestershire', *Country Life*, 19 September

Nash, T. (1782), *The History and Antiquities of Worcestershire*, I

National Trust (1991), *Lacock Abbey*, Over Wallop: Hampshire: BAS Printers Ltd

Nichols, J. (1811), *History and Antiquities of the County of Leicestershire*, (IV, part ii). London

Oswald, A. (1946), 'Radway Grange, Warwickshire, I', *Country Life*, 6 September

Palladio, A. (1570), 1716-20, 1721) *Quattro libri dell'architettura*, Ed Leoni, G., translated into English and French by Leoni, G. and Dubois, N. English edition published in 1721, London

Paulson, T. (1997), in Hogarth, W., *The Analysis of Beauty*, New Haven and London: Paul Mellon Centre for British Art, Yale University Press

Parnell, J. (1769), *Journal of a Tour through England and Wales*

Phibbs, J. (2003), 'The Englishness of Lancelot 'Capability' Brown', *Garden History* 31 (2), 122-140

Plumridge, A. and Cousins, M. (1998), 'Wotton House, Buckinghamshire: Playground of the 'Boy Patriots', and more than second fiddle to Stow!', *Follies*, 10 (2), 3-6

Pococke, R. (1888-9), *The Travels through England of Dr Richard Pococke volumes I and II*. Ed. J Cartwright, London: Camden Society. (First published 1757)

Pope, A. (1995), *The Works of Alexander Pope*, Ware: Wordsworth Editions. (Pope's works were published in the first half of the 18th century; the poem based on Swift's 'Imitations of Horace' was published *c.*1738, the Essay on Criticism was published 1711)

Pope, A. (1999), in Batey, M., *Alexander Pope, the Poet and the Landscape*, London: Barn Elms Publishing. First published in *The Guardian*, 1713, the *Spectator*, 173

Preston, C. (undated, *c.*1950s), *Gosfield Hall, the building and its history*, Essex County Record Office, G1

Ridgway, C. and Williams, R. (eds) (2000), *Sir John Vanbrugh and Landscape Architecture in Baroque England, 1690-1730*, Stroud: Sutton Publishing Limited

Roberts, J. (2001), 'Well Temper'd Clay: Constructing Water Features in the Landscape Park', *Garden History*, 29 (1)

Robertson, William (1797), *Journal of William Robertson of Kilkenny*, National Library of Ireland, MS.248

Robinson, J. (1990), *Temples of Delight, Stowe Landscape Gardens*, London: George Philip

Robinson, Sir T. (1734), Letter written to his father-in-law Lord Carlisle, 23 December, London, Historic Manuscripts Commission, Carlisle

Rorschach, K. (1983), *The Early Georgian Landscape Garden,* Catalogue to go with exhibition, Yale Centre for British Art

Rowe, A. (ed) (2001), *Garden making and the Freman Family: A Memoir of Hamels 1713-1733,* Hertfordshire Record Publications Volume 17. Hertford: Stephen Austin Ltd. for the Hertfordshire Record Society

Russell, B. (1946), *History of Western Philosophy*, London, Routledge Classics, 2004

Salmon, T. (1748), *The Foreigner's Companion through the Universities of Cambridge and Oxford*

Scott, S. (1995), *The Follies of Boughton Park*, Moulton, Northampton: Scott Publications

Shenstone, W. (1939), *The Letters of William Shenstone*, ed. Williams, M., Oxford: Basil Blackwell

Splaine, A. (1954), *Country Life*, 4 March, Letter ascribing the Ecton Pavilion to Inigo Jones. (The National Buildings Record)

Stembridge, P. (1996), *Thomas Goldney's Garden, the creation of an eighteenth century garden,* Bristol: Burleigh Press

Souden, D. (1991), *Wimpole Hall*, London: The National Trust

Spencer, C. (2004), *Blenheim, Battle for Europe*, London: Weidenfeld and Nicolson

Strong, R. (2000), *The Artist and the Garden*, New Haven and London: Yale University Press

Strong, R. (1992), *Royal Gardens*, London: BBC Books and Conran Octopus

Stroud, D. (1975), *Capability Brown*, London: Faber and Faber Limited, new rewritten edition. First edition, 1950

Summerson, J. (1990), *The Unromantic Castle*, London: Thames and Hudson

Summerson, J. (1993), *Architecture in Britain 1530-1830*, New Haven and London: Yale University Press. First edition 1953, Penguin Books

Summerson, J. (2000), *Inigo Jones*, New Haven and London: Yale University Press. First edition, 1966

Sweet, R. (2004), *Antiquaries, The Discovery of the Past, Eighteenth-Century Britain*. London and New York: Hambledon and London

Swift, J. (1714), *Imitations of Horace*, Translated from Horace's *Satires*, book 2, no.6

Swift, J. (1897-1908), 'Abstract of the History of England', *Prose works of Jonathan Swift*, ed. Scott, T., ed. Bohn, X. London

Switzer, S. (1718), *Ichnographia Rustica: or the Nobleman, Gentleman and Gardener's Recreation,* London

Symes, M. (1991), *The English Rococo Garden*, Princes Risborough: Shire Publications

Symes, M. (2005), *The English Rococo Garden*, Second Edition, revised and updated, Shire Garden History Series no.5. Princes Risborough: Shire Publications

Symes, M. (1996), 'William Pitt the Elder: The Gran Mago of Landscape Gardening', *Garden History* 24 (1) 126-36

Tait, A. (1980), *The Landscape Garden in Scotland*, Edinburgh: Edinburgh University Press

Tait, W. (1943-44), *Enclosure Acts and Awards Relating to Warwickshire. Transactions of the Birmingham Archaeological Society, LXV,* 45

Tavernor, R. (1991), *Palladio and Palladianism*, London: Thames and Hudson

Thacker, C. (1994), *The Genius of Gardening*, London: Weidenfeld and Nicolson

Thomson, J. (1727), *The Seasons*, Descriptive poem

Throsby, J. (1789), *Select Views in Leicestershire*

Trauzettel, L. (1996), 'Worlitz, England in Germany', *Garden History* 24 (2), 221-36

Turner, Roger (1999), *Capability Brown and the Eighteenth-century English Landscape*, Chichester: Phillimore

Tyack, G. (1998), *Oxford an Architectural Guide*, Oxford, New York: Oxford University Press

Tyack, G. (1994), *Warwickshire Country Houses*, Chichester: Phillimore and Co Ltd

Victoria History of the County of Berkshire (1923), Vol 3. London: Oxford University Press

Victoria History of the County of Gloucestershire (1968), gen.ed. R.Pugh, Vol 8. London: Oxford University Press

Victoria History of the County of Oxford (1957), gen.ed. R.Pugh, Vol 5. London: Oxford University Press

Victoria History of the County of Warwick (1949), gen.ed. L.Salzman, Vol 5. London: Oxford University Press

Walpole, H. (1753), *Horace Walpole's Correspondence*, ed. Lewis, W. (1937-83) Oxford and New Haven: Yale University Press

Walpole, H. (1764), *The Castle of Otranto*

Walpole, H. (1995), *The History of the Modern Taste in Gardening*, New York: Ursus Press. (First published 1780, as part of *Anecdotes of Painting in England*)

Walton, J. (1978), 'Agriculture 1730-1900' in Dodgshon, R. and Butlin R. (eds), *An Historical Geography of England and Wales*, London, New York, San Francisco: Academic Press

Watkin, D. (1983), *The English Vision, The Picturesque in Architecture, Landscape and Garden Design*, London: John Murray

Watkin, D. (1999), 'Built Ruins: The Hermitage as a Retreat', *Visions of Ruin, Architectural Fantasies and Designs for Garden Follies*, catalogue to go with the exhibition of the same name London: The Soane Gallery

Watkin, D. (2001), *English Architecture*, London: Thames and Hudson. First published 1979

West, G. (1990), 'Stowe, The Gardens of the Right Honourable Richard Lord Viscount Cobham' a poem in Clarke (ed), *Descriptions of Lord Cobham's Gardens at Stowe 1700-1750*, 37-51. First published, 1732

Whateley, T. (1771), *Observations on Modern Gardening*

Wheeler, R. (2000), ' 'Pro Magna Charta' or 'Fay ce que Voudras': Political and Moral precedents for the Gardens of Sir Francis Dashwood at West Wycombe', *New Arcadian Journal*, 49/50, 26-60

White, R. (1997), *Nicholas Hawksmoor and the Replanning of Oxford*. Catalogue to go with the exhibition of the same name. Norfolk: Witley Press for RIBA and University of Oxford, Ashmolean Museum

Williams, M. ed. (1939), *The Letters of William Shenstone*, Oxford: Basil Blackwell

Williams, R. (2000), 'Fortified Gardens' in C. Ridgway and R. Williams (eds), *Sir John Vanbrugh and Landscape Architecture in Baroque England 1690-1730*, 49-70. Stroud: Sutton

Williamson, T. (1995), *Polite Landscapes, Gardens and Society in Eighteenth Century England*, Stroud: Sutton

Williamson, T. (2000), 'Estate Management and Landscape Design' in C. Ridgway and R. Williams (eds), *Sir John Vanbrugh and Landscape Architecture in Baroque England 1690-1730*, 12-30. Stroud: Sutton

Williamson, T. (2001), 'Chatsworth, Derbyshire', *Garden History*, 29 (1), 82-90

Williamson, T. (2002), *The Transformation of Rural England*, Exeter: University of Exeter Press

Williamson T. and Bellamy, L. (1987), *Property and Landscape*, London: George Philip

Willis, P. (2002), *Charles Bridgeman and the English Landscape Garden*, Newcastle upon Tyne: Elysium Press

Wilson, M. (1984), *William Kent, Architect, Designer, Painter, Gardener, 1685-1748*, London: Boston, Melbourne and Henley: Routledge and Kegan Paul

Wilson, R. and Mackley, A. (2000), *Creating Paradise, the Building of the English Country house 1660-1880*, London: Hambledon and London

Wood, A. (1969), 'Sanderson Miller of Radway', *Cake and Cockhorse*, 4 (6), 79-98. (The magazine of the Banbury Historical Society)

Wood, A. (1983), *The Shire Hall, Warwick, Its Rebuilding in the mid-eighteenth century*, Stratford-upon-Avon: Warwickshire Local History Society. Reprinted, with additional material, from *Warwickshire History*, V (5)

Wood, A. and Hawkes, W. (1987), 'Radway, Warwickshire: the making of a landscape', *Journal of Garden History*, 7 (2), 103-30

Worsley, G. (1995), *Classical Architecture in Britain, The Heroic Age*, New Haven and London: Yale University Press

Worsley, G. (2000), 'After ye Antique': Vanbrugh, Hawksmoor and Kent' in C. Ridgway and R. Williams (eds), *Sir John Vanbrugh and Landscape Architecture in Baroque England 1690-1730*, 12-30. Stroud: Sutton

Worsley, G. (2004), *The British Stable*, New Haven and London: The Paul Mellon Centre for Studies in British Art, Yale University Press

Wright, N. (undated), *'John Grundy of Spalding Engineer, 1718-1783, his Life and Times,* Department of Recreational services, Lincolnshire County Council

Bibliography of Unpublished Sources, Maps and Drawings

❧·❧

RECORD OFFICES

COVENTRY DIOCESAN RECORD OFFICE
Radway
Miller, Sanderson (1716) Record of Miller's birth at Radway, Radway Parish Register, Coventry Diocesan Record Office, DR47/4.

ESSEX COUNTY RECORD OFFICE, ECRO
Gosfield
Preston, C. (undated but c.1950s) Gosfield Hall, the building and its history. ECRO Gosfield Archives.

GLOUCESTERSHIRE RECORD OFFICE, GRO
Stoke Gifford
Correspondence, G. Lyttelton to Sanderson Miller on behalf of Norborne Berkeley (1752) Refers to landscaping and waterworks. GRO Beaufort Mss, uncatalogued. Letter from W. Hawkes held in GRO referring to this correspondence, GRO EN/Hawkes, 1975

SHAKESPEARE BIRTHPLACE TRUST RECORD OFFICE, SBTRO
Adlestrop
Leigh Mss
Leigh, Thomas (c.1740s-1750s) Thomas Leigh's Account Books. SBTRO, DR12/13/18.
Agreement for first building phase (1750) This phase included two new Gothic bow window. SBTRO, Leigh Mss, Series B, Box 2, Bn.4.
Accounts (1752) Payment to Samuel Driver for drawing a plan for the alterations by the bow window. SBTRO, Leigh Mss, Series B, Box 2, Bn.4, Account Book.
Agreement for second building phase (1759) This phase included four octagon corner towers. SBTRO, Leigh Mss. B1517.

STAFFORDSHIRE COUNTY RECORD OFFICE, SCRO
Ingestre
Wood, T. Peploe (1836-7) Album of Sketches, containing drawing of the Pentagon Gothic Tower. SCRO D240/M/26.

WARWICKSHIRE COUNTY RECORD OFFICE, WCRO
Arbury Papers
Miller, Sanderson (c.1749/50) Two sketches of Gothic arches and bookcases, entitled 'Arbury Dressing room' and authenticated as by Miller in Sir Roger Newdigate's hand. WCRO, CR764/214.

Newdigate, Sir Roger (mid-C18) Account book. WCRO CR 136/V156.
Newdigate, Lady Sophia (1748) Lady Newdigate's Tour in the South of England. Memorandum book of Sir Roger and Lady Newdigate's tour. WCRO CR1841/7.

MILLER AND RADWAY PAPERS

Accounts (1742-1780) An incomplete collection. The 'Great Book' of Miller's accounts, c.1749/50, is missing. WCRO CR125B/1- 37. Nos. CR125B/1-5 cover much of the expenditure on Radway.
Conveyance of Radway Grange to Miller senior (12 Octobe, 1 Geo 1, 1715). Copy of the articles of agreement between Thomas Goodwin the elder and the younger, and Sanderson Miller of Banbury. WCRO CR1264/1, 105.
Library Sale (1863) Sale pamphlet detailing part of Miller's library WCRO CR1264/7.
Library Sale (1910), WCRO CR Films 866 iii reel 28.
Miller, Sanderson (senior) (1737) Entry in Radway Parish Register of his death, WCRO DR47/4.
Miller, Sanderson, correspondence (c.1740-1779) Collection of over one thousand letters kept by Miller. They consist mainly of letters written to him, but the collection also contains a few letters written by him and by his wife and nephew. Many have been printed in part in Dickens and Stanton (1910), *see* Bibliography. The letters referred to are given their reference numbers in the text. These are all held in WCRO CR125B/, except that on p.114, from Oswald to Miller, which has the reference WCRO CR125C/1.
Miller, Sanderson, marriage (1746) Record of Miller's marriage to Susannah Trotman, Swalcliffe Parish Register, WCRO CR1264/1, 52.
Warwickshire County Book (1959) Warwickshire County Council. Records Sanderson Miller as High Sheriff of Warwickshire in 1728.

MAPS

Arbury, attributed to Deeley (c.1680-1700) Map of estate showing old fishponds and formal avenue approach to Hall. WCRO CR1199/69.
Radway, Salmon, G. (1756) Pre-Enclosure map prepared for Miller. WCRO CR1596.
Radway, Wallsgrove, S. (1997) Map showing the allotments under the Enclosure Act for Radway, 1757. Prepared to illustrate footpaths in the parish at this date. WCRO Z939/2L.
Walton, Overton, R. (1762) Map of part of the Walton estate, showing the Bath House and the Bath woods. WCRO CR750/3.

LIBRARIES

Bodleian Library, Oxford
Chart Park, correspondence, Talbot, Mrs H. (1751). Letter from Mrs Talbot to Lord North, MS North, d.19, fol.68.
Wroxton, correspondence, Delany, Mrs M. (mid-C18) Letter comparing Wroxton favourably with Blenheim. MS North, d.14, fol.209.

British Library
Wimpole, correspondence (1750-51) Letter from Sanderson Miller to Charles Lyttelton, written from Gosfield, 16 September 1750. BL Stowe Ms 753, fol.146v.
Letter from Sanderson Miller to Sir George Lyttelton, written from Radway, 20 February, 1750/51. BL Add. Ms 35, 679, fol.55.

MUSEUMS, GALLERIES and other collections available to the public

Banbury Museum
Wroxton, (1729) Map of Wroxton Abbey grounds, too frail to reproduce.

British Museum
Unsigned (1751) Sir W. Stanhope's Ethrupe (Eythrope), drawing. BM King's Maps, xxx, 19, u-w.

Staffordshire County Council
Ingestre (undated) Ingestre Hall. Leaflet listing the chronology of the Hall.

THE NATIONAL TRUST

Farnborough
Land Use Consultants (1993) Historic Landscape Survey and Restoration Plan.
Sales, J. (1994), Report on Farnborough. Personal communication.
Lacock Abbey
Papworth, M. (1999), Lacock Rockworks: Excavation Report.
Pearson, N. and Associates Ltd. (1994), Lacock Survey, Figure 7, 'Lacock Estate Plan of the whole parish and
    part of the parish of Pewsham, 1764'.
Prior Park
Sales, J. (1994), Historical Report on Prior Park.

AUTHORS

Berger, R. and Hodgetts, C. (1999), *Upton House, Warwickshire*, Leaflet produced for the Warwickshire Gardens
    Trust
Goodchild, P. (*c.*1990), *An Historical Assessment of the Park and Grounds at Hagley Hall, Bromsgrove, in the County
    of Hereford and Worcester*, Personal communication
Hawkes, W. (1964), 'Sanderson Miller of Radway, 1716-1780', Unpublished thesis, Faculty of Fine Arts,
    Cambridge University. A copy is held in the WCRO
Haynes, S. (1998), *A History of the Eighteenth Century Gardens at Enville Hall*, Leaflet
Pafford, M. (1996), *Information on the sale catalogue of Belhus, Essex, (1923), Sale carried out by auctioneers Alfred
    Savill and Sons*, Personal communication
Phibbs, J. (1999), Draft report on Wotton Underwood estate, Personal communication
Piebenga, S. (1995), 'William Sawrey Gilpin (1762-1843) A review of his work as a landscape gardener', Thesis
    (in two volumes) submitted for the degree of Doctor of Philosophy, Institute of Advanced Architectural
    Studies, University of York
Rutherford, S. (1998), 'Middleton Park', Draft report prepared for English Heritage, personal
    communication
Rutherford, S. (1998), 'Park Place', Draft report prepared for English Heritage, personal communication
Rutherford, S. (1998), 'Wotton House', Draft report prepared for English Heritage, personal communication
Rutherford, S. (1998), 'Wroxton Abbey', Draft report prepared for English Heritage, personal
    communication
Wyatt, H. (2001), 'The 18th-Century English Landscape Park: its Functional Use and Management'. MA in
    Architectural Conservation, De Montfort University

Index

compiled by Susan Vaughan

❧·❧

Page numbers in bold type refer to illustrations.
Roman numerals in bold refer to colour plates.